A Good Deal

Selected Short Stories from *The Massachusetts Review*

Edited by

Mary Heath & Fred Miller Robinson

The University of Massachusetts Press

Amherst, 1988

Printed in the United States of America
LC 88-4734
ISBN 0-87023-639-3 (cloth); 640-7 (paper)
Set in Linotron Garamond No. 3
by Keystone Typesetting Co.
Printed by Thomson-Shore, Inc.
and bound by John M. Dekker & Sons, Inc.

Library of Congress Cataloging-in-Publication Data

A Good deal : selected stories from the Massachusetts review / edited by Mary Heath and Fred Miller Robinson.
p. cm.
ISBN 0–87023–639–3 (alk. paper). ISBN 0–87023–640–7 (pbk. : alk. paper)
1. Short stories, American. 2. American fiction—20th century.
I. Heath, Mary, 1931– . II. Robinson, Fred Miller, 1942– .
PS648.S5G66 1988
813′.01′08—dc19 88–4734
CIP

British Library Cataloguing in Publication data are available.

For Robert Garland Tucker
Editor, 1960–1982

Contents

Preface

When the editors of *The Massachusetts Review* were invited by the University of Massachusetts Press to collect fiction from a twenty-seven-year harvest, we asked ourselves what the criteria should be. The answer, reduced to essentials, was quality and diversity. These are the bases on which *MR* has always selected fiction, and we wanted the book to be representative—not to mention pleasing—to serious readers of short stories.

It would have been pleasant to pass the summer months (when we do not ordinarily read fiction manuscripts) browsing through past issues, choosing our favorite stories, those that offered us, to paraphrase Robert Frost, delight and even wisdom. But we thought it more responsible to assign randomly sixteen or twenty issues each to ourselves and to our four veteran fiction readers: Corinne Demas Bliss, Joan Bramwell, Julia Demmin, and Charles Moran. By the end of the summer we had compiled a short list, which we proceeded, painfully, to reduce further, to a selection of 20 out of a total of 244 published stories.

The number of stories sent to *MR* is astonishing. We publish an average of only nine a year (figuring in special fiction sections), and receive some forty every week. Other journals and magazines could report similar statistics. We can only hope that the interest in reading short stories is as keen as the interest in writing them. Clearly we are in a high period of fiction writing, by people from all walks of life.

Every story published in *MR* has aroused enthusiasm in any

number of editors and readers. But we are particularly happy with the range of subjects and styles in the twenty we now offer you. A man dies, awakens to a landscape at once ordinary and dreamlike, and begins a strange journey with instructions to avoid "going back." A lowly sweeper in a Nigerian health clinic goes into business dispensing medicine he knows nothing about, with occasionally fatal results. An assistant warden at a Mississippi prison needs to find a substitute executioner, and a shy widowed schoolteacher volunteers. A daughter accompanies her parents, in 1938, to the Polish shtetl where her father was born, and years later, hearing from the sole survivor of that shtetl, learns that sometimes you can go home again. Comic reminiscences of Stanford fraternity life in the 1950s are complicated by the presence of a Hungarian refugee. One story begins, "On November 6 of last year, at around 8:15 p.m., I was beaten and raped by a man named Raymond C. Moreau, Jr.," and goes on to recount the real damage and tragedy of such a violation. A young, pregnant black woman waits for her lover, a piano player named Time, to come back to her. A foundry foreman is forced by circumstances to learn what work in the "oven" is like, and to recognize the ovenmen as "brothers in fiery agony."

And so on, from the traditional realism of Rosellen Brown and Gayle Whittier to the Rabelaisian fable of João Ubaldo Ribeiro to the postmodern comedy of R. M. Berry. Like almost all the stories *MR* has published, these have come to us "over the transom": uncommissioned, unannounced, but never unwelcome. We are especially proud of having discovered many new writers. They found the way to say the story that had to be said that way, and we think that's a good deal.

Mary Heath
Fred Miller Robinson

A Good Deal

Rosellen Brown

A Good Deal

My father does not live in what I would call a "home." We'd never have considered anything that even resembled the word, with its hypocrisy built right into its name (home cooking, comforts of home). I like to think he is in a sort of benign arm of the Catskills out on Long Island, a brightly decorated and well-kept hotel complete with live entertainment and a built-in synagogue a few blocks from the ocean. The air outside his hotel has that sharp salty extra dimension that makes you realize you are standing in something nourishing, almost tangible, not transparent, nonexistent, like most air. He won't go out in it because for him the extra dimension he anticipates (besides mugging or murder) is germs—a cold, bronchitis, pneumonia: who wants to smell *air?* Not at his age.

When we visit, we take him walking once around the building as if "outside" were a destination in itself. He's got his hat—a pale yellow golf hat for our summer visit, a formal fedora for the winter, the kind the FBI used to wear before they started passing as hippies and stoned collegians. "Come on, let's go for a walk," I suggest as soon as I see my wife and the kids sinking into torpor on his roommate's bed in the room on the fourth floor.

This time we have brought him a little radio with earphones because the room-mate complains about noise, any and all, after 8:30 and the management will not "mix in," either out of scrupulous fairness or their (correct) suspicion that reason is destined for defeat here among the elderly with their habits that have turned to stone.

Jane has correctly predicted his reaction again—she maintains that my father is the only person she knows who has never said an unexpected thing. He is, for some reason I can't fathom, bewildered by the radio dials and I can see that it will go unused, he will leave it in its little blue box on his half of the closet shelf, another failed toy alongside the hearing aid and the electric razor. Inertia overpowers energy, impossible as it sounds. Entropy makes promises; someday I suppose I'll know what it is saying.

He has embraced his grandsons, offered them small dusty-looking cookies that he's saved from lunch in a napkin. They are touched, Timmy especially (he is the little one), at a sign of awareness that they were coming, that they might have needs or pleasures he could gratify. They don't ask or expect much—some rudimentary consciousness, a sign. They take one cookie apiece and chew it carefully, as if they are thinking hard. I ask more, although I don't get it. Well, I am his son, the remoteness of the third generation has not made me forgiving.

So we troop downstairs, Jane ahead of us, wearing her glorious red hair that made my father, when he first saw her, call her a Yankee; the two boys trying ceremoniously not to step on each other's heels, giving off, though, with every gesture the suppressed air of kittens in a sack, all frisky irresistible quenched movement. The elevator is one machine Pop seems to have mastered; not only does he hold the door, assured, while we file in, but he smiles and keeps his hand on the OPEN button for another tenant of his floor, a short, vividly-muumuued woman who hobbles on slowly inside a walker. As we move down the floors, sinking so hard our stomachs rise up into our chests and Josh says "Gulp" out loud, she looks at us, smiling, and then, apologetically at her aluminum contraption and shakes her head. "Don't get old, *kinder,* that's all I can say."

After she's gone—we politely wait for her to drag herself out and disappear around the elevators toward the gift shop—my father says "So who asked her? We need her opinion on anything, we'll remember to ask her."

Jane opens her mouth and closes it; so do I. We are going to berate him for his lack of generosity but instead we berate ourselves: the same impatience that bit her into speech bit him into anger. The hotel is fine, we assure ourselves, it is age that's depressing.

But no. I watch my father walk toward the door slowly but

securely. It is mostly women who are seated, watching, in the purple and yellow leather chairs on both sides of the aisle, because life seems for the most part to be a widowing. He has very few real complaints, considering what a man his age can expect—even the Bible would agree. It is all that has never changed that rankles: he is the same father I've always had, lacking a few appurtenances (teeth, hearing, hair, a wife) but otherwise stock still the same. "Kill me!" he pleaded after my mother died. "It's a mistake, how could such a mistake happen! I was always going to go first." I don't know how much losing her cost him. But he was terrified to face his life alone without a mother, that I know. He was bewildered, and he's still bewildered—how could it be that he has come through eighty-two years intact when strong men, men twice his size and a hundred times more vigorous and full of will, have died and left these women?

Timmy pushes on the hotel door with all his weight and the live air opens to us, edgy with salt, the sky bright blue as pure deep water. "Oy," my father says, turning his face back toward the building. "I'm climbing into my grave out here. What are you doing, Joey, punishing me with this cold?"

I wish I could find a sin in my father's past. I thought this once when I was embroiled in an episode of, what shall I call it, a brief unsanctioned lust—Janie never did find out, no harm was done—because I was caught in a paradox. My father didn't drink (a little schnapps on *shabbos,* gone in a blink) and neither did I; he was a dutiful breadwinner, earnest in his work, and so was I, give or take the moments of insolvency any writer is heir to. His shortcomings were all of omission, never of commission. He and my mother, however they had begun, had endured a marriage of convention and dependency. They mocked and quibbled, demanded and berated, my father thrust his neck out to be shamed and my mother enthusiastically did her best to shame him, and how they had me is hard to envision. As a teen-ager (like all teen-agers who have everyone experimentally in bed with everyone else, their teachers, their friends' mothers, the President) I could never manage to imagine them so much as acknowledging each other in the Murphy bed they pulled down from the living room closet. (It was a tiny apartment; their son got the bedroom for his more hallowed activities.) But just as people unquestioningly needed marriages in those days, so did those marriages need children. I suppose I was a duty and they did me.

But then, as I said, the moment presented itself when I was less than dutiful and I found myself gathering up the odd ingredients for a great stew of justifications. I found myself thinking, I am not my father repeated once down the line. Even though you could confuse us in the dark by the shape of our bodies, the nap of our hair, he is a man in whom the blood beats weakly, whom the traces bind. Admirable and not admirable, those things. I didn't know just where I stood on virtue just then. It seemed to me, but only in flashes, as if there were a blinking sign at the corner of my vision, that virtue was only safety and safety was timidity. Cowering. Then that sign would blink again and I wasn't so sure. I saw Janie's face, innocent of worry (though I tried to see it anywhere but in the bedroom) and I saw the blond, thoroughly gentile, slim-hipped woman (a student of mine, not, to be honest, as innocent as my wife) who wanted me enough to put a lot of foregone conclusions in danger, hers and mine; and it was my father who seemed, or at least ought, I thought, to be begging me to *do* it, leave the strait and narrow, seize the hour and be bad.

I was bad; I could achieve badness with the best of them (only perhaps not as a recidivist). As it happened, I didn't enjoy it much, either in anticipation or in retrospect, only in the single blinding instant, gone as quickly as that ritual fire-in-the-throat whiskey after *kiddush,* that drives all of us every time, in the dark, on the sly, the animal instant that slaughters reason. And perhaps I enjoyed this colloquy too: Pop, I thought, a man has to dare to dare. Then I would ask myself why. To be able to say he dared? Say it to whom? I wasn't telling *him.* If my father, who was too simple and decent to lie or even give short-weight, wasn't good, only frightened, what was a good man? Sometimes he seemed to me, all of a sudden, not so naive as I had thought: telling me about a gangster neighbor, a philandering cousin, his aunt who took in boarders and then took off with one. He had noticed there was a world out there. But his own record, I thought, that was clean enough to be an incitement. In retrospect I see I was averaging my guilt over two generations. In my own way I was a coward too.

A few months ago, the night before we were to make our biennial trip to the city to see him, he called me. A call up here to Providence—"the country," he calls it—is a long-distance affair, very daunting. He hazards it rarely and only in emergencies. His voice had broken through distance to me, quavering, when he went into the hospital with pneumonia a few years ago, and once when his brother Abie died in Miami, to weep for twenty minutes while he cursed himself for the bill he was running up. This time, hearing his voice saying "Joey?" as if he doubted it was really me, I was alarmed.

"What's the matter, Pop? Are you okay?" Our suitcases were already out on the bed waiting for our New York City clothes.

"I'm okay, a little cold, I cough, but I'm okay," he told me and his equivocal voice seemed to wait there for me to tell him why he had called.

"Listen, sonny," he said finally, "I got to ask you something."

"Couldn't it wait? We're—"

"I wouldn't bother you without a reason. I don't need a phone call on my bill, you know."

"Well—" I hadn't intended to be so uninviting. It was all to the good when he made himself push against the world; using the telephone was the challenge to him that climbing up a sheer rockface would be to me. I could see him pacing while he held the phone; I do that too.

"Listen. What do you think if—I want you should tell me if you think this is such a good idea."

"Right. Okay." I imagined he was going to ask to change rooms and be done with his room-mate's *mishugas* once and for all. Play the tv till midnight. Sing in the shower.

"What?" he asked.

"All right, go ahead."

"What head?"

"Nothing. Tell me what you want to tell me." Janie and the kids sometimes come running when they don't know I'm on the phone with him. "Who are you shouting at?" they ask. He must hear me as if we had one of those ancient undersea connections. "Pop. What idea?"

"I'm thinking I might get married, Joey. But I'm not so sure."

I bit my lips closed to keep from laughing. Then, guilty, I made my voice approximate simple interest and possibly even approval. "Married," I yelled. "Married?" The world was an astounding place; maybe if I leaped out the bedroom window I could fly.

"I don't want you should think this has to do with Mommy," he began, and I listened speechless while he explained. Then I went downstairs and told Jane he had finally said something surprising.

And so we were ready to meet Frieda the next day. "Is Frieda grandpa's fiancée?" Timmy asked, saying the words as if he were holding a fishbone by its repulsive tip. I said I didn't know. My father had asked my advice but I hadn't given any.

Usually he was seated just inside the front door of the hotel so that he could jump up anxiously at the sight of every clump of people who approached. This time, confirming my understanding that all his routines had changed, there was no one waiting for us.

The woman at the desk rang his room; no one answered. (His room-mate, he had told me incidentally, was in the hospital for tests—"He was falling down"—and, although such an intimation of mortality had always frightened and depressed him before, not for the room-mate's sake but for his own, this time he was too distracted by his own changing fortunes to take much notice.)

The receptionist suggested we try the card room where they were having their daily bingo. "He's in there a lot," she told us amiably. "And *she's* a hot one at games," she added indiscreetly. "Let me tell you, she wins real money!" We were dealing with common knowledge, then. The boys giggled and Jane looked grim.

We walked down the long hall that had the mildly antiseptic, beige, asensual ambience of a Holiday Inn. The door to the card room was open and I could see him from the hall, seated next to the cage in which the bingo pieces flopped and fluttered like lottery tickets, so that he could hear the caller with his better ear. Which one was Frieda, then?

On one side of him sat a dishevelled woman with hair twice as red as Jane's but slightly purple at the roots, as if it were emerging from a wound. She had the look of someone on loan from a back ward. On his other side sat a *ketselah,* a little cat, smaller, under what looked like a real lace shawl: my mother would have called her quality. She had a good hairdresser for her dry sherry curls (or was it a wig?) and a vaguely European tinge of irony, or tolerance, to her smile. Everyone here was European, of course, but I don't mean Poland, I don't mean Odessa, I mean, say, middle-class Prague or Vienna. *Cafe mit schlag.*

And she was raking in the chips. "Good Lord," Janie breathed at my side. She was thinking, I know it, of my mother's orthopedic shoes, the plastic flounce and flowers that spread like a rash to cover every undefended piece in the now-dispersed apartment, the Decline of Rome wall decorations, all pillars and crumbling temples, or Gainsborough ladies in gilt frames. She was thinking of the little piece of paper we had found in my mother's coat pocket when we were going through her "effects," the rain check from Waldbaum's for a 39¢ cauliflower. This Frieda, you could tell from a hundred yards, knew her antiques, her armoires, her netsukes; a hundred to one she kept sachet in her bureau drawers.

Pop introduced us but not until he had pulled everybody into the hall so that we wouldn't impede the next bingo round. "You look as if you've won enough for one day," I said to Frieda as pleasantly as I could. "You must have talent."

She laughed and shrugged self-deprecatingly. Even her teeth were a cut above the hotel average. Her winnings had gone into a delicate purse that closed with a businesslike snap of finality.

What had they agreed to? I couldn't tell—on the phone my father had simply said she had "asked him" and he was "thinking about it." She had been widowed fairly recently and was lonely living alone, and so she had (admirably? shamelessly?) come to see whom she could meet here. To make a deal. She had her own money and apartment and didn't need his, her own children and grandchildren ditto. On the phone that had made sense: a frightened little woman, permanent immigrant-class like Pop, toward whom, not on purpose, I had been—I and my generation, I mean—condescending since we were children.

But this Frieda was something else again. She entertained us. I had suggested we do something besides the usual tour around the shabby block and she suggested a nice little restaurant, "strictly Kosher"—with a calculating smile at Pop that would have passed, in his book, for "consideration." It was nearby, her daughter had found it and they'd gone there for brunch just last week. "It has privacy," she promised. "Booths. Nice. Upholstered."

The boys were ostentatiously enjoying all this. I could see they liked this new wrinkle in the dull fabric of their grandfather's life. She looked like the kind of grandmother who could reach into her purse or her pockets—not that she'd done so yet—and produce charming surprises, more interesting than plain butter cookies. At very least she was an impressive gambler. Or maybe it was relief at the chance to do something besides sit in the blank air of a dozen old people with their canes and cataracts and forced cheerful Happy-to-meet-yous and their self-absorption.

As I say, she knew she was charming and so she entertained us. She told stories, in a firm quiet voice, about her father who had been a scholar in Cracow (therefore a pauper here, untrained to do a days-work). Her husband, continuing the tradition of useless luxury—a philistine she was, but honest—had been a violist. Whatever are you doing *here,* I wanted to ask her. What do you want of my poor father? He will make a woman like you more lonely still.

Well, the violist had dreamed of music, as it happened, but worked in "clucks"—that's cloaks and suits—like the rest of his *landsmen.* A cutter, then a presser at Waranow Togs on 35th Street. An unhappy man, unreconciled. For forty years, music on the side.

And that was how she had met my father, all those years ago. Some kind of garment workers' union picnic, wives invited. A rare Sunday in a park on Staten Island. An unforgettable day.

"How you met my father?" I echoed stupidly. Pop was eating a bagel, trying to negotiate it in spite of his insecure teeth. He looked at me shyly, blinking.

"He didn't tell you? Sam—" She lay one wrinkled but manicured hand on his bare arm. She was a woman who made disappointment into a charming pretext for flirtation. How my mother would have laughed. "Sam! A *tschotskele!*" she'd have said. A little trinket. But Frieda turned her widened eyes on all of us with innocent enthusiasm. "Yes—he didn't tell you we knew each other in the old old days? So when I met him here, what a surprise. A shock! Children—" and she fixed them, unfairly I thought, in her softening gaze and put one hand helpless on her chest as if to still her heart's persistent amazement. "Can you imagine, this old tired lonely lady comes out here to a strange place, she doesn't know a single soul—but, you know, my daughter, my son thought it would be good for me to get out from my apartment, they said it wasn't healthy to be all the time alone. And they were right, now I can see that!" The boys were attentive to her gaiety even if it was the kind of love story that only brought forth from them retching noises when it concerned the young and the beautiful. "And who do I meet the very first day, I'm sitting next to him at supper, they put me there, you know, just like that, and they bring the soup and I look at him—"

My father is embarrassed. He struggles with the cream cheese, which will not spread evenly on his bagel. Timmy reaches across unsmiling and does it for him. "Thanks, sonny," Pop says, shamefaced. Do you know you will be a nursemaid? I want to ask this stranger. Do you know he gets lost on his way to the bathroom? He lived with us for a year after my mother died, and there wasn't a day I came home not expecting the house to have burned down because he'd left the gas on again, long after the kettle had gone dry.

I wasn't used to complex and contradictory feelings in my father's presence, I have to admit that—except for the contradiction of loving someone you don't respect. About myself and the way I live my life, he is impossibly ignorant, try as I might to enlighten him: beginning back when I first refused to put on my galoshes for the rain, that old story, I have been a confusing rebellious undutiful son whom he has loved, as I love him, in spite of all. (Had I been lovable on his terms I'd have killed myself long ago.) That I should have become (happy or not) an impecunious writer instead of a doctor or, at worse, a businessman, has been an unforgiveable affront to his dreams for me. My working wife, the dishevelment of our house—no bedroom set, no wall-to-wall—have only been corroborations. He is a straightforward little man desperate for solvency, invisibility, silence. Tit for tat, I failed him, he failed me.

Now what am I to think?

Why does this woman want him? He is a live male, in better shape than most—two eyes, however cloudy; two ears, however shot; vestiges of a sense of humor, though that was better when he could hear. No stick to lean on, no apparent illnesses. Perhaps that makes him a prize. Is he flattered? Does he want to get out of this hotel because, comfortable as it is, you live in public here? Does he see her as a woman? What would he *do* with a woman besides hand her his dirty socks, his underwear?

We do not talk marriage; or, that is, we talk around it by admiring her proferred proofs of ownership: pictures of her Sheryl, a teacher; her Arthur, a podiatrist with blow-dried hair and stunning practice; their children; a polaroid of her living room, which is not so different, actually, from my mother's: Italian Renaissance chairs, pseudo, only no plastic to protect them from the depredations of use. It is not so much her dowry as the bride-price, I am thinking, studying the stubborn hairs that sprout like weeds from my father's nearest ear.

Later, when we'd left her—awkwardly—in the lobby of the hotel where she claimed she had some business with a friend but hoped she'd see us again soon (were we off to Providence immediately or would we take advantage of the wonderful city, the shops, the shows?) I went up to my father's room alone with him. He looked deflated, though for a man who hasn't much wind in his small sails to begin with, that's a matter of conjecture. "You like her, Joe?" he asked me, afraid to meet my eyes.

"She's—fine, Pop. A lovely woman. Very well-preserved." I hated to say that, it always made me think of embalming, on the one hand, and a feat against great odds on the other. But I sometimes found myself purposely blunt with him, if not downright cruel. Partly it was to fulfill his disappointment in me, to rub his nose in it since he'd think it anyway. But also I think I did it out of disrespect, as if I knew his hide was so thick nothing I said could penetrate to sting him. How could I ask what she saw in him? I made it a question about calculation which he, ever the paranoid, could appreciate.

"What she wants? I don't know, Joey, but it's true. Living alone is no way. Especially a woman, all the way out there on Ocean Parkway by herself. . . . " He left the meaningful details to my imagination. "She's a good woman. Not selfish. Anyway, she's got her own."

"A little—fancy, maybe—in her habits? Do you think?"

He shrugged. "You know, I told her she wouldn't get much from me in the—you know—that department." He raised his eyebrows on "that," which made it sound like what my mother had darkly referred to as "dorten"—"down *there,*" that island that was to be isolated from thought, speech, and, most important, touch. "Not like before."

I assumed the "before" was his marriage. "Well, there are lots of ways men and women can be friends," I said, and wondered if that sounded as pious as it felt. "She's probably not interested in—she just sounds lonely."

"Before she was always very—she's a modest woman, considering she's what you would call attractive."

The conversation was getting deeper than I tended to expect with my father. "Before she was modest? Pop, what do you mean, before?"

"*Before.*"

"When you met her on that picnic, you mean?"

His eyes lit for just an instant with a warmth I had myself seen often before I was, say, twelve.

"You met her—more than at that picnic? You got to know her?"

He shrugged again, this time not for vagueness but for its opposite: detailed memory he did not care to discuss. I sat down gingerly on his room-mate's bright blue bedspread and clasped my hands between my knees. "A lot of things I wouldn't tell you, sonny. A father wouldn't tell his son certain things. You shouldn't be mad—"

"You knew her—well? For very long?"

He was looking out the window, though the blinds were three-quarters closed. "Oy, sonny," he said the way he did when something hurt him. "What can I say? Not long enough."

"Did—" I couldn't ask if my mother knew about it. "It" was not so very horrible, considering the facts of their marriage, or not even considering: my marriage is perfectly fine. But I had no memory in forty years of having addressed a single sentence to my father's back.

"Nobody knew it, Mommy never, you never. Not even Harry either."

"Harry."

"Her husband, Harry Abrahams. He was a nice man. He had some temper but when he wasn't mad. . . . Not what you call a hard worker but a nice man." He twirled the string of the blinds in his hand. "We only wanted nobody should get hurt." He looked at me briefly, to check my face. All I knew about my face was that it felt very red, hot, inflamed with confusion.

"What happened, then?" I managed to ask. I think I was stuck somewhere between laughter and a huge chest-clearing shout, a massive bleating beyond good or bad taste, beyond a son's discretion. "What?!" I wanted to yell. "What?!" like Archie's father in the comic strip.

"Once we almost—people were asking a lot of questions. So we couldn't take no more chances."

"Pop," I said from where I sat. I wanted to touch him, comfort both of us, but he was very calm, very distant from this tumult in my chest. "Were you glad? Did it—" I looked down, embarrassed. "Were you happy?"

"Happy? With her?" He hadn't mentioned her name once. He laughed. "I was all the time looking over my shoulder Mommy shouldn't find out. I don't know if that was so happy." He ran his hands hard along the sides of his head, where the remaining fringes of his grey stubble grew; it was not a gesture I recognized, probably something he did when he had a full head of hair. "So anyway, Joey, you children with your happy, all the time happy this and not-so-happy that—how do you know what this happy feels like?"

It was the thing that had separated us, really: my choice to be happy in my life, not simply "comfortable." "You'd have known," I said with a bitterness I thought nervy but couldn't take back. "Well, then, why did you do it? Why would you take such a chance?" If it wasn't for joy, I meant, if it wasn't for ecstasy. I saw him trudging up from the subway with the Journal-American under his arm, and sometimes the Daily News or the Post if he had found one abandoned on the train, summer, winter, all the time except the slack season when there was no work. I couldn't imagine the mechanics of an affair in the life of a man of such regular habits. Did he really go to union meetings when he said he did? Or to play pinochle?

"Why?" he echoed. He had sat down facing me, in his familiar defeated slouch. All his life my father has looked as if the chairs and mattresses he sat on were too soft. "Why?" He shook his head. "She was a nice woman, I told you. Very lively. A good talker. She dressed good, it was a pleasure to sit by her." He looked to see if I understood. "And miserable, all the time he made her sad. I don't know about his problem, what it was. Maybe the music. He thought he was a genius, a Heifetz, the world should see it, so all the time he was taking it out on her. How she suffered by him! I don't know what it was."

No matter what kind of English a man spoke he could be an adulterer, I thought. The word seemed hollow, as if its meaning had spilled out of it, leaving a dry pod with no mischief in it. I still felt as if I'd fallen hard on my stomach, though, the way I used to when I was a kid. And he was not apologizing. I was impressed.

"So are you going to marry her? Have you been dreaming of this ever since you were—"

He shrugged and looked into his baggy lap. "I don't know, sonny, it's not the same thing now. After all. Then I was, you know. . . . A man. Now." My father pulling his clothes off in a frenzy, not taking the bills and coins out of his pockets, his glasses, his comb, not laying his slacks scrupulously over the back of the fat brown armchair with the clawfoot legs to keep the crease, not putting on the pajamas my mother had ironed, striped or figured with one of those aimless silly patterns, green or gray. I used to run the drawstring through with a pin when it came out in the wash. No, my father locking the door, approaching her, this Frieda, slowly, to draw out the pleasure a little longer. I knew the dream ritual too in which everything moves incredibly fast and incredibly slowly, both. It is forbidden pleasure that leaves a scar. Memory heals ragged when it isn't repeated a thousand times. He would know, if I said that, he would recognize the crater where the shame and jeopardy lay, and the sharp ridge of healing. Everything in me heaved once, the feeling in the elevator that had made my son say "Gulp" and press his palm to his stomach.

"Well, think about it, then. You don't have to decide right now." I stood up as if this had been a routine conversation. I was glad to find my knees steady. "See how it feels to think about it. Waking up with somebody there besides old Morris." I hit Morris's bedspread with my hand.

"I don't know, Joe. Ocean Parkway, what am I going to do all the way out there?" Being with Frieda didn't seem to loom large in this proposal.

"What do you do here?" You can sit in a chair anywhere, I thought. You can wrap your *tfillin,* eat your poached egg, huddle out of the wind.

"If she could drive a car. I got my doctors' appointments, and the *shul* maybe isn't so close. Here it's convenient under one roof." He was teetering. A shove either way could do it. I embraced him, showed him how to work the radio one more time, went down to the lobby by the stairs two at a time, agitated, while he stood bewildered beside the elevator whose button he had pushed for me hospitably, the way a host watches till the car departs, taking you with it.

We began the drive toward the city in silence. Jane asked me what was wrong and I snapped at her. "Why are you angry?" she said, though I swore I wasn't angry. My father rising from the warm rumpled bed and pulling on his rough layers of clothing, shrugging on his coat, his muffler, his gloves, and coming home to the Bronx, to me and to my mother standing over the endlessly steaming *tup* of soup. Steam coming out of his mouth as he turned the corner from the hilly avenue and headed toward me where I sat in front of the apartment house, on its two wide brick steps, in exactly the same place every day, even, preposterously (and to my mother's irritation) in the dead heart of winter. It was my challenge to myself, my hardship, my fifty-pound weights, my four-minute mile, my swan dive, to sit with my corduroy knees drawn up in the three-quarter dark, tears of cold in my eyes, my gloveless hands jammed in my pockets, waiting for him, knowing it was only my secret endurance that made him come.

Tim Gautreaux

Just Turn Like a Gear

Billy Willit hung up the wall phone in his kitchen and dropped hard into a vinyl dinette chair, spreading its chrome legs. He screwed up his face at his wife, Tilda, seated across from him at the formica table. "That was the warden. You know what I just got handed?" He pointed toward the phone over the back of his chair.

"You're back on the hoe detail," Tilda joked. "I told you not to take off so much."

"Aw, no. It's Miller Babin. Remember?"

Her pleasant expression faded. "So it's him." She placed her coffee on the formica and tilted her head. A small roller unwrapped down the left side of her hair, and she grabbed at it, winding a bleached strand around the plastic. "They've decided to electrocute him next month?"

"That's right. And I've got to find someone to do it." Billy put his hand on his round middle as though his stomach hurt. "Remember Farley, the old state executioner? He's in Baton Rouge for heart surgery and Marvin is scared to pull the switch." Marvin Trouple, warden of the regional penitentiary, wore tailored three-piece suits, trying to hide his weakness which the inmates could sense under the expensive cloth. The small number of prisoners who ever caught sight of him called him Marvy-Babe.

The inmates showed more respect to Billy Willit. He was a fifty-year-old executive assistant warden who started his career as a type-writer repairman in Natchez, Mississippi. He lost his first job because of his temper. One hot afternoon he was unable to get the tabs to work on a manual office model after two hours work, so he threw it through a closed sixth-story window and watched it tumble to street level and crush in the roof of a parked sedan. The next month his brother-in-law got him a job as a tower guard at Bisley, a regional prison farm. After twenty years he outlived enough prison officials to get to his present air-conditioned but unimportant office. The prisoners called him Blow-Up, or sometimes, Fat Blow.

Tilda lit up a cigarette and blew her first lungfull of smoke at the telephone. "Don't they have a standby executioner?"

"We got enough deadheads out at the farm now. Why do we need a standby person for a job we haven't done for years and years? Trouple's not sure the chair even works anymore."

She tapped the edge of a purple glass ashtray with her Lucky. "Can't you get an executioner from out of state?"

"Trouple says he's tried. None of them wants to fool with our old system. I guess they're not sure they can get a clean kill out of the machine." He wagged his head. "Hell, I don't know. I just got told to find someone to pull the switch. Trouple said he'd worry about the electronics."

"He wants a volunteer," Tilda said. "He thinks a volunteer will look better to the newspapers than a paid executioner."

Billy thought about this for a while, staring vacantly at the sugar bowl. "He worries about bad press, all right." He turned, looking through the glass of the kitchen door over to a new brick house across the street which looked exactly like his own. "Anyway, I've got to advertise, Marvin says. But how?" He scratched his bald head and ranged his gray eyes over at his wife.

She pursed her lips. "Have it run as a news item in the Pilotville paper," she said. "Last time Utah executed somebody they used local volunteers."

Her husband thought about this. He could count on Tilda for a clear-cut vision to the heart of any problem. He had no such decisive force and usually fretted and worried about each of his minor problems out at the prison until he lost his temper and smashed something. Sometimes his frustration at not being able to make a decision caused him to throw an inmate against a wall or into a ditch. One hot day down at the prison machine shop, unable to decide whether to junk the prison lawn tractor or to order it rebuilt, he shot the machine through the engine with a tower guard's rifle.

He stood up and kissed his wife on the neck before banging

through the kitchen door on his way to Pilotville a few miles up the road. At the newspaper office he gave a statement to a reporter who promised she would write a story which would appear the next day. He left the office relieved. He had made a decision and done something.

The next morning Billy was dimly pleased at the terse article appearing on page one of the Pilotville Journal. The logical thing to do after all, it seemed, was to advertise locally. His white prison sedan climbed the long low rise to gate one, a breach in miles of towering galvanized chain-link fence topped with razor-like concertina wire. After checking in with the guard, a drowsy old man nursing a Winchester pump shotgun, he drove up the asphalt a mile to his office in a squat rectangular brick building. He went in, sat down and called Marvin Trouple to tell him what he had done.

"That's a strange way to get an executioner, don't you think?"

"It's a strange business to begin with," he retorted. "You want me to ask for resumés or something?"

"All right, don't get so damned snappy. When did you set the interviews?"

"I had the article state after lunch today, here."

"O.K. But be careful." There was a long silence after this statement as Billy tried to figure out what the warden meant. He was always saying things like, "Whatever you think is best," or "That would work all right, I guess," statements which indicated that the warden really did not know what he was doing half the time. He often left the important decisions up to his assistants so they could be pinned for any mistakes. Billy's temper made his decisions for him, but the warden never made any decisions by himself.

"Be careful about what?" Billy asked, flushing slightly.

"You know. The press is going to cover this thing pretty close. Pick somebody that doesn't look crazy. Somebody with, uh, with . . . "

"Class?" Billy said, wincing.

"Yeah. That's right. Class. I guess. Give me a call when you get someone. Babin is scheduled for March 17 at dawn."

Billy hung up and loosened his tie; although it was a chilly day, he felt hot, and he walked over to the radiator by the window, turning the valve to shut off the steam. He threw up the window and looked over the grassy grounds of the office compound to a stand of gray hardwoods, huge pin oaks about two hundred yards distant. One oak, inside the wire fence, twice as large as the rest, stood out from the ranks, its empty branches soaring into a milky sky. In the many idle hours his job afforded him, Billy had studied this one tree as if it were a statement of nature, a decision the forest had made for the groundskeeper. The tree had begun to die about three years before. The gray bark was splotched with orange mold, and a white, scalloped fungus burst through the dead skin of several upper branches. Turning away he went to his desk where a pile of federal forms awaited him. He dawdled over them until noon, carefully filling them out in longhand, grateful that they would not allow him to think about the afternoon. When the hoarse whistle roared from the sugar mill across the rich alluvial soil of the farm, he left for the cafeteria.

The building where the employees ate was a one-story brick slab a few hundred feet from Billy's office. Already the tower guards were lining up their trays on the railings, talking to the few white-collar employees who came in early. The clerks and supervisors were never as hungry as the guards who stacked their trays with extra drinks, extra salads, and double helpings of meat. Taking a ham sandwich and a glass of milk, Billy sat down next to a window. Cyrus Ditts, a horseback guard who watched over prisoners working the soybeans, sat with him, his tray overflowing. He put his straw cowboy hat between them on the table.

"I saw the paper," Cyrus said, squinting a red-veined eye as he squeezed his lemon into one of his glasses of tea. "It's a shame when you got to go outside to get someone like that."

"Marvin said nobody here'll do the job," Billy responded, a hint of accusation lingering around the edges of his voice. "Not even Black Raoul."

"Black Raoul is one of us," the horseback guard said, carefully buttering his cornbread. "He'll call us to shoot a man going over the fence because he knows that man knows that's how it is. That's the rules." Black Raoul was a long-time trusty guard of the death-house exercise yard.

"Babin broke the rules," Billy said, looking through the foggy windows at his oak. "What's the difference?"

"Ain't the same." He ran his right hand through his greasy black hair to sweep it out of his weathered face, the face of an Indian, the face, Billy thought, imagined by boys out of the side of a mountain.

"Babin'll be sitting still when he gets it. It's kind of religious. If you're struck dead in the middle of sinning, you go straight to hell. But if you're struck dead after a while, when you're just walking along the road or fixing a broke water pipe, nobody knows."

"I don't know what you're talking about." Billy tucked the last piece of sandwich into his mouth and stared at Cyrus, waiting for explanation. The guard was a man who, if you stared at him long enough, would keep talking, as though to be looked at was to be questioned.

"It's kind of a code. I'd shoot Babin in the head if he tried to go over my fence. But not if I found him in my shack on the other side watching my portable TV." Cyrus rolled his veined eyes at Billy as he popped a forkful of hamburger steak into his mouth.

"You don't think he ought to fry?"

"I somehow think he ought to. None of us can forget those babies, none of us who read the paper. But I won't do it. Don't ask me why not."

"I'm fixing to meet some people who will, if anyone shows up," Billy said, wiping his big mouth and getting up slowly.

Five minutes later he was seated at his desk, and there was a knock at the door. He got up, letting in a small man dressed in khaki pants burned through in several places by either cigarettes or welding. His shirt was a washed-out cotton rag covered by either stains or faded design.

"Lo," the man said. "Name Earnest Quartenberry. Someone told me about the paper." His eyes were tiny and very far apart. His hair was gray, combed straight back from a sloping, sun-blistered forehead.

"Have a seat there." Billy sat down and immediately remembered warden Trouple's "Be careful."

"This feller you burning a nigger?" Quartenberry sat hunched over with his hands pressed palms together, pointed down. He asked the question as though he were asking the time.

"No. He's a white boy."

"Who'd he kill?"

"Five children," Billy said, feeling that he was wasting his time. "White," he added quickly.

"Well, sir, I'll throw the juice to him awright, if that's what you want. Things won't straighten up in this state unless we start hangin' and fryin' again." The man's eyes, which seemed weak at first, took on a certain power as he spoke, as though he convinced himself of something as he spoke it. They were the eyes of a crazy man, Billy thought. He imagined the reporters photographing Earnest Quartenberry at the switch, imagined what the liberal press would do to the prison administration, imagined Marvin Trouple in his blue three-piece suit crying like a baby as he prepared to meet the governor.

"I tell you what, Earnest. Just give me your number where I can get in touch with you, and I'll give you a call if we need you." He turned a pad around and pointed it at the other man who sat slumped into an S shape staring at him with sudden suspicion.

"I don't use no phone," he said, waving a skinny hand studded with greasy fingernails at the pad.

Billy turned the pad around again and prepared to write. Maybe the man couldn't. "Then give me your mailing address."

Quartenberry leaned back and stared at the wall above Billy's head. "Don't take no mail," he said. "I'll tell you where to find me, though."

"That's good."

"You know Mr. Ellis McFarland's property?"

"Yes."

"The road that goes straight back two mile to the levee? You get on that road and go to the tractor shed don't nobody use no more. In back that they's a cane truck on its side. In back that they's a tool shed don't have no windows. I stay there."

"OK," Billy sang. "When we need you we'll send out a car." He stood up.

"Better send a truck. Can't a car get back where I'm at," he said, sliding out of the chair.

When Quartenberry got into the hall, Billy saw another man rise from a folding chair and stride toward him. This is going to be a long day, he thought. The other followed him into his office and sat down without being asked to. He was a tall, well-built man who did not take off his cowboy hat nor his mirror sunglasses even though the old office, cheaply paneled in dark, imitation wood, was as dim as a tunnel. He wore a wooly jacket, blue jeans and black western boots. He seemed to be about thirty-five. "I hear you want that murdering son-of-a-bitch to scream," he began.

"We need an executioner, Mr.?"

"Sallet," he said. "Lacy Sallet."

"Are you related to or have you known any of the victims of this man?" Billy began to pull a form out of his desk drawer.

"All men are related someway, mister. Except for Babin who ain't related to nothing."

Billy stared at him and made a face. He hadn't counted on a philosopher showing up in this part of the state.

"I mean, I ain't adverse to killing the bastard at all. I was in Nam. I killed every day God sent, so I know how to do." Sallet stuck his legs straight out in front of him and folded his hands over his belly. It was impossible for Billy to see his eyes. He didn't know why people wore those glasses; as a matter of fact, it made him angry to have someone in his office staring at him at such an advantage.

"Why don't you take off your glasses," Billy said, a slight edge in his voice.

"Don't see why I have to," Sallet snapped.

"Look, stud, you got any eyeballs behind there?" Nobody could outsnap Billy Blow-Up.

The cowboy peeled off his glasses and showed a pair of surprised ordinary eyes. He looked like any of the local young farmers, almost normal.

"Just write your number on that pad," Billy said. "If we need you, will you be around on the seventeenth of next month?"

"Sure will," he answered, standing up and sidling toward the door, all his power stripped with his sunglasses. He wrote on the pad as he moved.

"You got a suit?" he asked as an afterthought.

"A suit?"

"Yes. A suit. This is a pretty sober occasion."

The cowboy thought for a while and handed back the pad. "Will Babin have to wear one?"

Billy let out a long sigh. "No."

"Then why . . . "

"Thank you. We'll call you if we need you."

The next man he interviewed was Horace Clemmons, a bank officer at the local savings and loan. As the old man sat down in the office, Billy looked him over and thought how pleased Trouple would be. Clemmons wore a three-piece suit, his gray hair was neatly combed, his Florsheims gleamed, and in his face was an aura of upper-middle-class composure. People would see his picture in the paper and know that the man who pulled the switch on Miller Babin was a gentleman. Billy knew Clemmons personally. He knew him as a life-long resident of Pilotville, as a run-of-the-mill Presbyterian, a Rotarian, a veteran. There was nothing the press could do with him.

"Horace, I'm kind of curious about why you're volunteering for this job," Billy said, settling into his padded office chair.

Clemmons looked down at the tile floor as though the question embarrassed him. "I'm not sure that I know myself. I'm afraid that Babin will get out someday, I guess. Somebody might lose another child. I don't know." He got up and walked to the window, looking out to the woods. "I think about him when I look at my grandchildren."

"Do you know the families of anybody he hurt?"

"No. I guess you think it's crazy to want to kill someone without a personal reason." Clemmons' gray eyes seemed to focus on something out on the grounds.

"Some people might say you're brave. If you can spare the time next month on the seventeenth, I think you might be our man. I can't tell you for sure right now because I have to interview the rest of the folks that show up today."

"I won't be sorry if you find somebody else." He kept looking out to the woods as though something was bothering him there. Billy walked up next to him and followed his gaze.

"It's dying," Billy said after a minute.

"Such a big tree. So symmetrical and heavy of limb. I don't see a lightning strike."

"It's not lightning. It's not disease. No one knows what went wrong with it. Black Raoul says a tree is just like a man. It can't live forever."

Clemmons looked away from the tree. "Black Raoul the murderer?"

"He's a trusty in DR."

"Yes." He turned and walked slowly toward the door. He was a man who knew when business was finished. He did not have to be told to leave.

"I'll call you," Billy said.

"I hope you don't have to," the old man answered, pulling the office door shut.

That afternoon, the interviews continued. There was Lloyd Buntin, a pest-control man from St. Francisville, Wilfred Boineaux, a garage mechanic who wanted the job seemingly because he was bored, Alexis McCrory, a black undertaker who wanted two jobs, and Xavier Guz, a simple, red-faced man who relished the chance of killing someone.

Billy usually left the office at four, and at a quarter to four, when he saw no one waiting in the hall, he began to clear off his desk. There was a knock at the door and he grimaced, imagining another sour volunteer intent on wasting his time.

"Come in," he moaned, pausing with a handful of papers in midair. A woman, perhaps forty-five, dressed in a navy-blue skirt and jacket over a white blouse, walked in and stood in front of the desk, waiting to be asked to sit down. As Billy looked at her he worried that she might be from the parole board.

"I read your statement in the paper," she said.

Billy was suddenly rattled. "Sit down." He wondered what Trouple would think. She was slim, about five-and-a-half feet tall and looked like a librarian, a graceful, pretty librarian. "You mean you're here about the execution?"

"Yes," she said, crossing her legs in a slow, smooth motion, the way a polished woman does, showing nothing to a man looking at her head-on. "I'd like to volunteer."

"Is there any special reason you would like to do this?" He read in her ordinary brown eyes an unease which might signal that she was hiding something. He was not good at spotting hidden things in women. This he knew from twenty-three years of living with Tilda, who behaved stupidly at all times except when it mattered that she did not.

"I feel that Mr. Babin would be better off someplace else."

"I see," he said, puzzled at the spirituality of the statement. "You don't know any of the families of the victims, I guess."

"No." She shook her head gravely, folding her hands over her knees. "Do you really want a reason or are you merely trying to find out if I have a grudge that the press can exploit?"

He shook his head. He had underestimated another woman. "It's just that we need a responsible person to do this for the state, someone not, uh . . . "

"Crazy?"

He turned in his chair and looked out the window at the lengthening shadows on the lawn spreading from his oak. If she was going to finish his sentences, she could invent her own questions. After a moment's silence, she cleared her throat. He did not turn around.

"What are you staring at?" she asked.

"That big oak. I've stared at it for so many years I feel it belongs to me."

For a long time she looked past him through the window. "It is an impressive tree."

"Yep. It's some tree all right."

She let out a pent-up breath. "I want to do it because it needs to be done, Mr. Willit. I don't have young children, so it's not a protection motive. I'm not militant about anything. I'm just a schoolteacher from Pilotville who wants to do something definite, something to put things in order. Mr. Babin will never be eliminated if he lives past his execution date."

"That's for sure. His lawyers will invent a case for a new trial in two months for some reason or another." He turned to look at her again. "What does your husband think about this?"

"My husband died five years ago. And I don't care what my children think. The youngest is twenty and beyond my influence."

He thought of his own twenty-year-old son presently in the woods east of Vicksburg at a four-wheeler mud rally. His twenty-five-year-old son had recently quit his job at the power company to open a head shop in Shreveport. "I see," he said in an understanding tone.

He interviewed Evelyn Wright for half an hour. She told him that she had taught math four miles away in Pilotville for twenty-four years. She was not depressed, not on drugs, did not owe a large sum of money, was not ill, did not have a depraved family. There was a subtle irony bordering on the dark side of humor in many of her statements about her career and life in Pilotville. Billy looked at her smooth skin and dark, silver-veined curls and could detect no sign of anything the press could seize and exploit. There was no fire in her eyes as there was in Earnest Quartenberry's murderous balls. He wondered what the warden would think of her. Then he thought of Horace Clemmons. The uneasy realization that he would have to make a decision filtered down on Billy's balky mind.

He thanked the woman for the visit, jotted her address and phone number, and followed her into the parking lot. He wanted to see her car. She walked over to a four-door Oldsmobile, started it and drove off in an ordinary manner, doing nothing to indicate that she was crazy, and Billy nodded to himself. He went inside and called the principal of Pilotville High School, who told him that Mrs. Wright was indeed an ordinary teacher, a woman who did her job loyally.

"But would you say she had any, what you might call, idiosyncrasies?" Billy liked the word and was finally talking to someone who would not find it odd.

"No," the principal said. "She seems a bit bored lately. In the past two years, I mean."

"Nothing else?"

"No, Mr. Willit. She's a good teacher."

He drove home to Tilda feeling satisfied. But that night he woke up on his coil-suspension mattress next to his delicately snoring wife. He lay on his back and folded his hands behind his head, staring at the sheetrock ceiling in the glow filtering in through the curtains from the streetlight. He thought how sheetrock was a thin covering of the bones of the house, the ugly studs, pipes and wires. It was like Evelyn Wright's face, giving no hint of what was underneath.

He thought of Horace Clemmons, wondering if he should tap him for the job of executioner. The fact that Clemmons was a man comforted him because Billy understood men more than he did women. He felt a bit guilty about questioning the woman's motives more than he questioned those of the men. Was it because killing was more of a man's job?

The thought caused him to sit up in bed and stare through the sheers into the lawns of the subdivision. He had come across many women during his experience in the prison system who had killed, and he attempted to assemble a representative catalogue to prove something to himself. He thought of five women quickly, all convicted of knife murders, crimes of passion. Three more came to mind who had done in their boyfriends with guns. There was Martina in the women's division across the river who had backed over her husband with the family station wagon immediately after he had told her he was leaving for good. Woman after woman came to Billy in the dark, and they were all guilty of killing by passion, in the heat of the moment's passion. He could think of only three who had planned the murders they were involved in, and they were sent up with male accomplices.

It seemed that unless a woman became angry, and damned angry at that, she was unlikely to take a life. In contrast Billy could think of dozens of male killers, nearly everyone in Black Raoul's exercise yard, who had planned their crimes or who had not been particularly excited when they had carried them out. He thought of Willie Sid, an accountant who had arrived at a used car lot to do the place's books and who shot the manager, took his keys and started up several cars before he found one he liked the sound of, driving off to Florida.

He rolled over against Tilda and tried not to think; soon he was asleep, her hard body working a charm on him.

The next morning he was a flurry of indecision, totally ambivalent about the choice between Horace and the Wright woman. He told everything to Tilda over his third cup of coffee, even about his nighttime list of women murderers. She sniffed like a horse. Even though she was not coarse, but in fact, fine-looking for a tall middle-aged woman, Tilda carried the womanly traits of the community: she cursed, suffered from sinus and burned holes in everything with her cigarettes.

"You're right," she said, sitting down across from him at the breakfast table and crossing her legs smoothly, but with some difficulty, rocking on her round bottom to give momentum to the act of hoisting her right leg over her left. "When you boys look at one of those bad ones out at the farm, all you see is a son-of-a-bitch. When a woman looks at a son-of-a-bitch she sees him for what he is, all right, but then she sees him as somebody's boy, somebody's baby a long time ago." She took a drag on her cigarette and blew the smoke between Billy and the door. "I don't know, Billy. A lot of women just worry more about bringing sons-of-bitches into the world than they do about taking them out."

He looked more perplexed. "She worries me, but she sure would make good press. When those liberal paper boys get through with her somebody'll be after her to do lady cigarette commercials in magazines.

"Go over to Pilotville and talk to her after work." Tilda said this in a quiet voice as though she might have wanted Billy to think he was hearing his own thoughts.

"Hold supper for me."

Cyrus Ditts, the horseback guard who often ate lunch with Billy, was waiting for him when he walked into his office.

"What can I do for you, Cy?" he asked, falling into his desk chair.

"Kiddie day," he said.

"Oh my God." Kiddie day was a quarterly event. The youngest offenders from the state's city slums were brought in every three months for a tour of the prison. "I'd forgotten." He walked over to a metal file cabinet and from the top drawer retrieved his large-billed cap which had the word *Bisley* spelled threateningly across its white crown. He followed Cyrus who was holding his Winchester pump in his right hand, and together they walked across the compound to the visitor's parking area. They came to a blue school bus in which thirty pairs of eyes looked warily out at the drab buildings and miles of galvanized wire. Cyrus nodded to the driver who told everyone to file out and stand alongside the bus. Thirty young boys between eleven and fourteen came out into the sunshine. This part of the event, the filing off the bus, was something Billy never got used to. He was always struck with the young faces of the offenders. He assumed some link between innocence and youth, and here in the dowdy line-up was a contradiction he never could understand. One short black youth looked like a baby, his short curls shining as though his mother had just lifted him from the bathtub.

It was Billy's job to greet the bus and to tell the children what they would do before being brought back to their city. He gave his spiel, told them what cell blocks they would go through, told them that they would go out in the field in the hot sun to see what the work was like for a prisoner. When he finished, he asked if there were any questions. A tall boy whose jeans were three inches above his ankles said, "Yeah, man." Billy nodded at him.

"We gonna see the 'lectric chair, man?"

Billy wondered if anyone had ever shown Miller Babin an electric chair when he had been a boy. He wondered if it would have made any difference. The chair was part of the tour they saved for the older delinquents. "Why do you want to see that?"

The boy shrugged his thin shoulders. "I just wants to, you know?"

Billy nodded to Cyrus. "Throw it in the tour. Let him sit in it if he wants to and pray that that's the last time he'll sit in it." Everybody stirred uneasily when he said that, even Cyrus, who shifted his shotgun from one hand to the other.

"Any other questions?" Billy saw a small black hand rise above the head of the smallest boy. He had the face of a cherub. "Yes?"

"We going by cell block O?" he asked.

"No. Why?" Block O was a minimum security area to the north of the farm.

"That's where my daddy be," he said. "I thought maybe I can see him."

"No." he said again, looking over the top of the bus as though the answer cost him nothing.

"Oh." The boy looked sideways, sticking his hands into his pockets.

Another little boy with a mouthful of crooked teeth and a shock of uncombed blond hair asked a question. "Someone tried to run out this place, will you kill him with that gun there?"

"That's the rules," Cyrus drawled, narrowing his red eyes at the youth.

"Would you kill a convick just for fun?"

"No, boy. What kind of question is that? It's them that kills for fun what we got locked up here. Somebody's got to be on the fence before I shoot him." The old horseback guard was flustered. He turned away and faced cell block A, their first stop.

"All right," Billy announced. "Move them along. Come lunchtime, let them eat under the sick oak." He went back to his office and sat in his chair looking over the lawn at the dying tree. Its branches were puffy in places, and when he looked close he saw raw spots where pieces of bark had fallen away. Last spring the leaves had been thin and uneven, the color too yellow. He wondered if the tree would become dangerous, if the big limbs would fall off.

He knew he must decide who the executioner would be as soon as possible. Staring out the window was doing him no good, and in desperation he called Warden Trouple's number. He quickly explained his problem. Trouple insulted him, told him that he shouldn't be afraid of a woman, that she would be a good choice, he guessed. Billy countered with the attributes of Horace Clemmons and Trouple grew abusive, asking him what he was requesting his opinion for if he wasn't going to make use of it. The conversation degenerated quickly until Billy grew so angry that he was yelling into the receiver. "OK boy, I don't need no damned advice from you. I'll just go ahead and pick somebody and you'll see them March seventeenth for the first time." Marvin Trouple said something nasty about going to work for Smith-Corona again and Billy slammed the receiver down so hard that it bounced onto the desk. He mashed the button with his thumb to kill Trouple's whining and then dialed a number written on a pad next to the phone. He spoke with the secretary at Pilotville High School, got the woman's schedule and then walked out into the oily parking lot to find one of the farm's official cars.

The high school was a modern one-story brick-and-tile building, a labyrinth of halls and classrooms. At five-to-twelve he finally located her room and took off his hat, leaning against the wall to wait for the end of class. He could hear her lecturing inside, a steady, professional voice, the voice of someone who knew her subject almost too well, the voice of a recording. The classroom had two doors, one at the head of the class, one at the rear. Looking through a glass slot cut vertically in the rear door he saw several students who were either asleep or gazing out onto the playground. Two were carrying on a subdued conversation, and two others were drawing in their notebooks. He could not quite see Evelyn Wright but could hear her trying to teach the class about quadratic equations. For five minutes he listened and understood, the old facts coming back to him like unimportant memories. The bell down the hall rattled alive, and the somnolent class jumped to life and began to file through the door, bumping past him into the uncomplicated air of the corridor. When the class was nearly empty, he walked in. She saw him and didn't change her expression.

"What brings you up here, Mr. Willit?"

"Hello. I'd just like to talk some more about our meeting the other day." Standing before her desk, he felt suddenly subordinate. He folded his hands before him. "Is there a place around here where we could have lunch?"

"I'm afraid not. I have a sandwich waiting for me in the teacher's lounge, but the place is crowded now. No place to talk." She stepped from behind her desk and sat down in one of the metal and formica student desks, her stockings whispering as she crossed her legs. He sat next to her.

"I guess I just wanted to make sure that you wanted to do this," he began. "It happens at dawn on March 17."

"I'll be there. Do you want me to come to your office?"

"I'm afraid it'll be early. About five or a little before."

"OK," she said. "Now I suppose you want to know why I want to do it?" She looked at him almost viciously, as though baiting him for a fight.

"No, lady. I just wanted to be sure you'll show up." He forced a smile which wrinkled his bald forehead. He began to play with his hat like a cowboy. Tilda often said he looked like Gene Autry.

She looked away, and in an instant her eyes misted over. "You're lying. You want to know, don't you? You can't fool me. What person in his right mind wouldn't be curious?"

He began to feel queasy and foolish, as though he had bought something and realized suddenly that he had paid too much for it. Pulling out his handkerchief he wiped his forehead.

She looked at him closely. "Don't let me upset you."

"Upset me?"

"My husband used to wipe his face with a handkerchief when we would begin discussions." Outside the window two boys passed, bragging about their video game scores.

"Aw, it's just hot, that's all." He looked down at the floor tiles, feeling a fear mount inside. He wondered where the conversation was leading.

"I'm a very private person, Mr. Willit. I don't like to define my reasons for doing things." She stopped and looked away, seeming to try to get control of her feelings, momently biting her lip, raising her eyebrows. "Just don't worry about me."

"That's the advice my wife gives me."

She looked at him with new interest. "Is your wife still with you?"

"Oh, yeah. She's just a big country girl, but we get along real good."

"I hope you never lose her, then." She ran her fingers through her dark hair as though she had to touch herself to prove she was real. "My husband and I were very compatible. After he died, I tried to rely on my children." She stopped speaking abruptly and threw her gaze out over the playground as though to visualize her children years before in the tumult of play. Her look became an expression of longing, and Billy saw her right hand open and close in a gesture that had meaning only for her.

"Look," he began, "you don't have to tell me anything. I just don't want you to let yourself in for something you really don't want to do. I've got half-a-dozen fellows on a string that want to pull the switch."

She almost smiled at him. "Is it really a switch or do they just say that?" Her eyes fastened on his own.

"Yes'm. A double knife blade."

"You mean like in the old Frankenstein movies?"

"An electrician will set everything up and he'll show you what to do."

She sat up stiffly and uncrossed her legs. "I'll be there on time."

Billy let out a breath noisily. "I'm glad. I just wanted to make sure how you felt about this."

Evelyn Wright ran her eyes over him, his large bald head, his sloping wrestler's shoulders that she knew were all fat. Reaching out she gave him a playful slap on the arm. "Don't worry, Mr. Willit. Whatever my reasons, I'll show up."

He didn't change his expression when she touched him. People in this part of the state were fond of slapping each other affectionately. He stood, taking her hand as she offered it, helping her out of the cramped desk. "I don't want to take up your lunch hour."

"It doesn't take me long to eat." She gathered up her books and notes from the wooden desk.

"I'll be going now. I'll call you the day before the seventeenth."

"That's fine," she said, putting her right hand into a pocket of her blue skirt and pulling out a tissue to wipe her nose.

"Maybe you can come over and have dinner with Tilda and me after this thing's over."

"What a strange request. Dinner with the executioner." She laughed.

He gave her a worried smile and walked with her down the hall to the teachers' lounge. There, she touched his arm and several teachers looked up at him, causing him to flush like a teenager. He started to say something to her but they were both distracted by a class of first graders marching past their legs, going to the cafeteria. When the woman saw the flock of bright faces, her expression froze into a poisonous frown.

"Miller Babin," she said to herself. "Would he like to be here?"

Billy nodded slowly, wiping his forehead again. "Five of them together in the same room." He stared at the children in disbelief, having forgotten how small and fine-featured first graders were, having forgotten what Babin had done. "What are they doing at a high school?"

"Field trip," she said, folding her arms and leaning against the wall. "First graders go everywhere in town. The railroad station. The phone company. They just follow where their teacher leads without a thought. They never have to make a decision."

"That must be nice," he said longingly, looking after the line of children as it wove down the hall and out of the building into the sunshine.

That night at supper Tilda asked him how his interview had gone.

"Oh, all right, I guess." He was feeling fine. He shoveled at a plate of sliced ham, greens, potatoes and string beans. "She turned out to be a pretty agreeable girl after all. She's sure she wants to do it, anyway. She slapped my arm real hard."

Tilda didn't miss a chew. "Those Pilotville women like to think they're more polished than most, but they're pretty mean, deep down."

The night before the execution, Billy could not sleep. He lay in bed and watched the ceiling, wondering if he was doing something wrong. He questioned whether finding an executioner was as bad as pulling the switch himself. Getting up at two o'clock, he wandered into the kitchen and stared into the refrigerator. Deciding that a beer would calm his nerves, he grabbed a can of the sale brand Tilda had brought home from the one-stop. He put a forefinger through the little aluminum ring and it broke off the tab without opening the can. He stared at the metal circle in disbelief. He rummaged through the hill of utensils in the kitchen drawer for three minutes before he found a rusty beer opener. The tool would not grab the rim on the top of the can, and there was no rim on the bottom. He turned the can around four or five times in the dim light of the refrigerator, and torn between putting the can back and stabbing it with a fork, he made a roundhouse swing and slammed it onto the kitchen floor. It skittered across the tile and banged into the wall. It was deformed, but unopened. Tilda appeared, leaning on the doorjamb. "Get dressed and go out there," she said.

"Til, my stomach hurts so bad." He backed up against the counter, his hands folded over his belly.

"It'll all be over in four hours. Four hours won't kill you. Not you."

He could not see her in the dark kitchen, but he could feel her presence give him strength as though some intangible power passed between them. "I'm just wondering if what I'm doing is right," he said. "What do you think, Til?"

From behind her an orange star appeared as she swung a cigarette up to take a drag. "Who do you think I am? God? If you didn't go out there today, they'd still do it. You're just a little gear in the machine, and if you don't turn with the big wheels, Trouple will strip you clean. Think about Babin. There are as many reasons to do it as not." She walked over to him and rubbed his bald head, finding it in the dark like a doorknob in a familiar house. "Honey, are we smart enough to figure out the best set of reasons? We could think and fret the rest of our lives and then never be sure the decision we made was the right one." She took a long, painful drag on her cigarette. "Just turn like a gear. A gear don't know where the power comes from. It just turns because of it."

He relaxed under Tilda's cool, soft hand like a curled-up morning newspaper. "Where's my blue suit?" he asked, squeezing her behind.

Death Row was a stone building of three stories built in 1883 and topped with countless spirals of Viet-Nam era concertina wire. At five-thirty, two news artists, a photographer, three reporters, Marvin Trouple, Black Raoul, a priest and three guards waited at the gate to the Death Row exercise yard, all watching Billy and Evelyn Wright walk across the grass toward them. Only two reporters were to be allowed at first, but Trouple was so pleased with the idea of a woman executioner that he permitted one more. The photographer snapped his picture and Trouple smiled broadly, adjusting the lapels on his immaculate brown suit, checking his silk tie. As Evelyn Wright approached, introductions were made to the amazed pressmen, and photographs were taken of the woman from several angles.

"Remember, boys," Trouple said expansively, "no pictures once we're inside for the, ah, event."

Billy nodded to Black Raoul only. "What you doing here?"

" 'Lectrician wouldn't work on the panel, so they got me to check it out. Make sure it work right." When he grinned, four gold teeth shone in the mercury-vapor lights of the exercise yard. In the centers were white stars.

"That's right. You were a licensed electrician," Billy said.

"Twenny years ago. Senior trusty got to go anyway," Black Raoul said.

Billy looked up at him as they walked side-by-side. "Are you the senior or just the biggest and the blackest?"

Black Raoul showed his stars. "I be the oldes' and the stronges', Fat Blow."

"Take the lead," Trouple commanded, falling in behind the big trusty. The woman walked ahead of Billy and the reporters and guards came last.

They went through an iron mesh door, up a sour-smelling stairwell to the third floor. There they passed through a double-locked set of barred gates, down a cell block for two hundred feet to a steel wall. Black Raoul produced a small key and opened an ordinary steel door distinguished only by thousands of smudges and scratches covering its tan paint. Through this door was a short hall, three cells on the left, a wooden wall with a black door in its center to the right. The group marched quietly down to the last cell and looked in on Miller Babin, who was sitting on his cot masturbating.

"Aw, shit," he said as the group gathered quietly outside his door. He danced around his cell jerking up his pants, trying to keep his back to them, fussing with his fly.

Trouple blushed and turned to Evelyn Wright to apologize, but she stared at him, not seeming to know what he was talking about. Billy went into the cell behind Black Raoul and checked to see that Babin had been shaved properly. "You want to see the priest?" he asked.

"Naw. He can kiss my ass. I can't believe you're really gonna do this to me. What did I ever do to you people?" He began to cry, and Trouple motioned for two big guards to grab him and pull him into the hall. When they dragged Babin whimpering past the woman, she began to get wild-eyed.

"Easy," Billy said, squeezing her arm. "Easy. It'll be over in a few minutes."

"He's so short. His nose is big," she said in a subdued falsetto.

Miller Babin began to scream as they tried to shove him through the black door. He caught his feet in the door frame, and it took Black Raoul and both guards to force him through. Once inside, Billy held on to the woman as though she were a talisman. The reporters were told to line the wall on the right twenty-five feet from the chair which was on the opposite wall. To the left was an electrical panel eight feet high with controls on the side away from the chair. The panel, which had a small window in its middle, was turned slightly toward the reporters. Black Raoul tended to the controls as the guards fought with Babin. He bit one on the neck and the injured man fell back howling, but the other one slammed his shoulder into the shaved man and thrust him into the seat. Another guard locked the electrode clamps around his ankles while the biggest guard, sweating and cursing, sat on Babin and locked in his arms. When they finished, they backed off and looked at him. The smallest guard, blood streaming down his back, lowered the head electrode onto Babin's slick scalp.

Trouple glided around the room like a butterfly. His shoes were noisy and he was smiling too much. "How's the panel, Raoul?" he asked.

The black man raised a huge, scarred arm and flicked two switches which started the generators, old, black, heavily-wound motors which spun quietly, giving off a mild scent of ozone. He adjusted two sets of rheostats and frowned. "This old thing ain't been used in sixteen years. The amps is wrong."

"It checked out yesterday," Trouple said, a whine in his voice. "Can we still use it?"

"I can't believe it." Babin began screaming. He cursed everyone in the room.

"Sure," Black Raoul said, glaring at the man in the chair through the tinted window of the control panel.

Billy shook his head, thinking of the power of words, how Babin was a doomed man long before he had killed anybody.

Trouple peered at the amperage gauge which fluctuated wildly for a few moments but then calmed down and rested close to the required level. He looked at his watch, then the reporters, then Evelyn Wright. "It's time," he said to her.

She now clung to Billy, her eyes on Babin who writhed and cursed in the chair. Billy knew he would have to lead her over to the panel, but he hesitated. He felt that he was betraying her, sending her out to do something awful that she did not really have to do. He forced himself to move toward the control panel. Be like a gear. Just turn like a gear. He pushed and she walked slowly over to the controls. Trouple showed her that double-blade knife switch that she had to push, one time for twenty seconds, disconnect, and then again for ten seconds.

When Babin saw her walk toward the controls, he stopped struggling. "You mean a bitch is gonna do it? What you got against me, lady? Why ain't you home looking after your kids, huh momma? I can't believe this," he shrieked. She looked at the black bakelite handle of the switch and then at Miller Babin. Tears began to roll from her eyes. She grabbed the handle and looked over at Billy, who was biting his lip. She opened her mouth. "I can't do it," she sobbed.

Trouple stood next to her, behind the panel out of sight of the reporters. "Now just push it to," he coaxed.

"You do it," she said. "I tried, but I can't." She placed a hand over her mouth.

Trouple stalked over to Billy and said something through his teeth. The two of them walked back to the panel where she was sitting on a stool Black Raoul had provided. "Evelyn," Billy said. "Are you going to go through with it?"

She shook her head slowly, crying into her hands. "I thought I could. I don't know what's wrong. He's horrible."

Billy looked over at the reporters, who were busily drawing and writing. "Raoul?"

"No, man. I won't," he said, squinting at the voltmeter.

Trouple looked like a man whose ship was sinking. "I'll have your desk for this," he said. "You'll be back in a tower with a rusty carbine when I get finished with you. Sunshine and mosquitoes, you like that?" He kept his voice low enough so he would not be heard by the reporters, who were absorbed with Babin.

"What do you want from me?" Billy asked, flushing. "I sweated blood over this choice. You think I just went out in the street and grabbed the first person I saw?"

"I should have known to trust a dummy with this job. A typewriter repairman. It takes someone with good sense to choose an executioner. What do you think those press boys are going to say about this if we don't go through with it? Talk to her."

Billy squatted, looking at the woman, and when their eyes met, she shook her head in a delicate, pleading fashion, the way only a woman can.

"One of you screws cut me loose," Babin yelled. He could not see the woman, and like the reporters had no idea of the conflict going on behind the panel.

"Please," Trouple said, getting down on one knee and grabbing the woman's hands. Again, she shook her head. The warden stood up. "You really screwed my life up," he said. "This'll cause me months of paperwork. Do you know how many legislators are on my ass?"

Still squatting, Billy leaned around the panel to look at Miller Babin. The prisoner uttered a curse that made even the big prison guards look at each other in astonishment.

"Talk to me," Billy said.

Babin screamed something which made Evelyn Wright move her

hands to her ears. Black Raoul stuck a long screwdriver into an open panel on the control cabinet to adjust a rheostat. The amperage needle waved like a reed in the wind.

"Talk to me."

"Let me go. Let me go, you fat maggot."

Billy jumped up to say or do something, he didn't know what. He bumped Black Raoul's arm and the trusty dropped his screwdriver into the cabinet. The two men looked after the tool as it fell into the mechanism and lodged between two copper brackets, producing a small blue spark as it did. In thirty seconds they had fished out the screwdriver using two long pairs of insulated pliers. Billy looked up through the tinted glass and found that Babin was dead.

The reporters began scribbling more furiously as the physician walked forward to check for a pulse. They were unaware that Babin's death was an accident. The doctor nodded to Trouple and the warden smiled. Two guards winced as they touched Babin's hot body to unbuckle him. It seemed that everybody wanted to leave at once, to get through the black door. Billy held Evelyn Wright from behind by her upper arms, keeping between her and the reporters, even nudging a couple away when they tried to ask questions. Black Raoul left the group at the third floor gate, turning back to help the guards with Babin, and Billy made sure the reporters were escorted down two landings before he followed. The priest left at the first floor entrance, turning silently into the first floor cells, asking the double-lock guard for permission to give visitations. The reporters, curiously quiet, escaped the exercise yard, running for their cars. Marvin Trouple, casting Billy a grudging smile, stalked off toward his office. Evelyn and Billy walked across the lawn under a new copper sun.

"I am so sorry," she said, leaning heavily on him. "I am so sorry."

"Don't fret about it," he said dully, looking over the lawn for something.

"But you killed a man and you didn't want to do it," she sobbed, realizing the enormity of what had happened. "You killed for me."

"Aw, don't say that. It was kind of an accident. You saw." He was perspiring heavily, even though the air was cool. Stripping his pretty blue coat, he slung it over his shoulder.

"That's how it always is," she said. "Men killing for women." She disengaged her arm from his and walked ahead a step as though to prove that she was strong and separate from him.

"Don't say that. Don't worry about pulling the switch or not pulling it. He didn't die because of you or me." He thought a moment, then added, remorsefully, "Not because of you, anyway."

"We all killed him. Lawyers, guards, there must have been hundreds of people involved." She turned back to him and they linked arms again. "I feel so shaky still."

"Maybe it was the children," he said. "Everybody wants to protect them. There's nothing that will make somebody angry like the death of a child. Even Trouple likes kids." He thought of the shiny faces on the prison bus that rolled up near his office every three months.

"I can't believe I put you through this."

Billy scanned the tree line past his office building. "It's not over, either. Never will be. Just don't worry about it. Not you." He had walked her to a point from which they could see the tall oak he studied endlessly from his office window. They stopped walking and watched a crew of prisoners unpacking chain saws, axes and cans of gasoline from a farm truck parked under its branches. From a hundred yards off they could see that the spring head of leaves was thin and yellow. Several large branches were barren.

"Why, that's the tree you enjoy so much. They're going to cut it down. Isn't there something you can do?"

"I ordered it cut," he said, catching her brown eyes with his own. "It was getting to be dangerous."

Her hand tightened on his arm. "You made a hard decision."

"Yeah, but my wife says I'm not smart enough to figure out what's right and what's wrong."

"We'll never stop wondering," she cried.

"Take it easy on yourself." He patted her hand like the good guy in a cowboy movie.

"How can we ever know? I'm just a math teacher and you're a, a . . ."

"Typewriter repairman," he said, smiling sadly into her face as between them passed the feeling that even though they might not forgive themselves, they would forgive each other. From a distance they looked like brother and sister stopped to talk, the dawn sun gilding her dark hair, lighting his bald head in a bronze glow.

From across the prison lawn came the dark and raspy sound of a big saw warming up.

Andrew Horn

The Making of Musa Maikudi

Musa Maikudi was hardly the best advertisement for the Local Authority Health Clinic in which he worked. His cheeks were hollow; his pale green *riga,* stained and threadbare; and he spat constantly through what few kola-reddened teeth he had retained to the age of forty-three. He looked well set to pose for Oxfam posters. But beneath the crushed and faded cap, embroidered "Nigeria—1978—*Madalla,*" beneath the shaved and vein-ridged skull lay a mind which Musa felt would be the envy of any chauffeur-driven Alhaji. The agents of this mind, his long, incongruously elegant and uncallused fingers, moved with great economy, calm yet ready, as were Musa's large but heavy-lidded eyes.

Musa was the sweeper. Within the highly stratified world of the Clinic—microcosm of the town outside, with its "Sarki" Doctor, "Waziri" Nursing Sister and several Health Assistants, in a great descending social cone—Musa lay at the very bottom, almost invisible to those near the apex. But that was only how it looked from above. Because there was a layer beneath even Musa, a layer which broadened out into the community itself—the patients. Certainly not all of the patients, for many of them were wealthy and influential: shopkeepers, civil servants, teachers. But most of the people who came to the Clinic were not so worldly wise: the farmers from outlying villages and the nomadic cattle-Fulani. Particularly the Fulani. Unused to the Westernized *bature* ways of the towns and only temporarily encamped on the grassy plains to the north, the Fulani would usually enter the Clinic with a bemused look that was their emblem of rusticity. The men were gaunt-faced with arms and calves whose contours showed no sign of muscle, as in a child's drawing, and dressed in indigo-dyed homespun, with broad minaret-shaped grass hats and baggy-seated pantaloons that tapered sharply to the knee. The women had a fine and unselfconscious beauty which aged quickly into a gnarled cadaverousness and, unlike the well wrapped Hausa women, cared little that their breasts were exposed. Bedecked with brass and iron bangles on wrists and ankles, they made music as they walked. The Fulani were a great source of derisive wisecracking amongst the other patients in the Clinic, to which they never responded. "Fulani, your child is pissing on the floor. *Haba,* Fulani! This is not your village-that-walks"—from town women whose own children were just as likely to urinate wherever they stood. They seemed as indifferent to this ridicule as was old Binta Usman, the moon-faced mad woman who had appeared on the Clinic verandah one day in the Harmattan season and had returned daily ever since, to brew her tea, smoke twig-like cigarettes of greasy newspaper, and languidly beg coins or food from patients and staff.

But to Musa the cattle-Fulani and the village farmers were no joke. They were the linchpins of his financial scheme. Musa was not a man of great ambition. His father had wished him to become a *malam,* a religious teacher. But as a boy in Koranic school he could never quite separate the curls, dots and arches which passed across the Arabic text like the sand tracks of small worms. And so he became a sweeper for the Local Authority, under generations of white and black polo-playing provincial officers.

There is not really very much to sweeping. A concentrated and theatrical swirl of dust at 7.00 a.m. and a sluicing of the latrine at noon could be separated by several hours of congenial conversation on the shop-front verandah next door, or even by a quick visit to the market across the road. But some six months after Musa had been transferred to the Clinic from an identical job sweeping an identical "Native Authority Pattern D" building which housed the Tax Office, the Doctor had announced that the Clinic was to be "rationalized." Musa thought that meant a Ministry of Works paint job, overdue now by six years, which would guarantee no sweeping for at least a week. But it soon became clear that "rationalizing" meant more work. The Senior Staff were being overburdened by jobs that others could do and, somehow, pieces of the Doctor's clothing would now have to be worn by the Junior Staff. (That was how it came out in

Hausa, at the far end of a tortured catena of translation.) In the end, what it added up to was that the Attendant, having inherited several responsibilities from above, would divest (this was the inscrutable word) himself of the task of issuing empty bottles to patients who had been directed by the Doctor to the Dispensary. This crucial step in the process of curative community medicine was now to fall to the tapered fingers of Musa Maikudi. And it was to change his life.

He had never thought very much about the Dispensary, a small cluttered room with shelves warped by the weight of bottles—large ones which often contained brightly-colored capsules, but were usually quite empty; small brown ones from which the Sister drew liquids into her syringe for injections. The Dispenser, a rather pompous and toad-like man who wore a white lab coat and a frayed blue dacron tie, had never let Musa sweep the hot and windowless little room unless under the close and jealous scrutiny of the Dispenser's amphibious eyes. Musa assumed that the bottles' contents must be valuable, but he had no idea to whom, exactly.

Now Musa was to be a part of the Dispensary, or at least adjacent to it, for the shallow counter behind which were stored the patients' bottles stood in the corridor, alongside the Dispenser's narrow galley-hatch.

It was on a Monday in the rainy season that Musa took up his new responsibilities. After sweeping the Clinic and the verandah and instead of retiring to the shop-front next door, he stepped behind the yellow counter and faced a small queue of patients with prescription forms. He handed to each the same number of bottles as there were blue ball-point entries on the form, for, although demonstrably illiterate in two alphabets, he was by no means innumerate. Midway in the queue was a young Fulani girl, beaded, bangled and bearing on the crest of her high buttocks a tiny immobile lump that must have been a baby only days old. The rains had brought the Fulani; the queue had brought the young girl to Musa's counter. As he handed her two brown bottles she turned her eyes to him and asked flatly, "How much?" Musa paused. He knew the bottles were given free to all patients. He carried cases of the bottles from the Sister's car and had been told that even the Clinic got them free from some overseas office. But for the first time in his life Musa had something to sell—something to sell that, unlike the worm-marrowed yams and stringy chickens he raised with signal ineptitude, he had not worked to produce, or even to procure. "*Kai, malam!* How much?"

the girl's voice now impatient. In a semi-whisper audible only to her as he bent, apparently to straighten the rows of bottles, he said coolly, "Kobo, kobo." As the girl reached to place the two copper kobos on the counter, the long fingers of Musa Maikudi caught them soundlessly and the chink of the coins as they met in his pocket were unheard even by him as his voice, with the professional blasé he had observed daily in the Dispenser, called down the queue, "Next."

Musa was in business. Two kobo was, granted, not much of a start. But the principle was clear. He knew as well as any man that something for nothing is something indeed. It was what his neighbor Hamza Taleda called "frofit"—when you get more than you give. That this two kobo was profit, there was no doubt. And, as in an epiphany, the full potential was revealed of that paint-peeled shelf of brown bottles and of the cases yet to come from the boot of the Sister's old powder blue Deuxchevaux.

By the end of the first day Musa had entered into his imagined ledger thirty-one kobo. By the end of the first week he had discovered two things: (1) that people were willing to pay up to three kobo per bottle and (2) that in the narrow space between his counter and the corner of the Dispensary there was taped, with surgical strapping, a key. By the end of the second week, during which the Dispenser had been ill, he had discovered that this key in fact opened the Dispensary itself. Although he then only dimly perceived it, Musa Maikudi was about to become a doctor.

Before his elevation to purveyor of medical glassware, Musa had thought little about what the Doctor and the Sister did. He had, of course, overheard the endless interrogations, the dialogues in three voices distortedly echoing, English-Hausa-Hausa-English, as in a dream:

> Where does it pain you? Show me.
> *Ina ne yaha make chio? Nuna mine worin.*
> *Yanu nan.*
> For how long?
> *Tine yawu she?*
> *Sati biyu.*
> Two weeks,

and then some scribbling on paper and a few routine phrases of instruction: "wash dishes . . . another tablet tomorrow . . . injection over there."

Musa was a good imitator. He had entertained his children when they were small with the sounds of birds and animals and had picked up the condescending tone of the Dispenser with little effort. As his voice could imitate, so could his long, agile fingers. He could sew a torn *riga,* tie complicated knots in rope and, when young, had once surprised his family with delicate designs he had shaped with his hands in the fresh mud wall of his father's *gidan soro.* So for the next week he watched. He watched closely the Doctor's lips as they paused and pursed before pronouncing medication; the Sister's hands as she chose the quadrant of a buttock and slipped the needle at an acute angle into the taut skin; the Dispenser's most frequently issued tablets and syrups.

One Friday afternoon, when the Clinic staff had dispersed, either to the Hospital, the Mosque or, unofficially, home, leaving only Musa and the Attendant, Musa unpeeled the taped key from the wall, waited until the Attendant had gone outside to chat to the young girl who sold kola and matches on the road, and slipped into the Dispensary. He needed only a few moments, for he knew clearly what he wanted: the white tablets with the deep groove, the black-and-red capsules, several small bottles sealed with rubber stoppers, a syringe and some disposable needles. Just a few, so no one would notice.

That evening, not wanting to waste his small bottles of medicine, he filled the syringe with well-water and slowly eased the needle into the flesh of a large, green mango, having first with a flourish mapped out the upper right quadrant.

Musa's demeanor, both at home and in the Clinic, had changed noticeably. While still obsequious and crouched before his near and distant neighbors in the Clinic's hierarchy, he became to the patients more aloof, more histrionically sage and judicious. Everyone in the district knew he worked in the Clinic and had access to both the knowledge and materials of the *bature* (European) medicine. When he began dispensing drugs and administering injections in his *zaure* most evenings after prayers, no one was surprised. A visit to Malam Musa was more comfortable than queuing at the Clinic and, anyway, he spoke Hausa and was much more approachable and willing to listen to elaborate complaints than the abrupt and harassed Polish physician. Nor did Malam Musa charge very much more than did the traditional herbal doctors and yet he offered imported and powerful *bature* cures.

By day Musa sold empty bottles to the unsuspecting Fulani and village farmers; by evening he sold full bottles of chemicals he did not understand to townspeople who thought that by side-stepping the accustomed Clinic procedure and paying for the luxury, they must be getting something as good, or better.

So far, Musa's imagined ledger had entries only in black. All "frofit"; no expenses. But when, after several months, the District Health Office was also "rationalized," a new pattern was imposed upon Musa's regime. Heretofore all drugs and supplies had been delivered to the Clinic by the Health Office van, a rattling Renault held together only by the will of the driver and the fathomless ingenuity of his brother's son, a fifteen-year-old roadside mechanic. When, having survived the military vehicles of two armies in three wars and civilian vehicles under a succession of governments, the Health Officer driver was killed in a taxi on the Kano road, the old and mystically faithful Renault, as if in sympathy, ceased forever to rattle. It was impossible for the Office to tax its staff by making deliveries on foot to all the clinics and equally awkward for the overburdened Sister to shuttle between the Clinic and the Stores in her own car.

It was therefore decided that Musa would, twice weekly, walk to the other side of the old walled City, to the Health Office behind the brown brick Alkali Court, and return with the Clinic's allocation of supplies. Although he demonstrated great displeasure when dispatched on the first of these treks, with a soft sucking of the teeth and a gathering of his leathern brow, Musa learned in time that no one noted very closely his departures or arrivals and that these afternoon trips to the City could be the occasion for a rich round of socializing along the laterite paths and avenues of the ancient Hausa settlement. Nor did it interfere with his forenoon bottle trade at the Clinic.

But on a cold Monday in Harmattan, when the desert dust was thick as a sea fog and white mucus caked the noses of the children wrestling in the small humped car park, Musa arrived at the Clinic to find the Senior Staff in great agitation. Even mad Binta Usman had moved closer to the double-door entrance and was watching perplexedly. During the weekend, explained the solemn Attendant with the precision of an engineer, the Electricity Board had released one of its unparsimonious surges of power through the town's overhead pylons and had decimated the worn and fragile mechanism of the Clinic's antique refrigerator. Despite the wintry nighttime temperatures, the cases of sensitive vaccines were about to go off. Eventually, after several futile probings of the machine's arabesque interior, an order was passed from the Doctor down the web of authority that Musa be immediately commissioned to summon technical aid from the Health Office. For this he was especially permitted to use the official Clinic bicycle, a black Raleigh with unmatching tires like an old "tuppence-ha'penny."

The sun was bright, if somewhat veiled by the morning dust, as Musa stepped into the close and evening gloom of the Health Office, its windows fortified against the day by yards of lank cotton curtaining printed with sketchy and inverted representations of apples and Cinzano flasks. A single unshaded light globe of low wattage hung arbitrarily near the doorway, revealing a large number of oddly assorted desks, most unoccupied save by an open newspaper or a rusted lazy-susan of lint-clogged rubber stamps. Musa felt the strain of his irises wrenching open and blinked as he knelt low before the first manned desk. *"Ranka ya dade,"* he said, raising his right fist in the traditional gesture of salutation, virtually all that remained of his spear-bearing horsemen forebears. "How is work?" inquired flatly the voice of the clerk, beginning the elaborate choric catechism of greeting, during all of which Musa, in modest acknowledgement of his social station, stared resolutely at the leg of an adjoining table.

The formalities concluded, Musa asked if the Electrical Technician, Malam Isa Makarfi, was "on seat," and was waved towards a low curtained opening in the wall, which led out again to the long verandah. Half-way down the narrow avenue of dozing messengers, he turned into another door, along an unlit and circuitous corridor and arrived, like a termite in the depths of a dying baobab, before a wooden door marked with the durable lacquer of the long departed Native Authority: "Cloak Room—Senior Officers." Malam Isa's workshop was a clutter of dismembered and unattended machinery, like an automobile graveyard for matchbox cars. In the far corner a water tap dripped mercilessly into a thick cracked porcelain sink.

The Technician was bent over an eviscerated tea kettle, his screwdriver chinking against the plaque of chalky mineral deposits like coins in a beggar's bowl. He greeted Musa in a listless repetition of the customary formula, without raising his eyes from the kettle. "*Ranka ya dade,* sir," Musa tentatively approached Malam Isa, "but Doctor says you must come now to fix the fridge." The Technician paused before replying. "You can see I'm busy. Orders from Alhaji. Must fix this kettle before he comes back from the Council meeting."

"But, *ranka ya dade,* sir, Doctor says to come now. It's an emergency." A whine entered Musa's voice, "He will be very angry with me."

The Technician looked up at Musa for the first time. "You see, if I leave this, then Alhaji will be angry with *me.*" Musa stared forlornly, turned and left.

He chose the long route back to the Clinic, skirting the edge of the central market and following the irregular mound of the eroded City wall, thinking all the while of how he could avoid the impact of the Doctor's temper. But when he had dismounted the battered Raleigh and entered the bench-lined anteroom of the Clinic, it was clear that no matter how subtle his strategems, he was in for it.

The Doctor himself approached and asked Musa directly, in a splintered and fruity Slavic Hausa, where the Technician was. "*Ranke ya dade,* Dobtah, sah," Musa had rashly stumbled into that uncharted forest of language he tried always to avoid, "Mala Isa no on seat, sah." At this the Doctor briefly closed his angled Tartar eyes and then exploded in a scatter-shot of English which struck Musa's ears like a June storm.

When the Doctor had retired into the crowded consulting alcove, the Sister collared the gaunt Attendant and came over to Musa. Translation amongst the semi-literate usually means a radical condensation, and the Doctor's paragraphs of vituperation, filtered down through the funnel of authority, produced a pungent precipitate: "Get that electrician here before 10 o'clock or I will have you and your seat transferred to the Hospital."

The Doctor did not know how sharply this threat would strike Musa. Transfer now would mean not only the end of his bottle trade but, more alarmingly, the end of his access to the Dispenser's key. "Dobtah" Musa would be sent to fish clotted dressings from the sewage sluices and to hose down the fetid interiors of surgical dustbins, as did other sweepers at the Hospital. He looked at the queue of patients awaiting medication, at the shelves of large-mouthed bottles in the Dispensary, and walked deliberately back to the bicycle.

Once again inside the fixed confusion of Malam Isa Makarfi's Cloak Room, Musa explained the urgency of his mission. The repaired kettle sat somewhat precariously atop a mound of electrical detritus and the Technician sat before the exposed workings of a large

Sanyo floor fan, clearly from the private home of one of his superiors. "You can see," he gestured firmly towards his splintered wooden table, "that I have a lot of work here." Musa tried to argue, respectfully, that the fridge was a very small one, that it would require only a few minutes' attention and, finally, that it would be bad *wahala* for Musa if Malam Isa did not come before 10 that morning.

The Technician picked up his screwdriver, turned to the fan motor and in an off-handed tone, as if to no one in particular, said "Of course, if it were worth my while to take the risk, I might be able to consider it. But Alhaji wants his fan today." With great apparent concentration, he loosened a small bolt that had just been firmly tightened.

Musa froze. The man wanted "kola," a "dash," a bribe. "But it's not for *me,*" Musa spoke quickly, "it's for the Clinic. For the Doctor." "And this fan," answered Malam Isa, "is for Alhaji and he must have it before closing time, *wallahi.*"

Musa listened to the relentless plosives of the dripping tap, to the numismatic clatter of the screwdriver and then turned to the Technician: "How much?"

"Only two Naira. For expenses. I use my own tools."

"Kai!" Musa thought of how many bottles he had to sell, how many illicit tablets he had to dispense to put together two Naira. Slowly he hiked up the frayed yardage of his *baban riga* and ran long fingers deep into his greying underclothes. There, in the sequestered safety of his lean loins, the only bank he had ever known, he found two Naira notes, faded and furled like a cigarette. He unrolled the notes, flattened them with careful haste on the workshop table and stepped backwards to the doorway.

"I'm coming," said the Technician to the fan.

On reflection, Musa thought as he sat that evening on a folding wooden chair in the tiny courtyard of his compound, two Naira was not really very much to preserve his little business. Still, it was the first red entry in his ledger, the first "cost" to be set rudely against the thin but firm columns of "frofit." And he teased his mind, as he slipped into a light doze, to find the blind corners of mischance which might conceal similar liabilities.

They were shortly to reveal themselves. When, after the great Sallah celebrations of Eid-el-Kabir, Musa made his first visit of the new year to the Health Office Stores, he found that another of the periodic staff reshufflings had brought in a new man as Store-keeper, a slight, wall-eyed Fulani from Transport. Within a fortnight the new Store-keeper had revealed, indirectly but unmistakably, that certain inducements would be necessary to ensure the reliable delivery of supplies. Again Musa tried to marshal the argument that the order was not for him personally, that it was only part of his job. But, in the end, more rose-veined Naira notes had been drawn from the cleavage of Musa's limbs.

Musa's little economic miracle, his role as medical savant and pharmacist to the community of the narrow lane in which he lived, in itself brought burdens beyond those imposed by his venal colleagues at the Health Office.

He had been able, somewhat later than many men, to take a second wife, the plucky 14-year-old daughter of his near neighbor, and was now saving slowly towards meeting the heavy costs of making the Holy Pilgrimage. As Alhaji Musa Maikudi his mean post as sweeper to the Local Authority would no longer be the primary tag of his identity. But he was distressed to find that each time he deposited some "frofit" into his money tin, he heard the same high leaden ring. The money was not, somehow, accumulating. Perhaps it was the pair of platform shoes he had bought at great price in Kano. The shoes, of black and red leatherette, their soles now worn down to a curious angle, asserted themselves beneath his long *riga* like twin snub-nosed VW Beatles. Or perhaps it was the Panasonic radio, with its profusion of knobs and inscrutable FM button that produced only the ragged sound of a rocky waterfall. But these, surely, were the things his money was for. What it was not for was people like Malam Isa and the parasitic Fulani Store-keeper. Somehow he had to outpace his costs, to bring more paper and less copper to his money tin.

Ever since the establishment of the College, on a hill overlooking the shallow river, it had been common for students, pressured by the atavistic competition for University places, to seek in the City charms and powders to increase their powers—powers of memory, of concentration, of physical endurance. Musa sat in his low slung deck chair, his long fingers flicking through a string of plastic amber prayer beads. These students, he thought. These students will put me before the House of Allah itself, the sacred Ka'ba in Mecca.

In various discreet ways, through the hall porters and kitchen workers at the College, Musa put it about that he had access to certain medicines—not the traditional herbs and roots, but proper *bature* medicines from overseas—which could not only cure the usual illnesses, but generate startling strength in even the most obscure body organs. The pressed-paper suitcase of bottles in his small domed bedroom now included substances of many colors and consistencies, their labels impressively ornamented with Cyrillic, Fraktur, Arabic and Roman runes.

Through the hot season a few young men, troubled by insomnia or disheartening essay marks, found their way to Malam Musa's thatched *zaure* and were given, for 50 kobo, a single iron tablet, an injection of Sulfa, or a dose of whooping cough vaccine. They rarely returned.

But in the rains, as the year-end examinations approached, there was a sudden increase in Musa's trade. Often the boys came late at night, after studying, causing Musa to be more than usually torpid at work the next morning. His syringes were now cracking and the disposable needles had grown as blunt as a donkey prod. He would need to restock from the Dispensary.

On an evening in late April a boy arrived at Musa's house. He was about seventeen, quite tall and beak-nosed, and when he spoke, with a glottalized Kano accent, Musa noticed a strong stammer, which made the boy blink and pause and sometimes shift from a stubborn fricative to a less troublesome synonym. It was from this maddening stammer that the boy wanted relief.

Now, it is relatively easy to inject most weak men with strength. The patient, convinced of the power of Malam Isa's medication, could often will himself quite quickly into health. So too with other fleeting complaints, like sleeplessness or headache. But this stammer was a problem of another water entirely. It drew attention like a pendulous goiter and its continuance, if the *bature* phials failed, would be very evident. Musa shook his head sagely and explained with studied patience that it might require several treatments and that success, even then, could not be guaranteed.

But the boy, clearly the focus of brutal adolescent jokes, was insistent. With considered care, Musa's delicate fingers sought and opened the speckled suitcase. He made a series of sharp noises with his tongue, to signal the contemplation of a serious decision, and chose from the case a rubber-topped bottle of Glaxo Triplopen penicillin. Piercing the diaphragm cap, he drew the milky liquid into the shaft of the syringe and held it up to the candlelight, as he had seen the Sister do thousands of times. Drawing up the sleeve of the young man's Indian cheesecloth shirt, he rubbed a spot on the exposed arm with his tobacco-tarred thumb and drove the needle lightly into the smooth caramel flesh.

Musa rolled down the boy's sleeve, finely assaying the shirt's value. He turned to his suitcase and, rather more slowly than necessary, replaced the syringe unwashed in its powdered-milk tin housing. As he began to push the suitcase towards the far corner of the room, Musa heard from behind him an abrupt burst of heavy breathing, like a dog's after chasing goats. As he spiraled up from his crouch he saw the boy stumble against a shelf and, with labored gasps, slip to his knees. As Musa approached, he saw in the weak candlelight that the boy was beginning to tremble, a series of localized flutters which within moments became convulsive.

Musa deliberately scanned his carefully stored Clinic observations, like upright bolts of cloth in a shop, but no precedent presented itself. "Maybe it will pass," he thought and, knowing it would not, whispered a jumbled sequence of imploring prayers. After a very few moments the boy stopped convulsing, stopped moving entirely. At this hour, when most of his neighbors were asleep, the only sounds from the street were the soft tide of the obstructed, rain swollen gutter and the rustle of dogs on a distant rubbish tip. Musa bent to the boy, turned the harrowed young face to him and listened for any sign of breath.

Musa's compound was only a few roads down from the Clinic and from the small, squalid market which backed onto it. This market, animated during the day by shoals of people at commerce, became at night a rather fearsome place, the unchallenged turf of madfolk and otherwise unhoused itinerant beggars. There were recurrent tales of innocents venturing in at night and being killed, even eaten, by the desperate and deranged. By some strange concordat, even the most incoherent of the City's lunatics came to know this market as their own, once the last trader's stall had been shuttered and the past Peak Milk-tin paraffin lamp extinguished.

It was the only place Musa could think of. He felt sorry for the young man, he explained as if to an audience of lip readers, yet there was nothing now but to get the boy as far as possible from anything that could connect him with Musa Maikudi. It was Allah's will that the boy should die, but not necessarily that his family in Kano should revenge themselves on Musa.

The flooded streets had been empty as Musa walked determinedly towards the market under the weight of a shapeless bundle of coarse hessian trussed up with thongs of knotted leather. A new white sedan, emblazoned with a Learner's *L,* had passed him near the dye pits, stippling his *riga* with droplets of red mud. But the driver was too preoccupied by the mysteries of his machine to notice a lone, stooped pedestrian in the slivered-moon light of early morning.

As he reached the passage between petrol station and tailor's shop, through which he usually entered the market, Musa angled his head and listened. But by this hour even the clack and suck of the scullery vultures had been stilled.

Amidst the telegraphic crackle of his own dry-tongued invocations, he stepped carefully down the path, worn by generations of foot flesh, that curled into the market's caecum. He had decided that he would leave his parcel near the herb and incense sellers' stalls, at the western edge of the metal-workers' foundries. From there he could quickly regain the main road and return directly home.

Crossing the wooden plank over a deep and reeking drainage ditch, Musa heard a sudden scuttling, too loud to be a rat. Deliberately, he stepped under the wooden overhang of Alhaji Danladi's barbering stall. A pyramid of hand-painted faces in profile stared, each with its one scleraless eye, at a point several yards in front of Musa. Under each head, like an Egyptian hieroglyph, was the name of the hair style it bore: "Native," "Been-to," "City-boy." Musa followed the determined line of their rigid gaze, looked again at the battery of eyes and stepped into the slender channel of pale night light.

The spot was at the base of an old acacia tree, as fixed and broad-bottomed as the Yoruba women traders of Sabon Gari. The tree was set apart in a small open square which, amply shaded, was a favored meeting place of the merchants. Musa could remember how as a child he would chase his older brothers around the deep-grained trunk until Alhaji Danladi's father would drive them away with a croak and a gesture.

He dropped his load in the sand beneath the tree and was chilled by the rigid bounce that shifted the hessian slightly from within. Dragging the bundle nearer the dark indigo interior of the tree's deep arbor, Musa suddenly heard the same scuttle, now louder and just beyond him. As his eyes desperately searched the tree's inner night, a stunning shriek, like car brakes before an accident, splintered the market's silence and a face, flat, red-eyed, fish-breathed and slack-jawed, started up before him, like the *dabo-dabo* handpuppets that had terrified him as a small boy. It was the round face of a woman, whitened with ash and sand. It was the face of mad Binta Usman, unnoticed fixture of the Clinic verandah.

"*Kai,* Binta," his voice was breathy, hoarse. "Ah . . . ah," he rattled and then, bizarrely, he greeted her—"*Sannu da hutawa*"—and bolted towards the main road like a goat in traffic.

For the two hours before dawn Musa cravenly fought his fears. When he arrived at the Clinic, Binta Usman would be there. Would she broadcast to the whole community where she had seen him that night? But then, who would ever take her seriously? But, if the boy had been found, they might.

By 7 he was exhausted and, in hopes of staying the confrontation until he had put his thoughts together, sent off his youngest son to the Sister to explain that Malam Musa was ill this morning and that he would certainly be in tomorrow. And when the boy returned with the Sister's injunction against sick leave without a Hospital note, Musa felt he had gained a day.

But the next morning brought no greater confidence as Musa walked reluctantly towards the Clinic, his eyes raw with fatigue, his mouth as grainy as the bottom of a birdcage. As he stepped up onto the verandah he did not immediately see Binta Usman. Then the round face and the slack jaw which had hung like a lantern in the tree two nights before turned itself up to him. The eyes, a batik of burst capillaries, squinted, lingered for a long moment on his embroidered cap, on his long tapered fingers and then, like the signal lights on an airstrip, passed on indifferently to a three-legged dog in the car park. "*Allah kiyaye,*" she mumbled the blessings of a beggar, "*Abinci. Abinci, maigida.*" Musa looked back at her, as if to thank her for the dullness of her ruined mind, let out a breath and quickly entered the Clinic.

Shaking out his thatching-grass broom, he reminded himself that today the Dispenser should be going to the Ministry and that he was himself much in need of some new syringes. From the broad, rank fundament of the great social cone, Malam Musa Maikudi, like a small white ant, was eating his way upwards.

Lloyd Zimpel

Ovenmen

Nightly, Prokop watched the mixer, its hum in his head and throb in his bowels. Even when he slept he heard and felt it, the hot sun under the blind his wife never pulled quite down all the way enough like the oven heat to sweat him awake certain he had somehow, impossibly, dozed off on the job. Then children shouting in the sun-struck street told him where he was.

Nightly he walked the high catwalk with the sand mixing in the huge open drum at his feet. Between the mixer and the archway to the now-dark foundry worked his crew in the white light of the coreroom alley and the shadows of the oven; the operators of the half-dozen blowers, their helpers, the rod-men and dippers, the loader, the ovenman. What went into every job, what that job took out of man, Prokop knew. At one time or another in his eight years—except for the oven—he had put in a solid stint in each. Did something go amiss? With a buffaloing nudge of his shoulder he moved the incompetent aside and demonstrated with flourishes how sound cores were blown, stacked and dipped, just so. "Show him how, Prokop!" came the cry then, to needle the fellow who needed showing no more than they needled him, the pushy foreman.

The foundry's contract for five months past with three months to run was for tractor transmission housings. In eight years Prokop couldn't remember an easier job. No tricky spots on the cores to crack, even the housing neck was thick and easy to blow. Piecework rates, set early, remained unchanged; the crew made money and stayed happy.

It was not a bad crew: a half-dozen family men who could be counted on, a dozen others who bore some, but not overly much, watching. The ovenmen though, that was a different story. They came and went so often that Prokop was tired of breaking them in. One after another, a new one every week, stood around awkwardly flexing his fingers in the thick asbestos gloves, gauntlets to the elbow, or cracking his knees on the dolly jack-handle, while the loader, Tony, did the work of showing how. All too often Prokop loaded his own sand, letting Tony bail out the greenhorn who in his first night jammed seven racks in the back of the oven which held six, all needing to be got out at once. Just the same, Prokop preferred throwing his own sand all night to a half-hour's killing oven work. It damn near scared him how the ovenmen took it—even for the short time each hung on. And short it was—he hardly learned the name of last week's ovenman before that suffering fellow, his skin dried and cracking, his scorched hair sprung like steel wool, shuffled up beneath the catwalk perch and called in a voice baked harsh, "This's the last shift I'll roast my ass! Get me my time tonight!"

The mixer stood next to the open-sided shed housing the raw sand. Tony, plying his wheelbarrow between sandpile and mixer hopper, kept the door open. A breeze worked in and into its path the ovenman, whoever he was this week, found his way between cries of "Rack! Rack!" for a moment's cooling. On the catwalk Prokop looked down as the poor son-of-a-bitch swallowed another salt tablet, retied the sopping sweat rag around his forehead and trotted back to the heat.

"How's the new man doing?" It was Prokop's most frequent question to Tony, no matter who the new man was. "So-so." At the lunch break they were sitting with sandwiches and beer in the cool sand under the high roof of the shed. It reminded Prokop of the majestically vaulted ice-houses of his youth—great mounds of brown wet sawdust and tier after tier of sawdust-sprinkled ice in perpetual twilight; the great ceiling high above where pigeons cooed in the rafters and sparrows fluttered. If all the machines in the coreroom were quiet and the oven turned down and not a person spoke, he could hear pigeons move restlessly above on their night perches. Where they fouled the sand the runner on the morning shift would scrape it clean.

"Ever seen one of those old ice-houses?" he asked Tony, who was—what?—twenty-one, half Prokop's age.

"What? Ice-house? I guess not. How about ass-house?"

From the near darkness of the shed Prokop looked back into the coreroom where the crew ate sitting on sand-slicked benches or hunkered against the base of the blowers. Now he heard the ripping of the chain as it raced through the tackle to raise the oven door. An ovenman took his lunch break on the run, between bites hauling out the racks before the cores burned. Even outside on the sand, thirty yards away, Prokop heard the throaty roar of the oven's burners and felt a great hot breath subtly increase the shed's temperature. Then came the quieter ratchet sound of the dolly as the ovenman pumped down another rack to cool for the dippers.

Prokop dug out a dollar and car keys and sent Tony for more beer, than pressed the buzzer to send the crew back to work. He loaded his own sand, replacing all that had crusted in the mixer over the break, tossing in the binder and water and climbed to the catwalk to observe the mix. He ran a handful through his fingers, brought a pinch of it to his nose. No one believed him but he swore that an off mix smelled bad.

"I hadda wait at the store," said Tony, returning a full hour later. The beer went into its cool hideaway in the sand.

"Well, hell," Prokop warned. "You better not take advantage."

Tony winked, saluted, and ambled down the alleyway to offer the apprentice ovenman a word of advice. It was this newcomer's third day. Prokop, preferring to avoid ovenmen until they had stayed long enough to blend with the crew, had hardly noticed him; that was Tony's job.

Now from his vantage Prokop marked the ragged carrying-on of the new man scurrying in the hot gloom before the oven. He was an odd foreign fellow, with an ear-bruising accent the one or two times Prokop had heard him, and hair that bristled out at the sides like a wild man's. His baggy overalls and oversized khaki shirt were not so different from what the others wore, but his short TB-like slightness seemed more properly wrapped in a European suit, thick and ill-fitting, of the kind Prokop remembered from 1946 Berliners trudging to their gray jobs past the entrance to the compound where Pfc. Prokop pulled guard duty every damned third day.

Baum was his name, Tony told him. Usually ovenmen were gone before anyone got past calling them "Buddy."

The shadows before the oven leaped now with a spurt of activity. The ovenman jumped first to the clock, then to temperature gauge, then to tackle, then to dolly. A flurry of racks were due out at the same time and Tony was nowhere in sight. Baum dashed in and out of the oven while great billowing waves of heat shot back to Prokop and beyond. With his gloved hands flapping like wings, the ovenman was all awkwardness. Whatever set procedures Tony had shown him he'd not yet learned. One arm flung before his face to partly ward off the heat, he entered the oven peeking from under the crook of his elbow, as cautious as a man edging into a knife fight, his other hand pushing the dolly by its long handle and apparently hoping for the good luck to get its wheels under a rack. But the dolly jackknifed and he pulled out to make another pass. By now he'd been boiled clear through. He dropped the handle, ran out, cooled for a few moments, and desperately tried again. And failed again.

Prokop knew that with luck a good man with some experience could get into the oven, pump up the rack and have it out, door closed, in ten to twelve seconds. That was all a man could stand. One trip per rack had to be the rule. Baum was taking three. Once Prokop counted four.

He finally found Tony combing his hair in the toilet. "What's wrong with that guy? He takes three or four passes at each rack. The door is up for two, three minutes. We can't have that."

Tony shrugged. "He don't understand too good. That's what you get if you're gonna hire refugees that can't talk English." But he went without complaint to give the greenhorn another hand.

"Look here," he pointed out to Baum the sharp swings up and down on the temp graph. "They should be like this." He made a gentle waving line with his hand. "Door's open too long, see?"

Sweating heavily, his eyes burned red at the rims, the ovenman nodded, nodded, nodded, but said nothing. He kept licking his lips as though they were parched beyond relief.

"You understand?"

"Ya, unnerstan'," said Baum.

Left to himself again he rushed into the oven only to fly out as if struck by an invisible hand that knocked the air out of him. Gloves flailing before his face like a man battling hawks at his eyes, he tried again. Then, suddenly remembering, ran to the temp graph to see how much heat he'd lost for leaving the door up too long.

Watching, Prokop itched all over. From the looks of it, Baum was addled by the heat. He climbed down the ladder, and dug a beer from the sandpile. The usual 3:00 A.M. breeze was up, but it could not counter the warm suffusion that came with each opening of the oven door. Given a few more days the poor bastard might come around, Prokop told himself, not hopefully.

He put off talking to Baum, even the next night when the dippers came up with the first of the complaints about hairline cracks in the cores. The necks came off in their hands. Instead of easing the racks down the last crucial half-inch, Baum was dropping them off the dolly, jarring, cracking, the cores.

"What the hell you teaching these ovenmen anyway?" Prokop asked Tony. "No wonder none of them last, they never learn their job right."

"It ain't my job to do the teaching," Tony grumbled, but he dropped his wheelbarrow and shuffled through the sand-drifted alley back to the oven for a long earnest conversation with the nodding ovenman.

Prokop watched: The runt keeps nodding sure, sure, but he don't understand a word, I bet. He was stung by what Tony had said—it was after all the foreman's job to see that the new men were properly broken in. Yet he'd told Tony more than once, you've worked the ovens, you know more about them than me. Hell, it was a good foreman who knew who to get to do a job. Did he have to do it all himself?

All the same, he vaguely told himself he'd talk to Baum when the chance came up, and in the meantime practiced his criticism on Tony, who dropped his wheelbarrow in the alley and spread his hands to look up at Prokop. "Why you yelling at *me?*" The loader still went for beer, but later found business elsewhere when Prokop pointedly headed for the sandpile at the break; then, casting injured glances at the foreman, slunk about for an hour after.

Far from Baum having gotten handier in his tasks, Prokop glumly judged that two weeks, three weeks on the job had in fact lent him greater clumsiness with the dolly and no more adroitness in getting in and out of the oven. He worked at not much less than a dead run all shift just to meet his minimum and still was a good forty-five minutes catching up after the shift ended, and all strung out and exhausted so that the foreman never expected to see him make it in for the next shift.

But he always did. In four weeks Baum had put in more time than the previous four ovenmen altogether. He was almost permanent. For that alone Prokop owed him something, and on a night when the poor bastard inexplainably had time enough to pause to catch his breath in the breeze from the shed, Prokop guiltily rose out of the darkness of the sandpile and held out a beer. "Have a cool one," he said. "That's sure hot work."

But in a calm gesture with the hand that held his sweat rag, far different from his herky-jerky way with the dolly, the ovenman refused the offer. He fixed Prokop with quick dark eyes, recalling to the foreman the house-to-house gypsy furnace repairman who had talked his way into the basement from which Prokop had all but to throw him out. "It make *sweat* too much!" the ovenman declared.

"Hell, it's healthy to sweat, get all that poison out of you." But Prokop saw that whatever lay behind that thin harrowed face with its three day growth of black beard never varying in length and the eyes which sunk deeper and deeper into the skull with each day in the ovens—that would not compromise for a can of beer.

"Too much *heat,*" Baum wagged his finger sternly. "No drink." Then he turned and hastened back to his duties, as if the foreman had taken up his time much too foolishly.

Later Prokop said to Tony, "I didn't realize the guy had lost so much weight. He's all bones."

"That's why they all quit. Remember Randall? Lost seventeen pounds in six days. You sweat it out."

Indeed you did, thought Prokop. What hellishness was this that could reduce a man by three pounds or more per day—in thirty days a man would be a stick—and leave him looking sad as Christ crucified?

Later that week when the superintendent came by on his semi-weekly stroll, Prokop told him, "We ought to take a good look at that oven job. It might be set too tough. We can't keep a man on it any length of time."

The super gingerly plucked his sweat-stuck white shirt from his armpits. "Can't be too bad. We studied it with all the others."

Prokop admitted that was so. "But we keep losing the men."

"Tell you what—I'll have personnel send you some colored boys. See how they take the heat."

"It's not that we need anybody right now. We've got a guy who's trying, but who can say how long he'll last?" He wouldn't take up this subject with the super soon again. The old boy would be lining up whatever unemployables personnel could find, and sending them in for Prokop to fry. He saw himself yelling *next* and pointing each new man on to the oven where the last ragged geezer had just fallen, swollen tongue between cracked lips, after fifteen minutes in the heat. He watched the super's fat back retire from the coreroom, and took his problem out to the sandpile.

There Tony, resting in the gloom, turned away Prokop's offer of beer and got at once to what was eating him. "Seems like what I've really got is *two* jobs, don't it?" he said darkly.

"I'll put you in for goddamned doubletime," said Prokop.

"Okay," the loader said in a wounded voice. "Okay." He started back to work. "You know it's not my fault we're all losing money on the bum cores he turns out."

"Nobody said it was."

Tony stopped at the door to the coreroom. "Well, I sure as hell get treated like it was. Hell, I try to tell him but he don't understand English worth a damn. That's what you get for hiring a Jew just off the boat."

"It doesn't take English to shove those racks in and out of the oven," said Prokop, brushing past Tony to climb to the catwalk.

He shunned the loader the rest of the night, then paid for it next shift when Tony failed to show. Without his coach the ovenman dashed about like one demented; somehow he got through the shift. Prokop did all his own loading for the first time in years. His hands, when he squirted soap on them to wash up, were tender from the shovel, all the old calluses had worn away in years of nothing but pushing the mixer button.

The next night Tony was back with no more than a nod for the foreman. Nursing sore hands, Prokop had little to say to him anyway. Or to anyone. When two of the dippers came up he met them with a scowl.

"Hairlines comin' through worse than ever, Prokop." They were from the batch the ovenman had baked last night on his own.

The foreman waved them away with a grunt. He started the rounds of the operators. "Blow 'em tighter, you guys, we're getting too many hairline cracks."

They stared in amazement. He knew as well as they where hairlines came from. But he brushed off their questions, leaving them to turn dirty looks back toward the ovens and to bitch about the matter amongst themselves during the break.

When the super came up that evening, he leaned on the rail to the ladder, plucked at his sweaty shirt and talked about the weather and his kid who was due home from college next week, and somewhere amidst it all warned that *hairline cracks were getting through.* He smoothed over some spilled sand with his polished oxford. "Your piece work rate has been going down steady for three weeks. Hate to see it happen. You know how the men get to feeling."

Prokop raised his hand in a little never-you-fear gesture, as if he and the men were totally at peace over the whole issue in a way a front office man would never understand. But as soon as the super was gone he angrily signalled to Tony.

"We're getting more bad cores than ever—"

"You blamin' *me?*" cried Tony in exasperation. "Well, just shove it all up your rear, Prokop!" And he walked off the job, owing the foreman God knows how much for beer and favors over fifteen months.

For three shifts until personnel sent him Tony's replacement—a man seeing his first foundry coreroom—the foreman not only did his own loading but tried as well to provide advice to the frantic ovenman. All those years he had successfully avoided the ovens and no one the wiser and now look. He lay awake days, like a man knowing his dread time would come: the oven door would open and he'd have to walk in. As Baum did dozens of times a shift, night after night.

"I shouldn't be getting back here in this heat so much," he told the ovenman one night when called to direct the rescue of a rack that had angled and jammed in the oven's deepest corner. "It's a matter of my health."

This drew only a befuddled stare from the ovenman, and Prokop hastened away from the opened door feeling laid waste no more by the heat than by his duty to keep a man in that desolate job.

Hardly had he gained the healthier atmosphere of the catwalk than he heard a cry and turned to see Baum come trotting unevenly toward him, his usual cornered look now twisted with anguish. He held one hand carefully before him, as if balancing an egg in the palm. He had stumbled, caught himself with a good firm grip on a rack not ten seconds out of the back of the oven, the glove on that unfortunate hand off as he went to mop his forehead.

Prokop hated to look. The sweat-moistened hand had cooked. "You *gotta* be careful. No question about it. For God's sake, watch your step!" Outraged, sickened, he fetched the ointment tube from the tin box where the bandaids and the extra salt tablets were stored. Now he had a one-handed ovenman. "Come in early tomorrow and have the first-shift nurse take a look at that. I'll get some help for you the rest of the night."

But he couldn't find it. When he had gone down the line with no success and came at last to blower six, even Arnie, usually easy-going, was as hard-nosed as the others. It would screw up his piecework. What would the union say? Prokop was ready to hold aloft Baum's puffed hand and cry, "Help me while this heals! Don't you think of anything but money?"

Swearing, he accompanied Baum back to the oven where the ovenman examined his chart and told Prokop which racks were due. But Baum had to retreat quickly from the area, his bad hand far too sensitive to take the heat.

"Everybody handles their own for the rest of the night!" Prokop yelled. The bitching began. With three hours to go it meant several trips apiece into the fire. Nobody wanted it. "Screw the complaining!" Prokop shouted. "Do what I say or get the hell out!"

He'd made a dozen enemies, piecework was shot to hell, a quarter of the cores were ruined, but he got through the shift without having to brave the oven himself, and he was ready to admit that that alone was worth whatever it cost.

When he came on the next night he found a note stuck into a joint on the catwalk rail. It was written in what looked like a foreign language. At last he puzzled it through: "She sent me to go home two days the nurse. Herschel."

Well, wasn't that damned nice of her to do for old Hersch! He looked furiously out over the coreroom. The crew was coming on; not one of them looked his way, as if afraid of what he might ask if he caught an eye. As soon as he had pushed the buzzer and they were all at work, he walked through the silent, dark foundry to the other the side of the building where the super sat in his office behind his cooling fan, framed pictures of wife and kids on his desk.

There were, the super told him, no extras on tap for tonight; maybe tomorrow a temporary would be available; it wasn't a promise.

"Well, what about that oven? Who's going to run it?"

"You," the super calmly said. "It's no big deal."

Just what he had expected; they'd get him yet. He came back through the silent foundry toward the bright light of the coreroom trying to tell himself there was nothing sinister in the fat old bastard; it was only logical, he was the logical one. On a good night the mixer took hardly ten minutes of work; let him put that spare time to constructive use. It was logical, true enough, but he came down the alleyway as scared as if an ugly unknown torture awaited.

From the hook on the wall by the temp graph he took Baum's old khaki shirt and the big asbestos gloves. Instead of joshing him as he half expected, after last night the operators and helpers seemed not to see him. He had seven hours to go: it seemed to him the sum of his life.

The first racks filled. He set the dolly under one, rolled it before the black oven door, stood back and grabbed the chain tackle, pulled hand over hand. He had never felt the heat this close before; the shock of it took his breath away. In spite of himself, he backed off. The roar of the burners was so loud they must surely be turned up too high; he raced to the gauge: no, they were down as low as the valves would go. He got behind the dolly, quickly lined it up and shoved it at the oven. It had to roll all the way to the back—ten or twelve feet into the oven. He kept close to the rack, as if it would protect him, wrapped one arm around his head and guided the dolly beneath the door, into the depths.

He tried to hold his breath but couldn't and his lungs ballooned with pain at the seared air. Even behind the protection of his free arm, his eyes clouded and he could not see how far into the black oven he had yet to go. His toes sought to curl away from the burning soles of his shoes. Only for an instant did his clothing shield his body, then it seemed to take fire, his skin puckering away from it. Panic rose; in another instant he would have dropped the handle and fled, as it had annoyed him to see Baum do so many times. But instead, some lucky reflex let him trip the dolly; the rack settled evenly enough if a bit out of line, and he burst free of the oven, giving the dolly a fierce tug and letting it roll off by itself. He grabbed the chain to keep from stumbling, and with one strong jerk brought the door down to cut off the heat. It was like a return from the grave.

He turned away to wipe his face. There was no sweat on it, it had burned away. Out of the gloom, shot with brilliant spears fed into his vision by his scalding eyes, he saw the operators and helpers gladly watching. He turned his back on them. "Rack here!" It was like a vengeful curse meant for him. Then, almost simultaneously, from the other operators came the call, "Rack! Rack here! Rack!" He set himself against an impulse to flee, grabbed the dolly and went to get them, every goddamned one.

Salt tablets corroded his belly, water did not help. His face took fire, and hands went raw inside the asbestos mitts so that he could not grip the dolly's hot handle squarely, but hooked it with the heel of his hand, butted it, made fists and caught it against the knuckles, finally insulated it with a two-inch wrap of gunny-sack.

It all took too much time. Happy to see his fumbling the operators grumbled, called angrily for speed, a little speed, how about it? Even Baum was faster.

Into the oven he dashed and each time fled gasping. In his nostrils the mucous fried; his eyes framed themselves in stiff red rims that pinched when he blinked. Vision blurred. His sweat stopped; from Baum's example he figured it would start again in time. At the water fountain he splashed his face, but water brought no relief. He could not spit, his body refusing to give up that moisture. The operators yelled at his dallying. They had been yelling all along, wasn't he listening?

No sweat, no sweat, he mindlessly told himself, trotting the alley like an obedient dog. The dolly jounced behind him. No sweat.

At the lunch break he went out back to the sand. Normally cool it now burned like all else. Surprised but willing, the new loader went for the beer Prokop desperately ordered. "What's your name, kid?"

"Louie."

"You're doing okay," Prokop said bleakly.

The beer boiled like lye in his throat and he could not finish the first can. In disgust he threw it into the dark and turned to see the super pause at the doorway, his eye thoughtfully following the can's glinting arc into the tall weeds.

"How's it going on the oven?"

Prokop leaped up to tell him. "It's a regular bitch. I never really knew." It seemed like there should be much more to say.

The super nodded, almost smiling. "Do what you can." For the rest of the lunch break he hung around the blowers, pinching the sand, checking the seams of the molds, sneaking a glance into the shed for signs of more beer. Prokop nudged the remaining cans out of sight, downed salt tablets and water, and checked the mix. Before he pressed the buzzer to summon his crew he put in five minutes noisily wrestling racks into place at the blowers. Far from standing by to note his extra work, the super had disappeared. With a groan Prokop impelled himself back to the oven. Still yards off his tender skin wrinkled away from the heat. The clock-watching operators griped at him for a fast buzzer.

Through that night and the next he ran and staggered. His skin dried and flaked, grew dark and leathery, his hair like wire. "What's the matter?" his wife asked uneasily on the second morning, not sure if she should be bothering him. "Why didn't you eat your lunch?" He had brought the black bucket home unopened.

"I'm on the oven!" he cried.

"Why you?" she said. "You're the foreman."

Distractedly he waved her away and stumbled unshaven to his bed, his sleep all nightmarish tossing, and the children with their shouts outside woke him again and again.

On the third night he came to work knowing the ovenman would not be there again. Yet in despairing weariness he tried to forestall that certainty. If he made three stoplights running, then the ovenman would be there. He made four, but in his belly knew it was no use. A fifth would be the clincher. He didn't make it. So then he knew. Tears came to his eyes.

The oven wouldn't wait. He came to it as heavy as if filled with his own wet sand. "Rack!" cried the operators. "Rack! Rack!" deliberately bunching them to keep him scrambling. Enough's enough, he wanted to tell them. But he held no malice; they didn't know how tough the oven was. If they did they wouldn't push him—but he wasn't sure.

On his first trip of the night beyond the door one shoe sole split from the heat. He leaned against the wall to look at it—cracked straight across the middle. The material was artificial, plastic, not leather. They weren't cheap either. To protect his foot he wound a gunny sack around the busted shoe, wet it at the puddle under the fountain for traction. Two steps into the oven and the bulky bandage began steaming; he came out trailing smoke, like something from a swampy wilderness; the hot burlap stink cut like acid fumes into the dried tissues of his nostrils—one thing more to endure. All the hollows in his head were already expanded to their limits, stretched by heat and the smell of scorched sand. His joints creaked like the ratchet of the dolly, as if the moisture that greased the bone hinges had boiled off. How could he last the night? He leaned his weight—how much had he lost the past two shifts?—against the dolly handle to bring out a hot rack and found the burlap had steamed dry and gave no grip. Down he went on the oven floor, struggling instantly to his feet, unburned but with the flesh of one flank now stiff as with a good sunburn and sensitive to heat. He turned that side away from the oven door, and into his pained vision appeared the white shirt of the superintendent, behind whom came Baum.

"Keep this man off the ovens for another week at least," said the super, pointing to the hand.

Sagging, Prokop looked at neither visitor, but fixed his gaze on the wounded hand, bound in a light gauze strip and not the pillow of bandages he had somehow expected. Baum held it limply before his chest as if an invisible sling supported it.

"Put him on dipping," said the super. "Something like that." He gave Prokop a last long look, from the scraggly two-day beard on the tanned face to the bulb of sacking protecting his foot, then turned and with a fat, splay-footed gait strolled out of the foreman's anguished sight.

Baum slowly flexed the fingers of the offending hand. "It is the nurse, she say," he said sadly, as if he personally did not agree with her.

Prokop kept his eyes on the burnt paw. He recognized apology and sympathy in the voice—this was the only other one around who knew the oven. They were brothers in fiery agony. No consolation there, but at least the balm of recognition between men who knew their duty.

Heat-addled and guilty, Prokop flung himself at the chain tackle, and above the racket of the door's ascent and the fearsome roar of the burners croaked out through his dried windpipe, "Go dip!"

Sherley Anne Williams

Tell Martha Not to Moan

My mamma a big woman, tall and stout and men like her cause she soft and fluffy looking. When she round them it all smiles and dimples and her mouth be looking like it couldn't never be fixed to say nothing but darling and honey.

They see her now, they sho see something different. I should not even come today. Since I had Larry things ain't been too good between us. But—that's my mamma and I know she gon be there when I need her. And sometime when I come, it okay. But this ain't gon be one a them times. Her eyes looking all ove me and I know it coming. She snort cause she want to say god damn but she don't cuss. "When it due, Martha?"

First I start to say, what. But I know it ain't no use. You can't fool old folks bout something like that, so I tell her.

"Last part of November."

"Who the daddy?"

"Time."

"That man what play piano at the Legion?"

"Yeah."

"What he gon do bout it?"

"Mamma, it ain't too much he can do, now is it? The baby on its way."

She don't say nothing for a long time. She sit looking at her hands. They all wet from where she been washing dishes and they all wrinkled like yo hand be when they been in water too long. She get up and get a dish cloth and dry em, then sit down at the table. "Where he at now?"

"Gone."

"Gone? Gone where?" I don't say nothing and she start cussing then. I get kinda scared cause mamma got to be real mad foe she cuss and I don't know who she cussing—me or Time. Then she start talking to me. "Martha, you just a fool. I told you that man wan't no good first time I seed him. A musician the worst kind of man you can get mixed up with. Look at you. You ain't even eighteen years old yet, Larry just barely two and here you is pregnant again." She go on like that for a while and I don't say nothing. Couldn't no way. By the time I get my mouth fixed to say something, she done raced on so far ahead that what I got to say don't have nothing to do with what she saying right then. Finally she stop and ask, "What you gon do now? You want to come back here?" She ain't never liked me living with Orine and when I say no, she ask, "Why not? It be easier for you."

I shake my head again. "If I here, Time won't know where to find me, and Time coming; he be back. He gon to make a place for us, you a see."

"Hump, you just played the fool again, Martha."

"No mamma, that not it at all; Time want me."

"Is that what he say when he left?"

"No, but. . . . "

Well, like the first night we met, he come over to me like he knowed me for a long time and like I been his for awmost that long. Yeah, I think that how it was. Cause I didn' even see him when we come in the Legion that first night.

Me and Orine, we just got our checks that day. We went downtown and Orine bought her some new dresses. But the dress she want to wear that night don't look right so we go racing back to town and change it. Then we had to hurry home and get dressed. It Friday night and the Legion crowded. You got to get there early on the week-end if you want a seat. And Orine don't want just any seat; she want one right up front. "Who gon see you way back there? Nobody. They can't see you, who gon ask you to dance? Nobody. You don't dance, how you gon meet people? You don't meet people, what you doing out?" So we sit up front. Whole lots a people there that night. You can't even see the bandstand cross the dance floor. We sharing the table with some more people and Orine keep jabbing me, telling me to sit cool. And I try cause Orine say it a good thing to be cool.

The set end and people start leaving the dance floor. That when I see Time. He just getting up from the piano. I like him right off cause I like men what look like him. He kind of tall and slim. First time I ever seed a man wear his hair so long and it nappy—he tell me once it an African Bush—but he look good anyway and he know it. He look round all cool. He step down from the bandstand and start walking toward me. He come over to the table and just look. "You," he say, "you my Black queen." And he bow down most to the floor.

Ah shit! I mad cause I think he just trying to run a game. "What you trying to prove, fool?" I ask him.

"Ah man," he say and it like I cut him. That the way he say it. "Ah man. I call this woman my Black queen—tell her she can rule my life and she call me a fool."

"And sides what, nigga," I tell him then, "I ain't black." And I ain't, I don't care what Time say. I just a dark woman.

"What's the matter, you shamed of being Black? Ain't nobody told you Black is pretty?" He talk all loud and people start gathering round. Somebody say, "Yeah, you tell her bout it, soul." I embarrassed and I look over at Orine. But she just grinning, not saying nothing. I guess she waiting to see what I gon do so I stand up.

"Well if I is black, I is a fine black." And I walk over to the bar. I walk just like I don't know they watching my ass, and I hold my head up. Time follow me right on over to the bar and put his arm round my shoulder.

"You want a drink?" I start to say no cause I scared. Man not supposed to make you feel like he make me feel. Not just like doing it—but, oh, like it right for him to be there with me, touching me. So I say yes. "What's your name?" he ask then.

I smile and say, "They call me the player." Orine told a man that once in Berkeley and he didn't know what to say. Orine a smart woman.

"Well they call me Time and I know yo mamma done told you Time ain't nothing to play with." His smile cooler than mine. We don't say nothing for a long while. He just stand there with his arm round my shoulder looking at us in the mirror behind the bar. Finally he say, "Yeah, you gon be my Black queen." And he look down at me and laugh. I don't know what to do, don't know what to say neither, so I just smile.

"You gon tell me your name or not?"

"Martha."

He laugh. "That a good name for you."

"My mamma name me that so I be good. She name all us kids from the Bible," I tell him laughing.

"And is you good?"

I nod yes and no all at the same time and kind of mumble cause I don't know what to say. Mamma really did name all us kids from the Bible. She always saying, "My mamma name me Veronica after the woman in the Bible and I a better woman for it. That why I name all my kids from the Bible. They got something to look up to." But mamma don't think I'm good, specially since I got Larry. Maybe Time ain't gon think I good neither. So I don't answer, just smile and move on back to the table. I hear him singing soft-like, "Oh Mary don't you weep, tell yo sister Martha not to moan." And I kind of glad cause most people don't even think bout that when I tell em my name. That make me know he really smart.

We went out for breakfast after the Legion close. Him and me and Orine and German, the drummer. Only places open is on the other side of town and at first Time don't want to go. But we finally swade him.

Time got funny eyes, you can't hardly see into em. You look and you look and you can't tell nothing from em. It make me feel funny when he look at me. I finally get used to it, but that night he just sit there looking and don't say nothing for a long time after we order.

"So you don't like Black?" he finally say.

"Do you?" I ask. I think I just ask him questions, then I don't have to talk so much. But I don't want him to talk bout that right then, so I smile and say, "Let's talk bout you."

"I am not what I am." He smiling and I smile back, but I feel funny cause I think I supposed to know what he mean.

"What kind of game you trying to run?" Orine ask. Then she laugh. "Just cause we from the country don't mean we ain't hip to niggas trying to be big-time. Ain't that right, Martha?"

I don't know what to say, but I know Time don't like that. I think he was going to cuss Orine out, but German put his arm round Orine and he laugh. "He just mean he ain't what he want to be. Don't pay no mind to that cat. He always trying to blow some shit." And he start talking that talk, rapping to Orine.

I look at Time. "That what you mean?"

He all lounged back in the seat, his legs stretched way out under the table. He pour salt in a napkin and mix it up with his finger.

"Yeah, that's what I mean. That's all about me. Black is pretty, Martha." He touch my face with one finger. "You let white people make you believe you ugly. I bet you don't even dream."

"I do too."

"What you dream?"

"Huh?" I don't know what he talking bout. I kind of smile and look at him out the corner of my eye. "I dreams bout a man like you. Why, just last night, I dream—"

He start laughing. "That's all right. That's all right."

The food come then and we all start eating. Time act like he forgot all bout dreams. I never figure out how he think I can just sit there and tell him the dreams I have at night, just like that. It don't seem like what I dream bout at night mean as much as what I think bout during the day.

We leaving when Time trip over this white man's feet. That man's feet all out in the aisle but Time don't never be watching where he going no way. "Excuse me," he say kind of mean.

"Say, watch it buddy." That white man talk most as nasty as Time. He kind of old and maybe he drunk or an Okie.

"Man, I said excuse me. You the one got your feet in the aisle."

"You," that man say, starting to get up, "you better watch yourself, boy."

And what he want to say that for? Time step back and say real quiet, "No, motherfucker. You the one. You better watch yourself and your daughter too. See how many babies she gon have by boys like me." That man get all red in the face, but the woman in the booth with him finally start pulling at him, telling him to sit down, shut up. Cause Time set to kill that man.

I touch Time's arm first, then put my arm round his waist. "Ain't no use getting messed behind somebody like that."

Time and that man just looking at each other, not wanting to back down. People was gon start wondering what going on in a few minutes. I tell him, " 'Got something for you, baby,' " and he look down at me and grin. Orine pick it up. We go out that place singing, " 'Good loving, good, good loving, make you feel so clean.' "

"You like to hear me play?" he ask when we in the car.

"This the first time they ever have anybody here that sound that good."

"Yeah," Orine say. "How come you all staying round a little jive-ass town like Ashley?"

"We going to New York pretty soon," Time say kind of snappy.

"Well, shit, baby, you—"

"When you going to New York?" I ask real quick. When Orine in a bad mood, can't nobody say nothing right.

"Couple of months." He lean back and put his arm round me. "They doing so many things with music back there. Up in the City, they doing one maybe two things. In L.A. they doing another one, two things. But, man, in New York, they doing everything. Person couldn't never get stuck in one groove there. So many things going on, you got to be hip, real hip to keep up. You always growing there. Shit, if you 'live and playing, you can't help but grow. Say, man," he reach and tap German on the shoulder, "let's leave right now."

We all crack up. Then I say, "I sorry but I can't go, got to take care of my baby."

He laugh, "Sugar, you got yo baby right here."

"Well, I must got two babies then."

We pull up in front of the partment house then but don't no one move. Finally Time reach over and touch my hair. "You gon be my Black queen?"

I look straight ahead at the night. "Yeah," I say. "Yeah."

We go in and I check first on Larry cause sometimes that girl don't watch him good. When I come in some nights, he be all out the cover and shivering but too sleepy to get back under em. Time come in when I'm pulling the cover up on Orine two kids.

"Which one yours," he ask.

I go over to Larry bed. "This my baby," I tell him.

"What's his name?"

"Larry."

"Oh, I suppose you name him after his daddy?"

I don't like the way he say that, like I was wrong to name him after his daddy. "Who else I gon name him after?" He don't say nothing and I leave him standing there. I mad now and I go in the bedroom and start pulling off my clothes. I think, that nigga can stand up in the living room all night, for all I care; let Orine talk to German and him, too. But Time come in the bedroom and put his arms round me. He touch my hair and my face and my tittie, and it scare me. I try to pull away but he hold me too close. "Martha," he say, "Black Martha." Then he just stand there holding me, not saying nothing, with his hand covering one side on my face. I stand there trembling but he don't notice. I know a woman not supposed to feel the way I feel bout Time, not right away. But I do.

He tell me things nobody ever say to me before. And I want to tell him that I ain't never liked no man much as I like him. But sometime you tell a man that and he go cause he think you liking him a whole lot gon hang him up.

"You and me," he say after we in bed, "we can make it together real good." He laugh. "I used to think all I needed was that music, but it take a woman to make that music sing, I think. So now stead of the music and me, it be the music and me and you."

"You left out Larry," I tell him. I don't think he want to hear that. But Larry my baby.

"How come you couldn't be free," he say real low. Then, "How you going when I go if you got a baby?"

"When you going?"

He turn his back to me. "Oh, I don't know. You know what the song say, 'When a woman take the blues, She tuck her head and cry. But when a man catch the blues, He grab his shoes and slide.' Next time I get the blues," he laugh a little, "next time the man get too much for me, I leave here and go someplace else. He always chasing me. The god damn white man." He turn over and reach for me. "You feel good. He chasing me and I chasing dreams. You think I'm crazy, huh? But I'm not. I just got so many, many things going on inside me I don't know which one to let out first. They all want out so bad. When I play—I got to be better, Martha. You gon help me?"

"Yes, Time, I help you."

"You see," and he reach over and turn on the light and look down at me, "I'm not what I am. I up tight on the inside but I can't get it to show on the outside. I don't know how to make it come out. You ever hear Coltrane blow? That man is together. He showing on the outside what he got on the inside. When I can do that, then I be somewhere. But I can't go by myself. I need a woman. A Black woman. Them other women steal your soul and don't leave nothing. But a Black woman—" He laugh and pull me close. He want me and that all I care bout.

Mamma come over that next morning and come right on in the bedroom, just like she always do. I kind of shamed for her to see me like that, with a man and all, but she don't say nothing cept scuse me, then turn away. "I come to get Larry."

"He in the other bedroom," I say starting to get up.

"That's okay; I get him." And she go out and close the door. I start to get out the bed anyway. Time reach for his cigarettes and light one. "Your mamma don't believe in knocking, do she?"

I start to tell him not to talk so loud cause mamma a hear him, but that might make him mad. "Well, it ain't usually nobody in here with me for her to walk in on." I standing by the bed buttoning my house coat and Time reach out and pull my arm, smiling.

"I know you ain't no tramp, Martha. Come on, get back in bed."

I pull my arm way and start out the door. "I got to get Larry's clothes together," I tell him. I do got to get them clothes together cause when mamma come for Larry like that on Sadday morning, she want to keep him for the rest of the weekend. But—I don't know. It just don't seem right for me to be in the bed with a man and my mamma in the next room.

I think Orine and German still in the other bedroom. But I don't know; Orine don't too much like for her mens to stay all night. She say it make a bad impression on her kids. I glad the door close anyway. If mamma gon start talking that "why don't you come home" talk the way she usually do, it best for Orine not to hear it.

Orine's two kids still sleep but mamma got Larry on his bed tickling him and playing with him. He like that. "Boy, you sho happy for it to be so early in the morning," I tell him.

Mamma stop tickling him and he lay there breathing hard for a minute. "Big mamma," he say laughing and pointing at her. I just laugh at him and go get his clothes.

"You gon marry this one?" Every man I been with since I had Larry, she ask that about.

"You think marrying gon save my soul, Mamma?" I sorry right away cause mamma don't like me to make fun of God. But I swear I gets tired of all that. What I want to marry for anyway? Get somebody like daddy always coming and going and every time he go leave a baby behind. Or get a man what stay round and beat me all the time and have my kids thinking they big shit just cause they got a daddy what stay with them, like them saddity kids at school. Shit, married or single they still doing the same thing when they goes to bed.

Mamma don't say nothing else bout it. She ask where he work. I tell her and then take Larry in the bathroom and wash him up.

"The older you get, the more foolish you get, Martha. Them

musicians ain't got nothing for a woman. Lots sweet talk and babies, that's all. Welfare don't even want to give you nothing for the one you got now, how you gon—" I sorry but I just stop listening. Mamma run her mouth like a clatterbone on a goose ass sometime. I just go on and give her the baby and get the rest of his things ready.

"So your mamma don't like musicians, huh?" Time say when I get back in the bedroom. "Square-ass people. Everything they don't know about, they hate. Lord deliver me from a square-ass town with square-ass people." He turn over.

"You wasn't calling me square last night."

"I'm not calling you square now, Martha."

I get back in the bed then and he put his arm round me. "But they say what they want to say. Long as they don't mess with me things be okay. But that's impossible. Somebody always got to have their little say about your life. They want to tell you where to go, how to play, what to play, where to play it—shit, even who to fuck and how to fuck em. But when I get to New York—"

"Time, let's don't talk now."

He laugh then, "Martha, you so Black." I don't know what I should say so I don't say nothing, just get closer and we don't talk.

That how it is lots a time with me and him. It seem like all I got is lots little pitchers in my mind and can't tell nobody what they look like. Once I try to tell him bout that, bout the pitchers, and he just laugh. "Least your head ain't empty. Maybe now you got some pictures, you get some thoughts." That make me mad and I start cussing, but he laugh and kiss me and hold me. And that time, when we doing it, it all—all angry and like he want to hurt me. And I think bout that song he sing that first night bout having the blues. But that the only time he mean like that.

Time and German brung the piano a couple days after that. The piano small and all shiny black wood. Time cussed German when German knocked it against the front door getting it in the house. Time want to put it in the bedroom but I want him to be thinking bout me, not some damn piano when he in there. I tell him he put it in the living room or it don't come in the house. Orine don't want it in the house period, say it too damn noisy—that's what she tell me. She don't say nothing to Time. I think she half-way scared of him. He pretty good bout playing it though. He don't never play it when the babies is sleep or at least he don't play loud as he can. But all he thinking bout when he playing is that piano. You talk to him, he don't answer; you touch him, he don't look up. One time I say to him, "pay me some tention," but he don't even hear. I hit his hand, not hard, just playing. He look at me but he don't stop playing. "Get out of here, Martha." First I start to tell him he can't tell me what to do in my own self's house, but he just looking at me. Looking at me and playing and not saying nothing. I leave.

His friends come over most evenings when he home, not playing. It like Time is the leader. Whatever he say go. They always telling him how good he is. "Out of sight, man, the way you play." "You ought to get out of this little town so somebody can hear you play." Most times, he just smile and don't say nothing, or he just say thanks. But I wonder if he really believe em. I tell him, sometime, that he sound better than lots a them men on records. He give me his little cool smile. But I feel he glad I tell him that.

When his friends come over, we sit round laughing and talking and drinking. Orine like that cause she be playing up to em all and they be telling her what a fine ass she got. They don't tell me nothing like that cause Time be sitting right there, but long as Time telling me, I don't care. It like when we go to the Legion, after Time and German started being with us. We all the time get in free then and get to sit at one a the big front tables. And Orine like that cause it make her think she big time. But she still her same old picky self; all the time telling me to "sit cool, Martha," and "be cool, girl." Acting like cool the most important thing in the world. I finally just tell her, "Time like me just the way I am, cool or not." And it true; Time always saying that I be myself and I be fine.

Time and his friends, they talk mostly bout music, music and New York City and white people. Sometime I get so sick a listening to em. Always talking bout how they gon put something over on the white man, gon take something way from him, gon do this, gon do that. Ah shit! I tell em. But they don't pay me no mind.

German say, one night, "Man, this white man come asking if I want to play at his house for—"

"What you tell him, man, 'Put money in my purse?' " Time ask. They all crack up. Me and Orine sit there quiet. Orine all swole up cause Time and them running some kind of game and she don't know what going down.

"Hey man, yo all member that time up in Frisco when we got fired from that gig and wan't none of our old ladies working?" That Brown, he play bass with em.

"Man," Time say, "all I remember is that I stayed high most of the time. But how'd I stay high if ain't nobody had no bread? Somebody was putting something in somebody's purse." He lean back laughing a little. "Verna's mamma must have been sending her some money till she got a job. Yeah, yeah man, that was it. You remember the first time her mamma sent that money and she gave it all to me to hold?"

"And what she wanna do that for? You went out and gambled half a it away and bought pot with most of the rest." German not laughing much as Time and Brown.

"Man, I was scared to tell her, cause you remember how easy it was for her to get her jaws tight. But she was cool, didn't say nothing. I told her I was going to get food with the rest of the money and asked her what she wanted, and—"

"And she say cigarettes," Brown break in laughing, "and this cat, man, this cat tell her, 'Woman, we ain't wasting this bread on no non-essentials!' " He doubled over laughing. They all laughing. But I don't think it that funny. Any woman can give a man money.

"I thought the babe was gon kill me, her jaws was so tight. But even with her jaws tight, Verna was still cool. She just say, 'Baby, you done fucked up fifty dollars on non-essentials; let me try thirty cents.' "

That really funny to em. They all cracking up but me. Time sit there smiling just a little and shaking his head. Then, he reach out and squeeze my knee and smile at me. And I know it like I say; any woman can give a man money.

German been twitching round in his chair and finally he say, "Yeah, man, this fay dude want me to play at his house for fifty cent." That German always got to hear hisself talk. "I tell him take his fifty cent and shove it up his ass—oh scuse me. I forgot that baby was here—but I told him what to do with it. When I play for honkies, I tell him, I don't play for less than two hundred dollars and he so foolish he gon pay it." They all laugh, but I know German lying. Anybody offer him ten cent let lone fifty, he gon play.

"It ain't the money, man," Time say. "They just don't know what the fuck going on." I tell him Larry sitting right there. I know he ain't gon pay me no mind, but I feel if German can respect my baby, Time can too. "Man they go out to some little school, learn a few chords, and they think they know it all. Then they come round to the clubs wanting to sit in with you. Then, if you working for a white man, he fire you and hire him. No, man, I can't tie shit from no white man."

"That where you wrong," I tell him. "Somebody you don't like, you supposed to take em for everything they got. Take em and tell em to kiss yo butt."

"That another one of your pictures, I guess," Time say. And they all laugh cause he told em bout that, too, one time when he was mad with me.

"No, no," I say. "Listen, one day I walking downtown and this white man offer me a ride. I say okay and get in the car. He start talking and hinting round and finally he come on out and say it. I give you twenty dollars, he say. I say okay. We in Chinatown by then and at the next stop light he get out his wallet and give me a twenty dollar bill. 'That what I like bout you colored women,' he say easing all back in his seat just like he already done got some and waiting to get some more. 'Yeah,' he say, 'you all so easy to get.' I put that money in my purse, open the door and tell him, 'Motherfucker, you ain't got shit here,' and slam the door."

"Watch your mouth," Time say, "Larry sitting here." We all crack up.

"What he do then?" Orine ask.

"What could he do? We in Chinatown and all them colored folks walking round. You know they ain't gon' let no white man do nothing to me."

Time tell me after we go to bed that night that he kill me if he ever see me with a white man.

I laugh and kiss him. "What I want with a white man when I got you?" We both laugh and get in the bed. I lay stretched out waiting for him to reach for me. It funny, I think, how colored men don't never want no colored women messing with no white mens but the first chance he get, that colored man gon be right there in that white woman's bed. Yeah, colored men sho give colored womens a hard way to go. But I know if Time got to give a hard way to go, it ain't gon be for no scaggy fay babe, and I kinda smile to myself.

"Martha—"

"Yeah, Time," I say turning to him.

"How old you—eighteen?—what you want to do in life? What you want to be?"

What he mean? "I want to be with you," I tell him.

"No, I mean really. What you want?" Why he want to know I wonder. Everytime he start talking serious-like, I think he must be hearing his sliding song.

"I don't want to have to ask nobody for nothing. I want to be able to take care of my own self." I won't be no weight on you, Time, I want to tell him. I won't be no trouble to you.

"Then what you doing on the Welfare?"

"What else I gon do? Go out and scrub somebody else's toilets like my mamma did so Larry can run wild like I did? No. I stay on Welfare a while, thank you."

"You see what the white man have done to us, is doing to us?"

"White man my ass," I tell him. "That was my no good daddy. If he'd got out and worked, we woulda been better off."

"How he gon work if the man won't let him?"

"You just let the man turn you out. Yeah, that man got yo mind."

"What you mean?" he ask real quiet. But I don't pay no tention to him.

"You always talking bout music and New York City, New York City and the white man. Why don't you forget all that shit and get a job like other men? I hate that damn piano."

He grab my shoulder real tight. "What you mean, 'got my mind?' What you mean?" And he start shaking me. But I crying and thinking bout he gon leave.

"You laugh cause I say all I got in my mind is pitchers but least they better than some old music. That all you ever think bout, Time."

"What you mean? What you mean?"

Finally I scream. "You ain't going no damn New York City and it ain't the white man what gon keep you. You just using him for a scuse cause you scared. Maybe you can't play." That the only time he ever hit me. And I cry cause I know he gon leave for sho. He hold me and say don't cry, say he sorry, but I can't stop. Orine bamming on the door and Time yelling at her to leave us lone and the babies crying and finally he start to pull away. I say, "Time. . . . " He still for a long time, then he say, "Okay. Okay, Martha."

No, it not like he don't want me no more, he—

"Martha. Martha. You ain't been listening to a word I say."

"Mamma." I say it soft cause I don't want to hurt her. "Please leave me lone. You and Orine—and Time too, sometime—yo all treat me like I don't know nothing. But just cause it don't seem like to you that I know what I'm doing, that don't mean nothing. You can't see into my life."

"I see enough to know you just get into one mess after nother." She shake her head and her voice come kinda slow. "Martha, I named you after that woman in the Bible cause I want you to be like her. Be good in the same way she is. Martha, that woman ain't never stopped believing. She humble and patient and the Lord make a place for her." She lean her hands on the table. Been in them dishes again, hands all wrinkled and shiny wet. "But that was the Bible. You ain't got the time to be patient, to be waiting for Time or no one else to make no place for you. That man ain't no good. I told you—"

Words coming faster and faster. She got the cow by the tail and gon on down shit creek. It don't matter though. She talk and I sit here thinking bout Time. "You feel good . . . You gon be my Black queen? . . . We can make it together . . . You feel good . . . " He be back.

Gayle Whittier

Lost Time Accident

Don't get that stuff near your mouth!"

"Why not? What'd happen?"

"It could kill you." But he deals this out easily, a man who moves daily among fatalities. My mother, fixing dinner, frowns: "I simply fail to see why you bring that poison home!"

He winks at me. "Why, that's not poison you're lookin' at, Lizzie, that's money."

"Oh, *sure.*"

"Besides, Annie'll be the only kid in her class who's got *samples* for her project," he justifies. "Even Old Brown's daughter won't have nothin' like this!" A smile bonds him, the father, me the girlchild: Old Brown may be his boss's boss, but in school I get higher marks than Nancy Brown in every subject. In school, we get even. "Brown wouldn't even know where to *look for* samples," my father adds complacently.

"I still don't like it."

What she doesn't like lies in front of me: little vials of soft-looking abrasive dust, in various grinds like coffee or like spice; the lethal bead of mercury which, if smashed, reforms itself at once into a chain of smaller spheres; sharp green and black and rose-colored, manmade crystals, products of Diamonid, where my father works. A public relations booklet, "How Diamonid is Made," lies on the kitchen table too. But I already know that story.

"They heat up all them chemicals in furnaces—you know, you

seen 'em—till it gets harder than diamonds. They even use this stuff to *cut* diamonds. What d'ya think of *that?*"

Reverently, my finger tries the needle tip of one of the crystals. It feels true: HARDER THAN DIAMONDS. That is the electric promise on a big sign between the factory's twin chimneys. Below it, a smaller legend swings in the cloudy wind along the riverfront: "__ Days Since the Last LTA." LTA stands for "Lost Time Accident," my father says. As the crystal dimples my fingertip, imminent danger draws me nearer to my father and my father's world. I imagine how close to the surface our blood is.

He works in dangers, where a man should work, and wears the steel-toed "safety shoes" to prove it. So do my uncles and my male cousins, those who are old enough to quit school and get a job. "Wouldn't catch me in no office!" they all boast. Looking down now at the luminous bead of mercury, a bead pregnant with my own suddenly possible death, I feel the strict enchantment of my father's otherness; and I divine the high and final line where violence marries beauty. Risk is my father's legacy to me: my mother's will be different.

"Don't breathe!" she always cries out, in those nights when we drive homeward from a family party or a movie, following the ancient crescent of the Niagara River which will outlast us all. "Don't breathe it! Hold your breath!"—distrustful of the silicon and pungent air around the factories, blind to the terrible loveliness of their smoking, glowing slagheaps in our ordinary night. When the stench begins, my mother and father both take big, ostentatious breaths; he plants his foot down hard on the gas pedal; the car jumps forward as if at the sound of a starting gun. A mile later, just beyond the row of factories, they surface, gasping. But although I always join them at the start, always draw my deep underwater-swimmer's breath too, I can't resist knowing what danger tastes like. Surreptitiously, I breathe them in: rancid, acid, strange odors that beg analysis even when they most disgust me. My throat is full of them, their sharpness and their exotic new complexities. Tasting them, I taste as well my coming sensuality, which will set experiment ahead of judgment, pleasure above safety, every time. That is why I disobey them both so secretly, seeming to gasp too, for the air which we pretend is safe again.

They would be worth a life or two, those alchemical fires glimpsed over my shoulder as we drive away. I try to read by colors what is smelted there: yellow for sulphur, framed in blue; the neon green, leafbright, to speak for copper; and a mysterious quiet mound, banked and smouldering pink as roses. Full of wonder, I feel myself moving towards a prayer in praise of my own humankind, rash dreamers and builders of all that I behold. The words of awe rise upward on my young but going breath. In my mouth they turn back into air just as I start to speak them. Music, sometimes, even now, revives those visions and the troubling, stubborn veneration that I feel yet before the face of power.

Power is my native city's rightful name. The Power City. It rides on the neck of the rough white river, deadly too, like a leash on the leviathan. My father's maleness goes with it in its power, runs outward from the city's metal core into the country's infinite iron body. The river clasps Grand Island in a dread embrace, then parts like the branches of the human heart. But it feels nothing. America—this was my earliest lesson after God—is built on what he does.

But what exactly *does* he do? Like all my other childhood mysteries, this one will never yield its final name. "My husband works for the Diamonid," my mother merely says. Her brothers and his do, too—or for Hooker or Dupont or Olin. "He works at Olin." That's my Uncle Joe.

"What does he do?" I ask.

Her answer trades me word for unknown word. "He works in Shipping and Receiving. On the night shift now." Or, "Why, he makes *big money.* He's getting star rate now."

But what does he do? The proud-eyed men in my family come back to mind: their serious, important look, the rare and hefty laughter salvaged when they "let themselves go": Thinking of their splendor, physical and brief, their dignity mined somehow from a day of taking orders—thinking of my childhood love which has outlasted them, I see that I am blessed not to know. They sold the only thing the poor have to sell, their breath and blood. And I confess the child I was. I would have loved my Uncle Casey, that night singer, less if I had known he spent the workday heaving sacks of concrete from a platform to a shed. And what if I had numbered, even once, my own father's compromises, counted out the daily spirit-killing facts behind his "steady job?" His pride is my pride too. If I had known, I could not have volunteered, when the teacher went around the room asking what all the fathers did, I could not have answered with such easy, innocent pride, "*My* father works for Diamonid."

"That filthy place!"

Whenever the industrial stench, the greasy dust, invades our house, my mother curses and mourns her missed life elsewhere, with another sort of man, in another sort of place. "I could have married Leonard Price. My mother *begged* me to. And he's a lawyer now, he lives on the Escarpment. Oh, I was beautiful, just beautiful. . . . "

"Goddamighty," my father reminds her wearily, "that dust is what we live off, Lizzie. You can thank your lucky stars for it, if you got any sense." He has "seniority" now, then a promotion and another one. No longer paid from week to slender week, he gets his paycheck once a month, like the management. "Unless there's a big layoff," my father promises, he will always bring home his paycheck and his bonus at Christmas, every month, every year, for as long as I need him. Forever.

"Oh, they just give you a fancy title and less money," my mother sneers. "Why, my baby brother on the assembly line's earning more than you."

"Yeah, and doin' what?" he counters.

"Don't you insult my brother! Good honest work and nobody can say it ain't!" I listen to her slip back into the dialect she hoped to leave behind her.

"I'm sorry, Liz. By God, I'm sorry."

"I should hope so!" she tells him. "That filthy place. Why. . . . "

"Ahh, stop bitin' the hand that feeds you." He strides out of the room.

"Mr. High-and-Mighty," she mutters behind his back. Then she notices me. "Why, that man owes everything he is to me! When we got married, he couldn't even read. I used to teach him. Don't you ever tell him that I told you."

"I won't," I swear, I who will remember this forever.

Our day turns as evenly to the whistles of Diamonid as a monk's day to bells. It opens in my sleep. Sometimes I rouse myself dimly when my father leaves. The noise of his Studebaker unsettles my deep child's sleep long enough for me to feel and mourn his absence in the house. Later I wake up to find him gone. And until he comes home again, nothing sits in its right minute or right place.

"When's supper? What're we having?"

"Don't call it 'supper.' It's dinner; we aren't farmers."

No. Coal miners, my father's people were, used to laboring in blackness and in early deaths. Hers marched a safe and charted course as civil servants. The stamp of these ancestral trades imprints them both, but she has married him, drawn to that breakfree energy that sent him to Diamonid, that promoted him through the war, that brought him, finally, a crew of men.

Our family begins, then, only at four-fifteen in the afternoon, on the shrill distant note of the quitting whistle. My mother, newly fragrant with Friendship Garden, her pin-curled hair unfurled around her solemn face, pretends to leisure, ties a ruffled apron over her clean dress. Then his car rushes into the driveway, the door's lock gives way with a click of metal like a broken bone. His footsteps. They are unique; the man himself is in them—a man no longer young, a man too old, really, to have a child as small as I, an accidental blessing.

"*Was* I an accident?" I dare to ask my mother once.

"Who told you that?"

"Nobody. *Was* I?"

"You were a big *surprise,*" she finally allows.

"Surprise!" my father shouts, bursting through the door. Behind it, almost flattened, we stand silently. SHHH, pantomimes my mother, raising a newly manicured finger to her lips. Something like an old, remembered joy brightens her features momentarily.

"Hey, anybody home?" he asks, pretending to look for us. "Hey, where is everybody? Ain't nobody here?" Mock worries. Then, "BOO!" he's found us. And in his hand, a chocolate bar, a suitor's rose: for me, a sunset sheath of scrap papers, or carbons the color of midnight. Out of the giving and his old return, even my obdurate loneliness melts. "Daddy!" I shout, and we are home.

"Well, will you just look at my two beautiful ladies!" he lies. "Don't you look good enough to eat!"

"Oh, blarney," my mother says, but smiles a younger smile. I feel his lie, a long one by the time that I am born and stand beside her, sharing unevenly in all of his old compliments.

"Somethin' smells good! You got somethin' in the oven, Lizzie?" And he winks a broad vaudevillian wink.

"Herb!"

"Well, have ya?"

"Don't you hold your breath," she tells him, eyes snapping.

I understand them just enough to know that their teasing predates me, that they are remembering each other as they were alone. I am lonely again myself. What does he mean? What could be in the oven except one of my mother's thrifty casseroles, almost unsalted and tending towards one even color? Suspicious of daily pleasure, she cooks "plain." But we must be grateful for it because of all the children who are starving in Europe. Not even Grace can sweeten what she serves.

Now, "Don't get any of that filth on my clean floor!" she warns, as he pretends to lunge at her. "And don't get *near* that carpet! Why, it'd cut it all to pieces. Go wash up," she commands, turning into his mother too. And their flirtation is over for the day.

The Company follows him home. *Don't breathe it.* But the silent, ubiquitous black Diamonid dust collects invisibly in the folds of his clothing, sifts out unseen into a fine glittering shadow which outlines the place where he has stood. All at once you look down and see it there, pooled around his safety shoes with their steelcapped toes ("Company rule, cuts down on accidents") covering his own crooked, comical ones. Diamonid dust destroys whatever it touches; but every night my father comes back to us preserved, saved by his safety shoes and by his ready Irish wits. He comes home "on the dot," my mother boasts to her less-fortunately married friends, the wives of "ladies' men" or drunkards—which is the worst thing a man can be, because if he drinks he will not be a "good provider."

"I'd trust him anywhere," my mother sings. But she too clocks his fifteen minutes between the company gates and our back door. Suddenly, in the midst of one of their quarrels, I will hear her cry, "You work in a filthy place! Your secretary . . . " before his hand bruises her into silence. And I understand that there is moral filth, too, just outside her jurisdiction, in the subtle colors of the air where our livelihood inhales and exhales.

"Back in a jiffy," he tells us now, disappearing into the cellar. Bent over the washtub, he violently scrubs away the company dirt, puts on fresh clothes for the second half of his daily life.

Above him, just as energetically, my mother sweeps up the dark dust. It winks and glistens in her dustpan among our duller household kind. "I want to be sure I get it all," my mother says, as if acknowledging that it is aristocratic, powerful as if it had fallen from a magician's pack stamped with an open trademark diamond around the letter D.

"Diamonid," I try the latinate word, echoing an inventor who named, but did not make, that terrible powder with his own two hands, his nostrils, or his broken lungs. "Diamonid." I am softly in love with its strangeness. When I touch the dust my finger leaves its print, and the dust sets its shiny smudge against my skin.

He washes it away with a soap hard and yellow as a brick of amber. Coming back upstairs, he smells of the soap, acid and golden-brown and potent as the man himself. "Clean as a whistle," he supposes.

But in my father's lungs, invisibly, the black pollen settles, cutting and hardening into what will be his distant death. Some other day, coming back ashen from the doctor's office, "Oh, my God," he'll cry to us, "I got emphysema. Advanced, he says. Do you know what that is? That's just a new name for Black Lung, that's all. That's all." And he will recount, over and over, his grandfather's tortured death, the miner's death he thought he had outrun, until my mother ends it: "For the love of God, shut up! You think that you're the only one . . . ?"

Now, that day unguessed, my mother serves dinner to us, I set the table, he lifts up his voice to tell us about Work. He spins stories out of it, takes male sustenance there, and somehow, miraculously, dreams a tall and fugitive pride in what he does. After the second story, or the third, I imagine that I stand in the stone and concrete of his masculine world. Sometimes, crushed, he seconds my mother's bitter knowledge: "Christ, what a hole that place is!" But, "You'll never have to work in a place like that, Annie," he promises us both. "You're real smart. Your teacher said. *You* won't end up in there."

It puzzles me. No other woman in my family works anywhere at all, except the wife of my uncle-the-gambler. *Men* work. Women marry them. Why would I ever have to work? Listening to my father, I suddenly guess that I am not pretty. I feel a confused shame, but he goes on: "You're college material. Get yourself a real good job," he is advising me. "Something clean. You got what it takes . . . I'd be right up there now, if I got an education."

Briefly, our lives ascend together. We exchange laurels. I recount the prizes that I win in school; he, a boss, tells stories about his men.

"What'd you do in school today? What's that you're reading?"

"French. I'm reading French."

"I'll be damned! Go on, say something in French for me."

"Ma plume est sur le bureau," I tell him, waiting until I make him ask for the translation, then: "My pen is on the desk."

"Me, I know some Polack and a lot of Eyetalian," he boasts. Then he says, "Eh! Ven'aca!" which means "Come over here," or "No capeesh?" for "Don't you get it?"

"You say it after me," he instructs, proud of my agile tongue and that textbook—stilted French, passwords into a world unlike his own, where he will not be welcome. Obeying him, I taste the flavor of my father's role at Work. The spoken phrases teach him to me. I see him merciful but just, commanding them in their homespoken tongues: *Come over here. Hey, buddy, don't you get it?*

"I got my men's respect," he always finishes.

They have simple, children's names, those men: Little, Big, Young, Old. Little Carl brings in the spring each Easter. He brings it tied up in a stout bag full of hard anise-seed cookies, the predictable chocolate rabbit that I am too old for now; a big bottle of bright red wine for my father, and a littler blue bottle of Evening in Paris perfume for my smiling mother. My father laughs, holding the wine up the light. "Dago red!" And Little Carl laughs at himself, too, while my father claps him on his rounded back. "He's a pain in the ass, that guy," my father says, but says it chuckling.

"Why don't you fire him? *I* would," my mother vows.

"Ah, he's all right," my father redetermines.

Then the war lets go of us, and one day—no holiday at all—little Carl runs shouting and weeping towards our house, waving the first telegram from a brother he had thought was dead. In our staid Northern European neighborhood, people come defensively to the railings of their porches, grimace at him, and go back inside. Final judgment. But, "Hey, buddy! Eh, paysan!" my father is already running out to meet him, infected with his joy. They embrace, Italians together, in the back yard, while indoors my mother hardly needs to ask, but does, "What will people think?"

I watch them through the glass. They are clasping and dancing their fellowship. "You get damned close to guys, workin' with 'em," he has often said. But men don't hug each other like that, do they? Do they? I ask myself if what I see is love, workborn. My mother, as if she has heard my silent question, states, "Blood is stronger," looking at them too. Jealous now, "Blood can't be broken," she reminds us both. "*His* men indeed!"

She herself maintains a distance which my French lessons have not yet taught me to name *noblesse oblige.*

"Wouldn't you like a nice cup of coffee?" she asks, moving already towards the speckled coffee pot on a back burner. "It's only this morning's heated up, but I think it's still O.K."

A bearish blond giant stands shy and huge against our kitchen door. One black-mittened hand wrings another, warming him against the late November cold. He has just delivered our winter kindling.

"No, t'ank you, missus," he says roundly and severely.

"Oh, dear! Well, at least sit down for a minute. You look chilled to the bone!"

Wearing a darker shadow even than my father's, he maintains his statue's pose against the yellow door.

"No, t'ank you, I get your floor all dirty. Anyway, got to get to another job." Only, "chob" he says.

"They sure keep you busy, don't they? What's the next one?"

The silence lengthens. I wonder whether his language or his wits can run so slowly. At last, "We dump barrels in that old canal," he remembers.

"Oh? What're they dumping?"

"They don't tell *me,* missus."

"Well. Well, I guess you've got to run, then," she dismisses him. "Now you tell 'the boss,' " my mother winks, "I said, 'Hello there!' " She thinks it is a joke that both of them work for the same boss. He does not.

"Be seein' you, missus," he tells her. Then, still unsmiling, he lifts his denim cap, work-blackened, to make a courtly gesture that starts me laughing inwardly. But my laughter dies unborn. I take in the strip of forehead underneath the brim: pure and white as day. Beneath the dusty skin, the shadow of his livelihood, another man is hiding, a man all pale and gold: a Viking or a lion.

Only one of the men, Shorty, ever stays. Anomalously black as a junebug, delicate and maimed, with a glass eye to match his equally freakish blue one, and one elegant leg made out of wood, he calls my mother "Miz Elizabeth." His stump is aching, he tells her, as she pours her coffee in his cup; he thinks that it will rain or snow, that's how he knows.

My mother bends, easy in her sure superiority. From below the cupboard she lifts up an almost-full bottle of brandy for emergencies. She adds a dollop to the black coffee in his cup. "Don't you tell a soul!"

One September afternoon, while my mother was taking down her steel-colored hair, the telephone rang. "Your father!" she knew, although he never called home.

For once she loved him, she rushed so quickly to the telephone. But she let it ring one more shrill time, while her hand endorsed her breastbone with the sign of the cross, as if she were putting on perfume.

"I just knew it was you! What's happened?" she spilled into the receiver. " . . . Oh, *no!* Who is it? . . . No, I didn't, *don't* . . . Just where is he now? Is he still . . . ? Oh, Oh. . . . I see. And when are you coming home?" Just as I thought she was about to hang up, she added gently, "Honey," as if her love must make some kind of difference now.

"What is it? Is there a strike?" I asked excitedly.

"No, there's been an accident at Work. Oh, your father's O.K., just shook up," she said. "But one of his men got badly hurt."

"Which one?" I warmed to the drama, selecting a victim in my imagination. "Shorty? Little Carl?"

"No. His name is Stash, Stanley . . . Wuh . . . I don't know how to say it," She added, "Be awful good to your father when he gets home."

"Sure."

But I hardly had the chance. He walked in, giftless and mad, deliberately striding right onto the forbidden linoleum with his abrasive dust, then even into the hallway where my mother's sacred expanse of new carpet started. He moved tight and fast, dramatically ignoring us. Then, angrily too, he tore a number into the telephone dial.

"Hello, is Mrs. Wyczolaski there? . . . Oh. Well, this here's Herb O'Connor. I'm Stash's . . . Stash and me, we work together," he said. "You just tell Stella if there's anything she wants, *anything,* why, us boys'll give blood or whatever else . . . ? I see. Yeah, I understand. I'd feel the same damned way. Well, like I said, *anything.* I'll call back later."

In the kitchen my mother was already sweeping up the fine black silt behind his rage. But she swept slowly and gently, so as not to anger him, I felt, or, perhaps, so as not remind that it was there. It made a dark and gritty sound in her dustpan.

"There's dirt all over here!" I imitated her.

But, "Never mind," she said. And when he returned to the kitchen, my mother did not mention it, only, "Tell me what happened," and a moment later, "Your paper's over there on the chair," as she always said, as it always was.

"Yes, tell us about it!" but I felt my enthusiasm for a story thrown back at me by their silence. Ashamed, I stopped, and heard my father speak only to my mother, to himself.

He documented it, how, in the hot September afternoon, Stash and the other men were out in the yard, "sweatin' like pigs," he said. He would have called to them to quit work early, it was so damned hot, only a bigger boss walked through, inspecting. Just as the whistle blew, "Put 'er down!" he shouted. And Stash, tired, hot himself, carelessly leaned over the pallet of the forklift and pushed the release button. The whole load flattened him.

"Oh, Jesus," my father recalled. "Everybody's shoutin' and yellin', nobody even remembered to get that fuckin' thing off of him. 'Herb, help me!' he's screamin'. I push this button and it lifts up in the air, takin' part of him with it, I swear to God. Joe Vetucci, he fainted. And there's this sound out of him when I did it, like a crunch, only . . . "

"Oh, don't!" my mother cried. "No, no, that's all right. No. Tell me."

"Softer," he said. "Like a deep breath when it goes out." His face sealed itself over the trace of the mystery, the failure of his own description of it.

My mother's hand reached out for him as over greater space, but his words bore him away, back to the yard, miles from us, back to quitting time, centuries ago.

"You couldn't tell his shirt from his chest. Blood everywhere. Mrs. Prince, she's the company nurse, she come runnin' from the clinic with her bag and give him oxygen. They called the ambulance. Then she started cuttin' his shirt away, and he was screamin'. No. It wasn't a *scream,*" he corrected. "He couldn't scream. It was more. . . . " And his voice left off in a chugging sound as his own mouth filled up with vomit. Keeping it back with an unwashed hand, he rushed into the bathroom. We could hear him vomiting there, wildly trying to get rid of what he had seen that day, or saying it.

"Shouldn't we go in?" I asked.

"No, leave him alone," my mother said.

After a while the vomiting dried off into sobs. The sobs stopped too. Finally, he came out angry.

"I'm gettin' the hell outta here! I'm goin' for a ride!" he shouted in my mother's direction, as if she meant to stop him.

"Herb, be careful! Please!" Futile. The door slammed; he punished the car, its parts shrieking and grinding against each other; it squealed down the street, him in it.

In the silence that gathered thickly where he had stood, I asked, "Can't that man get better? Can't they fix him?"

"Now, what do you *think!*" I heard my mother cry. Then, seeing that my question had for once been almost innocent, she added more kindly, "Oh, I doubt it." She took my father's plate away from the table, heaping it with portions of dinner, then putting it in the oven to keep it warm. She glanced at the kitchen clock, adjusted a dial, then moved our two remaining plates side by side. "Why, it would be a miracle if that man got well!" she afterthought.

But I lived then in a climate of miracles as of dust. First there were the stained-glass cures that had entertained my Sundays since my babyhood: "Take up thy bed and walk." These, however, I had recently understood to be ancient, outgrown events, mere precursors of the newer miracles, which my century's god, science, was dispensing. Through science—they told me so at school—we were getting an edge on death and illiteracy: also on other kinds of darknesses, bigotry, for example, and communism. Surely one of these hoarded miracles could save Stash.

Out of the clustered silence, my mother's voice awoke me. "Of course, *his* wife'll get a bundle."

"What? Oh."

"Because he died on the job," she explained. "That's why."

"Even if it was an accident?"

"Why, that's true," she considered. "He was *careless,* after all. Maybe she won't get anything." And now her voice took on vindication. "After all, it was his own fault, he didn't look what he was doing." *Careless.* I startled into shame, I who was accused daily of negligence and a child's innocent amnesia before the world. She had called me by my own secret name. Was death a kind of carelessness too?

Eight o'clock. Nine. The night went on without my being sent to bed. My mother turned on the radio, set sewing against its background of ventriloquists and organ chords. I, defying sleep, lay listening, raised my head to see her golden thimble twinkle as she stitched, magically recalling my father, thread by thread. At last her simple magic worked, and he came home.

The car gently ("Don't wake the neighbors") in the driveway; the careful clasping of the garage doors; the snap of the familiar lock. His older, lonelier steps came towards us.

"Are you feeling any better, Herb?" she asked.

"Oh, shit," he said. "Shit. I seen him. I went to the hospital and seen him."

"How . . . uh, what hospital is he in?"

"Memorial. It was nearest. She wanted St. Catherine's 'cause they're Catholics. But they can't move him anyplace, shape he's in. I seen him. He's so bad off they got him strapped to the bed, tubes goin' in and out. Givin' him blood. . . . " The uncaring tone began to take him away from us. Perhaps to prevent it, my mother cried too empathetically, "*Oh that poor man!*"

"He says to me, he says, 'Herb, I wanna die. Honest to God, I just wanna die,' is what he said. 'Just let me go.' Well, he mouthed it. I couldn't hardly make it out."

"Why, for heaven's sake!" My mother strung her words like counted beads. "Didn't they give him something for the pain, those people?" An alert, outraged expression stuck to her face.

"Oh, sure, sure," my father answered bitterly. "But they can't give him enough, is all. I seen his doctor, I says to him, 'Doc, why the hell can't you people deaden this man's pain?' What were they there for, I asked him. And you know what? He told me they *would,* only that much pain-killer might kill Stash too. Dying anyway, I says. And the doctor just froze me out, said that's *different,* it's the *law.*"

At the word "law" my mother faltered. "Well, maybe he's right, Herb. I mean, it probably *is* the law, isn't it?"

"The law can go fuck itself, far as I'm concerned."

"Now, Herb," my mother went on academically, "you have to see it from the doctor's side . . . "

"No, I don't. Why should I? Goddamned legalized thieves's all they are!"

My mother touched his arm. "Maybe he's got a chance, though . . . Stash, I mean."

"Oh, hell, Lizzie, you'd a seen him you wouldn't talk like that. The man's crushed to a pulp, that's what. A pulp." (The cliché tried to come alive in my mind, but didn't.) "And his wife's standin' out in the hall cryin', and his son . . . well, Jesus. 'I just wanna die,' he says to me."

"Son? I didn't know the . . . Wuh. . . . "

"Wyczolaski," he spat at her.

"I didn't know they had *two* children," my mother said almost brightly. "I thought there was only that one girl who goes to school with Annie. Annie, what's her name?"

"Wanda," I replied, disliking my mother. "Her name is Wanda."

"Of course," my mother acknowledged with the littlest of her smiles.

"Yeah, two kids. That poor woman. What's she gonna do now?"

My mother suppressed something sharper than she said. "Why, she's got Compensation coming, hasn't she? She'll do all right."

"Well, she gets it if I testify it happened on company time, before quitting," he said. "Or that the machine slipped."

In the length of silence my mother picked her way among the thickets where we lived. "A lot of people saw what happened, though," she finally ventured. "I mean, they'd know if you were lying, if you swore it happened on company time. Or was the equipment." His look, which I could not see from where I sat, must have embarrassed her. "Well, I *mean,* he *was* careless, really. It was his own fault."

"Own fault! Who the hell wouldn't get careless, all day in that heat?" He brought his fist down against the table. There was an interval of tiny chimes as her porcelain knick-knacks trembled against each other. "Anybody'd get 'careless,' that's all. That's *all.*"

"But suppose you lose *your* job? You're not even in the union any more. There's witnesses."

"Now, Lizzie . . . "

"What about us? Have you ever thought of that? Oh, no; not you. And there's *witnesses,*" she repeated, her voice rising. Her finger rose too and pointed him out, one red nail gleaming blood-drop pure.

"You make a better lawyer than a wife, Lizzie. Now shut up. It was on company time, and that's that."

"But it wasn't. . . . "

"I said shut up, Lizzie, and I meant it," he commanded in a stonedust voice. Then my father's eye caught sight of me. "What the hell are *you* doin' up? Ain't you got school tomorrow?"

"It's not her fault."

"Well, go on. Scoot. Go get your beauty sleep," my father said. As I escaped the room, his large hand lightly told me of the shape of my child's head.

Through my door, half open to let in the whisper of the cooler early autumn night, a long finger of light crossed the thin yellow varnished floorboards and pillared up the wall. There a wallpaper lattice lifted up its repeated clusters of white roses, stale and old.

I slept a white sleep.

Later in the night, half conscious and alone, I heard the customary thunder of their household quarrel. It no longer frightened me. I could identify their cadences like phrases in a symphony. Sometimes I even fell asleep, while they still raged, as constant and as changing as the sea, beneath my painted bed. This time, sitting up alive, I sorted out new and different sounds.

Against the rocking of their human voices, he was throwing things. Their dense thuds declared them heavy, breakable. They rang out dully. They reverberated against the floor. Once, I remembered, he had gotten angry at my mother and had thrown his breakfast at the wall. The plate splintered. But the fried egg slid slowly downward to the baseboard, a cartoon sun. Watching its descent, I held back my laughter, lest I disrespect the enchantment of my father's violence. But fear brought more laughter bubbling to my nervous lips. He had only broken the plate that one time, though. This breakage went on and on.

Where usually my mother's voice climbed, sickening, to half-evasive pleas, it kept instead a low and reasonable horizon note, a stranger's tone. They walked the circle of the rooms below, my father pacing heavily, erratically, my mother keeping up while he shouted: "That goddamn bastard! Polack son-of-a-bitch!" Crash—an object seconded his rage. "Stupid fucking idiot! If I told him once, I told him a hundred times: *One slip* and it's curtains, buddy! Yeah, I told him. . . . " Something struck the floor. "You, you gold-crowned son-of-a-bitch . . . " (even my mother's voice protested it) "Be-all, know-all fucker of the rest of us! . . . No, no, I won't, I won't . . . " And his body bore his words away, stepping through the stairwell to the kitchen to the dining room, almost never used, then the circuit of the downstairs floor. His muffled voice remained; against it, my mother's preserving obbligato. From time to time he climbed above language, and then I heard another heavy thud, and tried to imagine what it was he threw.

Slowly the intervals lengthened. At last, exhausting things to throw, he broke himself and cried. I lay in my changed bed, shocked in my hearing and my heart, while the night air carried up to me his foreign male weeping, wholly of this earth. I felt that my father's sobs would go on unbearably forever, but he was diminished too. In astonished meditation on the edge of sleep, I knew that he was less my father than he had been before. Aware of his abandonment, I abandoned myself to dreams.

There was a next day, and on it, everything resumed functionally but awkwardly, like a broken machine. Breakfast brought gluey oatmeal, acid orange juice, and lukewarm milk in the old chipped cup with a hair-thin crack through its pale wall. A lump of breakfast in me, I underwent my regimented schoolday. But through the getting dressed and the roll call, through the Products of Peru and our spiritless public school singing of "The Volga Boatman," I waited. Something else must happen, I assumed. Nothing did.

When I got home from school, home was still there, a semaphore of well-known laundry strung behind it. My mother, newly powdered, wearing the set, severe expression of a woman living out a holy but mistaken life, ran her finger over a few inches of windowsill: "Just look at that! Third time today I dusted it!" she said. Then, at four o'clock exactly, she disappeared to put on a fresh dress, to brush out her cold hair. Even her face in the center of it all was her old face, rigid and alone, the face I remember her by, even now: my mother.

"Wash your hands, Annie," she commanded absently. "And put on another blouse; that one's just covered with ink. How do you ever do it?"

Coming in to us, me with my clean hands, my mother in her unmarked apron, my father made no jokes at all that night, but went downstairs at once to scrub himself. I could hear the water rushing into the washtub, could sense his muted gestures as he changed into clean clothes. I felt his feet, my father's feet, measuring the steps deliberately as he climbed, purified, to the kitchen. Only then did my mother look at him questioningly, gently.

He shook his head. No. And again, as she asked, "Is he . . . ?" No, but only with his eyes.

"Is Stash dead?" I asked, voicing what I knew must be her question too.

"Mr. Wyczolaski," he corrected me. "No."

"I suppose he's in a coma," my mother said.

"Still conscious."

"Oh, that's good," I tried.

"It isn't good at all! What do *you* know . . . !" my mother scowled.

"Somebody oughta do something," my father said only to her.

"Well, they won't," she answered him. "You know it and I know it. Your paper's over there on the chair," she said.

Proving what nobody would do, they separated their lives from the dying man's. Humming a little, even, she set our dinner plates in their three places; we thanked our same God for her utilitarian food, which was not really the same every night, but seemed so. Only our voices, by an unspoken accord, stayed deep inside us, and we did not talk.

After dinner, while I laid out my assignment book and papers to do homework, my parents briefly whispered together in the kitchen, murmuring low enough for mourning in our altered house. " . . . a collection?" I caught, and then my father said, "Oh, flowers, sure," loud enough to carry easily to me. "Hey, Lizzie, did you know they put coins on their eyes, them Polacks? Honest to God. It's to pay their way into heaven."

In the outer room, always my room, with my books and my unbidden fear spread out around me, I felt myself only fraudulently theirs: my untapped excitement, my young urgency against their casual resumption of our life. A man was dying. And it was their fault, I decided. Too easily, too carelessly, they had let go of him, just as if they had let go of my hand in a crowd and I was lost forever. They had not kept him in their minds, they had excluded him. I felt a spirit sympathy between the man and myself; but even more warmly, a learned and rancid sense of drama took possession of my imagination, phrase by rehearsed phrase, as I tried to encompass him. "He's in God's hands now." "His life is hanging by a thread!" Where had I heard those words, those keys to my unwritten drama? Which would work, would open it? "Nothing tried, nothing gained . . . " "Perseverance wins the crown" (my mother's favorite). And "if at first you don't succeed. . . . " So that was it. They hadn't cared to try for the magical third time. And that was why he was dying so invisibly.

Somebody should do something," my father had admitted. *I* would, I answered to myself.

I did. Leaving my homework and my parents' voices in the rooms below, I put my own small upstairs bedroom in close to perfect order. The rug, a worn pink pile, I placed equidistant from the headboard and the footboard of my narrow bed. I spat on a turned-up corner of the chenille bedspread for luck, as if it were my skirt hem, and then I smoothed it into place. The windowshades, I saw, jogged awkwardly, one up, one down: I evened them.

Then I took up my last thing, my prayerbook, white leather stamped with a delicate gold cross. A recent Christmas present, it smelled like nothing else in the house, papery and new. Its thin pages clung to my clumsy fingers, and its scarlet bookmark lay silkenly against last Sunday's portion of the Psalter, accusing me of the early place where I had let my attention wander from the text. I was sorry now that I did not pray every day. I promised myself and God that, starting now, I would. I would read the Bible too, each morning, if only—but even I stopped short of bribery.

Almost at once, I turned to the right prayer, but, like any browser, kept my finger there to scan the nearby titles. "For Social Justice," I read, "For the Navy," "For Rain." And I kept on reading, delaying as long as possible the moment of what I now suddenly saw to be a test. At last nothing but the moment of my trial remained, and I resorted to my destined prayer: "For a Sick Person." Briefly its Renaissance cadences helped me on, but then I stumbled from the archaic words, falling back into my century and my place. Perhaps, I reconsidered, spontaneous prayer would be better? Yes.

Still I had to find the name of God.

I meant to choose a title which best suited my petition and my own unaccustomed voice, used only to a bedside "Our-Father-who-art-in-heaven" run off proudly and not even consciously, the same way I recited multiplication tables or conjugated French verbs. But by now my knees reminded me of time, and all the names of God began to sound ponderous and strange. I could not even repeat some of them without hearing, over mine, the priest's majestic voice drawing out vowels and clicking consonants shut to speak God's grandeur—or his own.

"Most Gracious God," I imitated. But I felt at once remoter from Him than I had ever known myself to be. "Our Heavenly Father," then. No. I was only one abashed person speaking, no "we" at all; and anyway, "heavenly" felt too distant, and "father" too close in. "Lord" avoided these degrees, but struck me as bare and abrupt, almost rude. And I passed over "God Almighty" embarrassedly. Except when a priest said it, it was a curse. In our household, where everyone but me blasphemed with Celtic latitude, I had often heard that title eased into a punctuating "Goddamighty!" I could not now make my own tongue disobey these family cadences, replace them with the unctious elevation of the priest's. They were in me, my people's voices. Hearing them, the others, I stopped altogether, afraid that my mouth might name God wrongly and undo my prayer.

Finally, on my numb knees and exhausting God's known names, I shifted my felt weight and got familiar: "God," I said, "please . . . " (minding my manners), "please take care of, of . . . " But here again I hesitated like a child in a spelling bee. I practiced the word in my head, then spoke, "Mr. Wyczolaski," out loud, fast and right. Borne on my confidence in the victim's name, and in my own power to pronounce it, I next told God why he should save Stash, "*Stanley,*" I reminded God, although He would know a nickname, too, I reasoned to myself. "Save him for his daughter Wanda, who's the same age as me, and for his wife . . . " I had forgotten her name, but chanted bravely on, since God knew everything, "and for himself," I said. After a moment I added, "In Thy Infinite Mercy . . . " I felt the thrill of my translation. The extemporaneous prayer sounded almost like those in my book: I knew that it was good. But with this recognition of my composition's quality, I almost praised myself, the speaker: suddenly I knew that God must save Stash for my own sake most of all. It was for my words that I wanted the miracle to happen: to make them good. The prayer was for myself. Before this forbidden fact, I arrested: and the prayer's lost momentum fell away from me, inexorable as dust.

"Not just for *me,*" I tried to get it back. "For everyone, O God." But I doubted that He would be taken in by this patchwork charity: I did not believe it myself. It opened falsely onto my new world, which was flat, not round, no matter what they said, and had an edge where heaven ought to be, and big deaths even for its smallest, most accidental men.

Almost dumb with loss, I waited out my first time of nothingness. It felt like death, that space between the outgrown child who had dared to pray and this self-conscious stranger who suddenly could not. Then the image of the careless, crushed man formed itself in my mind, textbook clear. I knew he must lay smashed—"like an egg," my father had described him—beneath a hospital sheet; and so I started there. I envisioned it whiter and coarser than my mother's sheets, decently containing him. The room around him smelled of purity and pain.

I drew nearer to that invented bed. But I did not open his eyes. They closed on his unimaginable expression, which I did not know how to see. His iconic head, I saw, resembled my father's, was not a young man's head; and his imagined features came to view both personal and sure, as if I had seen him many times before. Then—even now—I knew I really saw Stanley Wyczolaski's face. Safe white bandages held back his damage, like the swaddling on the porcelain Della Robbia in my new classroom.

I wanted to know more. In my mind's chamber still, I folded the silver bandages aside, neat as a lifted page. Underneath, everything showed itself smooth and charted, the proud high cage of ribs, the shadow of male hair. "There, there, you'll be all right," I comforted. Then, for the first time, I heard my own voice say, "Darling," in a whisper. At the word his body, a lattice in a birthday card, answered me by opening up. I saw all the mysteries that I had only read of: this, the four-chambered heart, but still, so still; here the arteries and veins running blue into it and red away; there the lungs, pink as shell. They lay as real as my eye, but unreal, too.

By now I had forgotten God. My dreaming hands moved in circles over the dying man, and in my vision they restored his life. Veins and arteries, collapsed, sprang full and fresh as stems after rainfall. I bent to kiss him better, and my borrowed breath lifted new roundness in his flattened lungs. I gave him my voice, too. "There, you see," I proved to him out loud.

Then my real hands began to move tenderly over the chenille ridges of my bed's coverlet. I breathed faster, conscious of a drum of pulse, my own, and of my will contracted tightly to a concrete thing meant to uphold him. The unguessed power of my life ran free, and with it, sadness older than the earth.

I could not know yet that my caresses, my reverence, and—when I moved—my newfound exactitude of care, made me a lover. But I knew that everything I did was futile, that I could not really mend: only I made the gestures of the healer all the same, defiantly. I felt my own bones age against the hardness of the floor, and, breathing for us both, for myself and for the dying man, I tasted my own mystery. In that dark way, among my vanquished gods, I began my work in the world.

João Ubaldo Ribeiro

ALAINDELON DE LA PATRIE

I do not understand him who has a liking for bulls and cows. There was a time here when they used to raise a great many humpbacked Indian cattle, which to me have faces signifying deceit, lies, crimes and shamelessness. In addition, most of them have dark circles around their eyes, which shows them to be evil-minded perverts not to be trusted. Any man who has found himself in the pasture or even in the corral in the company of a humpback knows he cannot turn his back or allow himself to be off-guard, because the humpback may get him, and if he does will not treat him sympathetically. As far as I am concerned, being otherwise employed at this farm mostly for general duties, the only bull that gets along fine with me is the one known as Big Butt, who is already a bit stricken in years and a very gentlemanly Dutch bull. In Big Butt's case, when the need arises I go and take care of him, and if I am not joy itself when I do it, at least I do it in peace and quiet, since the Dutch bull is by nature a civil and well-versed creature, and one can readily see his dutchness. This must be because in his homeland they have kings and queens and ever since bulls have been bulls in Dutchland they have been brought up to observe the proprieties. So the Dutch bull covers his cows with a great feeling for his obligations, and it is a beautiful thing to watch, because Dutch cows are also most well-mannered, and so when Big Butt is doing his job with one of them even our visitors enjoy watching, because he dismounts the cow with much elegance and almost a thank-you and a smile from her. It is a most polished thing. This bull Big Butt, by the way, enjoys a few peanuts in the *bagasse* whenever I can oblige him, since he is getting old and needs to be able to unfurl his instrument in order to maintain steady employment—for when Big Butt is no longer a swordsman, good-bye Big Butt, and maybe I shall even miss him for although he is not really anybody's close friend, he treats me in a way you would think he has a degree from at least secondary school. If someday I eat a stew made of some part of Big Butt, I shall eat it with sorrow. I shall eat it because life is one eating the other, and it is better that we eat the bull than the bull eat us; it is a political matter, even more so because the bull does not speak.

In the old days it did not used to be like this, I mean, we did not have all this organization. The humpback formerly in charge of servicing the cows was very outrageous. Called Nonô of Bombay, this humpbacked bull would keep hoofing up the dust among the cows of his race, and when one of them would forget to keep an eye on him, you would think he was a paying customer entitled to the whole works and the cow would not even have time to get into the proper position because Nonô would dart at her snorting smoke and ready for action, and one thing I thank God for is that He did not bring me into this world to be one of that humpback's cows. In fact, there were more than a few times when the cowhands had to adjust him for a proper entrance because he did not pay attention to how things were done, he would dab any part of a cow wherever he found one. A very backward type, the king of uncouth. When I remember Nonô of Bombay intercoursing with his cows I shiver, for the cow suffered much. When a man compares the way Big Butt treated his Dutch cows to the way Nonô treated his humpbacks, he sees the difference between a blond, cultured person such as Big Butt and an unprincipled, mulatto person such as Nonô. This is one of the many reasons why in my next reincarnation, God willing, I will come back white and well-educated. I do not wish to act like Nonô, who almost tore his cows apart, even though he is quite well-admired around these parts and the story goes that to this day there are women who, enthusiastically playing the two-backed beast, praise their men by saying, "Let me have it, my Nonô!" but I consider those women to be a bunch of humpbacked cows, that is what I consider, because I am in favor of tenderness, and blows should only be used when pleaded for or truly deserved.

However, with all the Nonôs and Big Butts and a few more stud-bulls of some repute in this land, such carryings-on have always been pretty standard. The rooster sometimes seems to be conversing with his shadow or discussing elections or something when all of a sudden he flares up with great brilliance and begins pecking the chickens back and forth and folding himself in the direction of their tails, and thus he does all his work in something like five minutes, spark-like. The eggs that follow are brown, not white, fertile, not barren, and quite good for one's health, or else out come little chicks and all the chickens go on with their chickening as Our Lord wished. Thus the little lizard has two rods, one at the right, one at the left, so that any female lizard can be well provided whether she be left or right, and it should be said that the lizard only catches one lizardess at a time, not taking advantage of being able to serve two. For it is not a matter of vanity, it is a question of not wasting time, because if it is true that the lizard has many flies to eat, it is also true that there are many other creatures desirous of eating the lizard, so he cannot afford to take it easy. The hummingbird makes it in the air, sometimes just in passing, sometimes giving a greeting and profiting by the opportunity, since the hummingbird's heart beats so fast it buzzes, and he dies an early death, his heart buzzing, his flowers being kissed. Jenny donkeys and mares much appreciate being mounted by the male, and there are cases of she-donkeys that keep on giving a jackass little kicks all afternoon until they get him, and then they grind their teeth and drool a little and become great admirers of the male, if it turns out he knew how to answer those little kicks well. The land tortoise grunts when he is on top of the female, and she shows great patience because their construction does not make things easy, and that must be the reason why he grunts. The pig and the drake apply screws, and there are those who say the screws are to stupefy the female, for she stares and stares until the screws get the better of her. The cat produces thorns which make the she-cat bleed as he withdraws, the bleeding however being necessary for her to become pregnant. The praying mantis stands motionless, and even before she is finished she begins to chew him up and there is room for all of him inside her belly. All of this can be seen here and many more things, from the lagoons with their toads and frogs getting married all across the waters to the noises of the bigger creatures. This is the way Nature was made and in each and every coupling you can feel her strength.

Well then, in these modern times we have been unnaturalized. Although I, disliking all kinds of bulls, did not know very well what was happening until everything started changing and we began being visited by many doctors and important persons. And it so happened that after many pronouncements and great nervousness, we took the large cage to the train station, like a party lacking only a musical band, to greet the great French Charolais bull who even before arriving here had been given the name Alaindelon. All French names end in *on,* and the name was supposed to be Napoleon, another tremendous Frenchman, who invaded England, chased King John the Sixth out of Portugal and all in all raised a great perturbation everywhere and wouldn't let anyone get away with anything. But Alaindelon was the final choice, being the name of a French movie star of very great reputation and from what I hear about this Alaindelon one would expect the cows here to be celebrating vastly.

Now, it seemed to me as soon as I saw him that this here Alaindelon was a wholly sorrowful animal, wrapped in darkness and appearing to be in mourning. At first I thought it was just the nature of French bulls, because it's well known that Frenchmen have a strong penchant for lechering but always with the utmost decency, not like what Nonô of Bombay used to favor. But even so how could this bull be so sad, since it was also well known that from now on he would be installed like a monarch, with massages, special food, stroking and vitamins? and if the cows he was supposed to work with were not French cows of the highest upbringing, they were not something you would throw out the window either, and it should be added that it was the beginning of summer and a general carnality was taking over in all parts of the farm, even the blowflies giving the lady blowflies their best, the boy earwigs with the girl earwigs and so forth, not to mention others, such as the cavies, which as everybody knows are always either eating or employing their lovemaking tools, be it summer or winter. And sometimes a man dresses in black like this but it does not mean a thing, witness for instance Father Barretinho, God keep his soul, may more words on this never escape my lips.

A job such as this many of us spend our lives praying to find, and now he arrives with all this sadness and showing himself to be almost disagreeable. An animal as big as a stocky elephant, all in black and with a disheartened countenance one could not help feeling sorry for, when the natural thing for him would be to be swishing his tail, drooling a little and preparing his gear. But this is evidence that the animal also has intelligence, because our Alaindelon already had a perfect knowledge of what was going to happen, which was why he was not rejoicing and, poor fellow, he had reason completely on his side.

When I found out, it staggered me. For about a week or two Alaindelon had been installed in his apartment with ventilation and all perquisites, including an American apparatus to stop the flies from bothering him, and then, as I passed by to fetch a few buckets and some troughs, I asked when his holiday would be over and he would go out to work on some cows.

"Given his great fame, everybody here wishes to get a look," I said. "He must be a thing of great competence."

"But he won't be working on any cows," answered Dr. Crescêncio, who works here as a kind of cow engineer, giving directions, and has a college degree in cows.

"So, what is he here for? Isn't he a stud?"

"Do you think we would waste an animal like him directly with the cows? No sir! Everything that comes from him is worth gold. What we do is to extract the material, put it on ice, and stick it in the cows with a needle. That way nothing is wasted."

At this point I saw Alaindelon's face poking out of an opening, and I realized that he must already know Brazilian, maybe he studied it in France, because he understood the whole conversation and became even more downcast than before, and such a grief it was that it made one's heart bleed. I inquired as to how the material was to be extracted, whether it meant that they would stick a needle in the poor animal's masculine pouch, but Dr. Crescêncio said no. Every so many days, he said, the people in charge will come to do the manipulation.

"How does this manipulation work?"

"You can watch if you wish for we are going to collect a few minutes from now."

"And does it not upset the bull, Doctor?"

"Not at all, he is accustomed to it."

And, indeed, Alaindelon, if he was not enthusiastic, did not raise any difficulties either, one could see he was practiced in his profession. As soon as he caught sight of the manipulation team, he spread his legs apart and looked the other way and then let himself be extracted, everything very businesslike, without so much as a little sigh. By then one could not help feeling very, very sorry to see a prestigious, medal-covered animal subject to being called a virgin stud. At the very end the manipulators even gave him a little squeeze, but he never protested, he stood there putting up with such humiliations in the best possible mood. How can a mortal endure such a situation—especially a Frenchman?

Maybe his profession is more respected in France than it is here, because here things are the way they are, so he received several nicknames—Five-against-one, Cold Hose, Knows-no-cow, Wind-fucker, Drip-in-the-jug, Hand Sausage, a whole lot of them—and we laughed but we also felt that it was not right to make fun of somebody's misfortune like that.

That was why we decided on a plan to do Alaindelon a benefaction, this benefaction to be carried out by the cow Honey Blossom, short on breeding but with a strong rump and a good build, and also a cow of much experience in life, having even been, according to some, Nonô of Bombay's mistress, and people say that the two of them used to eat a couple of hemp plants, also known as Angolan tobacco, better yet marijuana—what are we trying to hide—which grows here like so much bristlegrass, and not a few take a little smoke now and then, well, people say that the two of them would eat a couple of saplings and get into a great deal of indecency. This was before Nonô caught foot-and-mouth disease during a binge and died old and sore in the mouth and disapproved of by everyone in general. One acknowledges therefore that Honey Blossom was no young maiden, but in the first place it is known that Frenchmen appreciate aged females. And second, Honey Blossom was always in the mood, which is something you cannot say about all cows, even if they are cows or maybe actually because of that.

So Emanuel and I and also the boy Ruidenor agreed to take Honey Blossom to the small corral which is close to Alaindelon's apartment, and during the night we would go there and release the Frenchman. No sooner said then done, and we even had moonlight to make things perfect. We startled him when we opened the door, he was not used to that. And there was no way to make him come out, even with us doing a lot of explaining. Emanuel went as far as to suggest we flick his thingamabob to see if that got him in the mood, but we all feared he might presume one of us to be a manipulator and then wish to have the job finished, and a bull of this size one should try not to displease. But we tried so hard that he finally inched out into the corral, just a little suspicious. At that point Honey Blossom, proving herself to be quite a hot-blooded old girl, flared her nostrils toward Alaindelon and came closer and closer, but he did not even seem to notice.

"Do you think they manipulated him just a short time ago and he is now weakened?" Emanuel asked.

"No way, no way!" said Ruidenor, who was dying to see the whole business take place. "Pull him closer to her, pull him closer."

I do not know how many tons a dunderhead like that bull weighs, but we went on pulling and tugging and "go Alaindelon, go Alaindelon!" and Honey Blossom standing by more than willing, and the only thing we did not do was to put a heavy duty jack under the unfortunate to make him rise, all to no avail. And then, when everybody was already about to give up, he looked one way and then the other, looked at me and then at Emanuel, and made a weak little motion upward to climb on the cow's back, and quick as a wink she put herself in the right position, because the old she-devil still wanted very much to enjoy the Frenchman.

"There he goes, there he goes! Have faith, Alaindelon!"

But it seems that French bulls are bulls of little faith, because halfway through that weak little rise that everybody doubted would ever reach Honey Blossom's height, Alaindelon rolled his eyeballs, made a little noise in his throat and spilled his stuff all over the dirt.

"Holy Mother, there must be more than seven hundred thousand in good money sprinkling the dust right there!" Emanuel said. "Let's take that bull back inside!"

And truly, in a situation like this, the only possible thing to do was to take him back looking very ashamed and Honey Blossom most annoyed and as far as we know feeling quite nostalgic about Nonô of Bombay. The next day, not a word from us because of how Alaindelon's raw material had been wasted. But apparently no one noticed because, although we were nervous when it came time for the next manipulation, Alaindelon worked just the same as usual and nobody complained about his output. Only we three noticed that whenever he saw us he became quite discomfited, but we understood and respected it, so no one made any comments. And anyway it was revealed that Alaindelon was a kind of corporation, because no one had enough money to buy him all for himself, so he spent some time producing on a certain farm and then another and another and so on. And the day came for us to put him back in the same cage and take him back to the train once again. It cannot be said that he made friends here, but neither did he make any enemies. And all three of us knew for sure that he was born to his profession, and that was the only way he knew how to work—he was a specialist—there was nothing anyone could do. Just the same, Emanuel stroked his head at boarding time and said, "May God help you find a good hand, Alaindelon." And the owner of the farm overheard, but did not ask about it, happy as he was with the money he'd made from the Frenchman's work. When the train rolled on, he sang in a soft voice:

"Alaindelon de la Patri-i-i-e!"

He thinks I didn't understand, but I did. He sang a piece of the French anthem, only substituting Alaindelon for Napoleon. In French, it means "Alaindelon of our motherland." Theirs, not mine.

Translated from the Portuguese
by the author

Bernice Lewis Ravin

Cabin Class to Pubjanice

It was my father's idea that Mama and I make the journey with him to the Polish shtetl where he was born. I was fifteen that summer in 1938 and by my standards would lose face if I travelled with my parents. Besides, my father and I didn't get along; he would drive me wild. And who cared about Poland, I agonized. But the Eiffel Tower thrust its steely bands upwards into the sky of my imagination and Avon flowed sweetly at its base and they were locked into one landscape with Pubjanice near Lodz.

Above all, I wanted to seek the world beyond our middle-class Jewish ghetto in Boston. So I let my aversion to family sink behind the celestial horizon stretching across Europe. The trip was my father's idea and my dream.

But while I dreamt, didn't he think of pogroms and war, in 1938? He never spoke of it; I never asked him. And now he's dead so I can no longer put the question to anyone but myself.

Wasn't he taking a risk, this man who lacked the courage even to cancel in person an appointment he didn't care to keep? (He delegated the job to his wife, his child, or his employee.) Sometimes my father asked a nephew, beholden to him for cash favors, to return merchandise purchased and regretted; he feared a painful confrontation with the salesperson, as if his change of mind would be tagged a shameful inner lapse in the records of the department store. My father cried easily. We all looked away.

I have always believed he went back for a visit to the "old country" sentimentally, like a successful professional man returning to the broad lawns of his youth for the twenty-fifth college reunion. The safety of his sisters and their sons was a grafted-on reason, it seemed. In 1938, who could have known Poland would succumb to Hitler by the next year? Yet the pogroms of my father's childhood might have quickened his conscience to dangers mine was too ill-bred to discern. I do not know. He never spoke of it.

Was my father a fool or a hero? He'd tied a passel of neuroses in a bundle when he was in steerage, I used to think, and carried it on his back like a bindlestiff for the rest of his life. No matter how much money he made—and he made it—it was never enough to help him feel secure. He spent big out of one pocket, buying expensive cars and clothes and taking luxury trips like the one to Europe; and he dribbled pennies from the other pocket for home and furniture and allowance money for the kids, to keep faith with the command of his puritanical Jewish conscience: he was aghast that he was squandering the fortune he would surely need someday to get him across the border.

He travelled heavy; the bindlestiff bulged with shame and personal concern. So much personal concern: we were subjected daily to a punctilious accounting of what he ate, how he slept, what he remembered, what he forgot, what he should have done, and why we should have done what we hadn't.

He travelled heavy. To Europe he took all the baggage he needed to make the trip positively comfortable: suits for spring and warmer weather with ties and shoes to match; shirts, enough until the shirtmaker in Paris could measure him for more; Serutan taken nightly for the bowels; other assorted medicines for headaches, gas, and ulcer, and a hernia truss and back brace for chronic problems. No presents for the relatives: they'd prefer money.

He was stooped low under the heavy burden of his personal concern. Did such a man know he was taking a chance? Was he prepared to slip some Serutan in a uniformed pocket at an enemy border? Why did we go to Europe just before the war and the six million?

My father went, of course, for family. If he had been educated, he could have written his dissertation on the family: that was his second field of specialization, woven in and around his delicate appreciation of matters of personal comfort. He believed some simple truths about the family: the family is sacred; every member is equal except the father, who can never receive enough respect nor, to be sure, the fetch-and-carry kind of affection children owe the parent; the wife deserves as much consideration as the husband's daily business and Saturday night card games provide time for; a sliding loyalty to the family *is* permissible in cases of disputes with other members of the father's family or with the father's friends: in all such disputes, the "others" were probably right if they said so.

I grew up knowing my father felt strongly about the family, even though, as you see, his feeling sometimes sent all five of us mixed signals. His intentions for his family were confusing and still are, but his presence, like his thick shoulders and gravel voice, commanded consideration.

On that trip to Europe, I gave him no consideration. Except for comments on the "cute" boys I was encountering, my travel diary in the epoch of Anne Frank concentrated on spilling vitriol on "Pa." Later, in my twenties, before the American romance with the shtetl, I called my father "Daddy." Now "Pa" seems more at home with organic foods and ethnicity. "Pa" is "Father Ashkenazi" seeking to transform his long white butcher's coat into the industrial vestment of the "beef merchant." In that coat, he labored in the sawdust stalls of Boston's old marketplace where the canvas-covered, horse-drawn teams unloaded the heavy sides of beef and the railroad's shipping men came to call on him. Success American—that is zesty with cash, that dish. He ate of it without regard to whether it agreed with his stomach. It didn't, but he thought the fault was his, and he was ashamed that others seemed to collect more cash in the plate they passed in the temple of American commerce.

His stomach ached with fear: he might fail. Each day, the teams unloaded, and loaded up again with the loins and strips my father's men had carved so gracefully out of the great sides of beef they aged in the freezer after delivery. Each curve of the knife glinted like steel in the corner of his eye: they might fail, they might fail him. He would die a failure.

But then in 1938 he entered the shtetl, triumphant, carrying his wife on one arm, his young daughter on the other, bowing to right and left, the rich and famous uncle from America. Inside the door of his sister's tiny butcher shop he watched his brother-in-law bone out a rib for a village customer on the narrow butcher block counter. He smiled in disdain. They used cow beef, not steer beef. He traded only in western dressed steer beef. But how could *they* get western dressed steer beef—piled on the delivery vans at the railroad station where the freight cars arrived from Chicago, the Hog Butcher for the World?

But that was in America where beef itself was prime, its rich rosy juices bubbling up as a vital source of its people's energies. That was in America where people were mobile upward and sideways and the Jew from the shtetl could tell the railroad men who came to visit him what he wanted, show it to them, the Irishman from the railroad who came to the elegant dinner—New Orleans recipes—Mama-cooked at Pa's request. Pa could show the Irishman the exquisite veining of the beef side from Chicago, marbling unimaginable in the cow meat his brother-in-law boned out for the shtetl customer in Poland before the six million.

Carrying his women on his arm, my father held court in the one-room "home" at the rear of the butcher shop where his sister, her husband the butcher, and their sons, grown slaughterhouse workers, ate and slept. Outside this room, near a few greening shrubs, was the odorous privy.

I was resentful: the trip had taken us from a comfortable two-family house ghetto in Boston to Pubjanice, a tiny Polish village where the bedbugs had long ago claimed as theirs the only lodging house available to passers through. We travelled on a famous French luxury liner, connecting with Europe's fabled deluxe trains. Both conveyances carried "cute" boys to Europe and in and around its playgrounds. Pa let me know, using Mama as interpreter, that I could look but not talk to boys. He had not noticed they were cute. We got to the Polish ghetto many vitriolic diary pages later: the bedbugs were waiting for my choice adolescent flesh in the rambling old lodging-house room which, like my cousins behind the butcher shop, I'd share with parents.

I was rebellious and blamed the bedbugs on my father. I blamed these pests and the noxious "relatives" on my father: why had he permitted the bedbugs and the relatives and forbidden the boys? But my personal concern did not concern my father. He requested a special board for his bed.

The bugs brought out my rising blood. The relatives brought out the snob in me. Each morning a new contingent came to call. They kissed us each on both cheeks. Their clothes carried the smell of their bodies. I shrank from them in devotion to the American way of clean flesh. With open curiosity they pointed to our suitcases: they wanted a fashion show. My mother opened our suitcases. They pawed through our things, our middle class cotton underwear and rayon crepe dresses, fondling in their fancy the costumes of movie stars, lamé and sequins, satin and ermine. They held up our modest garments, held them against their heavy scented flesh. They wheeled about, Jean Harlow, Joan Crawford—bosomy, fleshy-armed, chunky-limbed. With deep throaty voices they called out in Yiddish "Look at me! Look at me!" They laughed. And then, in sub-titled English, "I wuv you! I wuv you!" In their sleazy acetate print dresses they pranced about, modeling my new dresses, my first high heels.

They handled my belongings. The snob watched in horror. My mother and father were both laughing at the vital flesh—unleashed, unashamed in the pleasure our visit had brought them. They were glad we had come. I hated them.

On the threshold of climbing up to the stylish world of the goy across the sea, I had gone off Cabin Class to Shangri-La, waved on by envious friends. Unwittingly, they had sent me off to bedbugs and privies and fat Jewish ladies who snatched my new grown-up clothes and cavorted with them around a shabby shtetl room.

I watched and hated; but I was dumb. They spoke only Yiddish or Polish; I had to stifle my anger. I had no ally, not even Mama who had always derided "Euro*peen* ways," taking care to stress her high school education. Through Junior Year, mind you. Mama was really lovely to the "relatives" and tried to help me bear with them for just two weeks.

They were heavy with life; they brought out the lady in Mama, the snob in me; by the next fall they were gone "adressat unbekannt," leaving me in America ashamed of my geography, desperate that I had patronized them. I would never be able to make it up to them.

Following our matinal spree, we went to the butcher shop and squeezed by the cutting block to the "house" in the back. Pa held court there for a constant stream of visitors—sitting legs spread wide, his smooth-shaven cheeks and his bald crown gleaming clean and dry in the June heat.

I turned my back on the privy which I had vowed to boycott. Then Itzhak, my young cousin, returned from the slaughterhouse for his dinner. The smell of his trade was upon him; I had never smelled it on my father, who sat clean, gleaming, expansive, holding court. The huge sides of beef in my father's market next to Faneuil Hall passed by his spotless white coat, sliding frozen on their great hooks in the Artic cold which freezes smell. Maybe only cow beef smelled.

My cousin leaned toward me and whispered "I wuv you." He had just seen a Tarzan movie from a folding chair in the schoolhouse.

"I wuv you," he teased. Then he winked. The wink was sexier than the romantic "love" I thrilled to from the upholstered movie seats in my America. Threatened, I turned away.

My father caught the scene and laughed with his nephew. Smelly boys permitted! Bedbugs, dancing ladies, and earthy nephews too old for romance—at least twenty-one—all permitted. I had never seen my father so convivial.

The unintelligible chatter thickened the air of the little sanctuary behind the butcher shop. I listened to my father, King of the Universe, switching from Yiddish to Polish. Not a word for me, his "baby," mincing about the little village in high heels I had wheedled out of Mama before the trip, though he forbade them, and my lipsticked mouth pouted near him in forbidden red but he didn't notice. He was too busy slapping all his fraternity brothers on the back, I thought. After all, only the really successful ones came back for reunions. Especially when they had lady wives and pretty babies.

Suddenly conviviality was at an end. Pa had been summoned to Lodz where his cousin, Shlomo, a successful lawyer lived. In the shtetl, they spoke of him with special reverence. He was a leader of the Jewish community in Lodz and mingled with gentiles as well. My father and Shlomo had been close friends, Itzhak told me. When they were sixteen, seventeen, Pa had begged his cousin to come to America with him. Two of Pa's sisters were already there and had written to him.

"Shlomo, Shlomo, come with me," he said. "No more shtetl. No more slaughterhouse. No more Peilishe anti-Semits. We'll be our own men!" Shlomo was silent.

One day, Shlomo came home from "cheder," put down his books, and said shyly: "I've been accepted to the Gymnasium in Lodz. I'm going to be a lawyer." His mother kissed him. A shtetl Jew in the Gymnasium! His father kissed him, tears in his eyes. Such an honor!

My father was bewildered. He couldn't understand why Shlomo should prefer cluttered, cobble-stoned old Lodz and higher education to glittering New York. A passion to move on had possessed him. Anyway, he'd had enough of books in the extra hours at the "cheder" his parents had insisted on. He left for America before Shlomo went off to his new life in the city, so long forbidden to Jews.

Itzhak's story sounds like Pa but I don't remember that he ever spoke of how he came to America and I never thought to ask him.

Shlomo, now Stefan, the noted Polish jurist, was said to be a member of many official committees in Lodz, the big city, as big as Boston. He lived like a goy in a big house, they said. He sent us a message, asking us to visit him in Lodz. Pa was unnerved, but his ancient Jewish prompter cued him into action and we made ready to go to Lodz for a few days. My father had misplaced his brown socks and his ulcer pills, and we all searched for them, even me, though I dreaded coming upon the bugs, countless Dracula insects, hovering in their secret hideouts for my scented, tainted blood.

Finally we were waiting at a bus stop just outside the shtetl. We were standing on a wide sidewalk. Our trip was beginning. A man, pale and thin-lipped, walked toward us and stopped deliberately, inches from us as if clicking his heels before asking us to dance. His chin jutted into our breathing space. Now my father was pale as they exchanged harsh Polish syllables. Pa was shaking his head in refusal. Mama and I realized the man coveted the piece of sidewalk we stood on and would not pass in front or behind us. He wished to pass through us. We must part like the Red Sea and let him through.

Pa's fair-skinned face and smooth pate were blushing fiercely. Mama put up a hand to calm them both, but the man flung his arm out, caught her hard on the shoulders and sent her reeling back towards a brick retaining wall. My father grabbed my arm and lunged for Mama just before she managed to regain balance. Coolly satisfied, the man surveyed our forced retreat and walked away in triumph.

I have always realized Pa knew the guts of that man immediately (as if he never left for America thirty years before). I could see then Pa hadn't held back when he was young. I'm sorry now that he had to have a face-to-face encounter with an "anti-Semit," a "Peilishe," so soon after all the reunion frivolity. Only the presence of his women must have prevented him from hitting the man.

What with the socks and the "anti-Semit," Mama had to pat Pa's arm quite a few times, once we were on the bus to Lodz. We both told him we were proud of him; but he was inconsolable. He wished he'd roughed up the bastard. He was upset that he was in his fifties and no longer the ready fighter he used to be. So Mama told him he did the wisest thing. We'd get our visit over. We'd do whatever we could for people in trouble. (Shlomo must want to talk to us about trouble, maybe about Pa's cousins in Berlin. What could one expect from the Germans if American Jews couldn't even stand on a little piece of Polish sidewalk?) And then we'd get off to Paris, Mama went on, to Switzerland, and London. I was in a heat to leave for my European paradise and forgot the unpleasant incident.

Cousin Shlomo's face was blurred beneath more and darker hair than my father's. He was quiet and spoke English better than Pa did. I was ashamed of my father for letting us lose points like that on our own terrain.

Shlomo's brick house was enriched underfoot by dark red and blue oriental rugs. Some were Chinese rugs, Mama said, marveling that "Euro*peen* Jews" could own such treasures. The walls were alive with books, moroccan bound, reaching to the ceiling. The mahogany furniture in the huge beamed rooms gleamed from fine polishing. Pa was quiet, thinking like me perhaps of our modest two-family house in Boston—a wise investment since the flat downstairs brought in rental income, a welcome but unneeded extra. Pa might be wrestling with the evidence that staying behind did not mean deprivation for everyone.

We had dinner at a long table. Cousin Shlomo sat at the head and carved a juicy roast with confidence. Later Mama confided that Shlomo had asked our help, for him and his family, and for our mutual cousins in Berlin. Pa'd have to take immediate steps to get American visas for everyone and travel money for the shtetl sisters and their families. All of the others had money, already deposited beyond Nazi jurisdiction, and jewels and other moveables for easing passage at borders. But we'd have to go to Warsaw, to Danzig, and to Berlin itself to get the papers we'd need. Berlin? Would we have difficulty? Pa looked pale again. I guessed he was worrying about getting a bedboard in all those places. Or he was counting the number of times he'd have to pack and re-pack. It was such a trial chasing down socks each time. (Was he thinking of sidewalk bus stops?)

But, then, what about me? Would I see Mont Blanc? The Champs Elysées? Shakespeare's cottage? (Could the Germans do anything to us?)

At breakfast the next day, Shlomo urged us to return to the shtetl and pack for our journey. I looked at Pa, intent upon his eggs and toast. Had he agreed to trail around a Europe in seige, bald gladiator, ready for any derring-do, with his women on one hand and his butcher knife in the other?

I never asked Pa why we had to follow an itinerary by train to Warsaw, Danzig, and Berlin. I don't recall wondering about it, and he never spoke of it.

He packed and re-packed and inquired about good hotels. Then he visited consulates. He argued with pale, tight-lipped Polish soldiers who ransacked our luggage in search of smuggled currency. Mama tried to pull him away, told him to make do.

I mistook Warsaw for Paris: I thought my continental tour had begun at last. But the Nazi banners fluttering over the buildings in Danzig and the stiff cardboard signs in shop windows forbidding Jews to enter baffled me. Certainly Berlin would send us home in terror, omitting at the last the visits to Paris and Stratford. But the handsome German soldiers at their border waved us on smiling, barely glancing at our luggage. They had no intention of ruffling visiting Americans whom they greeted with a salute and a "Heil Hitler." I feared the greeting, but their charm bewildered me.

Suddenly Pa was speaking to the tall blond inspecting officer in his untutored (Yiddish-flavored) German. Their charm had bewildered him too. Mama had forewarned him; knowing his pride in languages learned in transit, she had begged him to speak only English. I pulled his coat from behind and he stopped, looking sheepish.

Our Berlin cousins were richer than Shlomo. They were younger, very chic. Karla looked like Carole Lombard: she could pass, so we drove brazenly around the wide, impressive avenues of Berlin in her little Fiat. The directional signal was a little flag clicking up and down. My real trip had begun—in Berlin! This was the elegant life, dashing around one of the world's great capitals with Carole Lombard. Pa was very taken with her too: he tried his German once again and she complimented him, seductively, all woman. Her handsome quiet husband and Mama exchanged amused glances at the playing out of the roles.

But Leon warned us in a low voice during dinner in their luxury apartment that their own maid was a spy. They knew officials who could be bribed; they needed visas urgently.

Before we left, we dined in a restaurant where the waiters whispered in a corner, turning to look at us, not sure about serving us. We were served, but evidently we three didn't pass as well as Karla and Leon, Polish expatriate entrepreneurs, who had stopped in Berlin on their way to America more than ten years before.

Well, we did the promised trip to Europe. Pa refused to walk on the Champs Elysées with us, preferring to nap in his hotel room. But he insisted that we all go to Stratford because I'd played Queen Gertrude in *Hamlet* at school. How could he be so wrong and so right?

So I went home, holding my head high before my friends for having seen the promised land. I went back to school and was caught up in a new dream of going away to college. Then before the letters with the wanted visas for Pa's family in Pubjanice were re-routed to us, stamped "adressat unbekannt," Karla and Leon arrived at our home, having displayed the visas Pa sent to them, in all the right places. They had known someone in the Berlin post office. They had given away a fortune in bribes and still had money to invest towards a new fortune in America. For a few days we celebrated their wily escape.

On the third day, the gay romance with Carole Lombard dissolved into a Betty Davis horror story. Mama showed me the bathroom after Karla's weekly bath—the collected perfumed deposits on Karla's flesh transferred to Mama's pure white porcelain tub and left for Mama to wash. Mama never spoke of her again without reminding Pa and me of the shameful ring around the tub—and the nerve of her. Euro*peen* ways. And the nerve of her to put a hand on my older brother's knee the time he took her out for a drive. My father was silent and I never really knew what he thought of Karla.

And the nerve of her, I felt, to make an issue of *my* bad manners. On the fourth day she cornered me. I should stand up when my parents entered the room: hadn't I smirked visibly at one of my aunts? She intended to arrange for me to go to school in Lausanne the next year. She had to get me away from my impossibly bourgeois parents. Outraged vanity and submerged family loyalty came together like crashing cymbals and I grinned at her ungrateful back to think that a finishing school in Switzerland, on the continent she'd barely escaped, would help me make my way in America.

So Karla went to New York in 1939 with Leon and their young son. Within two years they were wintering in Palm Beach, though I think they're in Mexico most frequently now. I'm not sure because I haven't seen them in years: they didn't bother to come to my father's funeral. Once, in Florida, when Pa was beginning to feel his age,

Mama told me, Karla said he tried to cheat her at cards and she refused to have anything to do with him after that. I don't know too much about it because my father never spoke of it to me, nor mentioned his cousin Shlomo, now Stefan, whose visas got him and his family to England. We heard from him once in 1939 in a thank-you letter written in impeccable English. He must be dead now.

After the war, a woman wrote my father from Israel that she was the sole survivor of Pubjanice. Everyone else had been taken away. As he read the letter, I turned from the tears on his cheeks, remembering with shame then and for a long time after my aversion to the family in Pubjanice. Pa wrote the woman a letter in Yiddish, and I don't know what he said. Perhaps he told her that he remembered her and that he was glad he went. He'd done what he could. (I would have said to her Why you? Why me?)

Yet, once I became a woman and claimed him as my own, with smiles at foibles that used to shame, I might have asked him why he went in 1938.

They say you can't go home again, I might have said. So why did you?

I went to visit, he would have said, to see the people and places of my youth. Then they were taken away, so it's even better that I went . . . What do they mean, you can't go home again? Why not? I did.

W. D. Wetherell

Calm Seas and a Prosperous Voyage

I always imagined my maiden great uncle at one of Gatsby's parties—a slender, athletic young man in a sand-colored suit standing unnoticed by the pool. Couples would be walking past. Girls in white dresses who glanced lazily in his direction, then turned just as deliberately away. Men who may have nodded, called out each other's names. A blonde who teetered her way along the diving board with a bottle tucked under her chin—an old man dressed like a minstrel who suddenly ran up and pretended to push her off . . . people he didn't know, laughing past his noncommittal smile with drinks in their hands, on unsteady way to the house strung with balls of silver and gold.

After they were gone he would be left watching the cloudy, strangely unappealing water of the forgotten pool. Little bits of flotsam swept by just under the surface, flowing in the same order as the guests toward the end nearest the house. Coasters from the offering girls, cigarettes from the condescending men. A silk cuff from the minstrel's costume, a yellow strand from the girl who had almost fallen in. And during the self-pitying moods even he was subject to that last summer Colin must have felt an overwhelming temptation to follow them, to add a button from his shirt to the pool, then join the swarm of bodies climbing the sides of the distant patio in mock attack on Gatsby's walls.

Like a lot of people Colin must have been supporting a double life in those years. Traces of it survived through the time I knew him—he had the fastidious air of a reformed adventurer, a retired explorer who had never found anything remarkably profound, but who had gone far enough in the search to spare himself any remorse. The kind of man, for instance, who might once conceivably have been involved in a shoot-out between bootleggers, but not the kind of man who would ever miss a train.

But bachelor, businessman, explorer, the balance had been resolved years before and we never heard him talk about his youth except to explain about the night it finally came to an end.

"I simply got the tracks mixed up," he would say, with the same casual, apologetic tone someone uses in mentioning a long ago try at suicide. And, knowing him when I did, missing a train seemed the most desperate thing he was capable of. He would talk at revealing length about the way the station was that night, as though he knew this was the hardest part of the story for us to believe, as though he was circling for himself, trying to remember a convincing reason that wasn't there . . . how he usually left his roadster parked on the corner of 32nd and Seventh where the boy who always did his shoeshines would watch it for him while he took whichever girl from Long Island he happened to be going with down to her train. How it took ten minutes to get uptown from the apartment on 18th Street he was already sharing with his two unmarried sisters . . . the sound of an organ coming from the veranda of a walk-in brokerage house at the end of Platform Eighteen and how you could never count on finding an empty phone booth in Penn Station, especially when it rained.

Why was he on the train at all? For a long time we tried to give him a reason, using the little we knew. Girls he had met in the summer he saw off on their trains back to the Island. Could he have envied them, going out in the fall night, sometimes for good, the tickets he had bought for them twisted nervously between their cotton gloves as they waited to say good-bye? He was already living at home. Could it have been a premonition of all the years he would spend taking care of Lydia and Adie when they got sick? My grandfather told us about the fast life he was supposed to have led. Was he simply drunk? Was it just a curiosity about how the great shore places looked now that summer was over, just a confusion over tracks on a journey that may have been intended for nowhere more distant and exotic than Queens?

"I simply got on the wrong train," he said. There was nothing else for the first hour except what seemed an endless series of tunnels and underpasses debouching into concrete platforms . . . this in a blur of chalky neon peopled by men in premature overcoats getting off at suburban stations much closer in than they are now. There were long stretches when the electricity failed and the lights coasted out, letting him see through the window past his own reflection, but only to familiar, staring billboards fronting town after identical town, all of which he had been to before, with "Manor" or "Park" tagged onto their original Dutch and Indian names, priding themselves *country* for the few years they had left. But they were already as good as city and they bored him, just as the eager commuters did who sat down next to him to try and start conversations about their jobs.

One of them had left his paper. Colin rolled it up behind his head, taking off his suit jacket for a blanket and leaning sideways against the glass. They were old cars—they hadn't been cleaned since the end of summer and grains of sand skidded across the floor with every curve, first left, then right. As he sat there he noticed a pattern of scratches across the grey paint on the back of the seat in front of him. At first he thought they were names of towns further out on the Island he had never heard of, but then he recognized them for what they were—places in the South and Midwest, bayonet-carved by bored, homesick doughboys a decade ago as their regiments shuttled from camps on the north shore to embarkation from the dark ports of Jersey. GARY, one read. OH FOR GOOD OLD GARY INDIANA. And it was reading these that he finally fell asleep, with suggestions of long grey rides in overfilled troop trains, the prospect of great distance ahead and behind.

He had no idea how long he slept. When he woke up it was almost midnight, but his watch had stopped. He had a bad taste in his mouth, his head was aching. There was a ticket on the seat beside him but the part listing the destination was ripped off and he couldn't remember paying the conductor. Except for him the car was entirely empty.

He groped his way toward the head of the train with the vague intention of finding someplace to wash up. The swaying was worse than it had been and he had a hard time keeping his balance. When he got outside to the platform between cars he decided to rest until his head cleared.

They must have been well out by now. The only lights came at a road crossing where the beams of a waiting auto cut briefly against his knees. On long curves he could see the faint shade of the locomotive, trailing sparks that flew out from its sides, then unaccountably disappeared—suddenly, as if doused. It gave him the feeling they were at sea, waves lapping across the tracks, the train threading a narrow causeway between small islands . . . abandoned stations burning solitary lamps where the trains never stopped.

It was cool, almost cold. When the train slowed for a moment near another crossing he lit a cigarette and tossed it experimentally toward the water. It flew alongside for a moment, then cartwheeled away without going out. And it was only then he remembered Long Island was famous for its potatoes and that it was endless, empty fields they were speeding through and not the sea.

He lit another cigarette and started for the head of the train. The next three cars were completely empty. The fourth—it had once been the club car—was empty, too. New seats had been fastened across the floor in place of stools and the playful nymphs painted on the ceiling were draped in advertising. A bar hugged the left side windows, then billowed out around a rack of year-old magazines. Half of it was covered with timetables, the other half by empty bottles, tops off, labels peeling, held in place by shallow indentations in the bar's metal trim . . . the remnants, he assumed, of a lavish charter hosted that summer by someone who thought trains were fun.

It was two more cars before he found anyone. Slumped across a sat in the last aisle was a conductor, staring listlessly out the window, a pile of tickets waiting to be sorted on his lap. He still had on his light summer uniform, but there was a heavy woolen muffler wrapped around his neck. He sat up straight when he spotted Colin and began snapping at the air with his ticket punch.

"I was just wondering what time we would be getting in," Colin said.

The conductor smiled, nodded.

"Are we on time?"

The conductor smiled, nodded . . . didn't say a word. Colin's passive mood was wearing off—he was just about to grab one of the tickets away from him when he felt a tap on his shoulder. It was another conductor, this one much older and dressed in a heavier uniform.

"Cancer in his throat," he said simply, drawing a line across his own throat with the tip of his index finger. "We're taking him home."

The young conductor smiled—he seemed embarrassed at causing so much trouble. Colin mumbled an apology, then walked back toward the next car, mad at himself for not asking where they were going.

But at least someone knew he was on board now. The train had begun making stops again and at each one the conductor with the muffler came to the end of the car to try and shout out the station's name. This went on for a half hour or more. The stops were getting closer together—he assumed they must be running out of land, getting out toward Montauk Point. At least he hoped that's where they were going; he'd never seen it before and had always wanted to. There was another long stretch without stopping, then suddenly the train braked short, in two sharp jerks that almost spilled him out into the aisle, followed by a terribly high-pitched screech from up toward the engine, as though the sick conductor had finally found his voice.

Colin positioned himself by the door, half-expecting the train would soon start up again. It was very cold, very quiet. The train had stopped well short of the platform and to get out he had to jump into a bank of cinders. There were no signs but wherever it was had an immensity he felt the moment he got free of the tracks. An expanse of something . . . the stars overhead . . . the cold . . . but something else too, something just beyond the row of clapboard buildings that fronted a narrow macadam strip on the station's right.

Colin was in one of those rare moods that sometimes come upon men in illogical circumstances when you can refuse nothing. He wandered down the narrow highway in no particular direction, open to anything. If the road veered right, he veered with it; if a rutted driveway branched off to a boarded-up garage he would circle it before coming back to the macadam, feeling it was simply a part of the night's progression. Likewise the occasional lamp, likewise the blackness. At a point where the road came to the top of a gentle rise he stopped to rest for a moment; turning, he felt with a breathtaking rush of exhilaration a fresh breeze blowing untouched from the sea.

At first he felt staggered—he shaded his eyes with his hand as though staring into a bright sun. In the city he was used to only hints of it, spaced over long stretches when it was easy to forget the sea even existed at all. Bon voyage parties when the frantic interval of water between ship and pier lay sprinkled with confetti and wadded, bobbing balls of notepaper departing passengers had written last messages on to throw toward the widening gap . . . Restless nights when he lay awake listening to the sounds of tug horns on the East River, echoed across the city by a fainter horn from the Hudson, the tugs moving slowly their opposite ways.

But now it was all there, all at once. He left the road and started through a moor-like tangle of low vines and fir. It was hard going at first, but he had all the momentum of his trip behind him now and there was no stopping—he emerged on a high sandy bluff overlooking the ocean and started laughing like a ten-year-old, laughing despite himself just from the sheer beauty of it all.

Ocean stretched as far as he could see in both directions, lighter than the sky overhead, darker than the horizon. There was no surf, just a clumping sound from tiny breakers folding themselves in threes across a wide, traceless beach. Further out a current was sweeping past—the surface skipped alternate bands of white and black. When he ran down to the water to rinse his face he found it much warmer than the air, with an indescribable mildness to it, a tropical promise that seemed to belie the sharp autumn air, the hard bright sky.

To the right the beach seemed to grow broader, the bluffs flattening out to admit a few block-like houses sticking up from the moors. To his left the bluffs steepened, the beach receded as if the coastline was tapering to a point. He started off in that direction, walking near the water's edge to take advantage of the hard-packed sand.

He had gone about a half mile when a man detached himself from the shadows of the cliff ahead of him.

"Hopper?"

But he realized his mistake instantly and started shaking his head.

"Gee, I swore it was Hopper!" he yelled. "Never saw anybody else keep stopping like that to look over waves like that. People from here seen too many of 'em I guess. Had me fooled leastways."

When Colin finally got close enough to see his face he thought at first it was a boy dressed up like a sailor. He had the collar of his pea coat pulled up around his ears and he kept taking off his cap to wipe his nose. A few steps behind him was a track of deep gouges leading toward the water.

"No hard feelings, right? There's only one Hopper," and he stuck out his hand. "Norman McCann, U.S. Coast Guard retired. Or will be anyway."

Before Colin had a chance to worry about sounding foolish he came right out and asked him where they were.

"Montauk, where else? You walk much further and you'll run smack into the light. Course you can't see it from here. Too low. Out there," and he pointed toward the light and dark swerves. "Been in now for three years and my old man was in for thirty before that. I guess you can say the McCanns know Montauk all right."

There was a pause while he wiped his nose. Then, completely without warning, he took Colin by the arm and whispered something savagely in his ear.

"I hate it!"

And a moment later he was standing over the gouges, as boyish as before.

"Wasn't so bad at first. Sarah used to meet me with a bag of sandwiches. We'd sit here and . . . Well, we'd sit there before I had to finish patrol. She's sick now. Two kids, a sick wife and a dead-end job, that's me. She keeps telling me move to the city, move to the city. What for? I tell her. It's out there," making a quick shrug toward the sea, "It's out there where the big money is and soon Hopper's going to take me."

Colin nodded sympathetically—"Out there. I see what you mean"—then asked if there was someplace nearby where he could find a drink or something to eat. For some reason Norman thought this was funny; it was a minute or more before he regained enough possession to point up the beach.

"Well, guess you look okay to me. Keep going this way and you'll come to a house. It's the only one between here and the light. They'll probably give you something all right," and he started giggling again. "Only whatever you do, make sure you come up to them on the beach side. You come over the dunes and brother it's trouble, understand?"

Norman took him by the arm again and guided him through the gouges—Colin saw now they were marvelously detailed sand castles built in a line across the beach.

"Keeps the time from seeming so long," the coast guard explained, with a sheepish little shrug. "Listen. You tell Hopper not to forget me. He can't get by without me seeing him but you tell 'em not to forget, case he does. Sometimes he's got his head up too high if you know what I mean. Just like that old lighthouse. I'm down here low and you tell him that, okay?"

Colin promised he would. There was a last warning about the moors, then he was threading his way through the castle moats, the night finally resolved into some definite direction. He could remember being taken as a boy to Rockaway Beach on summer holidays and being told by an older cousin that if you kept walking along the sand out away from the city a hundred miles or more that eventually you would come to a place called Montauk where the land ended at a tall red lighthouse. It must have made a tremendous impression—his parents would tell of the time they discovered him suddenly gone, then spotted him way up the beach, a little figure trudging stolidly for the distant lighthouse and crying when they made him stop.

Now he was almost there. The beach was closing in on itself. The light on the water moved further out. The bluff grew steeper, the tide seemed moving in. There was an anticipatory, billowing white shine to the sand, as if the entire shore was about to set sail. He was beginning to wonder if he shouldn't veer inland after all when he noticed a light streaming through a tunnel-like opening in the cliff ahead of him. At the same time a girl stepped out, framed herself against the hazy yellow beam and started waving.

He stopped, then waved tentatively back. Like the coast guard she had obviously mistaken him for someone else and he didn't feel like disappointing her. He stood watching the water for a while before continuing up the beach, trying to maintain her illusion for as long as he could.

Colin was never happy with his description of the girl. He would mention something, then think of something else that seemed to contradict it. Her long dark hair—the way she wore it cut boyishly short over her forehead. The proud, assertive way she stood watching in the sand—the yielding kind of curtsy she made when he got close enough for her to see who it was. Most girls he knew always held their eyes back coyly in reserve, letting you have glimpses only later, as rewards. But right from the start hers met his without any hesitation. At first he thought, not without envy, well, this look is for whoever it is she's waiting for. Then, not a second later, it occurred to him that maybe it was for him after all, that she was standing there waiting for him. And still later he began wondering if it wasn't a trick she used on everyone, that turning her eyes away from yours would be in her the same sudden kind of admission a less vivacious woman would make in staring you full in the face.

She was wearing a long terry-cloth robe that came just far enough off her shoulders to reveal the bathing suit underneath. It was too cold for swimming and he couldn't decide if it made her look very daring or very silly. He just never could decide. . . .

"It's so beautiful. He left it there three days ago. With a message. Wait for me. . . . He wrote it across the sand. All in capitals! By the time we woke up, the tide was erasing the me. But then we saw the boat."

She pointed and for the first time Colin realized she was talking about something behind them more tangible than the sea. There was a small runabout pulled up on the beach behind a slight rise in the sand that had hidden it from him before.

"Do you play tennis?" she asked suddenly.

"A little," Colin said, in his noncommittal way, still confused about the eyes. It could have meant he played a lot or didn't play at all and she caught him at it.

"Do you play or don't you? They have a court here and it seems such a waste not to. But we can't find the racquets . . . " and back she went, silly again, as though she had been standing there waiting for a tennis partner, nothing more. But by the time she started in toward the lantern, motioning him to follow, he had decided he somehow preferred her silly to daring.

At first the path was just sand, then arrow-shaped beach grass matted down by overlapping brown crates piled three high on either side. A few yards of this and they came to a house of weathered, cedar-like shingle, set low on a dune with its back to the sea. There was a lantern hanging above the door; the door was open. They both emptied the sand from their shoes, then went inside, passing a porcelain sink and then the stove, a hammock strung between them stuffed with an assortment of old cardboard suitcases, souvenir decals plastered across their sides.

"Watch your feet," she warned. "Cuba spilled the oranges."

A step around these and you were in the living room. It was large and attractively furnished, mostly in wicker. There was a balcony running around the entire circumference—doors branched off into what he assumed were bedrooms. Against one wall was a fireplace; a man's swimming trunks hung across the screen. To the right was another pile of crates, topped by a lantern less bright than the one outside . . . Everything was scrupulously neat, slightly out of place. The chairs were arranged in artificially straight rows, the wrong throw rugs seemed mated to the wrong end tables which in turn seemed matched with the wrong lamps. It gave the impression of a summer house that had been rented for the season and was about to be returned to the original owners by tenants anxious to give it back to them just the way they had left it, but who had somehow forgotten exactly where everything was supposed to go.

There was a sofa overturned in front of another door behind which leaned two men smoking cigarettes, their backs against the couch. One fairly old, dressed in tie and overcoat. The other small and dark, dressed in overalls. They didn't see Colin when he first came in and for a moment they made him think of officer and soldier sharing a last smoke in the trenches just prior to going over the top.

It was the soldier who saw him first but the officer who jumped up to greet him. He was at least sixty, maybe older—he had the flexible look of an actor used to a variety of ages. He came up so fast, with such evident goodwill, that Colin stood there expecting a hearty slap on the back, a strong, testing handshake. But the second it took to cross the room must have been time enough for him to gauge his man and change his approach accordingly. His handshake was courtly, his tone lightly earnest, with just a trace of self-depreciation and cynicism that seemed left over from a previous role.

"Ahh, another recruit!" he said, making an exaggerated bow toward the tops of his white-tipped shoes. "Welcome to our tent, sheik . . . sheik? . . . Welcome to our tent sheik Colin, I'm sheik Doyle. You haven't by chance seen Hopper tonight?"

Colin hadn't. The man frowned, cupping his hand over his chin so the others wouldn't see it.

"Well, never mind. Never mind. You must be thirsty. What's it going to be?" and he gestured munificently toward the pile of crates. "We've got the best money can buy. Or at least Mario's money. You haven't by chance seen him tonight? Runs Detroit. The entire city. He steals from the local citizenry, Hopper steals from him. Just a little of course. Nothing compared to what Mario's own men steal from under his nose every day without his caring. But there's something about Hopper . . . You'll see for yourself. He's Mario's torment. Every time he relaxes, every time he's about to feel too satisfied with life, he thinks of Hopper and imagines him sneaking away with another portion of the empire. Out he goes, goons in tow, chasing all over creation. Keeps him young he says and he's probably right. Hopper reminds him of his youth. The way he was. Or at least the way he would have liked to be. It's envy more than anything. Pure envious love. What else would make a man his age leave family and fortune to crawl through some miserable bushes a thousand miles from home just to recover a few boxes of scotch? He'd shoot Hopper just as quick as he'd shoot you or me. But with Hopper he'd feel very bad afterwards. Very bad. . . . "

All this time he had been prying at one of the boxes in an unsuccessful attempt to open it. Colin told him not to bother. He made one or two more tries for form's sake, but seemed relieved to give it up. He paid Colin back with what obviously was intended to be a realistic summation of the way things stood.

"He left us the boat three days ago and not a sign of him since. Mario almost had us in Syracuse and he damn near had us in New York. His boys are out there somewhere right now so he thinks he's got us in Montauk. Got us at last with our backs to the wall and nowhere to run."

Here he hesitated, as if making sure of his irony before allowing himself the ironic little smile.

"Nowhere to run. . . . Wouldn't know how to handle a boat by any chance? That's great. We'll need someone to spell Hopper at the wheel. Nowhere to run . . . Poor Mario!"

The girl had disappeared—Colin had the feeling she had gone out looking for the tennis racquets. The man in the overalls had never left the shelter of the sofa. But now instead of leaning behind it he was on all fours with his chin against the window . . . quivering, as attentive as a pointer. He whispered something that Colin didn't understand, but Doyle just shrugged. He seemed unconcerned with whatever it was.

"Cuba Libre. Another recruit. Traitor of sorts. The good kind. Fought on the wrong side at San Juan Hill. Waited until the Americanos were all around, then grabbed a Mauser and started charging with them, screaming Cuba Libre! at the top of his lungs. He and old Teddy himself. Thirty years ago and he still talks about it. Liked their uniforms, didn't you, Cuba?"

The man only smiled.

"Soy imigrante," he said and immediately Doyle began yelling at him in an affectionately gruff voice.

"Emigrante! How many times do I have to tell you! We're all emigrantes now." But at least he went over to the window to see what it was he was pointing at. He stood there for a few minutes, then motioned Colin over.

"Look there. Over the horizon on the left."

There was a vague line of shrubbery beyond the window just light enough to make out. By following this until it disappeared Colin found the horizon; turning left he saw what Doyle meant—a bright red glow standing as straight in the sky as a candle.

"Cross burning," Doyle said matter-of-factly. "Last picnic of the season. Oh, I never knew they were out here either. But fear is fear, right? You start seeing things. From what I hear last time they burned one it sank a freighter. A foggy night and whoever was at the helm must have thought it was Montauk light. Kept it on the starboard like the pilot book says and hit a reef. Coast Guard had a hell of a time trying to hush it up. At first all the local people felt bad, being seamen, but a few days later a nigger washed ashore and they all felt justified. They took their kids out from school and pointed at him. See, they said. See. And besides, they found out the ship was owned by a Jew."

He said all this in an emotionless voice, the same he would have used if it had been a deer they were talking about, running free over the moors. The light seemed emotionless, too. It was too far away, the night was too cold for it to give off anything but a kind of wistful, amateurish hate.

"Don't bother with politics. Vote temperance every year because it's good for business, but other than that. . . . So you want to be an imigrante to this?" he suddenly yelled, giving Cuba a healthy poke in the ribs. "Welcome to America, that's what it says. Welcome one and all! We're emigrantes now, Cuba. Say it!"

"Soy imigrante."

Doyle threw his hands up in despair, then prodded Colin back toward the kitchen. He still felt bad about not offering him a drink, but he swore he'd do better with eats. He sat him down at the table and started rummaging around the cupboards.

It was very cozy in the kitchen, very domestic. Except for his curiosity about the girl Colin was feeling very content. She came in once or twice, never for long. Seeing them all together—Doyle in his overcoat, Cuba in his work clothes, the girl in her bathing suit—made it seem like they had come together from widely different places, or were about to depart for separate destinations, with separate expectations of what they were going to find there.

Doyle must have noticed the way he watched the girl. He talked about her in an offhand, avuncular way while he heated up the frying pan, starting with something he liked about her, then tagging on some broken-off qualification.

"She's proud in a lot of ways. If I were you. . . . "

And this was as far as it ever got, Colin never sure if he had been subtly encouraged or subtly warned.

The old man had found some eggs and was just on the point of cracking them into the pan when Cuba screamed something in Spanish and pulled out a gun. Doyle cursed, dropped the pan and ran over to the couch, yanking a revolver out from beneath his coat. The girl came in from the beach and quickly blew out the lamp. There was the sound of breaking glass, then the two men started shooting . . . wildly, from the hip, not bothering to aim, empty cartridges skipping across the floor to where Colin watched, one eye on the girl to see how he should behave. She covered her ears with her hands. He covered his. She smiled. He smiled. Neither one of them bothered to duck—there didn't seem to be any shots being returned and he had the feeling they were indulgent parents watching their spoiled children playing some make-believe game.

Just as quickly as they started the two men stopped. Cuba fell back against the couch and started reloading, no longer bothering to hide his gun. Doyle staggered back to the kitchen, trying to act calm. But he was still too excited and when he tried to crack the eggs they fell on the floor. The girl came over and made him sit down. She wiped his forehead with the sleeve of her robe, then gently pried his fingers away from the spatula.

"That showed them!" he yelled. "That showed them! They won't try that trick for a while!" and he tapped the barrel of his revolver triumphantly against his knee.

The girl brought the eggs over with bread and coffee. They both sat watching him while he ate. Once Doyle took the girl aside and whispered something in her ear. Later she got up to take some coffee in to Cuba. When Colin finished eating Doyle made a great show of helping him to seconds—he seemed on the verge of asking him some favor, but not sure how to begin. . . . Three nights without sleeping, he said. Tired. There were really too many for them and since he was junior recruit now . . . as though he was simply trying to get up the nerve to ask for help in washing the dishes. But when he actually volunteered they wouldn't hear of it.

"No, no! You'll be standing first watch, that's more than enough," and instead of handing him a dish towel Doyle handed him the gun. Before he could say anything he had been led over to the couch, Doyle and Cuba disappearing up the stairs with a vague promise about relieving him in an hour or so. "Watch the dunes," Doyle said. "Yell if you need us" and they were gone.

It was a few minutes more before he realized the girl was still there. She pretended to straighten up the room, coming closer and closer before finally sitting down beside him against the couch. She tucked her knees up under her robe and tilted her head towards his shoulder.

All night he hadn't said more than a few words. He'd never entirely gotten over the dream-like mood of the train and a dream is mostly silent assent. But now he felt like talking about everything that had happened. Missing the train, the long ride, the way he had always wanted to see Montauk ever since he was a boy, how he always had kept putting it off for one reason or another.

"Maybe you were saving it for last. Everyone should save one place for last."

He nodded. Maybe that was it. Maybe he had been saving it for last. But now he was here. Accidentally here and what did that mean? He had been to Europe, had been to Brazil, but neither seemed as far away. Montauk seemed the very edge of the world.

"The start. Can't you see that? Here is where it starts."

"Yeah," Colin said, turning away. "It really seems like a long way from everything out here."

The girl tilted her head even closer to his shoulder—strands of her hair brushed his jacket.

"Can I ask you something? Doyle asked me and I wasn't sure. Are you chased or are you chasing?"

Colin could see she was serious. He thought about it for a while.

"Neither," he said. "Neither. Maybe I was once, but tonight . . . Right now I feel very content."

"He thinks chased. I said chasing. Everybody's one or the other. Most are both . . . Neither is what Hopper says too. But he's lying."

"He chases you," Colin said instinctively—when she mentioned his name her eyes had left his for the first time.

"Oh, sometimes he pretends. But I'm too easy. Too very easy," and here her voice fell off into a whisper. "Hopper chases himself. He'll never be caught. . . . Let me see your hand."

He held it over her lap. She didn't take it, but instead put her own hand a few inches above it.

"How's that?"

"Too far away," Colin said.

"Is that better?"

"Closer," Colin said. "Move it closer."

"Now?"

They were almost touching. "There," he said. "What do you feel there?"

"I feel . . . sweaty," and she instantly covered her face with her hands and began to laugh, rocking helplessly towards the floor like a little girl does when she has the giggles.

"Oh, I ruined it! I ruined it!"

"I'm not talking to you anymore," Colin said, pretending to be angry. She apologized and reached for his hand—he pulled it away. She pretended to pout, Colin pretended to look out the window . . . pretending this and that until each of them grew tired of it and became quiet.

"Do you want me to sit here with you?"

Colin told her no. She must be tired, it was a long night. He didn't mind.

"Are you sure? I'd like to."

He was sure. But in the same instant he said that he saw something in her look—a faint hurt self-controlled into an even fainter scorn—that made him wish he hadn't. Before he could call out to her she was gone up the stairs, leaving him with the feeling that he was the one who had ruined it, not she, and that whatever promise there might have been between them was now irretrievably gone.

He sat watching by the window until dawn, holding Doyle's gun on his lap in the same feigning way he used to hold his drink at parties, one hand rubbing circles around the rim. The red glow was gone. There were stars where it had been but they seemed somehow tainted, seemed like sparks flung loose from smoldering wood. Closer to the house he could make out the tennis court. To its left was a small grove of pine. Beyond that the moors began . . . all very monotonous, all with the flat scrubby sameness, seeming to ebb without interruption back toward everything he detested.

He left his post only once—to get some coffee—and while he was in the kitchen he heard a noise out by the beach. He went outside to look but could see nothing except the grounded runabout, the sandy impression of its keel shingled by overlapped black waves. Watching them he felt a sudden anxiety that came over him like a chill—he actually remembered shivering—and he hurried back to the couch.

It was almost daybreak before anything happened. His nerves were strained from watching all night, he was feeling sorry for himself, mad at Doyle and the others for not coming down to relieve him . . . tired and cold. There was a slight motion near the tennis court, then another—as if some invisible player had fallen into the pine trees in an effort to return a lob that was wide.

He reached for the gun and brought it up to the window, tapping the barrel against the loose glass to clear it away. Again the slightest movement, the same slight pause. At the same time there was a sound from the balcony behind him. A low voice he didn't recognize atop a girl's teasing giggle. Both stopped almost at once—he wasn't sure he had even heard them and all his attention was concentrated on the short, blurry trees that bordered the house. He cocked the hammer on the revolver, wondering whether he should run upstairs to warn Doyle. The pines moved again . . . they seemed about to open to reveal a whole army of dark, menacing men crawling on their bellies towards where he waited, absolutely unable to make up his mind.

He raised the gun. Again the same chill, the same unbearable anxiety he had felt facing the sea. He held his breath, his finger tightened. Should he shout? Should he run? Whatever it was moved closer, the grass moved, had definitely moved. They were flanking the house, moving to cut them off. The bastards! he thought. The bastards!

"Shoot!"

And the gun went off, kicking loose from his hand out the window. He spun around instantly toward the voice but no one was there. In the same recoiling motion he turned back to the window but no one was there either. Just the same quiet stars and unending moor. Nothing moved inside or out. He knelt by the broken glass, not at all sure what had happened, feeling only release, an overwhelming urge to collapse beside the couch and go to sleep.

Recalling that night in later years he would sometimes wonder what had happened to that bullet—whether it had flown straight and true into one of Mario's crouching goons, whether it had embedded itself harmlessly in the bark of a nearby tree. Remembering the unknowing bitterness he must have been burdened with that night—the store of jealousies and betrayals anyone accumulates in growing older—he sometimes imagined it must still be flying out over the moors, ricocheting endlessly in angry, random patterns among the pines . . . or whether, more realistically, it had merely flown on a way before falling safely spent to the earth in a puff of dust, the one brief passion of his youth.

He couldn't have slept more than an hour but it seemed much longer and there was an even longer time when he tried to force himself awake. It was just after dawn and foggy. He remembered hearing voices, then the sound of crates being pushed along the floor, then more voices further away, all as vague and insubstantial as the fog. The first definite sight he made out was Cuba balancing a crate on top of his head as he disappeared through the kitchen.

"Hurry up!"

Doyle was running downstairs from the balcony, trying unsuccessfully to fasten a huge life preserver over his coat. He came to a momentary stop near the fireplace and Colin tried to explain about the gun.

"Don't worry about it. Hopper's here. Came in last night. Didn't you hear him? We're moving east."

He was excited as a little boy and before Colin could finish explaining he was on his way out the kitchen after Cuba. By the time Colin reached the beach he was already up to his knees in the water—there was no surf, the ocean was entirely still.

"Come on! What's keeping you?"

But when Colin still didn't move the old man shrugged and started wading out toward the waiting runabout. He had trouble when he got over his waist, but Cuba was there to help and together the two men reached the gunwhale of the idling boat, loaded low in the water with the crates, its stern swinging easily in the exhaust's gentle current. There were three people in it already. He recognized Norman straddling the bow with his legs, swinging his hand up and down against the side like a cowboy. The girl sat next to the driver, just close enough so that her extended arm rested lightly on his shoulder. She still had on her bathing suit; she didn't look back. The driver didn't turn either, except to glance half-amused at Cuba who was boosting Doyle over the side like a great, limp sack. He had one hand on the wheel—dressed in simple clothes that gave no hint as to destination, a strong man, gradually pushing the throttle forward, spinning the wheel around and starting east, a man in full possession of himself, lithe, tanned, enviously young.

The boat pushed off in a stream of white, gathered speed, and when Colin walked back up the bluff near the house and turned around it was gone.

He washed up in the sink. There was a crease across the back of his suit and he folded it over the table to smooth it out. He was hungry, but couldn't find anything except a tin of stale biscuits—he had them for breakfast, being careful not to get any crumbs on the floor. The bootleggers had left the house the same neat way they must have found it when they broke in. Sheets had been placed over all the furniture, someone had righted the couch and pushed it against the fireplace. In looking for more biscuits he even found the lost tennis racquets, piled in the corner of a closet near the stove.

By the time he was ready to leave, the fog was lifting. He stood waiting on the bluff until it was clear enough to see the lighthouse—it turned out to be only a few hundred yards away—then started along an overgrown path, enjoying the fresh breeze that came up underneath the rising grey, the sharp white clouds that streamed over it with the blue. Gulls spilled loose from the bluff toward the building surf, grass blew against his knees . . . wind and waves in the same parting flow.

It only took a few minutes to reach the light. It was striped in red and white bands, not as high as he had imagined, but located right on the very edge of the land, just as he had pictured it years ago. He walked very carefully up to the base, glanced briefly at the circling expanse of empty sea, then ceremoniously reached out and touched its side.

He would spend a long while talking about this moment, the time between going up to touch the lighthouse and starting back. He had seen everything with a supernatural clarity for these few seconds, from the white chipping paint that blistered the light at eye level to the small red flowers matted beneath his shoes. And I think what he was trying to tell us—why he lingered so long on this brief interval between satisfaction and regret—was that there is a point in a man's life when he has gone as far as he ever will go and where there is nothing left to do but turn around.

A few things more, his voice growing softer . . . the sound of the keeper's collie barking in the distance . . . a black roadster pulled up alongside the road to town . . . an old man with binoculars standing on its roof supported by three hulking men in leather coats, staring forlornly out to sea . . . breakfast in a luncheonette with fishermen who laughed over the ball scores and treated him to coffee . . . the train at the station . . . a seat by the window . . . and all the rest is simply going home.

Jincy Willett

Under the Bed

On November 6 of last year, at around 8:15 p.m., I was beaten and raped by a man named Raymond C. Moreau, Jr., who had entered our first floor apartment through a living room window while I was taking a shower. This is neither the most significant event in my life nor the most interesting; nevertheless it is a fact, around which cluster many other facts, and the truth is always worth telling. As I approach forty I am learning to value the truth for its own sake; I discover that most people have little use for it, beyond its practical applications, except as the glue which holds together rickety constructs of theory and opinion. As a rule the brighter and better educated select their facts with great care.

I teach philosophy at our mediocre state junior college. My husband teaches physics at the University. He is the real philosopher, like all good scientists, although, like most good scientists, he amiably resists this description. We self-styled philosophers window shop through metaphysics, epistemology and ethics, until we settle on those views which suit us, and then we tailor them to fit our idiosyncracies. The more cynical among us deliberately choose unpopular or bizarre philosophies the more easily to establish a reputation. My husband is a born verificationist. He does not ask unanswerable questions; he does not whine, or posture, or plead, or shake his fist at the stars. His agnosticism, unlike mine, is consistent throughout, utterly free of petulance and despair. It is he who taught me to hold the truth in such high regard, as he has taught me so many things. He believes in a rational universe. How I love him for that! He is worth a hundred humanists, a thousand priests.

My husband was at an evening seminar on November 6 (or, as we now refer to it, with some humor, "The Night of the Thing") and did not return until 9:00, when I was again alone in the apartment. Of course he blamed himself, especially at first, for having been away, for not coming right home when the seminar concluded. I am very glad he stayed for coffee. Had he interrupted us he would have had to do something, as would Raymond C. Moreau, Jr., who had a gun.

As it happened, and for reasons I shall try to explain, when he came home I was under our double bed, asleep. He did not notice that our television set was missing; there were damp towels on the living room floor, and the bedspread was considerably rumpled, but this did not alarm him so much (for I am not very neat) as the apparent fact of my absence. He was smiling when he opened the front door—I know this, because I am usually there to meet him, and he always smiles—but when he sat on our bed to puzzle out where I might be he was not smiling. I imagine that at that moment he looked his age (he is older than I) and that he let his shoulders sag, and that his expression was blank and vulnerable. I cannot imagine how he looked when, bending down to untie his shoes, he saw the fingertips of my right hand protruding from behind the gray chenille spread. Thank god he has a good heart. He dropped to his knees and took my hand and lifted the spread, at which point I woke up. A farce ensued. (Unfunny, as farces so often are.) I immediately realized, from the way his voice cracked when he called my name, that he was badly frightened, as who wouldn't be; since I did not want to frighten him further I determined not to let him see my face, which was bloody and ugly with bruises. "I'm fine," I said, idiotically, in an exaggerated reasonable tone. "What the hell do you mean," he said, and yanked on my arm. "Come out of there." I braced my other arm against the rail. "I will in a minute. I have to tell you something." Then, unfortunately, and rather horribly, I began to laugh, at the picture we would have made to an impartial observer, at our outlandish dialogue. This is usually called the "hysterical laugh," to distinguish it substantially from genuine laughter. Now my husband—and good for him—wasted no time, but gave the bed a hard sideways push. It flew on well-oiled casters and thumped against wall and windowsill; and for the second time in an hour I was well exposed. A pitiful and wrenching sight I must have been, clutching my old red bathrobe tight around me like a cartoon spinster, hiding my ugly face in the dusty green shag. (To this day a breath of dust makes me flush a little, with artificial shame. The body remembers.) Well, then there was reconciliation, and explanation, and generally the sort of behavior you would expect from lovers to whom such a thing has happened. These events were not extraordinary, except to us, and I shall not record them, here or anywhere else. These are private matters. We are very private people.

Raymond C. Moreau was twenty years old and looked thirty. He had long sand-colored hair, which hung in greasy ropes; small deep-set eyes, I don't know what color; thin lips and receding chin; and a rough, ravaged complexion: the right side of his face especially was seamed and pitted. I gave this information to the police artist and he drew me a picture of Charlie Goodby, a paperboy we had in Worcester when I was a little girl. He—the rapist—wore a soiled yellow windbreaker, an undershirt, beige chinos, and jockey shorts. Obviously he must have worn shoes, but I never noticed. His breath was terrible. He looked, as you would expect, like a bad man and a loser.

During the fifteen or so minutes of our association he said the following:

Get it off. Drop it.

In there, lady.

On the bed.

You got a husband? You all alone, you stupid bitch?

Spread them, bitch.

You're all alike. All alike. All alike.

Shut up. I'll kill you.

That's right.

Oh. Love. Love, love love, ahhh, love. Ahhh.

Stay there. Stay away from the phone. I'll come back and I'll kill you.

That he said "love, love, love" at the point of orgasm does not, in retrospect, strike me as ironic. On the back of his windbreaker the initials "CHSE" and the numerals "1972" were stencilled in brown. "CHSE 1972" is heavier with implication than "love, love, love." "CHSE 1972," now that I think of it, is eloquent as hell.

He never looked me in the eye. But he did not, I think, purposely avoid my eyes. He was not nervous, or ashamed, or fearful. It just never occurred to him to look there.

I used to be afraid of everything. That is, I was a functioning, relatively happy person with a great deal of fear. Spiders, heights, closed-in places—I had all the phobias in moderation. I never answered the phone without first composing myself for bad news—I always waited a beat before I picked up the receiver. (The ring of a telephone on a late sunny afternoon was particularly menacing to me.) Every time I got on a plane I knew I was going to die; and I was ever aware of the dangers inherent in any form of transportation. If I had to enter a dark room I hurried to the light switch, even though my night vision is excellent. At night I never let my hand or my foot dangle over the side of the bed.

Once or twice a year I would experience a few days of serious dread, touched off by something Walter Cronkite said, or a remark overheard at a sherry hour. Once a colleague mentioned a Roman Catholic legend to the effect that the last Pope would be the first non-Italian. "Then what," I asked him, with a false conspiratorial smile. "The end of the world," he said, and lifted his glass as if to toast this hideous prophecy. Oh, I despised him then, and all the laughing doomsayers, who spread terror all unmindful, precisely because they do not know what terror is. Cassandra never laughed.

It is not that I have ever believed the holocaust inevitable, or even probable; rather, I was forced on some occasions to admit the possibility. And on these occasions suicide had a certain appeal for me. I would lie beside my sleeping husband and try to think about a universe purged of human beings—surely there was some comfort in this concept; but then, I would be reminded, there would be no concepts either. A universe of particles, morally neutral: black, a pitiless black whole, with no memories, not even of the finest of us. I kept imagining the moment of purging, the dying, the knowing, and terror froze me so I could not even cry. I feared most that we would see it coming, that we would be spared nothing; that I would be separated from my husband, unable to get to him in time—in the last moments of time; or that we would be together but helpless to end in our own way. Plans must be made, I would think: emergency rations of cyanide. But even then we would not both die at once; one would have to endure alone, for however long it took. . . .

When I had had enough of this I always sought to calm myself, with craven prayer, and with the warmth of my husband's body, and the cool dry cross-grain of his skin; and magically, on the third or fourth sleepless night the terror would slip away.

And other nights, when nothing weighed on me at all, and fearless as a movie hero I lay in wait for sleep, I would suddenly have to rise on one elbow, just like a robot, and strain to hear the sound of my husband breathing; and if I could not be sure of it I would brush and push against him, as though by accident, until I had drawn out a sigh or shaken him into motion.

I was not so much neurotic as superstitious, as though through occasional ritualistic suffering I could save us all. I carefully hid this, and only this, from my husband, my talisman, because I did not want to worry or disappoint him; and if he ever suspected the depth of my perverse irrationality he kindly left me to it.

I am not superstitious now. Whatever else he did to me, Raymond C. Moreau measurably improved the quality of my life. My body sometimes jumps or shrinks from the unexpected casual touch, and this can be awkward. But I know no fear. I don't worry any more.

I used to have a good friend. Regina Montgomery is the only woman outside my family for whom I have ever felt physical affection. She is an Amazon, sturdy and large-breasted, with plain coarse features; she smiles like a big cat and is made beautiful. We are opposites physically, emotionally, politically; she is ten years my junior. She pleased me. She was exotic in her proportions and in her strength; earthy, passionate, intense, everything I was not.

She gave me two weeks to start talking on my own about my experience with Raymond C. Moreau. Actually I did not let her see me the first week, until the marks faded; and when she came to the door it was she, not I, whose eyes were red-rimmed and puffy. I remember she had part of a foil-wrapped fruitcake in her hand, and that she kissed my husband on the cheek and hugged him fiercely—it was so strange to see them embracing, she had always been so shy around him; and that she waited for some sign from me and didn't get it, for she kept her distance, fluttering like a great clumsy bird, saying how wonderful I looked. I was cruel to her, surprising myself; I was bland and cheerful and gracious, serving up the fruitcake, making light, maddening conversation, meticulously avoiding even oblique allusion to the single topic she had come to discuss. Her anxiety, so ingenuously displayed, was as comical as it was touching. I kept thinking that at any moment I would let down, but after awhile she left, unsatisfied and bewildered.

"I understood," she told me after, when we finally had it out. "You couldn't stand to be touched in any way." I let her think this. The truth is, I have a mean streak. Obvious people bring out the worst in me. I was not proud of having tortured her like that; I loved her for her genuine concern, her simple candor, her trust. I made a gift of my confession, describing the attack in detail, answering all her questions. It was not enough for her. "You talk as though this—this horror—happened to someone else. How do you feel? Or don't you even know?" "A total stranger invades my home, hurts me, rapes me, calls me names, turns my life into a melodrama. How do you suppose I feel?" She opened her mouth, shut it again. She had decided, I could see, that I was still not "over it." She would bide her time.

And she watched me closely, obviously, over the next few months, impatiently waiting, I suppose, for me to start drinking, or break into sobs at a faculty meeting, or something like that. Armchair psychoanalysis has always annoyed me, it is such an undisciplined activity. I deeply resented such presumption on the part of a friend.

We went out for wine one afternoon and had an awful fight. Our friendship has not recovered.

"All you can say is, you're not changed, not outraged, not afraid, not anything. Christ, you make it seem like a—an embarrassing *incident!*"

"Or a shaggy dog horror story?" I said, smiling, and poured us wine from our third carafe. Wine makes me happy and reckless.

"But you have changed," said Regina, who was not happy at all. "You're icy. Icy. Not like your old reserve. You've become rude, do you know that? Well, not actively, but I swear you look at people with such—I don't know—contempt—"

"You're just a bad sport," I said, teasing her. The difference in our ages was never more apparent. She was flushed, earnest and drunk, and childishly adamant. "Reggie, look. He just got me on a good day, all right? You know how sometimes a movie will make you cry, and other days you laugh yourself sick—"

"That's disgusting! You were violated! Violence was done to you!"

"You say that with such an air of discovery."

"And not just to you. To me. To all women."

"Oh, really?" I was angry now. We had argued the political point before, but this was personal. "Then why don't you tell me about it, Regina? It must have been a ghastly experience."

"You are bitter! You see." She was triumphant.

"Only about you. You want me to be a martyr, a role I find repellent in the extreme. I was victimized, yes, but I am not a victim. And I am not a symbol. I am not in the symbolizing business."

In the end I said she was no different from Raymond Moreau. Always willing to take a metaphor and run with it, she stared up at me, stupid and open-mouthed, trying to understand in what way she had been "raping" me. I could see clear into her skull. I threw my money down in disgust and left her there. I had meant only, she thought we were all alike, all alike. All alike.

I padded on damp feet into the living room, wrapped in a big yellow towel, another towel on my clean hair. I was going to turn on the television, for the comforting noise. He was winding the cord around its handle; a nice breeze came in the open window. I said, "Hello." I thought to say, "I've been expecting you," for this was true; I had been expecting him all my life. I thought to scream, but then the gun was out. Another woman—Regina—might have screamed without thinking first. I never do anything without thinking first.

I let my body have the fear. Bodies are designed to handle fright. It rippled and shuddered, the heart panicked, the blood scampered in terror. I watched. Really, it was not so bad. It was nothing like the end of the world.

He lay me on my back, arranged my legs this way and that, pushed against me like a vacant idiot child; his belly was soft and slack, it rested on mine light and warm and unmuscled; when my flesh shrank away it followed, spread thick, a cloying intimate layer of skin and fat. His upper body he kept to himself, propped up on rosy eczematous elbows. I could see each row in the machine-weave of his undershirt, the irregular rows of tiny hairs and diamond-shaped skin segments in his neck and jaw, the arch of his upper teeth, filigreed with silver. If there is a god, I remember thinking, he certainly attends to detail. He hit my face, alternating open palm and knuckles, with precise unhurried rhythm; and from my mouth came a terrible sound, as from a grunting pig. But I did not make the sound. I could never make a sound like that.

At no time did I need to remind myself that this was happening, and not a dream. There was no feeling of displacement. Nor did I wonder why he did it. After all, he never wondered about me.

Where is the tragedy here? He did not touch me. Of course, it was unpleasant and wearing, but I have been more deeply hurt by rude bus drivers. It was just a collision of machines.

When he left I was faced with the problem of how to tell my husband. It does not seem now like such a great problem but then I had been under a strain and could not think clearly. Once, when I was in college, I was playing bridge with some friends in my dormitory room when a girl from down the hall—a secretive, nervous girl, a bare acquaintance—shuffled in, in nightgown and slippers, asked if she could sit and watch. She was very pale, apparently exhausted from crying. She sat still for half an hour, peculiarly ominous but circumspect, until finally, blushing with shame, she confessed, in an offhand way, that she had taken a lot of pills and didn't know what to do. There is just no proper way to inform a roomful of strangers that you have attempted suicide. There is no way at all to tell your husband that you have been raped. Should I stay as I was, naked, unseemly? This seemed a gratuitously cruel method, almost amounting to accusation. Look what's been done to me! I put on my robe and wandered through the apartment, looking for a place to light. Well, I could sit down, on the couch for instance, with a single dim lamp on, and greet him that way—but with what words? For awhile I thought seriously of cleaning up, combing my hair; I could stay in shadow, avert my face, never mention it at all. But now my body, which had served me so well, let me down: I was tired and could not even lift a cloth to wash myself. I needed a hiding place, where decisions could be held in abeyance; a place of noncommitment. Intending to rest for only a minute I slid underneath the bed, where the monsters used to be; and there were no monsters there, just me; and I slept without dreaming.

To say the least I have never been effusive or easygoing, but before the rape I got along well enough with my colleagues. There was mutual respect. I have no respect for most of them now; they have shown little for me. We live in an age when self-control, competence, discretion—all are thought abnormal, symptomatic of dysfunction. "But how do you *feel,*" they all want to know; their eyes betray them, they are so obvious; some of them dare to ask. "I'm sorry," said our Kant and Leibniz specialist, a man I had always credited with sense. "I'm sorry!" "What for," I asked him, infuriated by his gloomy hangdog look, "are you responsible in some way? Did you once have adolescent rape fantasies? Do you believe in a common consciousness?" Shoddy, second-rate thinkers; bullies. Sentimentalists. *Why, look you now, how unworthy a thing you make of me!*

A police detective came to my office with a high school photograph of Raymond Moreau. After I identified him the detective told me he was dead, shot dead by some woman better prepared than I, a woman with her own gun. (What a stupid criminal was Raymond Moreau!) "Well, that's convenient, isn't it?" I said, and shook his hand. And even he, this stolid, unimaginative fellow, even he paused, surprised, disappointed, waiting for some further response. Tears of relief, perhaps; a primitive whoop of joy.

There are so many like Raymond Moreau.

My disgust is not unreasonable. I know, because I have talked to my husband, and he agrees with me. He does urge me, from time to time, not to be too harsh: they mean no harm, he says. He contends that people usually do the best they can. I suppose he is right, although I do wonder if this is not really a tautology in lush disguise. He has always been a compassionate man. He alone sees me as I am, and loves me as he loves the truth.

We are closer now than ever. We seldom go out; neither of us spends unnecessary time at school. Evenings find us here, laughing, talking into the night. We seem again to have as much to say to each other as when we first were lovers. I have fixed up the apartment quite differently—the bedroom is completely rearranged, with all new linens and a white bedspread and a thick white carpet. (I happen to like white. White does not symbolize.) Often we have picnics, as we did when we were young, only now we hold them indoors on the living room floor; and we drink good wine, '66 burgundies, '61 bordeaux, rich wines of every hue from purple black to brick red. And I have never been so content.

But lately, and too often, as we lie in the dark, I curled away from him, peaceful and fearless, he rises, stealthy, gentle, and leans over me, watching my face; I can feel his breath on my cheek; and I must give him a sign, a sigh, a dreamy moan to ease his mind. Just like a robot he must rise, prompted by my old foolish impulse, unworthy of him, as though by watching he could keep me safe; as though the universe concerned itself with us.

There's the violation. There's the damage, and the tragedy.

William Loizeaux

BESIDE THE PASSAIC

It has never been easy living here beside the Passaic River. In late winter, when the snow melts and the rain falls, the river comes over the back yard, right up to the step. Once, I built a small levee along the bank with railroad ties and sand bags. It held for a while, but I learned: you can't stop water. It goes where it wants to. Every two years, it seems, we have a hundred-year flood. I remember one morning six months after I had gotten the job at the college and Claire and I had moved here. We were in our robes, eating breakfast and looking out the kitchen window. The yard was all water, except for the tops of bushes that stuck up here and there like islands. "Look, Sam. Look," Claire said, and I saw our picnic table floating downstream, its legs straight up in the air. We had made that table. I had sawed the redwood; she had sanded and stained it. Still, we had to laugh. You learn to live with this river. The next table we chained to the willow tree. It's out there right now—a little warped, weathered. I can see it when I lean back in my chair.

For almost five years, we have lived beside the river. We found the house through an ad in the *Star Ledger:* a three-bedroom "handyman's special" with an "auxiliary apartment" off the end of the kitchen, an addition built years ago by the previous owner so that his aging father might live his last years with his family. The house was a bit more than we could afford, and clearly it needed attention. Some of the gray asbestos shingles had fallen off, revealing the tar paper beneath. Along the roof, the gutters sagged with years of dirt and matted leaves—grasses and maple seedlings had taken root there.

Even so, we liked the feel of it, especially the half-acre lot with the dogwoods out front and the wide back yard that gently sloped toward the river.

That was the spring of 1980. We moved in the following August. In January 1981 our first daughter, Deborah, was born, and our second, Carrie, came along almost two years later—a year and a half ago. All the while, we have been renting the apartment to students, Claire has been working part-time as an administrator at the County Health Clinic, and I have been teaching American History about a mile away at the college, one of the small state schools that are sprinkled throughout New Jersey. I don't have a fancy job. I am not on the "fast track," as it is called in academic circles. I am modestly paid. My students are so-so. I am here to teach rather than write books—and to tell the truth, it is better that way. Though Claire might disagree, at heart I am not a scholar. I spend more time in the yard than I do in the library. I don't work late into the night. I like nothing better than sitting here after dinner with Claire across the table. In the summer, the fireflies hover and blink in the back yard during the first hour after sundown. Later the moths bang against the screens and sometimes alight there, wavering, suspended as if by magic, so that we can see their feathery antennae, their muted colors, and the symmetry of their fragile wings.

At times like this, I can almost forget what the river is like in late winter. But of course I can't really forget. On a Saturday a year ago last March, when the river was slow but rising, we were caught up, it seems, in a strange current and swept through a narrow channel from which only now are we emerging.

Carrie was ten weeks old then. A friend had taken Claire and Debbie to see a puppet show at noon. I was sitting here in the kitchen. On the table before me, Carrie squirmed in the wicker basket, making her bubbling baby-sounds. With one hand, I was rocking the basket, trying to make her sleep, while with the other I lifted mid-term exams, one at a time, from a tall pile, corrected them, then dropped them onto the floor. The exams were horrible. Carrie cried, spat up milk. Her diaper stank. Outside it rained that cold, gritty rain that comes every March to New Jersey. So I thought about Florida. Sunshine. Spring training. The Grapefruit League. I hadn't seen a box score since October.

I remember taking Carrie from the basket and laying her on the table where I peeled off her diaper and wiped her clean. "Such a cute little pain in the ass," I said, and tickled her fat sides until her legs wriggled and her mouth made that toothless oval that meant she would smile. "Am I right?" I dusted her with powder, put on the fresh diaper, snapped closed the safety pins—snug, not tight—I'm an old hand at this. "Snuggins, let's go get a newspaper." Then I buttoned her shirt and zipped her into her snowsuit, her arms sticking out like stiff little wings.

In the garage I set the basket, Carrie bundled inside, on the passenger seat of our Volkswagen. The engine shuddered and started. It was getting colder, the sleet icing the windshield, the wipers grating. I turned on the heat. We drove along the river, over the plank bridge into town, and parked in front of the pharmacy. I reached over to tuck in the blanket and wiped her nose with my hand. She was sleepy, her eyes heavy, the slow lift and fall of her chest. "I'll be back directly," I whispered. "In a flash." I pulled the hood of the snowsuit up and over her ears. They were huge ears, alarmingly huge for a child I thought. But "relax," Claire had said, smiling in that mild way of hers. "She'll grow into them. Just give her a chance."

Chocolate Easter rabbits, eggs, and jelly beans were already displayed in the pharmacy window. I looked at the back page of the *Daily News* and bought the *Times*. I talked with Hank, the druggist. I was only in there a few minutes. Five at the most.

But when I got back to the car. Well, the basket was right there on the seat, wedged between the passenger door and the handbreak. The blanket was tight around her. But her face: it was pale and posed, like an old-fashioned photograph; her skin a bluish white, the color of porcelain.

I remember a roaring sound in my ears. I remember picking her up by the shoulders and shaking her. I didn't think of it then. I wasn't thinking at all. I should have yelled for Hank, but instead I folded her into my coat, wrapped it around her, and drove to the hospital, holding her against me with one hand, steering and shifting with the other, running lights, swerving, fish-tailing, screaming through the windshield, as though I could make her come alive again.

I called Claire from the hospital, but she wasn't home. ("Pneumonia," the doctors had said. "It comes on quickly. You couldn't have known.") Later, when I walked out through the swinging doors of the emergency room, I slipped on the curb and turned my ankle. I hardly noticed it then. But even now, it bothers me when I move it a certain way.

I don't remember much of the drive back. The river was as beautiful as I've ever seen it: the tall grass on the banks, the cattails, willows—all glazed, hanging down. And the water still and smooth. I wanted Claire to be home. I wanted to tell her, and I wanted to be with her. I think I wanted that more than I have wanted anything else in my life. When I went in the kitchen door, she was standing at the sink, sleeves rolled, her arms in the suds, her body long and graceful in the light from the window. Deb bounced in her highchair. On either hand she wore a puppet, and in the mouth of one, she held a spoon. Chocolate ice cream covered everything around her, including my exams.

"Where have you been?" Claire said, smiling and looking up from the dishes. "What's the matter?" Then, like a shade pulled down, I saw my own face in hers. I went to her, put my arms around her, caught her head in the curve of my neck. But she just stood still, her arms hanging down, the suds dripping off and pooling on the floor.

When I let her go and stepped away, she seemed a thing I didn't know. She wiped her hands on the dishcloth. She walked out of the kitchen, up the stairs and through our bedroom. I heard her lock the bathroom door.

Debbie was staring at me, her eyes wide, then she started to cry. I lifted her from the highchair. She was warm and sticky; her hair smelled sweet. Holding her, I ran up the stairs and knocked on the bathroom door. I heard Claire drop her clothes on the floor inside, the shower running, the curtain pulled, her feet squeaking on the tub. I'm not sure that I said it aloud: She. Carrie. She seemed fine, sleeping. She was bundled up with her hood and mittens. . . .

But the door didn't open. With Deb in my arms, I sat on the edge of our bed to wait. The water ran in the bathroom. Sleet tapped on the bedroom window. In a few days, a week at the most, the river would be over the bank and cover the lawn with that brown foam on top. Debbie's sobbing slowed, and suddenly she was asleep. I lay her down in the middle of the bed and pulled the quilt over her shoulders. A moment later the water stopped in the bathroom.

I heard Claire step out of the shower and pull a towel off the rack. In her blue terry cloth robe, she came through the door, her short hair combed back, shiny and black, her face sharp and refreshed. She looked at me with an expression I couldn't read. She sat beside me on the bed, her hands in her lap. She smelled clean.

"Tell me," she said. She wasn't demanding. Her voice was calm—everything about her was calm. But I could see her on an edge, as though with one foot, she was feeling the ground between us. It was as though we were back at the beginning, seeing each other. "Tell me," she said.

So I told her.

She asked me to tell her again.

I did.

And then we sat there, silent, not touching or looking at one another, the sleet still coming down outside, the steamy air from the bathroom, Debbie breathing quietly beside us.

"Sam," Claire said at last. She was right on that edge. "Sam, what are we to do?" And she didn't say anymore. Instead, she rocked slowly, forward and back, rhythmically, steadily. I put my hand on the back of her neck. She let it stay, then leaned against it.

As I think of them now, the next several weeks were a frantic blur, both numb and tumultuous. For a time we all had the flu. The phone rang; neighbors brought casseroles. The river came over the bank, up the yard, and lapped at the bottom row of shingles on the back of the house. Often I'd find myself doing something quite ordinary, like vacuuming the hall, and suddenly it was impossible to do—I just couldn't. One afternoon two policemen in boots and helmets appeared at our kitchen door. They had an "evacuation notice," they said, "the river's too high." "Well you have a hell of a nerve," Claire said, and she flew into such a rage that they retreated; they'd leave us alone. Then Claire curled herself in the corner of the living room sofa and wept for hours before she slept.

It was hard for us to gauge what we were feeling then. Claire was watching me carefully, I could tell, and I was doing the same with her. Sometimes I'd find her sitting out on the front stoop, looking at the dogwoods, and I'd stand in the doorway, searching for clues, as though by studying the back of her head and the slope of her narrow shoulders I might discover exactly what she felt. But I could only imagine her feeling my own sadness, my own upwellings of voiceless anger. We were encased, it seemed, each in our own grief. I think again of those willows along the river, glazed after an ice storm. They are still and silent, weighted with brittle hardness—a breath of air can bring them down. And so it seemed with Claire and me. We were terribly careful of one another. We barely touched. But still we watched and waited. While I stood in the doorway she would feel my presence, and without even turning around, she'd move slightly on the step, making enough room for me to sit down beside her.

We didn't talk about Carrie. Instead, by mid-April, we were trying to focus on living from one day to another. We made lists, went grocery shopping and checked things off. We took Carrie's crib and changing table up to the attic. In her room, we scraped and painted the walls that had mildewed and peeled with the steam from the vaporizer. Meanwhile, Claire and I returned to our jobs after a two-week absence, and soon I got back to my chores around the yard. The river receded, inch by inch, leaving behind a broken shovel, a log, a tire, and everything layered and reeking with sludge. One day as Claire was hanging out laundry, I raked the sludge in a long line across the lawn. The sun was warm, the river calm. The sludge was thick and had dried into a crisp brown crust that loosened in slabs. I raked it down to the river and wisked it over the bank, revealing the tender grass beneath. Claire and I were mending, it seemed.

But then there was that night in the river. It was June, when the evenings get warm and muggy. Carrie had been gone for three months now, Debbie was spending a few days with Claire's parents at their cottage on Lake Hopatcong, and I had come home late from a committee meeting. As I came out of the garage, I saw a spot of orange light far away on the surface of the river. I stood, briefcase in hand, and watched it. It moved slowly downstream, stopped, and moved haltingly back up. It glowed for an instant, dimmed, then glowed again. Now and then it would disappear, itself eclipsed, but its light reflected on the water around it. I was going to call Claire out of the house, but somehow this was my own mystery. So I walked down toward the river, avoiding our seepage pit to my left. A small haze hovered above the orange spot, caught its light, then dissipated. It didn't move as I approached, just glowed and dimmed. When I reached the bank, I could make it out: in the middle of the river, a cigarette. And someone treading water to keep it there.

"Claire?" I couldn't see, but you feel these things.

The cigarette glowed.

"Claire?" The word hung, dissipated with the smoke. "Is it you? Are you all right?"

I remember the sound from the river: a laugh, a giddy, uncontrollable laugh from another time—from before we had moved here, before the children—when we had first met at a party, drunk, and she on the floor in a red sweater, laughing, tying my shoelaces together; and I, hobbling, hopping kangaroo-style.

"What are you doing?" I called across the water.

Again the laugh. Then silence, except for the crickets, the peepers in a bog downstream.

"Why Sam, I'm smoking." Her voice—it *was* hers—had that old, odd teasing quality, as though she had a secret for me to unravel.

I felt like an idiot. "But Claire, you don't smoke."

An ash dropped off the end of the cigarette, disappeared on the water.

"You're right, Sam." She was serious now. "There are lots of things I don't do. Like smoking, like walking naked across the lawn, like swimming in the dark." The cigarette fell to the water. Claire's head, her hair straight down, was a dark silhouette. "Come on."

"What?"

"Come on."

"In the river?"

"Sure."

"We have neighbors. They have children."

"Who cares?"

"But Christ, there're things in there. Carp, catfish, polliwogs, snails—who knows? What if one gets in the wrong place?"

"Come on, Sam."

I stood there, where even at night the edge of the river is as clear, distinct as a boundary. Land. Water. Here a grassy blackness, there the rippling starlight. And still you can slide from one to the other as down a muddy bank, not sure of where the bank ends and the river begins, not sure of how or when or where you started sliding. Was it when I got out of the car? When I saw the orange light? When I turned toward the river instead of the house? Or was it now, as I thought of her smooth skin in the dark water? As I took off my sport coat, unbuttoned my shirt, stripping right there on the bank? Or was it then, the next moment, when she laughed once more and I dove, her sound swallowed by the river?

The water was thick and warm, the feel of things growing, multiplying; things taking in, consuming, excreting. On the surface now, it clung in my hair, ran down my face, the smell and taste so bad—manure from farms upstream, the gypsum factory, spillage, runoff, everything—so bad, and yet so rich and so alive.

I swam to Claire in the middle of the river. She was smiling and serious, something wild, a little scary. We side-stroked, face to face, upstream, beyond our own property.

"Claire, this is lunacy," I said, though I kept on swimming.

"Oh baloney!" She splashed water.

We were working against the current, breathing through our words. In glimpses, I saw her white breasts beneath the water, her legs scissoring, hands cupped, arms reaching, pulling the river, then reaching for more. Since Carrie's death, sex had not even been an issue, a possibility. Yet here we were in the river.

"But think," I said, "just how do we do this? There are some real logistical difficulties here. Like us even getting near one another. That's crucial, you know."

We passed the swingset in the Rittwigger's yard. Their dog barked from the porch.

"How?" I went on. "Tell me. There's nothing solid, fixed. Nothing here to hold onto."

We stopped.

"But ourselves," she said.

We drifted slowly downstream, coming awkwardly together, both of us treading water with our hands, her legs circling my waist, and Claire giggling, splashing, me catching her strange laughter, keeping that crazy balance.

And it was more, though, than sexual energy, I think—or at least I have come to think. There was a commitment in it, an intent, a kind of frenzied will. All of those impediments, qualms, reservations—the color of Carrie's skin, the stack of diapers in the bathroom closet, the twinge in my ankle—all of it was there, not drifted away, but coming down upon us now as water over falls. It was all there in that warm, rich water—the death of her—treading, kicking, rearing up and rolling under.

And yet we couldn't do it. We couldn't keep that balance. As we tried to lock, Claire went under for a horrible moment, then came up, crying and choking. It was just no use. We separated. Claire swam downstream to our yard, crawled out of the water and up the bank beneath the willow tree. I followed. Shivering, she tied my shirt around her waist, then wrapped my jacket around her shoulders and hugged her arms across her chest, folding in upon herself. Without a word, she walked away toward the house, her thin legs gleaming in the moonlight, bits of grass clinging to her ankles.

I have thought about that night in the river many times since then, and still its meaning is not altogether clear. I am a history teacher, and I am supposed to make sense of past events. This one, however, is more difficult than most. Something was unleashed that night in both of us. As it seems to me now, we were hysterical for a time, and that hysteria—or our awareness of it—made our union both more compelling and yet strangely distasteful, all at the same time. As I crawled out of the river, I felt unclean—and not simply because of the fetid muck and water. After months of careful nurturing and mending, we had suddenly lost all care. We had let everything go. We had gone too far, had tried too much, too quickly, and now that fragile thing between us, a web of finest filament, had broken. Neither of us had wanted that to happen. And both of us knew that when you thought about it rationally, if you considered the pure physics of it, making love in a river, particularly the Passaic, was virtually impossible—it couldn't have been done. But still there was that sense of failure and separation, that lingering distaste, like a faint odor that fills a room. Nothing in our lives was overtly changed. We cleaned the house, worked in the yard, and shopped on Saturday mornings. In the evenings we sat after dinner, then went upstairs together. If anything, we were more affectionate then. At night we would lie in bed beneath a thin sheet, silent and sleepless, holding like lovers, feeling an immediate comfort, and then a deeper sadness. It was as though we were reaching across an invisible gulf. Our skins were like boundaries. The more we pressed them together, the more they would resist, and the more it recalled that night in the foul water when we pressed with all that was in us—only to fall apart.

TOWARD THE END of that August I was in my office at school, getting ready before the start of the semester, when I noticed a young woman waiting outside my door. I asked her in, and she stood silently before me in a college T-shirt. She was a student of mine from the previous spring whose name, for the life of me, I couldn't remember. She had black hair, long and straight. Her eyes were dark brown, almond-shaped, and on her forehead, where she pulled back her hair, was a tiny scar, the shape of a crescent moon. I recalled that she had sat toward the back of my Colonial American History class, dozing sometimes. Though she had always attended, she seldom raised her hand or contributed to class discussions. She always came and left on her own. She seemed apart from her peers, older perhaps, though not measurably so. She was one of those rare students—quiet, intelligent, and self-possessed—who without any fanfare would take things in and understand.

"You're Sarah Morrison, aren't you?" I said, her name suddenly coming to me. "Have a seat."

But she remained standing. "I'd like to rent your apartment," she said.

"How did you know it was available?" I asked. "I haven't even advertised it."

She glanced at me with her dark eyes. From her purse she pulled out a check and handed it to me. It was made out to "Professor Collins" for $150, exactly a month's rent, and signed "Sarah L. Morrison." "I hope it's OK," she said.

There was something vaguely amusing, attractive too, in her combination of ease and determination. "Do you know what you're getting into?" I said. "It's not exactly a luxury apartment."

"I know," she said. "But it'll be fine for me."

That's how Sarah came to live with us that fall. The apartment into which she moved with a U-Haul full of odds and ends consists of three rooms: a central living and sleeping area with a door leading outside; a yellow-walled kitchen with an old Frigidaire, a sink, hot plate, no cupboards, and a window (like our own kitchen window) that looks over the back yard and down toward the river. On the end of the kitchen is a bathroom whose peculiar feature, other than its smallness, is a narrow door beside the toilet which, if opened, leads up one step and into our own kitchen just beside the washing machine. The previous owner, evidently, was as lacking for funds as we are. The whole apartment seems slapped together. It is heated by an old rust-colored kerosene stove that stands in the corner of the central room. The walls are thin, the wiring inscrutable. Routinely—whenever the hot plate is on in conjunction with any other appliance—a fuse blows, darkening the entire apartment and, by some bit of electrical wizardry, our own bedroom upstairs in the main part of the house. Come winter, the pipes freeze in the bathroom unless the tap is left on. In March the kitchen floods: boots and sneakers float over the linoleum. No amount of scrubbing or Lysol will get out the smell of the river.

As Claire and I are not exactly the landlord types, there was no lease for Sarah to sign, no damage deposit. I showed her how to work the kerosene heater and replace the fuses. And to better insure her privacy (and restrain Debbie's wanderings), I blocked off the narrow door between our kitchen and the apartment bathroom with an old armchair. During the fall, it became a favorite place of Claire's where often she'd sit alone, absorbed in a book or magazine, her legs curled beneath her.

For the first month Sarah was in our apartment, we hardly saw or heard from her. She never had company. Her telephone seldom rang. As far as I could tell, she rode her bike into school early in the mornings and returned sometime in the afternoons. We were all on different schedules, including Claire and me. "I need some time and space for myself," Claire had said. So on weekdays when she came back from the clinic at noon, I would take the car, drop Debbie at day care and go into school to teach my afternoon classes. In the evenings, of course, Claire and I would be together. Since that night in the river, we hadn't made much progress. Despite our efforts and intentions, we seemed to be drifting further apart. After Deb was in bed, we would sit here at the table and try to talk about what we were feeling. Yet somehow it was harder than we ever imagined. We would start out calmly, almost clinically. We might review what had happened in the last six months. We could say that it would take time to recover, that there were stages to go through. Then somewhere along the line, we would strike a nerve. Through the screen door we'd catch the ripe scent of the river. Or in Claire's eyes I'd see a hopelessness that I had never seen before. Then we would sit in a silence that sometimes I just couldn't bear. I would get up, go out the door and walk outside. There would be faint sounds of faraway traffic, the feel of loose gravel, the smell of damp, withered leaves along the sides of the dark road. When later I'd return to the house, the kitchen light would still be on, the door unlocked, but Claire would be upstairs, in bed, her head turned away toward the wall. As I'd slide in beside her, I could tell that she was wide awake, that while I had been out walking, she had been lying there, filled with the same fears—and yet we could do nothing to share them.

On a cool Sunday afternoon in mid-October, I began putting up the storm windows. I took them out of the cellar, and as I carried them around to the side of the house, I saw Sarah hop on her bike and pedal off. She wore a gray sweatshirt, her wire bike-baskets were stuffed with laundry, and when she went out the driveway, she turned and waved tentatively. Using the step ladder, I hung the windows, then went inside to hook them in at the sills. I started in Sarah's apartment.

I hadn't been in there since she had arrived. Though I knew she was out, it was strangely quiet—just the slow drip of the kitchen faucet which someday soon I'll get around to fixing. I stood in the main room for a moment. Beneath the window was a brown convertible sofa that Claire and I had picked up at a garage sale years ago. There in the corner stood the kerosene heater, warm to the touch, and over the stovepipe hung a pair of white knee socks, worn at the heel. I leaned over the sofa and secured the storm window, pushing the metal hook through the screweye in the sill. I went into the kitchen. The small formica table was covered with a red-checked cloth, and on it stood a vase filled with tasselled grasses that Sarah must have collected along the river. Beside that lay an open *Organic Chemistry* text book, a pencil in the binding, underscored passages, and an entire page circled by cryptic formulae. I hooked in the storm window above the sink. Though there were no windows in the bathroom, I pushed open the door anyway and turned on the light. It was cool in there, the smell of mildew and sweet shampoo. A damp towel hung on the rack, and on the tiled floor of the shower lay a strand of long hair, black and gleaming.

It is hard to describe the effect of seeing these things. It wasn't mysterious or surprising. These were the everyday items of Sarah's life—a lost strand of hair, calico curtains, a crust of bread on a dish in the sink. And yet it was as though for the first time I could actually see her living here: getting up in the morning, opening the curtains, folding the sofabed, turning on the shower to heat up the bathroom. In the evenings she must have cooked her dinner on the hot plate, then eaten on her red-checked tablecloth. Perhaps as she ate, she listened to the radio. Or perhaps she heard Claire and me talking in our kitchen on the other side of the wall. I know she stayed up late at night. When I returned from my long walks, I would see the beige light in her windows. She was probably reading a history assignment or wrestling with chemistry problems. When she got into bed, she must have read something lighter—flipped through a catalogue, a magazine—until she was drowsy and reached up to turn off the lamp.

One day during the next week, when I put my 50 cents in the Coke machine in the faculty lounge, I got two Cokes for the price of one. As I returned to my office, I saw Sarah come out of the classroom across the hall. She was wearing a denim skirt and those white knee socks. On impulse I said, "I've got two of these things." I held up the Cokes. "A miracle. Want one?"

"Sure," she said, smiling.

I turned into my office and she followed. I sat at my desk with my bag lunch. "Have a seat," I said, and this time she sat.

I opened both Cokes and gave her one. She drank hers slowly, her books in her lap. I asked her how things were going and if there were any problems with the apartment.

"No," she said. "It's not as bad as you said it'd be."

"Well, you must be getting pretty handy with fuses in the dark."

She nodded and we laughed a little. She looked around at my office: at the gray cinderblock walls, the maple outside my window, the filing cabinet, the disordered book shelf, and on top of that the piles of paper, manila folders, and the small photograph that I probably should have removed. It was taken last Christmas by my father. It was of Debbie, Claire, Carrie and me. Claire was smiling brightly. Awkwardly, I was holding Carrie who was wrapped in a blanket, her ears sticking out. She was a month old then.

Sarah studied the photograph, and I watched a question form in her face. She looked at me and I saw it dissolve as she understood. I thought she still might ask, but she never did. Instead, we sat quietly finishing our Cokes.

Three or four days later, I heard a cautious knock on my office door, though I always leave it wide open. It was Sarah again. She didn't have anything particular to say, but I was glad to see her. Soon she began stopping by my office every day at noon, right after her class.

She would set her books on the window sill and sit beside my desk with her hair fanned across the back of the leather chair. I knew she was our renter, a student, and only twenty years old; yet as we talked she seemed none of those to me. In her voice was a sympathy that I could not disbelieve. Without a word, she knew what had happened with Carrie, and she seemed to sense what was happening between

Claire and me. Nothing was said directly, but somewhere in the course of our conversations, she mentioned that her own parents had been through hard times, that for months they had lived together, virtually estranged.

Sarah grew up in Wrightstown, south of here, off the Turnpike, where the land is flat, the earth rich, and the fields of corn and alfalfa go on for miles. Her father was in the military; her mother was a nurse. And I remember one day in my office when she talked all about cranberries. They are grown in the bogs near her home. Workers pick them in late summer, and along the sides of dirt roads, Sarah would watch the men loading them into wooden crates with wide shovels. There were millions of them, like marbles, she said, shiny and red. You couldn't take what was in the crates, but what had spilled on the ground you could get by the bucket-load. . . .

Often, long silences followed our bursts of conversation, Sarah would gaze out the window. As the breeze blew in the maple, shadows would dance on her lap, and I'd watch her small hands molding her skirt around her knees.

It has always puzzled me, my relationship with Sarah. Strictly speaking, it was not an affair. We never touched. I never so much as made an "improper advance"—nor did she. And yet as we sat each day in the autumn light from my office window, I swear it was something like love. Anxiously I awaited her visits, and after she left, I went off and taught my classes with a strange exuberance that I hadn't felt in years. At home, however, she was as distant from me as she was from Claire. When I'd run into her in the yard, whether Claire and Debbie were there or not, Sarah would be friendly, but nothing more. As the semester went on and December rolled around, it seemed that this distance at home made our meetings at school increasingly intimate. In stages, Sarah opened her life before me, and I told her things that I hadn't told Claire in a long time.

When I'd return home in the evenings after picking up Debbie, I'd find Claire sitting in the armchair in front of the narrow door. She would have the lamp on beside her, a book in her lap, and it would strike me how little I actually knew of her life any more. We were giving up, Claire and I. Without saying anything about it, we had abandoned our talks after dinner. Instead, Claire would return with her book to the armchair. In silence I'd finish washing the dishes, while through the wall I'd hear—or thought I heard—Sarah moving about in her own apartment, washing her dishes, drying her hands with the fringed dishcloth. Then I'd go into the living room to read the paper. Later I'd hear Claire switch off the kitchen light and slowly climb the stairs.

The first flurries came in mid-December, and along the edge of the river, a sheet of ice, thin as cellophane, inched out a little farther each morning, then melted away in the afternoon. As the semester was coming to a close, we got a cold snap, the likes of which we have never had before. It was a deceptive cold. The sky was clear. There was no snow, no wind. If you had looked out our kitchen window, you would have seen the willow limbs, yellowy in the sunlight, and beyond, the warm shades of brown and tan, the crisp shadows, the tall grasses along the river, motionless as a photograph. But had you gone outside and stood on the hard ground, you would have squinted in the bright stillness, smelled the brittle air, then felt the twinge in your fingers and toes, and the dull warmth that follows it.

It was during that cold snap that I came home early one evening, at dusk, before it was time to pick up Debbie. As I drove down the driveway I could see that our curtains were wide open, and there wasn't a light on in the entire house. I was struck with a sudden fear: our home looked abandoned, rushed out of—Claire had gone. When I went in the kitchen door, the armchair was empty, the lamp off; yet there was a dark and lingering warmth in the room: the smell of tea, cinnamon, the dim blue ring of the burner beneath the kettle. I went over to the armchair. It had been pushed aside a few feet, and behind it the narrow door was open. I almost went through it, but something stopped me. On the floor lay Claire's shoes, side by side. The chair I usually sit in at the table had been turned around to face the armchair. On the seat was a gold bracelet that I knew was Sarah's.

I was reaching to turn on the light, when I heard faint laughter, like children playing, from somewhere outside. I went out the door and stood in the middle of the back yard, listening. The air was cold and clear. My breath came out in white plumes. Already there were stars in the twilit sky. I looked across the lawn and down toward the river. It had frozen smooth and pale, clear to the other side. I heard the laughter again, and from behind the willow Claire and Sarah appeared. They were skating on the glassy surface. Claire held Sarah's arm as Sarah made tentative strides. She let go and Sarah coasted off on her own, balancing, wavering, then flailing her arms and legs like someone in a Charlie Chaplin film. Claire tried to catch her before she fell, but together they went down in a heap on the ice, gently enough, their legs sprawled. They were like college girls off on a lark. Without noticing me, they unravelled themselves and sat there, looking at one another, shaking their heads, laughing.

And suddenly I knew: when Sarah left my office each afternoon, she came home to see Claire. While I was teaching, filled with that strange exuberance, they would be sitting in the kitchen, drinking their tea. Sarah would hold her cup in her lap, leaning back in my chair, her feet propped against the washing machine. Claire's shoes would be off, her legs folded beneath her in the armchair. Her face would be open, alive. They would talk softly and intently as steam curled up from the kettle and the dusk fell without them even noticing it.

I'm not sure just what I was feeling then. I thought of my own conversations with Sarah: her stories, her relaxed intimacy, the way she pushed back her hair, the bracelet sliding, then rested her slender arm on the edge of my desk and listened. There was something so pure about our meetings at school, so removed she seemed from my world at home. But now, to hear her laughter, to see her out on that river—and then to watch her, almost feel her, leaning on Claire as she righted herself. . . .

Sarah looked up to where I stood on the open lawn. I didn't know what to do. I turned to leave, but just then she called, "Sam." And the tone of her voice was as warm as it had always been in my office. I could see her there in the leather chair, her eyes wide with concern and sympathy. That was how she was looking at me now.

Claire's hand dropped from Sarah's arm, and she stared at me with a look of shock and disbelief. "My God," she said in a voice I had never heard.

I stood there silently. In the fields beyond the river, I could barely see the tall girdered towers that carry electric wires across the swamp and west toward Whippany. I had no idea what would ever become of us.

"Why don't we all go skating?" Sarah said, taking hold of the situation. She pointed at the wooden box of skates on the bank. "Yours are right here," she said to me. "Come on."

I looked at Claire, and for a moment I hesitated—was Sarah kidding?—but it was only a moment. There was really nothing else to do. I went down to the river, sat beside the box, took off my gloves, shoes, and laced on my old black hockey skates. The river was quiet, not even a rippling, an eddying sound. I stood on the ice, getting used to it, then dug in with one skate and glided off on the other, my ankle wobbling. Cautiously we all skated back and forth along the bank, watching each other, keeping some distance, mingling without speaking, like awkward guests at a cocktail party. Then, as I was coming up alongside of her, Claire just stopped. Her face was expressionless. Her skates were white, the blades glinting. She wore her red wool sweater with intricate cables and diamond shapes. She seemed poised, waiting, as though listening to something far away.

Suddenly she skated swiftly off in a wide arc, upstream and toward the middle of the river. Sarah and I, yards apart, stopped and watched her in open admiration. It had been a long time since Claire had skated, yet she was as graceful as ever. There was nothing forced or erratic in her movements. Effortlessly she gained speed, then keeping her momentum, turned and skated backward, weaving her legs, her scarf fluttering, her skates cutting long "S" marks in the ice. She glided between the willows and birches along the river's edge. She passed rushes, cattails and alders, brownish gray in the waning light. I will never forget the way that she moved on that flat, polished river. It was almost as though she was dancing.

Years ago, I recalled, when we were still in grad school, Claire and I would skate alone in the hockey arena. We were twenty-seven then, married for a year. On Fridays, after midnight, we'd take a bottle of wine, and with our skates over our shoulders, we'd sneak into the pine trees behind the gym. With a twisted coat hanger, I'd open the back door to the locker rooms. We'd feel our way along the wet, tiled walls, through swinging doors, and into the vast arena, cool and dark, where the ice lay like black marble. I'd find the switch box and turn on the banks of lights that hummed with electricity. The bleachers were blue. Brilliant banners hung from the rafters. We sat on the ice, laced our skates, and drank right out of the bottle. Then we'd stand, uncertainly at first, and skate wildly about in that flood of brightness. It was like being in the Olympics, Claire said. She curtsied and waved to the imaginary crowd. We held hands, went fast, tried ridiculous jumps, turns, double-axles, and spilled all over the ice. When later we stopped, giddy and panting, we'd finish the bottle, and I'd see the beads of sweat above Claire's lip, her face flushed, the wisps of moist hair that clung to the back of her neck. Leaving through the locker room door, we'd feel the sudden chill of winter air. Once it had snowed while we were inside—a fine, light snow—and everything was dusted, clean and crystalline. As we walked along the quiet streets, we looked up at the whirling constellations and tried to name them. Our legs were tired. Claire smiled and slid her hand into my coat pocket where I held it tightly. We lived in a small, third-floor room where the bed folded out of the wall. We didn't have regular jobs. Our lives were uncertain, but it didn't matter. We went up the long flights of metal stairs, shut our door and knocked snow from our feet. We hung our coats on the radiator, then lay in our clothes across the bed.

Beyond the Rittwigger's yard, Claire had turned and was skating wearily toward home. I looked behind me, but Sarah was no longer on the ice. While I had been watching Claire, she had quietly climbed up on the bank and now was taking off her skates. In her face was a sadness—and something else that I can only describe as love. I wanted to go to her and comfort her, but in a way that I didn't know and don't quite yet understand, everything had changed. As she stood with her skates in her arms, I felt at the same time an intense intimacy and an intense detachment. I saw her as I have seen our neighbors in their lighted windows when I go out walking at night. In that square of yellow light, while they eat their dinners or watch TV, I see their private mannerisms, their unseen faces. I know them, but they are apart from me.

And so it was with Sarah. When she turned, I didn't call out to her. I just watched as she walked away toward the house, leaving her small footprints on the frosted lawn.

After she went into her apartment, I skated out to the middle of the river. Claire was coasting, closer now. As she moved, her body was utterly still, open, her head thrown back, her face looking up, her spine arched like a bent reed. In a slow circle, she glided around me.

It has been four months since then. Another semester is winding down; the river has long since crested; and there are blackbirds now in the green sedge along the banks. Sarah left at the end of December and moved back into the dorms. For both Claire and me, it feels as though a love affair has ended, amicably, without regret, but still with an awkwardness and a lingering sorrow. Now and then I run into Sarah on campus; and last week, as Claire and I were driving through town, we saw her and a friend parking their bikes in front of the pharmacy. I suppose we could have waved, or stopped and said hello; we might have invited her over for dinner. But Claire turned to me and said, "Let's not," and I agreed. So we went on without Sarah even seeing us. At the light we took a left and drove toward home.

Ben Field

Three Sisters

Friday evening the family ate together. Every other evening Fay was busy giving lessons at the homes of her pupils, taking courses herself, or attending a concert or recital. And when Fay ate with the family everything had to be just so, and Essie, who came in to do the house cleaning, stayed on to serve.

The table in the dining room was set. The turquoise green tablecloth which Fay had bought on Fifth Avenue was spread, the silver was taken out of the Italian Renaissance sideboard, and the expensive salt shakers which no one dared call cellars were placed within easy reach of Fay, who could never have enough of salt in spite of her high blood pressure. In the center was a vase filled with marigolds, her favorite flower, resembling pieces of orange bath sponge.

Friday afternoon Papa and Mama climbed together into the bathtub—about the only thing they could do together without a frown from Fay—because he had to be kept from slipping and ripping his hernias again. Dressed in the clothes which they had bought for the High Holy Days, they waited for the girls to come downstairs. It was close, but they sat opposite each other as if they were caked or set in molds. The old man put his hand to his forehead and muttered, "Drops like beans." He did not rise to pull back the curtains, nets heavy enough to hold a school of fish, because Fay flew into a fury if the neighbors "looked into their mouths."

Only when the girls filed down and Fay pressed the button flooding the room with light did the old people relax. Then, as the girls seated themselves, Essie, who had been standing motionless at the door to the kitchen, stepped in with the tray. She wore a lacy apron no larger than a man's handkerchief, slippers colored like pigeons' feet, pearl-white earrings half buried by her hair, which was bleached brown and stood over her forehead in a hedge. Tall, graceful, almost white-skinned, she stepped so lightly that her footfalls could barely be heard.

Fay, who had shot sharp glances at her parents seated at each side of her, opened the letters and magazines which had been piled near her plate. Gert, generally restless and bored by all the fuss, propped up her head with her thick hands. Only Shirley, who was always unhurried, cool, spotless, gave her vague, dreamy smile and observed that Papa was probably hungry.

Without raising her eyes from her letter, Fay murmured, "Eat, eat."

They started on their fruit cocktails. With every mouthful, they swallowed every arch of her eyebrows and wrinkle of her nose, hoping that perhaps something had arrived by mail which would lift her black, bitter mood. Just last week, the dinner had turned into a storm when Gert had given it as her opinion that the only way to handle music teachers who muscle into other people's territories was for Fay to belong to the American Federation of Musicians.

Their mother kept stealing frightened glances across the table at the old man. He caught her look and gave her a reassuring nod. Her thin bloodless lips like frayed strings barely moved; she sighed, and the wrinkles grew deeper on a face that was cut like a well-used breadboard.

When Essie brought in the soup tureen and placed it before Fay, Fay asked, "Why don't you eat with us, Essie?"

The Negro woman would be uncomfortable and preferred the kitchen, but it was just like Fay to insist on having her way.

Essie hesitated.

"Set a place for yourself. I knew when I bought this tablecloth, I should have bought a sixth napkin also."

"I'll have a cup of tea."

"Good. You know you are always welcome to eat with the family."

"Thank you, Miss Fay."

"You're entirely welcome."

Mama, who had been hanging on to the conversation, blinked in bewilderment, and Papa, forgetting his manners, humped over his soup like a weary camel. Gert gave a snort. Shirley smiled vaguely through her glasses.

Essie served the beef flanken and the tea and sat down on the edge of her chair. She put her hands up to her earrings which looked like birds' eggs, and bent stiffly over her cup.

Papa couldn't control himself any longer. He said huskily, "Faygele, she sits on shpilkis."

"I know what I'm doing," pronounced Fay sternly, and then translated his Yiddish. The old man flushed behind his muzzle of a beard.

"Oh, no, Mr. Moscow," cried Essie. "I sit on no pins and needles. It's only I'm in such a blessed hurry to get home. You know my husband works nights. Oh, my, and I've got a rehearsal. Can I speak to them now, Mrs. Moscow?" And without waiting for the consent, she explained, "I told it to Mrs. Moscow a week ago, but she said it was a church."

The girls turned to Mama, who picked up her napkin and held it before her like a veil.

Fay stabbed a harsh glance at the old woman. "Speak up, Essie dear."

"It's true our church is giving it, Miss Fay, but it's not going to be held in the chapel. It will be in our auditorium. Now, what we're having," she said confidentially in her low, sweet voice, "is a song night and harvest home. We've got a good choir and wonderful solo singers, and during the intermission there's going to be a show of pictures, art work, sewing, and bake stuff members of the church is preparing. It's selling talent, that's what our pastor said. Tickets is only a dollar and a half a piece." She took four tickets out of the apron and handed them to Fay. "I know Mr. Moscow don't go out much or far. But I thought you ladies would enjoy yourselves, besides helping us. It's early next month. Besides we get prizes for the number of tickets we sell. And I do want to win a prize. Then, Miss Fay, other white folks I work for—I've told you about them, the doctor and his wife, who are from the top shelf—has bought tickets and promised to come." She had risen and paused, tall and confident. "I do know you as a music teacher and the ladies, your sisters, and your mother will have a good evening."

"We'll come," promised Fay, her grated, pock-marked face turning pink with pleasure. "And Essie, if you ever do want to do any rehearsing, don't be afraid to let me know. I can accompany you on the piano."

Essie thanked her and taking her cup of tea, turned to the kitchen.

"And if you are in a hurry, we can take care of the dishes."

Delighted, the young woman left her tea unfinished, got into her street clothes, and flew off.

As the door shut, Gert snapped, "Fay, I've told you a thousand times never to make decisions for me."

"You can skip going to that union once."

"My union is my bread, just as your music is yours."

"Are you afraid like Mama that it's a church?"

"Don't be a damned fool!"

Papa coughed behind his fingers, twisted as if they had been broken and then badly reset. "Please, children."

Fay sat stiff as a poker, her burnt-looking lips twisting around her teeth.

Gert disregarded the danger signs. "You're not the only one that's got his troubles. I got plenty in the shop, but I don't take it out on the rest of us when I get home."

"Girls, girls," begged their mother timorously.

Fay's eyes flashed. "I warned you that being the only woman in a dirty machine shop would be too much for even you. You could have come in with me, you could have been a physical education teacher."

Gert spoke slowly as if she were coating each word with lead. "Just keep your nose out of my behind."

"You with your filthy language!" Fay leaped up, jerking the table.

The horse-radish spilled, staining the turquoise green tablecloth, and as the old woman, moaning, dabbed at it with her napkin, and then became terrified as she spread the stains, Fay sailed from the room, her short, high-breasted figure swollen with rage, her hair-do high like a forecastle.

Shirley shook her head reproachfully. "Gert, you shouldn't speak that way when she isn't feeling well. You know you shouldn't." In her agitation she plucked at her full white throat, which was marked with a scar as if from a tight necklace.

"She gives me a pain with her airs. She plays the lady in front of Essie because she is a West Indian. If she were one of our Negroes from the South, she'd treat her differently."

Fay had slammed into the studio and shut the doors behind her.

The Friday evening was spoiled, and when the girls had finished eating, the old man with his hump of a nose and his great humped back and sandy face, got up quietly and began clearing the table, and the old woman rose with a groan to help him.

Shirley followed to reassure them and shoo them out of the kitchen. Gert and she would take care of everything. "Won't you, Gert?"

Gert nodded morosely.

After the girls got through with the washing and drying, Gert walked into the garden where her parents sat together on the bench. She said angrily, "Why do you look as if the world's coming to an end? So she got sore and didn't finish her supper." The sound of the piano could be heard. "The duchess!" In disgust she left her parents and walked out into the street.

She lit a cigaret, and with her hands in the pockets of her slacks, her blouse open so that her thick brown neck was exposed, she strolled past the synagogue and across the street to the tavern, which was broadcasting a ball game and where the bartender greeted her, "Hi, Gertie," and poured her a beer.

Fay left the studio after the family had gone to bed. She walked in the garden up and down the path between the fire thorns and the nightshade which her father had dug up out of a lot and transplanted, the flowers looking as if they burned tiny sulfur candles.

From the upper part of the house where Shirley and Gert shared a bedroom—Fay had her own—they could see her parading up and down in her trailing, flowered housecoat, teetering on spike-heeled slippers. Every once in a while she stopped and clenched and unclenched her fists: small-handed, finding it difficult to span C to C, she was always exercising her hands, using motions that suggested a wringing of the hands.

Shirley had undressed near the closet, standing modestly behind the door, which had a mirror. She slipped her nightgown over her soft, bulky, milk-white body. And then as she sat down to brush her hair, she murmured that Fay would be walking the garden all night long. "The neighbors—."

"To hell with the neighbors," grunted Gert. She was lying naked on her back, her short powerful arms, stained with oil blotches, were crossed under her neck. She glanced at Shirley brushing her long hair. "She's got to be told where to get off. I've taken enough from her." She yawned with a cracking of her jaws. "No wonder she could never keep a man."

"But, Gert, that's no way to talk."

"That's the only way. All you know is Fay. You've even turned Papa crazy. Because she gets mad and sits for hours chopping Chopin or prancing up and down the garden, the world ain't coming to an end. We got to live too. Maybe you ought to think about yourself for a change. She screwed up her life. All right, that's too bad. But why should you? You won't see thirty anymore, and for a girl like you marriage is the only way out. Soon you'll get overripe. You had chances but passed them by because you were afraid you were dishing Fay out. Nuts! If I were a man, I'd take you at the drop of a hat. Sure, any day in preference to Madame Chrysanthemum."

The blood flooded Shirley's face. "Gertie!" she gasped.

Gert snorted, "All you can do is squeak." She rolled over in disgust and fell asleep.

Their parents' bedroom was on the other side of the house, facing the street. The old couple in their twin beds could not compose themselves to sleep. The old woman sighed and groaned and muttered to herself. The old man got up for a drink of water, complaining that he had a sour stomach. Before he could take more than a couple of steps the old woman warned him about his hernias, and he had to lie down and put on his harness. Then, girded safely around his broken belly, he stole downstairs and opened the door carefully. He could make out nothing in the garden. There was a shelf of cloud, and finally the moon came up and hung there like a bitten bone. A bush rustled.

He retreated into the kitchen, waited for a while in the hope that Fay would stop her pacing, as if she carried her cage with her, and come to bed. In the dark he groped his way to the frigidaire and helped himself to seltzer and filled a glass for the old woman. On the way up he paused to peek into the studio. The street light slipping through the blind lit up the grand piano and the bust of Chopin. Hearing his wife's whisper at the head of the stairs, he labored up to her.

To her "Still out there?" he nodded and humped on the edge of the bed, his veiny swabs of hands on his knees. She gulped the seltzer down but that did not help. He shut the door though it was stifling hot and quietly got into bed with her. With a groan she turned to him.

They had always been close to each other. They had eaten from the same plate, slept in the same bed, and never said an ugly word to each other. All this had changed with Fay's growing up, with her persuading the girls to help her buy this house in the hope that she could establish a conservatory in it eventually, with a couple of her former students as instructors, poor substitutes for her sisters who had turned out to have no more feeling for music than hunks of wood. The house had not helped. Lately, Fay had begun losing lessons. The girls picked at one another, and to eat from the same plate and share the same bed was old-fashioned, not healthful, sinful. The old man stroked the withered, narrow shoulders.

They did not sleep all night. When the dawn was like a saucerful of milk, the door in the rear opened. There were movements in the kitchen, dining room, studio—Fay was the one who replaced the flowers in the vases, insisting that each upper room have a vase too—and at last she came up, drew a bath, and went to her room.

Reluctantly the old man crawled to the synagogue. The old woman remained, feeling guilty, having reassured him that she would be able to see to it that the girls did not get into another quarrel. Shirley, who worked half a day Saturday in the cafeteria where she was cashier, came down for her breakfast. She was followed shortly by Gert, who was going to spend the day at the union.

The old woman served both of them, almost trembling in her eagerness, afraid to speak up and yet desperate. Finally as Shirley rose, she spoke up, knowing that Shirley would support her. "Gertie, child, please try not to, try not to quarrel with Faygele. Please."

Gertie gave her a sour glance.

"Shirley, tell her it is necessary. Faygele is Faygele, but—."

Gertie grunted and lit her cigaret. "Let her keep off my back."

"Thank you, child." The old woman took Gert's head in her hands, hesitated, and kissed her on the lips.

"Why did you stop?" said Gert. "You know I never use lipstick."

Shirley beamed.

After both girls left together, the old woman sat down. She dropped her hands into her lap, the veins unravelling down her shrunken arms. She remembered with a start that she hadn't warned Gertie about smoking in the street on the Sabbath, and that she hadn't gone to the synagogue. The good Lord would understand. At least there was peace again. She dressed as if she were going out, in her white stockings and a small lace shawl, and throwing her shawl over her head in the corner of her kitchen, the shop in which she had machined her life, in which working for her family she had also labored for God, she opened her prayer book and gave a deep sigh.

At noon Fay found her in the corner praying. She leaped to her feet and was ready to prepare breakfast if Fay would light the gas, but Fay would have nothing but the juice of two lemons with a few drops of water from the tap. She drank without a grimace; her face, grated and pocked, looked like a stone in the highway. Rinsing her glass, she told her mother to continue with her prayers, and went into the studio.

At one o'clock the old man had not yet returned, and the bell rang and two of the students came in. The banging began, and one could hear Fay's harsh, impatient voice. The old woman rose from her chair, clutching the prayer book to her chest, hurried to the studio, raised her hand as if to knock at the door, reconsidered, and cried to herself, "Faygele, is that the way? You are driving them away. Soon you will be left with nothing."

After the lessons Fay got dressed and hurried off without a word, passing the old man, who was coming down the lane between the garden and the high hedges. He looked questioningly at his wife as he entered the house. She sighed. He rubbed his hands briskly. "Nu, let us have something to eat. You sit, I'll serve."

She smelled whiskey on his breath, and that added to her unhappiness. If she questioned him, he would answer that he had had a kiddush with the pious Jews, his eyes twinkling at the lie. For the truth was that he always felt more at home in the cellar of the synagogue than upstairs in the presence of God, always at ease with the janitor, a goy, a Lett of some kind, who had been a sailor and an engineman, a drunkard with a song and a story on his shaven lips.

So another week passed before Fay could spend an evening with them, and during that week the old people, helped by Shirley, used hints, persuasion, cajolery to have Gert promise she would go to the recital. The old man took her by the hand and looking into her eyes fondly said, "Remember when you helped me as a child. I had to fix something for a tenant, you went along carrying a hammer or a wrench. Fix it so you go along with Faygele," and Gert answered, "Papa, I'll fix it if there isn't something doing at the union."

And again when Friday evening came around, the old ritual took place. After the house had been dusted and washed and polished from top to bottom, the old couple took their bath together, got into their holiday clothes, and sat down in the dim room near the Italian Renaissance table. They waited patiently while the girls got washed and filed down, led by Fay, who pressed the button, flooding the room, the signal for Essie to come in with her good evening and her tray. Again Fay insisted that Essie have tea with them, which the young woman did in an embarrassed fashion, sitting in her chair as if on the edge of a knife. Once more after her first sip, she was dismissed and excused from her dishwashing when Fay remembered that she had to rush home for a rehearsal.

Only after the Negro woman had gone did the family speak up, and it was Gert who said, "Fay, you'll never learn!"

"Look who's talking. You don't care for Essie because she is cultured and light-skinned. The darker a Negro, the more Negro he is. The Negro you admire is the ignorant, dirty worker. The same with the Jew. The Jewish people can be destroyed if only a handful of Jewish workers are left. You and the workers!"

Gert saw the white, anxious faces of her parents and Shirley's plucking at her scarred throat. She contented herself with saying, "I got a close tolerance, Fay. The min. and the max. for me will always be the worker. You're damned right."

The old woman interposed, "Faygele, I like her. She is a good clean girl, but if it wasn't a church." Her eyes slid down to her worn hands. "You see, Faygele."

Fay twitched her shoulders. "But Essie said it is not being held in the church, in the chapel. In the hall there will be no crosses."

"It is a church, silly little one, and they will sing what is forbidden."

Wearily humped over his plate, the old man turned his sandy face toward her. "Why can't you go even if it is a church? A thousand churches and all the songs and dances in the world will never make you a goy. I'd go with you, but, no, I should stay home to watch the house, maybe somebody will run off with Faygele's flowers or a lesson will call up. Go with the girls. Shirley is going. Gertie also, I think." He looked appealingly at his youngest.

Gert said, "Papa, you miked me wrong. If there's nothing else doing that night, I'll go."

"See," cried the old man, brightening up, "you three will be stepping out as they say. Then go for once. See how it tastes. If you don't like it, you won't go out again. God will understand and forgive you."

"You and God. If you had spent more time in front of the Holy Ark instead of in the cellar—." The old woman stopped and faltered, "God forgive me."

The old man laughed. "Children, your mother will not stop until I become as holy as a ram's horn or the citron and the palm. The shool needed a new shamas, you know that. Your mother wanted me to apply for the job, but they picked Federbaum, a man almost my age. It is a small shool, said your mother, your friend the Lett does all the work. What does a shamas have to do? Well, when it is noisy during the prayers and the Jews let themselves go, all he has to do is bang on the table with his fists." And here the old man pounded the table the way the sexton did during prayers and bellowed, "Shah, Jews!"

As his great loose fist descended on the table, a glass of water was upset, wetting the turquoise green cloth.

"Ach." He jumped up in alarm.

"It'll dry," said Fay through tight lips.

"Fist I have," he groaned, "but where is the head?" He looked across the table. "Old woman, if only God weren't such a landlord."

Gert roared, Shirley gave her twittering laugh, while Fay patted her father patronizingly and protectively on the arm.

The old woman blinked at them like a hen at goslings whom she has reared only to have them taking to strange talk and swimming into all kinds of danger.

Gert grinned. "I suppose I can take one evening off. All right, I go."

The look of fright faded from the old face. "Thank you, child," she murmured gratefully.

Shirley threw her arms around Gert, hugged and kissed her fervently, then blushed at the excess of emotion. The last time the girls had been together for an evening had been so long ago that she could not remember; it might have been in their childhood. For once they would be together and forget all unpleasantness, strains, the fear of losing the house, the problem of Fay's dwindling students. Perhaps they could have their mother eat with them that evening, use that to draw her, but Shirley shook her head with both hands as one shakes a clock that's stopped going. The old woman wouldn't think of having a drop of water out of the fastness of her home.

Whenever the old woman was cornered and forced, her reaction was to bury herself in work. As Essie did the housecleaning and Fay frowned on her digging in the garden, all that was left for her was the cooking. She cooked huge meals, went back to the traditional Jewish dishes. Fay had been trying for years to teach her American cooking, had considered getting Essie to come in every day and do the cooking, and had given up her plan reluctantly only after Shirley had insisted that "it would kill Mama: she's got to do something." The food did not agree with Shirley either, but she was willing to burn for her mother. As for Gert, she had a stomach that could digest anything, and she was indifferent as to how or what she ate.

Fay laughed when the fat noodle soup was served.

Shirley commented that their mother was working too hard, an evening out, say, an evening listening to a little music would do her good.

"I am not working hard," protested the old woman. "You want me I should sit like a baron."

"That evening I won't come home from the synagogue. I'll eat with my friend the Lett," said the old man.

"Am I a child, afraid of mice and bears?" she cried. "You talk and talk, all of you, until I don't know in which world I am." And then she paled, frightened at the rebellion in her voice.

Fay's fork clattered on the table. The skin tightened around her nose so that it turned white. She rose and stalked into the studio.

Fortunately, a new book on Chopin had arrived in the mail. It was in Polish which she read and spoke, having picked it up as a child from the Polish families that had lived in the house where her father had been a janitor. Fay considered Chopin the greatest of all composers. She compared the original with the translation which she had drawn from the library, made notes, and as she read, the bitter expression on her grated face vanished, her lips parted, and a patch of color came to her cheeks. She did not walk in the garden all night where the neighbors could notice her. She spent the night on the book.

After this flare-up, getting the old woman to go along was given up as hopeless. The girls agreed they would meet in front of the church. Afterwards they might go out together for a bite.

The evening of the musicale Fay was the first to appear in front of the church. She wore a large straw hat, her white gloves, and was dressed in a gray suit. The doors of the church were open, people were streaming in. It was a large building, plastered with a brown stucco which was peeling in places. The grounds were covered with crab grass. The fence with its palings looked as if it had been built from the sides of dry-goods boxes. Only the cross on the bell tower seemed new and gleamed golden in the setting sun.

The girls were late. Fay walked to the corner, her hands opening and closing as if she were doing her finger exercises, and then she turned and saw Gert striding down the street, hands in the pockets of her slacks, blouse open at the neck, a cigaret in the corner of her mouth.

"Shirley hasn't showed up yet. Now that's strange." She spat out her butt, got herself another cigaret; her fingers were brown from oil and nicotine stains. She searched in her trouser pockets for matches.

Fay said in disgust, "Couldn't you have worn a dress for once? And where's the sterling silver lighter I bought you as a birthday gift?"

Gert ignored her outburst, scratched a match with her thumb, cupped her hands, puffed the smoke through her nostrils and gave the church the once over.

A "hello" sounded behind them. Behold Shirley crossing the street escorting their mother who was wearing Fay's old mushroom hat and carrying a big black pocketbook which resembled a market bag.

"How did you do it?" shouted Gert, running up to catch Shirley's hand, which she pumped vigorously. She stepped back. "Boy, what makes you look so pretty tonight?" Shirley had strands of white in her hair which matched the milk-white of her skin and her simple white dress. "You look like you've just come out of the stove, like one of Mama's old kalahs—I mean chalehs." She caught herself as she stumbled over the Yiddish for Sabbath loaf and pronounced it as though it were the word for bride. "Yes, a man could tear a piece off."

"Don't be vulgar," said Fay through her teeth. She was highly pleased, however, with her mother's coming. She examined her critically. "But, Mama, your stocking is wrinkled!"

Shirley knelt in the street and took care of the wrinkled stocking. She smiled. "I went home to get dressed. I knew then that Mama would change her mind. Something in my heart told me." She choked up. "You know this is our old neighborhood. I said to Mama maybe we would get a chance to take a walk through the streets again."

"What are we waiting for? Mama, now that you are here don't look like a kapoora hindel," said Fay.

Led by Fay, Gert and Shirley flanking their mother, they marched into the lobby. They handed their tickets to the smiling doorman, who directed them to take the stairs. Shepherding their mother as if she were under protective custody, they moved down into the hall. The old woman sat down, breathing heavily, her face assuming a wooden look.

The hall doubled as an auditorium and gymnasium. Up front there was a platform curtained off; on both sides against the walls there were cages for basketball, and several bucks and parallel bars. The chairs were folding chairs.

Fay's hooked nose with the spot on it like a grain wrinkled in disappointment. She looked sternly from under her broad-brimmed hat at the men and women filing in. They were Negroes, some of them in their work clothes. So far the girls and the old woman were the only white people present. There were tables in the rear around which there was much activity. "I wonder where Essie is. She said she'd look for us." She slipped off her gloves; her hands began their exercises.

Gert had risen to examine the apparatus against the walls. Several gangly boys were standing in back, laughing and gabbing and getting in the way of the women who were setting out cakes and preserves. Gert got into a conversation with the boys. She took out her cigarets and passed them around before returning to her seat.

The hall began filling up rapidly, but Shirley was dead to what was going on around her. Her eyes were moist, and there was a far-away look in them. "It's like—I just can't forget. Everything comes back, kids," she whispered to her sisters.

"Spare me the details," said Fay.

"What I remember is the cat smell," said Gert, turning as an usher came up to ask her please not to smoke. She crushed the cigaret between thumb and forefinger and dropped it at her feet.

The main had broken, and Shirley was being swept away, and as her sisters were little interested, she spoke to her mother. "Do you remember how we had trouble with the mice? One day you baked and Papa thought it was kimmel over your bread, but it was the mice. And Davey, he'd be twenty-five years old if he was alive, remember Davy's sickness and how they burned that sulfur candle in our two rooms in the cellar?"

Her eyes became suffused with tears, and she swallowed a sob. Fay threw her a sidelong look, and Gert muttered, "Hell, Shirley, why do you have to dig up what's best buried?"

"All right, I'll stop, but I just can't forget. I can't forget the convent across the street, the brewery down the block, and how Eve Metz, the one who had so much trouble with her family, ran into the convent and was given a home there. She became a nun. And when Mama slapped me, the only time she ever hit me, I remember it was when one of the nuns gave me a string of beads and a cross, a rosary. Do you remember, Mama?" She took the hand that had struck her and fondled it.

Her mother was looking across the aisle. There, directly opposite them, was a young Negro woman, who had just finished nursing her baby, first covering her breasts with a bandanna which her husband had given her. The rigid wooden look passed. The old woman's face seemed to loosen like a breast pulled out of a tight blouse. A gleam of understanding lit up her eyes. "Little mouse," she murmured.

A burst of applause from the audience greeted a short man who trotted up on the stage, pinching a cabbage butterfly of a bow tie and adjusting his pince-nez. This was the pastor of Essie's church. The curtain rolled up, revealing the choir, the women in white middies and black skirts, the men ranged behind them in their Sunday best.

The little pastor beamed at them and started telling the story of the preacher who, at the end of a sermon delivered to the inmates of a jail, said: "Brethren, I sure am glad to see you all here. I hope to be with you next year." As the audience laughed and clapped appreciatively, he introduced the professor who had trained the choir, a successful piano teacher, so busy that he had to turn away pupils. Essie had spoken about him to Fay.

Fay watched him intently, her eyes under her floppy hat burning in her long, caked face. For the man, big, easy, affable, at home with his people, gave his comments on the musicians with wit and humor and then turned to his choir which he conducted while he played the piano in accompaniment.

The first composer whose work was played had worked his way through college as a janitor. When she heard janitor, the old woman shook her head and sighed, remembering the gaslight fluttering all day like a rotten leaf, the bugs big as mice, the night one of the

Polish tenants went berserk with a butcher knife, and Gertie had wrestled him down and the old man had disarmed him, Gertie handling the ash cans every morning; and the time that Fay had the smallpox. . . .

"Is he a Jew, my child?" she asked as she pulled at Shirley's sleeve.

"The janitor who liked music so much?" Shirley examined the program notes and shook her head.

The old woman's shoulders sagged.

Fay reached out and straightened her mother's collar. "For God's sake don't look as stupid as a kapoora hindel. Must everybody be a Jew? Forget once you're one and it'll do your heart good. Please, do."

The old woman wrapped herself in her coat, drew a deep breath, and shut her eyes.

The music master tapped the stand with his baton. The whole audience seemed to move to the edge of their chairs when the choir rising as one burst into "Jesus Is a Rock." The Negroes in the audience—there was just a sprinkling of whites—swayed, their teeth shone, their eyes glowed. They lifted their voices ecstatically in praise of their great lord and savior.

In her bewilderment the old woman looked from one girl to the other. "What is it?" she faltered.

Shirley came out of her reverie. "That," she whispered, "is about Jesus. The music is nice. Listen to the music only. The words don't count."

The humming of the men and women in the audience grew louder, and soon the whole mass was chanting and rocking.

With a shudder the old woman pulled her mushroom hat down tight over her ears. "God punish me."

Shirley put her arms around her. "If you want to, I'll go out with you."

The old woman kneaded her hands, one in the other. "It isn't nice. In the middle of their song, you will hurt their feelings, child. Later, I'll go."

She had to sit back and reconcile herself to listening to the praises of the man in whose name a furnace of horror had been built for her people for hundreds of years.

When the chant was over, a young woman came up on the stage to recite a poem, "On with the Soul," and then the pastor's wife rendered several solos.

The intermission followed, during which Shirley sat next to her mother, her eyes dreamy and moist, the tip of her tongue caught between her full lips. Once she stirred, took out her vanity case and dusted her face, looked about her and then again was lost in the past.

Gert went outside into the street and stood with a bunch of young men at the gate, smoking and chatting. Fay teetered around like a ship with too much sail, ready to keel over any second, trying to find Essie in the press in the rear where the tables were spread with pictures, needle work, cakes and preserves, the work of members of the congregation.

When the program resumed, a slim girl rose from the first row of the choir. Miss Alberta Smith sang "Sometimes I Feel Like a Motherless Child." The simple words repeated again and again trembled in the old woman's brain like birds in a cloud. A smile moistened her eyes. A kiend oohn a mama. This she understood. And then as she turned, she saw the baby sprawling in its mother's lap, bouncing about, waving its fists.

"Talk to her, talk to the wall," was her comment. "It will make cheese in the belly."

There were a number of other songs and solos by pupils of the music master, and then the program ended.

As the audience broke into applause, down the aisle came Essie. Bright-eyed, smiling, she offered her apologies. She had looked for them, but she was one of the coffee-makers and had to go out to the store to buy more coffee. Then her little girl was sleepy, and as her husband had to go to work, she had to dash back home and have a neighbor take care of the child. "How did you like it, Mrs. Moscow?" she asked.

"About the baby without a mother, I enjoyed. It tore the heart."

"Alberta Smith was raised an orphan. That's why she sung it with so much feeling."

The old woman sighed.

As they had been seated in front, they were delayed in getting out. While they waited, several of the young men started folding up the camp chairs and stacking them against the walls. A boy in a jersey darted in with a basketball and dribbled it across the floor.

The family had stopped at the door, and suddenly Gert shot across the floor and whipped the basketball away from him. With a grin, standing in mid-court, she shot for the basket and made it. The young Negroes applauded.

"You've got a team, haven't you? Who plays center? I'll jump against him."

A gangling youngster, grinning sheepishly, came to the center; the boy in the jersey stood between Gert and him and tossed the ball. Gert had kicked off her shoes, and squatting, she leaped high, hit the ball, and then ran rings around the boys, daring them to get it away from her. Then she stood in a circle with them and several others and passed the ball, whipping it hard, hitting them in the stomach.

Many of the audience stopped to laugh and nod their heads in approval. She got into her shoes and walked to the family, having worked up a sweat.

In the lobby stood the pastor with the straining little white bow tie, greeting his parishioners and their guests. Shirley smiled and the pastor shook hands cordially with her. The old woman looked on as if she were drugged and failed to acknowledge his bow.

In her halting fashion, Shirley explained, "We are Jewish people, sir. Essie Jones, one of your children, sold us the tickets. We've had a wonderful time, sir. I don't remember your church being in this neighborhood when we lived here more than twenty years ago. I remember when the first Negro family moved in. I—." She saw the expression in Fay's face and, becoming embarrassed, hesitated before adding, "We want to thank you for an enjoyable evening."

The pastor bowed. "Thank you, thank you kindly, ma'am. Or is it miss?"

"You missed," said Gert. "We are all misses or near misses."

Out in the street Fay exploded. "Why did you have to say we are Jewish in such an apologetic way?"

"But I didn't, Fay," cried Shirley, blinking.

"What difference does it make what we are? And then 'Essie Jones, one of your children.' "

"If they call the priests fathers, are not the people children?" asked Shirley defensively.

The two continued walking toward the subway, Shirley trying to placate Fay. Some steps behind, guiding the little old woman, walked Gert, a cigaret in the corner of her lips, pleased by the way she had played rings around the boys.

Fay recovered her temper. She stopped in front of a restaurant. It was much too hot to eat dinner, but they could probably get frappes here; the treat would be on her.

Her mother said quickly, "This must be goyisch, Faygele."

"Mama, we'll order only frappes. Ice cream is ice cream."

The old woman looked doubtfully at her.

"I'm sick of this. This stinginess, this Jewishness is driving me crazy," she shrilled. "There isn't one minute we can get away from it. Haven't I had enough?" She brought her fist down hard on her bag and began beating it.

The old woman gasped and fell back a step.

Shirley chased after Fay, who had turned back and was heading wildly in the direction of the church.

"Mama," cried Gert, "you shouldn't have said anything to her. Don't you know her by this time?"

Shirley began calling from down the street. "I can't hold her, Gert. Help, Gert."

Gert raced up. "Snap out of it. Quick," she said sternly. She whipped her fingers across Fay's face and put her arms around her.

Caught in those strong arms, Fay buried her head against Gert's shoulder. Spasm after spasm shook her.

A taxi sped by. Gert put her fingers into her mouth and whistled shrilly. The driver swung around, stopped at the curb, looked curiously at them, and reaching out, opened the door. "Sick?" He nodded at Fay, who, head bent, got in first.

"Faygele, Faygele," whispered her mother fearfully.

Fay huddled in the corner.

The taxi lurched and went on.

"Faygele, child, you'll catch cold near the window. It is open."

Her jaw rigid, Fay moved closer to the window.

Shirley gave a guilty smile, touched the mushroom hat, patted the pocketbook which looked like a market bag. "Tell me, honest to God, Mama, how you liked it all, the whole thing, the being away from the pots one night."

Her mother's answer was a stifled sigh.

"Yes, Mama?"

The taxi stopped for a traffic light.

Gert spoke up in her husky voice. "How are you men doing these days?"

"It's a dog's life," said the driver without turning around.

"So geschaft's no good."

"Ulcers you get." The taxi shot ahead.

Even Gert did not have the heart to question him further, and again there was silence.

At last the old woman ventured timidly, apologetically like the kapoora hindel that she was. "The music was nice, children. Essie and her friends, they are good people." But before she could help it, out slipped, "But as I told you, it is a church."

"It's a taxicab," said Fay between tight jaws.

Shirley gave a nervous giggle. "Yes, Mama, the music is nice. The words don't mean anything. Listen." In her sweet voice breathlessly, she started singing one of the spirituals.

Gert stared at her, and then in her monotone, off key, she joined her, pounding at it, her stocky body behind it.

Fay turned away and stuffed her handkerchief between her teeth. And on the other side of the cab sat the old woman, her mouth open, no sound issuing, the mushroom hat bobbing over the dead wood of her face.

John J. Clayton

Cambridge Is Sinking!

The Sunday night telephone call from Steve's parents: his mother sorrowed that such an educated boy couldn't find a job. She suggested kelp and brewer's yeast. His father told him, "What kind of economics did you study, so when I ask for the names of some stocks, which ones should I buy, you can't tell me?"

"It's true, Dad."

George rolled a joint and handed it to Steve. Steve shook his head. "But thanks anyway," he said to George, hand covering the phone.

"Man, you're becoming a Puritan," George said.

"Stevie, you're getting to be practically a vagrant," his father sighed.

Susan kissed him in a rush on the way out to her support meeting. Where was *his* support meeting? He closed his eyes and floated downstream. "Goodby, baby."

A one-eyed cat pounced from cushion to cushion along the floor. He hooked his claws into the Indian bedspreads that were the flowing walls of the livingroom. The cat floated, purring, until Steve yelled—

"Che! For Christsakes!"—and Che leaped off a gold flower into the lifeboat. It wasn't a lifeboat; really an inflated surplus raft of rubberized canvas; it floated in the lagoon of a Cambridge livingroom. It was Steve who nicknamed it the Lifeboat and christened it with a quart of beer.

Steve scratched the cat's ears and seduced him into his lap under

Section 4 of the Sunday New York *Times:* The Week in Review. Burrowing underneath, Che bulged out Nixon's smiling face into a mask. Che made a rough sea out of Wages and Prices, Law and Order, Education. Steve stopped trying to read.

The *Times* on a Sunday! Travel and Resorts. *Voilà!* A Guide to Gold in the Hills of France. Arts and Leisure. Business and Finance. Sports. Remember sports? My God. It was clear something was over.

All these years the New York *Times* was going on, not just a thing to clip articles from for a movement newspaper, but a thing people read. Truly, there were people who went to Broadway shows on the advice of Clive Barnes and Walter Kerr, who examined the rise and fall of mutual funds, who attended and supported the college and church of their choice, who visited Bermuda on an eight-day package plan, who discussed cybernetics and school architecture. People who had never had a second-hand millennial notion of where we were heading—only a vague anger and uneasiness.

Steve tried to telepathize all this to Che under the newspaper blanket: Che, it's over. Hey. John is making films, Fred lives with eight other people on a farm. But it isn't a *commune,* whatever that was. The experiment is over.

Look: when Nancy cleared out of the apartment with her stash of acid and peyote and speed and hash after being released from Mass Mental, cleared out and went home to Connecticut; when trippy Phil decided to campaign for George McGovern and nobody laughed; when the *Rolling Stone* subscription ran out; when Steve himself stopped buying the *Liberated Guardian* or worrying about its differences from the regular *Guardian;* when George—when *George*—stopped doing acid and got into a heavy wordless depression that he dulled with bottle after bottle of Tavola—and said he'd stop drinking "soon—and maybe get into yoga or a school thing"—something was finished, over.

Che purred.

The lifeboat floated like a bright orange H.M.S. Queen Elizabeth sofa in the middle of the sunset floor. Steve sat in the lifeboat on one of the inflated cushions reading Arts and Leisure and listening to Ray Charles through the wall of George's room. As long as it was Ray Charles he didn't bother to drown it out with the livingroom stereo. As if he had the energy. He sipped cranberry juice out of an Ocean Spray bottle and looked through this newspaper of strange science fiction planet aha.

Ray Charles whined to dead stop in mid-song. George stood in the doorway and stood there with something to say and stood there and waited.

"Come aboard. I'm liking this old boat better and better."

George: hippo body, leonine face with a wild red mane. He ignored the boat. "Steve, I'm going back to school."

"School? To do what?"

"Get a masters."

"What in?"

"I haven't got that far yet. I'll let you know." The door closed. Ray Charles started up from where he left off.

Steve smiled. He stretched out in the lifeboat and let it float him downstream. They came to a rapids, he and Che and the New York *Times,* and he began negotiating the white water. George. George: school? Well why not.

George. One day last year when George was tripping he found his Harvard diploma in the trunk under his bed: he ripped it into a lot of pieces and burned—or began to burn—the pieces one by one. But halfway through he chickened out and spent the rest of his trip on his knees staring into the jigsaw fragments as if they were the entrails of Homeric birds, *telling him something.* Yesterday, when Steve went into his room to retrieve his bathrobe, he found the fragments glued onto oak tag: half a B.A. on the wall. Nothing else was any different: unmade bed, unread books, undressed George, sacked out in the bathrobe. Steve burned a wooden match and with the cooled char wrote R.I.P. on George's forehead. George did.

Susan was gone for hours. Sunday night. Steve sat crosslegged in his lifeboat and made up lists on 3 x 5 cards.

It was a joke that began when he was doing his honors thesis at Harvard. On the backs of throwaway 3 x 5's he'd write

> B-214:
> Steve Kalman cites Marx—18th Brumaire—
> "Peasants shld be led into socialism
> by being asked to do housecleaning once a week."

He'd tape that to the bathroom mirror so the early morning peasants, recovering from dope and alcohol and speed, could hate him and get some adrenalin working. It was therapeutic.

Now the lists were different:

B-307:
Steve Kalman tells us in his definitive
work on Engels' late period:
a) learn karate
b) practice abdominal breathing while making love
c) read Marx' *Grundrisse*
d) read something through to the last page
e) "Be modest and prudent, guard against arrogance and rashness, and serve the . . . people heart and soul" (Mao)
f) specifically: fight racism, sexism, exploitation (whew!)
g) practice revolution

When he felt it might be necessary to do something about an item on the list, he closed his eyes and meditated. Words sneaked in: what he might have said to Susan, what was the shortest route to Harvard Square, would he see his guru face to face the way Sam said he had, how many gallons would it take to do the kitchen. Aach, you should just get into the waiting, into this time without political meetings or leafletting at factory gates. Get into something.

In his mind's eye Steve saw Susan's face. All right, she wasn't Beatrice or Shri Krishna. But who was, nowadays?

SHE CAME IN late from her support group; Steve was in a gloomy half-sleep. She curled up behind him and touched her lips to the baby hairs on his back. He grunted and turned around: "And that's another thing—" he kissed her cheek, her nipple.

"What's another thing?"

"Your other nipple." Which he addressed himself to. "Listen. You come home after an exciting day at work while I've just swept the floors and wiped up the children's doodoo. Then you, you want to make love."

She held the cheeks of his ass and pressed him against her. They kissed. "Stephen, I don't have what you just said quite figured out, but I think you're making a sexist comment."

"Sexist? What sexist? I envy you your support group. You leave me nothing but the lifeboat and Chairman Mao."

"And a couple of years ago you'd have been up all night hammering out a 'position.' I think you're better off."

"We make love more, for sure."

"Let's make love, Steve."

And they did.

"Let's get out of Cambridge before it sinks. Cambridge is sinking."

Susan played with his curly black hair and beard, a Cambridge Dionysus. "You're silly. Cambridge is built on money. There are new banks all over the place."

"Then it's *us* who are sinking. We've got a lifeboat, let's go."

"Go where?"

"How about British Columbia? They need teachers. Or northern Ontario?"

"You'll get a lot of political thinking done up there."

"In exile? Look at Ho Chi Minh. Look at Lenin."

"Oh, baby. They were connected to a party."

"I love you. You're right. Let's go to Quebec and get away from politics."

"Away from politics? Quebec?"

"To Ontario."

"But baby, you're away from 'politics' right here. That's what you're complaining about."

"But Cambridge is sinking."

At night in bed it was funny and they had each other. But daytime after they breakfasted and kissed goodby and Susan would go off to teach her fourth grade class and Steve would go off to the library to read Trotsky or Ian Fleming or he'd sub at a Cambridge junior high and sit dully in the faculty lounge waiting for his class to begin, then he'd think again, like the words of an irritating jingle that wouldn't stay quiet, about whether to go on for his doctorate in sociology so he could be unemployed as a PhD instead of unemployed as an MA.

SUSAN WAS OFF at work. Steve washed the dishes this morning. MA. PhD. The dishes. If you called it karma yoga it was better than dishwashing. But he envied Susan her nine-year olds, even if she were being paid to socialize them into a society with no meaningful work, a society which—*watch it:* do the dishes and stop the words.

He did the dishes—then spent the rest of the morning at Widener Library reading Mao's "On Contradictions."

He was to meet George for lunch. On his way Jeff Segal passed him a leaflet without looking up.

> The press loves to boast that the student movement is dead. It's alive and fighting back. And SDS is in the forefront of that fight. . . .

My God—SDS. (Which meant, in fact, PL.) Well, Steve felt happy that somebody considered themselves a Movement, even a handful of people using the rhetoric of 1950's ad men.

Steve passed through Harvard Square—past the straight-looking Jesus freaks and the bald Krishna freaks dancing in their saffron or white sheets and their insulated rubber boots. In the corner news store, across from the kiosk (Steve remembered when they "took" the Square and people got up on the kiosk and the cops came. So the freaks charged off in all directions busting windows—called *liberating the Square*—while he, Steve, who'd helped organize the march and rally, walked quietly away)—in the corner news and magazine store there was George reading the sex books at the rear of the store.

"Hey, George!"

They got out into the street and stood blinking at the noon light like a couple of junkies oozing out of a basement. George took out from his army coat lining the copy of *Fusion* he'd ripped off. He thumbed through the record reviews and he headed down Boylston to Minute Man Radio. "You stay here, Steve. I know what you think about my ripping off."

Steve watched the young women of Cambridge pass. A lot of fine lunchtime arrogance that he delighted in; but, he considered, not a hell of a lot in their eyes to back it up. One blonde on the other side of Boylston, tall, with a strong walk and no-bullshit eyes: Steve fell in love with her right away and they started living together but she had kids and he didn't get it on with them and she had perverse tastes in bed and didn't understand politics so by the time she actually crossed the street and passed by they'd separated it was too bad but anyway there was Susan to think of and so on. But they smiled at each other. Then George came out with Bob Dylan—*Greatest Hits Volume II* and showed it to Steve when they'd sat down for lunch.

They ate in the Française under the painted pipes, ate their good quiche and drank French coffee. "George, I think this is a Hemingway memoir. I'm feeling nostalgia for this place while I'm still here. That's bad.

"I wonder where I'm going, George. . . .

"I can't be Raskolnikov, George, as long as I can afford quiche for lunch. But it's the direction things are moving."

George ran his thick fingers through his wild red mane. "Not me. I decided. I don't want to be a casualty. I'm getting my MA in English and moving into a publishing house. I've got an uncle."

"Could you get your uncle to help you get your room cleaned up?"

"It's a pretty hip publishing house."

"I bet, George, that they make their profits off only the most freaky books."

"What's wrong with you, anyway?"

Steve bought George an espresso. "Here. Forgive me. This is so I can take our lunch off my taxes. I'm organizing you into our new revolutionary party."

"You couldn't organize your ass, lately."

Steve agreed. "I'm into getting my internal organs to communicate. I'm establishing dialogue at all levels."

After lunch Steve called Susan in the teachers' lounge at her school. "Hello, baby? Cambridge is collapsing."

"Love, I can't do anything about that. 31 kids is all I can handle."

"Pretend I'm a reporter from the *Times* and you're a terrific genius. 'Tell me, Miss French, how did you get to be such a terrific genius? I mean, here the city is falling down and nobody can stop snorting coke long enough to shore up a building, and here you are helping 31 human kids to survive. How, how, how, Miss French?' "

"Steve, you know better, you nut."

"Steve knows what he knows; me, I'm a reporter."

"Well," she cleared her throat, "I take vitamins, and I make love a lot with my friend Steve. And I ask his advice—"

"Ha! Fat chance!"

"—and I owe it to my sisters in the women's movement."

Steve didn't laugh. "It's true, it's true. Ah, anyway, love, I miss you."

Steve went up to the raised desk at the Booksmith on Brattle Street to ask the manager whether the one volume reduction of Marx' *Grundrisse* was out in paper. The "manager"—long mustachios and shaggy hair like a riverboat gambler, $50 boots up on the desk where they could make a *statement*—aha, it turned out to be Phil. Hey, Phil.

Phil looked down from the counter, stopped picking his Mississippi teeth and grinned. "I've been meaning to stop by, Steve. You didn't know I had this gig, huh?"

"It's good to see you."

"Sure. I watch the motherfuckers on my closed circuit swivel-eye TV set-up, dig it, and I check out the Square when things are slow. It's okay. I'm learning. In a couple of months I'm going out to Brattleboro, open a bookstore. A hip, a very hip bookstore."

"In Vermont?"

"There's a whole lot of freaks in Vermont."

"You doing a movement bookstore?"

Phil began picking his teeth like waiting to look at his hole card. Grinned his riverboat grin. "My uncle's setting me up, Steve. I want to make bread, man. As much as I can make in two, three years, and then I'll sell and split for someplace."

"Where?" Steve played at *naif* to Phil's heavy hipoisie.

"Lots of time to work that one out."

Steve forgot to ask about Marx. But Marx was all right. He found a *Capital* and when the camera had swiveled away, he slipped it into his bookbag. Then a Debray. A Che. Mao's *Quotations*. A Kropotkin. Into the lining of his Air Force parka. If Phil noticed, he didn't say. They grinned hip gambler grins at one another and Phil said, "Later, Steve."

MARX, MAO, CHE, Debray, and Kropotkin. A complete infield, including catcher.

Steve pitched his winnings out of his lining, into the lifeboat.

"*You,* Steve?"

"Everybody's got an uncle, George. Wow. I remember Phil when we took the administration building. He was up on a car that night doing a Mario Savio. And now—" Steve told George about the *very* hip bookstore in Brattleboro.

"Everybody's got an uncle, huh?" George grunted. "And you're pure, huh?" He assimilated it into his computer; it fit. He swallowed once, then his massive moon face framed by red solar fire, his face relaxed. He went back to his room. Steve considered tacking up a 3 x 5 sign over the doorway: The Bestiary. Today he was a wall-eyed computer. Yesterday George was a griffin. Tomorrow he could expect a drunken red-haired cyclops.

What animal was Steve? Steve was *existentialops meshugenah.* Nearly extinct, thank God. Little survival value. Never looked down at the ground. Every bush a metaphor. Can't go for a picnic on a hillside without watching for a lion, a wolf, and a leopard.

He shrugged. Ask Chairman Mao. He opened the *Red Book* at random:

> We should rid our ranks of all impotent thinking. All views that overestimate the strength of the enemy and underestimate the strength of the people are wrong.

Good advice. But, plagued by impotent thinking, he climbed into the lifeboat and hugged his knees and sulked. He sat there till George, hammering up another picture on his wall, got to him. "George, will you cool it? Cool it, George. I'm miserable. The sky's falling down."

He tossed Mao aft in the boat, fitted real oars to the real oarlocks, and began to row in the imaginary water. It was smoother and easier than in real water—there was no struggle, and so, no forward motion. All things proceed by contraries. Blake or Heraclitus or Hegel or Marx. He rowed.

He rowed. Aha! It began to make sense. He was expressing precisely the "contraries" he felt in this year of the Nixon: him pushing, nothing pushing back but hot air from the radiators.

So. He closed his eyes. There was a forest on both sides. Tactical Police were utterly lost in the woods. Maybe it was a beer commercial. Inside his head Steve did up a joint and floated, eyes closed. The Tactical Police were stoned. Then he turned inside out and floated into a deep jungle world. There was a fat parrot with iridescent yellow and green, red and blue wing feathers. It was as big as a tiger.

George had a real parrot in his room, and it was the only thing George took care of. Including George. It wasn't very beautiful, certainly not iridescent or big as a tiger. It liked dope, ice cream, and Cream of Wheat. Like George. But now Steve floated while a very different bird floated overhead like a bubble or helium-filled crystal ball. He watched for the Good Witch of the West. Or for the Wizard of the East. But before any such visitation, he fell asleep.

Cambridge is a lie. Doesn't exist never existed. I am in my cups. The moon a cracked saucer. We are hardly acquainted.

In the graveyard of the Unitarian Church, sixteen-year old runaways slept, dreaming of breasts with amphetamine nipples. They are all the time tired. Cats prowl the graveyard lean and angry. They suck blood and fly moon-wards. The Unitarians under ground are coughing uneasily. They are pressed down by the weight.

He woke up. He pretended it was a Caribbean cruise, this was the ship's boat, his jeans were a dinner jacket and tuxedo trousers. Susan was off to the captain's table getting champagne cocktails.

When she came back they walked through the Square arm in arm with champagne glasses and a bottle of Mumm's. It was spring, they kissed in front of a Bogart poster and poured more champagne for a toast. The Beatles were on again at the Brattle. There was nobody else in the theatre. All the psychedelic flowers were fading, wilting dingy, like the murals on WPA post office walls. The submarine had faded to a rusty chartreuse. Steve remembered when it was bright yellow and Lucy looked just like an acid lady. You used to get stoned or drop acid and get into the colors.

The lifeboat was getting full. Harpo was asleep on a raccoon coat, and George and his girl, very stoned, were examining a wind-up see-through clock they'd ripped off at DR. Steve could hardly spread out his newspaper. It was a rush-hour subway except everybody had suitcases and guitars with them. "Is this the way to Charles Street?" The sign over the door said DORCHESTER.

They held on and on, the subway was behaving like a bad little boy they were disappointed and wrote a strong note home but his government didn't reply. They floated through Cambridge trying to find the exit. They shouted FIRE! but it wasn't a crowded theatre, and so they were stuck, everyone with their own suitcase and their own piece of the action.

Susan's key turned in the lock.

"Susan—hey, Susan! Let's go get dinner!"

THE NEIGHBORHOOD FOOD cooperative operated out of Ellen's apartment. Her twins crawled among the market boxes and noshed grapes. "Stop noshing grapes!" Ellen warned. Susan put an Angela Davis defense petition on the table for coop members to sign.

Chairman Mao sat crosslegged on a cushion slicing a California avocado with his pocket knife. He ate slice after slice of the creamy green fruit.

Coop members started arriving to pick up their orders. 23 member households came in; only five ordered Angela Davis. Steve threw up his hands: "Dare to struggle, dare to win!" Chairman Mao shrugged sympathetically. He'd had trouble of his own with Cambridge intellectual types. Ellen hugged her twins and said, "But it's people that count, not politics." She put a Paul Klee on the stereo and recited W. B. Yeats.

Early spring. Cambridge. Torpor, confusion, scattered energies. A return to sanity was advertised in *Life* and in the little magazines. Aha, you mean sanity's *in* again. Okay! The art show Steve and Susan took in after dinner so they could drink free wine and hold hands, it was all giant realistic figures and giant, colorful geometrics. He could imagine them in the lobby of the new, sane, John Hancock Building. They said EXPENSIVE, CAREFUL, INTELLIGENT, PURPOSEFUL, SERIOUS; but HIP. And look at the long hair on the doctors and PR men at the opening. Everyone was hip.

"They're into patchuli oil on their genitalia for sure!"

"Who're you kidding?" Susan laughed. "You don't want to see paintings, you came to kvetch. You're a silly man. I want a Baskin & Robbins ice cream cone. And I'm willing to buy one for you, too."

"You're throwing your wealth up to me."

"Well," Susan sighed, and took his arm like a lady, "some of us have firm positions in the world. Only Harvard Square trash does substitute teaching. This is a free country. Anyone with a little guts and brains and in-i-sha-tiff—"

"All right, I want an ice cream cone." He stopped and right there on Mass Avenue kissed her, because she was so fine, because her tight jeans made him want to rub her thighs, because she kept him going through the foolishness.

They walked by the Charles River with their bridges burned behind them. There was nothing but to shrug. An invisible demonstration passed them from 1969 waving red and black flags and shouting old slogans. So they marched too. Steve lifted a revolutionary fist and shouted, "Take Harvard!" Susan said he sounded like a Princeton fan from the 50's.

"In the 50's I was a kid waiting for someone to push a button and end my having to go to school. I wouldn't blow up: just my school. The walls. Then in the 60's I expected us to tear down the walls."

"Well?"

"Now? Ah, Susan, where will we end up?"

"In a clock factory?"

On the other side of the river the business students stood by the bank with almost long hair and fat empty pockets. They bought and sold dope and sincere greeting cards with pictures of couples walking almost naked by the edge of the sea. Since the bridges were burned, Steve could yell, "You think you smell any sweeter, baby?" The business majors at the bank ignored them. When they had their stock options, where would Susan and Steve be? In the bathtub making love? In their lifeboat on a stream in British Columbia trying to locate the Source?

They wanted to make love, so they went back to their lifeboat and opened a bottle of cheap champagne. "What should we toast?" she asked.

"The river that gets us out of here?"

Steve made love with Susan on a quilt in the bottom of the rubber boat, a raft made for saving downed fliers.

TUESDAY AT LUNCH George and Steve spent a bottle of beer mourning the casualties.

"I decided again this morning," George said. "Not to be a casualty."

"Terrific."

"It's been a war of attrition. You know, 'I have seen the best minds of my generation . . . '"

"And some of the worst," Steve said.

"Sure. But like last night. Lynne came in to crash at 2 A.M. She didn't want to ball, just have a place. I think Paul kicked her out. This morning I woke up to the smell of dope, and she was getting sexed up and so we balled, but she didn't even know I was here. I can't get into that sickness anymore."

"Well," Steve said, "afterwards Lynne came into the kitchen, you were still in bed, Susan was off at work. We had coffee. I asked about her children. Her mother is still taking care of them. 'But I'm really together, Steve.' She's told me that about three times this past year. 'I couldn't stay in that hospital; nobody knew anything about where I was coming from. My *supposed* therapist had never done acid, but he's telling me about drugs. But anyway, they detoxified me. Cleaned me out.'

"I asked her how much she'd been doing. 'Wow, too much,' she said. 'I was exploring heavy things, I was deep into myself. But back-to-back acid trips . . . Too much. I think the hospital was good. But this psychiatrist with long hair, you know? . . . About my father.' Her voice started fading out. 'I had to split. I had to get back to my kids. . . . ' So she signed herself out.

"I reminisced about her kids—one day Susan and I took Lynne and the kids out to the Children's Zoo. So I was blabbing and fixing coffee, I turned around, and Lynne was doing up a joint, and her clear blue eyes were really spaced out. She was fingering Nancy's old flute, recorder really, and she was talking to it: 'This side is blue, is Hegel, and the lower register is red, is Marx. The point is to listen down into the tone of God. Otherwise you're condemned to repeat the cycle.'

"I gave her a kiss on the cheek and went back to my lifeboat to read. I understand you about casualties, George."

The casualties. And what about Lynne's two little girls? Today Nixon was on TV from Mars. He toasted a new "long march" of the American and Martian people. Two years ago we thought it was all set to autodestruct: General Murders and Lying Johnson and Noxious Trixter and Spirococcus Agony and the Chase Banana Bank. Now we're out looking for jobs. Peter, who put me down for getting a degree. Offered a job at Michigan if he'd finish his dissertation. He refused, lived on welfare and organized at factory gates. Now he's still on welfare, but there's hardly a movement to support him. Two years ago he was right. Now he's another kind of casualty.

The bridge is burning while we stand in the middle. Our long hair is burning, wild and beautiful. We are the work of art we never had time to make.

I don't want to be a casualty.

FEELING RESTLESS, UNEASY, he sat crosslegged on a pillow in the orange boat. He tried paddling down a magic river of umbrella trees, giraffes with french horn necks, a translucent lady with hummingbirds flying out of her third eye. But the film kept breaking. To placate him or perhaps to make things more difficult, the projectionist flashed a scene out of his childhood: floating on a black rubber tube, a towel wrapped around the valve like the bathing suit that sheltered his own penis. He floated safe and self-sufficiently past the breaker rocks. Where nobody could touch him. Meanwhile his mother stood by the edge of the ocean waving a red kerchief she pulled out of the cleft between her heavy breasts. She called and called, she tried to interest the lifeguard in his case. Steve's lips and ears were sealed.

Steve opened his eyes. They burned a little from salt water although he was 24 years old, although this was a make-believe boat, a livingroom prop. He felt like a shmuck. Chairman Mao's face was red.

He didn't close his eyes again. "Hey, George? George!"

"I'm doing up a joint," George said from the other room. Then he came in and lit up. "Want a toke?"

"Listen, George—"

"I'm gonna get stoned and then get my room clean. Clean."

"George, first, come with me for a couple of hours. We'll wash our sins away in the tide."

They lifted the inflated rubber boat onto their heads like dislocated duck hunters. Through the french doors to the balcony, then by rope to the back yard. Steve lashed it to the top of George's '59 Cadillac. He wore a red blanket pinned at the collar, Indian style.

At the Harvard crew house they put the boat in the water and pushed off into the Charles. Metaphor of Indian so long ago no Prudential Center or Georgian architecture of Harvard. Nice to push off into the river wrapped in such a metaphor. But today there was oil and dirt on the surface of the Charles; perch, hypnotized or drugged, maintained freedom of consciousness by meditating on their own motion. Even the fish with hooks in their mouths were contemplating their Being and harking to a different drummer. That's all more metaphor, too, for who would go fishing in the Charles? Steve played a rinky-dink tune to the fish on Nancy's recorder, but they turned belly up and became free of their bodies and of the river. The smell was nasty.

George said he felt like Huck Finn. Steve thought that was possible. They floated under the Harvard footbridge and past the site of the future water purification plant to the River Street Bridge. Stench of traffic and COCA-COLA in two-story letters. The river curved. "I can see myself as Tom Sawyer," Steve said. "For me it wasn't quite real, getting Jim out of slavery. I always figured on Aunt Sally's investment firm to settle down into. But for you, George, it was a real plunge. You almost didn't come back out. You were almost a shaman who didn't return."

"What are you saying, you crazy fool?"

"We must steer the boat. Susan's school is by the left bank. She'll be getting out in fifteen minutes."

Kids in the playground on the other side of Memorial Drive waved at the young man in the bright red blanket. Steve leaned over the chain link fence: "Peace to white and black brothers," he said, spreading his arms. "Tell Princess Afterglow we have come." George and a small boy tossed a ball back and forth over the fence.

"You're silly," a little boy told the Indian.

"Call Miss French. Ask Mis French to come down to the fence."

Miss French came down to the fence. Two little girls held her hands as they led her to the fence. She laughed and laughed and gestured *ten minutes* with her fingers.

George took up the recorder. It squeaked. "Steve. Those kids. That's where it's at."

"George, I don't believe you said that. Listen, George. I may dig being crazy or playing at being a child, but I can tell you that won't save me. Or being a freak. Or being an Indian. Metaphor won't save me. I got to save my own ass, so to speak. I mean, it's not any kind of revolution to float down the Charles in an orange boat."

"It was your idea. And who's talking about revolution? You're getting incredibly straight."

"And there—see—you can't make it on categories like straight. It's all over—the time you could think of *them* as bread and wine. So everything turns to shit in your mouth. Is bound to." He tugged at George's matted hair. "Except I don't feel like that this afternoon. I feel pretty manic and joyful."

Susan leaned against her bookbag in the stern and stretched back, her face parallel to the sky, and took it all in.

"Just smell this water. Don't let's fall in, friends," Susan said. "We'd be pickled in a minute."

They paddled upstream towards Harvard. Downstream, upstream. Circle-line sightseeing: on your right is Stop and Cop, and the Robert Hall Big Man Shop. Fer you, George. Harvard crews raced each other towards the lifeboat; alongside was the coach's motor launch. The coach, in trenchcoat, scarf trailing crimson in the wind, stood droning into a bullhorn. For a second Married Students' Housing was upside down in the water; then a gust of wind shattered it into an impressionist canvas.

The shells raced by and the orange lifeboat rocked in their wake and in the wake of the launch. They shared an apple left over from Susan's lunch and didn't fight the rocking.

They rowed. They were rowing home. Home because

The cat has to be fed.
And the parrot.
Because we are hungry and
the place needs to be cleaned up bad.
There are lots of books at home, and a telephone.
Home doesn't smell as bad as this river.

No wild crowds on shore cheered this. From the footbridge no Radcliffe girls dropped white roses on their heads. Farther on, even more to the point, no marchers cheered them with raised fists, with red flags in the spring breeze, with a bullhorn dropped down off the Anderson Bridge so that Steve and Susan and George could address the crowd:

"Well, it's been a terrific five years. We've all learned how to make love and posters. We can really get into the here and now at times and we've learned to respect our fantasies. Yum yum. We're glad to be going home. We hope to see all the old faces tomorrow right after the revolution is over so we can clean up the paper we dropped."

After this didn't happen they paddled up Memorial Drive some more. The gulls were fishing. The shells raced past them going the other way and they rocked and bobbed, like a floater for fish. They sang,

Fish on a line
all strung out
If I cry the moon will go away.
Are you with me?
Plenty of conditions
Sold by the millions
Nice to tell you
can't hold water.

They drew pictures of fish in the water like visible ink to be recovered later and read.

"We can't get anywhere this way," Steve said.

"Just float, man. The trouble with you is you never learned to float." George shrugged and reversed his oar, so the boat circled after itself like a dog after tail, like Paulo and Francesca. Infinite longing unsatisfied. But this was merely parody. George knew better than to long. The river stank but he had a cold. Steve and Susan were kissing on the bottom of the boat. Who knows how this fairy tale goes?

Why are the bridges all falling down? Why are the boats floating against bars of ivory soap and turning over? It doesn't matter how the words go. They wound me up and didn't give me directions, Steve groaned, playing wind-up toy. But when he finished kissing his friend Susan, he took up paddle and coaxed George into rowing upstream past Harvard to the boathouse.

STEVE—OH GOD STEVE YOU'VE GOT TO STOP TORCHER-EENG YRSELF, Steve decided painfully. CHINA WASN'T BUILT IN A DAY. Steve closed his eyes and meditated, crosslegged in the wet lifeboat, on the career of Mao Tse Tung.

Susan and George carried in a brass tray with what was left of the champagne. But Steve was meditating.

"Join us, why don't you? We've got some heavy pazoola here on a fancy gold tray," George like a six foot three red-haired genie wheedled. "Cut the meditating."

"Who's meditating? I'm telephoning Mao Tse Tung in Peking. *Hello, Peking?*"

"Well, tell us what he says."

Chairman Mao, Chairman Mao, Steve said inside his head. Tell us what we can do in this year of the Nixon.

Ah, yes, Mister Nixon. . . .

It's been a long winter, Chairman Mao.

With no leaves on the trees, the wind shrieks; when leaves fill the branches, the wind rustles.

I think, Steve said, inside his head, I get what you mean.

The important thing, Chairman Mao said, is to get outside your head. Open your eyes. What do you see?

The rubberized canvas sides of my orange raft and a print of

Primavera on my wall. My friends are offering me champagne on a gold tray. A brass tray to be exact.

Chairman Mao supposed a difficulty in translation. You, you behave like a blind man groping for fish. Open your eyes. Study conditions conscientiously. Proceed from objective reality and not from subjective wishes. Conclusions invariably come after investigation, and not before. Open your eyes.

"Open your eyes and your mouth," Susan said. "Here it comes." She tilted a glass of champagne to his lips.

"Well, nobody can say those are elitist grapes. Those are the people's grapes," Steve said, pursing his mouth.

"Connoisseur! Drink up!"

Picking up the pieces. Picking up the check. Somebody got to pay before we split and all them lights go out. Ah, well, but it's time to clean up and start almost from scratch.

Susan and Steve helped George clean up his room: Two green plastic trash bags full of wine bottles and dustballs, moulding plates of spaghetti, old *Rolling Stones,* socks with cat spray, insulating felt strips chewed up by the parrot, Kleenex and Tampax and a cracked copy of Bob Dylan's *Greatest Hits Volume I* and a few cracked *ands* that broke open like milkweed pods and had to be vacuumed up in a search and destroy operation.

When George's room was swept and scrubbed, George decided to wash away the Charles River effluvium in the bathtub. So Steve and Susan sat crosslegged in the bottom of the lifeboat. Wiped out.

Then Steve pulled the plug. The boat hissed disapproval, deflated, expired. They were sitting in their own space, for better or worse.

Clara Winston

A Lovely Day

"Outing, Raymie," Mother said tantalizingly. "Outing?" Not that Raymie could understand, though he grinned toothlessly and kicked out with his wizened legs.

"There's nothing he likes better," Mother interpreted. "You were both crazy about outings when you were his size. I know it's warm, but we'll put Raymie in his bunting as usual. We don't want him catching cold when he's just got over one."

Constance agreed that this was wise. Raymie was cross when he was sick—the least little thing and it upset his bowels. But otherwise he was a wonderful baby, Constance maintained with Mother.

"I can't find my things," Rosalie complained. At this rate, Constance thought, it would be all afternoon before the three of them were ready. But finally they were, zipped into the old tired clothes of winter. "Rag, tag and bobtail," Mother said, surveying her brood. "Tell you what, honey, it being so warm you don't need to bother with the snowpants."

This was lucky, as Rosalie's, which had been handed down from Constance and had thus served three seasons, were all gone at the crotch. First it was only the lining, but now it was the cloth itself. Without the snowpants the girls looked a lot more presentable. It was almost the same as having new outfits. So the good weather was like a gift coupon, a premium, a Dollar Day—one of those happy cuts in the standard price of life—fixed by what combine or what giant trusts?—triumphs and miracles and commutations that figured so largely in the task of raising a family. These upswings of weather, godsent, when Constance's boots—too small for her fall-bought shoes and an agony to pull on, stamp down, but indispensable if the shoes were to give their expected wear—could be bundled away for Rosalie, year after next, and the fuel bill could be accepted philosophically: "Well, it's the last one." Time, for all its smuggling in of new problems, conspicuously cancelled others. Which made Mother an optimist, ready to say, "We'll get along," and take a cheerful view even of doctor bills: "At least we won't be having measles again."

"We could use a warm day," Mother said, as though she had ordered it from the catalogue. "Seems like it was years since we had a good outing."

The warm air struck Constance's liberated knees like the feathery ripple of joy itself. Even Mother found it hard to believe that the weather was as good as it seemed, that it had gone as far as it had—the clean sweep it had made of snow and ice that had become organic to their street. "Spring is here," Mother exclaimed as they maneuvered the carriage off the porch. "What do you know?"

It was the first warm day of the year, when the eye like a washed window disclosed an altogether transformed reality, scoured, focussed, spruced, shining with the particularized magic of common things seen in a picture. Everything looked glorious, outdoing itself like the salads in mayonnaise ads, the cold beaded bottles of coca-cola on billboards. "Off we go," Mother said, giving the carriage a big bounce. "Don't hold my coat, Rosalie, hold on to the carriage."

"Will we go to the country?" Constance asked. Past Wellman's Junk and Parts and all the way past the mill where, beyond a high wall and a moat called the Old Canal, Dad mysteriously worked; across the iron bridge and along the highway cleft between beetling walls of rock. Then at last the field which Constance called the country, the first and only unbuilt space she knew. An immense plain, all goldenrod and strapping burdock and affording a view of the burgundy fortress of the Old Mill, no longer used but still spilling white froth through three brick arches.

"Can't we go to the country?" Constance asked again. Last year they had been able to go. That is, they had been twice, and the second time Constance had discovered a cairn of concrete rubble and smashed crockery. A dump, Mother had said it was, but to Constance it was Johannesburg and the Klondike, for she had poked it with a stick to discover the lid of a sugar bowl almost unchipped, and a piece of purple glass. "It's amethyst," Mother had said, "for all we know. Do you know what that is, Constance? A precious stone. The kind they put in rings and necklaces. One little piece of it is worth—oh, anything." That had been in the fall, for Constance remembered now how there had been burrs like little hedgehogs in the folds of her socks, and other burrs like V's stapling the hem of Mother's coat. They had meant to come again, but Mother had started to feel heavy on her feet. "We'll go sometime in the spring, Constance," she had promised.

But last year Rosalie had been able to ride in the carriage. There'd been no Raymie then, and Rosalie took her displacement hard. "Remember the country?" Mother appealed to Rosalie. "Wouldn't it be nice out there, a lovely day like this?" One had to reckon with Rosalie, prepare her mind, sound out her attitude.

"I no want to," Rosalie said. "I no want to see the country." She gave herself one of her nasty stubborn twists. "It too far. It way way out of town. I hate that damn old country."

"Don't swear, Rosalie honey," Mother said. And Constance felt a twinge in the region of her temper—not so much at being thwarted—she was used to that from Rosalie—as at the insult to a place so rich in possibilities. For what did Rosalie know about the country—that little kid, though pig-headed and brash beyond her years?

The country, ruled out, flew off, like the balloon Dad bought for her at the Fourth of July parade, that she'd held only a moment before unbelievably she had let go. Or had Rosalie tweaked it from her hand? Off it had gone under its own precious, sky-seeking buoyancy, and she was left balloonless. And everyone had laughed and pointed. "Mine," Constance had thought, but was it, was it, when she hadn't had it a minute? So with her hope for the country. She couldn't feel regret for something that was only a longing.

"All right," Mother said pacifically. "If Rosalie doesn't want to—" But now Constance felt real alarm that the outing was going to boil down to a visit to the IGA store. Mother stood so undecided and Rosalie, sullen, victorious, stubbed the sidewalk with her shoe. That was how she ruined her shoes so fast, Constance was tempted to say aloud, but forbore.

"Then we'll just go and see the house where Constance was born," Mother said. "We haven't been by it for a long time, have we now?" She wheeled the carriage slowly down the sunlit street, and Constance felt quite overwhelmed. It was more than she had ever counted on, and she felt a new awe of Mother, who could conceive of such stirring projects.

Yet wasn't it terribly far away? For she remembered going there, oh long ago, when Rosalie herself was tiny, harmless, flat on her back in the carriage with the army blanket tucked tight. What a pilgrimage it had been—miles. No wonder they never went that far again. Was it emotion alone which had stretched the distance for Constance? Now that she had her wits about her, she could see that it was only a little way beyond the railroad underpass where the street took an ominous dip and became almost a tunnel, dusked over by the tracks and thronged with echoes. It was only a few blocks past there.

"There it is," Mother said. "The house where Constance was born." Their little party halted on the pavement. Constance, clinging to her side of the carriage handle, trembled with a deep gratification. It was in all respects as she had remembered it.

It sat across the street. The paint was alligatored on the yellow clapboards, but it was always proportion that counted, that gave an effect of majesty or meanness. The windows were benevolently spaced and there were columns across the front as high as the house itself, and little slabs of white wood mitering the corners. The house was up on a bank, too, which enhanced its stateliness, and far back from the sidewalk, all alone with big grounds to either side of it, aristocratic and exhausted lawns showing dun now that the snow had melted.

"See, Raymie," Mother said, jogging the big wicker carriage whose hood drooped on one side, "that's where your sister Constance was born." She had announced the same thing to Rosalie in the same tone, and Constance had sensed even on the previous occasion that at the foot of this place she and Mother were united by the same strong emotion, at once terrible and sweet, an endlessness of meaning, a long roll of consequences from which the younger ones were excluded.

Because it was Constance who had been born here and not they. It was so different from where they lived now, where every house on the street was much the same, bungalows weatherproofed with the Z pattern of Tilo, grey and grainy like wood, or the too-tripping lines of little sham bricks, which up close proved to be made of an infinity of tiny glinting slivers of mica, red or buff.

"Is that really where you lived?" Constance asked. For to be honest, it took a stretch of the imagination to see Mother going in and out the double doors of etched glass. Mother who lingered so bashfully now on the pavement on the further side of the street and seemed, indeed, faintly restless and ill at ease.

"We'll walk down a ways and then come back," Mother said. "It's a pretty street." So they strolled to the end of the block and Constance felt the house like a church dominating the whole scene and staring at her back. It was a thrill swerving around and looking at it from the opposite direction and nearing it, under the pretense of being an accidental passer-by.

"I want to go somewheres," Rosalie grumbled. "What we turning around for?"

"Hush, Rosalie," Mother said. "Be good now. Don't you care at all about seeing where Constance was born?"

"Stinking old Constance," Rosalie said. But Constance could overlook that, united with Mother in a mellowness which neutralized such acids.

"Don't tug back on the carriage, honey. You make it harder for me to push," Mother said absently. "Yes, we had a room there," she rambled, pushing the carriage at a snail's-pace and keeping her eyes on the house. "I used to tell your Dad before we were married that I wanted to have a room in that house. Not that they're anything special, when you come right down to it. Just rooms, like you might find anywhere else."

"A room?" Constance wondered. That seemed an enigma. "What do you mean, you had a room?"

"Well, that's what it is," Mother said. "It's all let out in rooms. You see that little sign there by the door. That's what it says—rooms."

Mystified, vaguely dismayed, Constance looked for the little sign. Yes, there was one all right, but she had to take Mother's word for what it said, since she could not read. But didn't all houses have rooms?

"Not like this," Mother explained inadequately. "Here everyone has a room to himself—every couple or single person as the case might be. Some of the rooms—they have a little hot plate in them so people can get their own meals. You see how it is, honey?"

Constance was still not sure. It seemed a perilous and queer arrangement and she kept looking at the house, trying to fathom its differentness. "A big barn of a place like that—no one family could maintain it. Why, the fuel alone—" Mother reflected. They were past it now, had to crane backward to keep it in sight—"I'd hate to be in the position of owning a house that size," Mother said. She stopped and brushed some strands of hair out of Rosalie's eyes. "Honey," she addressed Constance, "you didn't think we lived all over that big house, did you?"

Heaven knows what Constance had thought—she dutifully shook her head. The notions of childhood, so frail, so foggy, so shredded that any making-clear scattered not only the inexactitudes but even the memory of what had been imagined. She had not visualized the house beyond its façade, its pillars, its look of importance, nor thought about what kind of life went on in it.

"That vast thing?" Mother said. "Goodness, no. Why, we were barely—we hadn't a thing, not a broom, not a scrap of furniture. And they were talking about the Mill going on a four-day week. Oh well—" For the house lay well behind them now and they were in the cavern under the tracks, the bars of shadow and light rapidly striping sleeping Raymie. "What's the matter, Rosalie, what are you dragging your feet for?"

"My feet hurt," Rosalie whimpered. "I got a blister on my heel."

"Hole in your sock? Kneel down and see, Constance."

Constance ducked low to the ground. "Her socks are all right," she reported neutrally. She wanted not to joggle her impression of the house, wanted to walk in a state of exalted decorum, but that was asking too much, with Rosalie along. Who hit her in the face now. "Mind your own business, stupid Constance"—a blundering feeble blow more infuriating than painful.

"Now, now," Mother said. "That's no way to act. Don't hit her back, Constance. You musn't fight in the street."

Constance had no intention to. She had standards even firmer than Mother's, a horror of scuffles and plenty of practice in a bleak forgiveness. Having just seen the house where she had been born reinforced all these. But it seemed unjust that by force alone, and sourness, Rosalie could spoil the whole day. Constance went back to her side of the carriage and helped propel it. Stalking along, she told herself—"She doesn't belong to me. She's only my little sister. Why did we have to have her anyway?"

"I want an ice cream," Rosalie said. She had found a new grievance. "Oh God," Constance somewhere thought. Principally she tried to be blank, not to hear, not to foresee, sensing in the air that rising frenzy of egotism and miserableness which was Rosalie's special brand of self-expression.

"That's a good idea," Mother said. "Soon as we get to the drug store you can both have ice cream."

"Now," Rosalie said. She had her thumb in her mouth. Constance noted with some cynicism how Rosalie reverted to babyhood whenever she was being bossiest. "Don't notice," she warned herself. "Don't get mad." Yet in spite of herself and her effort to stay calm, her heart started to pound. It was as though Rosalie's tantrums were contagious—she could feel a slowly gathering pulse of hatred and fierceness, involuntary and overmastering. How often this happened—how she dreaded and was powerless before this savage onrush of feeling. "This is baseness," she thought, and she might never have known it but for Rosalie. If it weren't for Rosalie—they would still be living in the house where she had been born. Everything would be different, sufficient and calm.

"She's never stopped squalling since the day she was born," Constance recollected bitterly. "Not a moment's peace." Indignation filled her almost to bursting. It strained the limits of her being, and as it was too big for her to contain, it seemed also too big to have only herself for its object. "Mother either," she thought with anguish. "Mother either." Though Mother was saying meekly enough, "Just a bit more to go, Rosalie. We'll be downstreet in no time."

"I tired," Rosalie stormed. "My shoes hurt. I hot. I want to ride in the carriage."

"You can't," Mother reasoned. "It's Raymie's now. You're three. You're a big girl." An honor Rosalie repudiated. She stamped and bawled and squatted down on the curb.

"Come along, honey, sweetheart," Mother pleaded. "See, at the end of the block, there's Main Street right there." While Constance stood by, still holding on to the stock-still carriage and feeling almost blind with rage and sick with contempt for Mother's useless gentleness. She thought of the house where she had been born, so respectable and aloof, but since then, since—a thousand memories gathered to a judgment—there had been nothing but this, disgrace and noise and greed and disorder. Their life was hateful. If Rosalie had had to be born, then all that Constance could wish—it phrased itself for her just this way—Constance wished *she* had not been born upon this earth.

People were slowing down and looking at them, and Constance

could see how they must appear to strangers—Mother large and frumpy in her oatmeal-colored coat all wrinkled up the back and stretched over the hips—the ancient wicker carriage beginning to quiver with the first squirmings and faint trial whimpers of Raymie—who always woke up when the carriage stopped, and Rosalie in her crisis of woe. Rosalie was beside herself by now, sprawled out and kicking on the sidewalk. The beat of her shoes, her sobbing screams, were as loud to Constance's ears as the clamor in a small room of someone being murdered. Even though they were on an open street, it was as if they were pent up in a tight place, in the narrow horror of being a family. "People will think Mother's whacked her or something," Constance thought. "I wish she would whack her. Oh yes, I wish she would."

But instead Mother was bending over Rosalie and trying to soothe her. How large and rumpled Mother looked in the smart spring sunshine, cajoling, calming, trying to ease Rosalie stubbornly cemented and epileptically thrashing on the pavement. "The horrid little kid," Constance muttered from her fullness of acrimony. "I wish she'd be run over." She said it loud enough for Mother to hear, and held herself tight for the punishment she knew she deserved for such a bad thought. She was astonished to see the look Mother gave her. There was no blame in that look, none at all. If it were Dad, she would have been paddled for saying so much, but it was almost as though Mother's eyes, in their sanity and tiredness, confessed to an understanding. Could Mother ever have had such a thought, herself, when there was nothing more sinful than to wish for a person to die?

"Hush, my baby, hush," Mother was murmuring. "What will people think? The people in cars are noticing. Even that oil truck that just passed, the driver was looking at you. See, there's another truck with big high side boards. Maybe there's a horse in there—remember the time we saw a horse in a truck and its head was showing. Don't you want to look? You never know when there might be another. There's an old tomcat running along that wall—there by the shoe repair shop. Running so fast—what's it after, I wonder? Oh baby, honey, you go on this way, people will think you're sick. They'll send an ambulance to take you to the hospital. They'll send a policeman to see what's the matter."

The policeman did it. Limp and struggling for breath, Rosalie allowed herself to be lifted from the pavement. Sooner than risk standing her on her feet, Mother deposited her in the carriage. It lurched from the sudden imbalance. Mother righted it just in time and started to wheel it at a furious pace. Now it was Raymie, crushed down, who was bawling, as Rosalie, smug, her face all slime and sidewalk filth, occupied the carriage, looking obscenely gigantic, like a full-grown pig in a hen coop.

She had won again, and Constance thought her heart would break from the injustice and the shame. Her nerves were still vibrating from the conflict and she had a stitch in her side from the way she had to scamper to keep up with the carriage. Still she was glad that they were moving away from the place where Rosalie had put on her exhibition. Up here near Main Street they would not be identified as the same persons who had so shockingly broken down at the corner, and Mother was so bright and cheerful, singing a little song over Raymie's plaint:

Over bush and over bramble
Oh what fun with you to scramble
Hip, hip, hop,
Trot, my pony, trot.

"I learned that in Third Grade," Mother said. "We used to learn all kinds of nice songs, the school where I used to go." She rounded the corner with a flourish. There was the news shop with papers on a rack in front, their taut top pages pulling in the stiff spring breeze. "Dear, dear," Mother said, her eyes caught by the headlines—an auto crash near Pittsfield, a fire in a frame building in Chicago. There were the pictures—the wreckage, the charred beams. A tenement containing four families, Mother read. She shook her head and clicked her tongue against her teeth—propitiating Calamity, that jealous goddess, with some small tribute to her power, her caprice, her awfulness. How dangerous life was, at its most commonplace. What could people do but burrow down ever more humbly into the ordinary, in the hope that being nobodies, aspiring to nothing prouder than survival, they would be bypassed. Trials, shocks, losses, terror, physical pain. "Ain't it terrible?" Mother said to the world in general.

And there was the drug store with lobster red bags in its window same as hung on the bathroom door at home. "What'll it be?" Mother asked, borrowing from Dad that bluff manner, half frightening, half emboldening, with which he offered treats when they did their Friday night trading. "Chicken Dinner?" Dad would demand.

"O Henry? Hershey bar?" "What will it be?" Mother quizzed. "Strawberry?" "A double one," Rosalie said, looking headstrong and mean, and Mother flinched a little, for double ones were twenty-five cents these days, but went on smiling.

"I don't want any," Constance volunteered.

"Are you sure?"

In a way it was a shame to make Mother look anxious. "You always like ice cream. What's the matter, honey?" But there were higher imperatives than custom and it was the call of higher imperatives that Constance was hearing so clearly today. "I don't want any," she declared again, almost crossly. Mother meant well, but made it hard for Constance when she wanted to rise above herself. Hadn't they just been to see the house where Constance was born? Besides, it was necessary to show Rosalie that one didn't have to be hoggish—and then there was Rosalie's unreasonable demand for a double one. Things like that, Constance reasoned, had to be made up for somewhere. She had been out shopping with Mother long enough to have gained that impression. She was deeply disappointed at the way Mother missed all this which underlay her sacrifice.

"Nothing else you want, honey? Lifesavers? A package to yourself?"

She shook her head, stubborn in nobility. And really, it was not so hard, watching Rosalie bite into the firm spheres of cream veined with crushed berries like marble. It didn't take much, she thought, to content Rosalie. . . . The double cone, as could have been predicted, took too long to eat. The lower ball melted, the cracker became soggy and went all to pieces. Rosalie, fortunately, was stuffed and didn't care. "Goodness, you're a sight," Mother said, and tried to clean her up with a handkerchief. Suffering this, Rosalie fell asleep.

"That's what she needed all along," Mother said indulgently. "Now we'll just pick up some groceries and home we'll go."

A package of bread and a jar of marshmallow fluff. A half dozen miniature glasses of strained foods for Raymie. They were such a convenience, Mother observed, she didn't know what she would do without them. On the other hand she was looking forward to the time when Raymie could eat what the rest of them did. Coffee was up again. Mother deplored it. Mr. Bullard, who owned the IGA store, sympathized with her. It was the world market, he said, lest Mother should think it was his doing. But Constance observed that Mr.

Bullard, benign and white-haired, did not seem to mind half as much as Mother.

"When we started in housekeeping," Mother told Constance, "coffee was fifty-six cents a pound." And Constance stored away this confidence and bit of history with her other precious relics—the amethyst glass she had found in the field outside town, the farm where Mother's folks used to live, the brown head of a horse showing above the side boards of a truck—impressions, information, a small fortune of spiritual goods.

"I don't know how I'm going to manage the bag," Mother said doubtfully. For there wasn't the usual room at the foot of the carriage, with Rosalie toppled over and practically crowding out Raymie. Mother sprung the brake with her foot. "Maybe I can wheel with one hand and carry with the other."

"I'll take it," Constance said.

"But it's heavy."

"I can carry it."

"Then be careful, sweetheart. Mind you don't drop it—all those things in jars." She transferred the bag to Constance, who received it rather charily. She found it not heavy but bulky and her walking was incommoded by a new responsibility—she had never carried a parcel before.

"When we lived in that house, Constance, the house where you were born—" what harmony between them, walking in the now stale warmth of the afternoon. The hood of the carriage creaked, drooping on its bolt and bumping against the wicker side; the wheels made a continuous and lovely squeak. Outside the hardware store in galvanized pails were orange onions no bigger than marbles and dull dusty puckered peas as hard as pebbles which had appeared out of nowhere, this opening day of the earth's fruitful season. The metal of the pails flashed light from its countless platinum specks.—"There was a man lived up the hall had a little dog he trained to carry parcels. Carried them in his mouth in the carefullest way—Oh, his master's cigarettes and maybe newspaper. He wasn't a large-sized dog, one of these cockers, I guess, the kind with the long silky ears. Now wouldn't such a dog come in handy, times like these."

It abolished the weight of the bag and its perilous shape, as a small dog, ears dragging on the ground and a bag bobbing in its black-lipped jaws, bounded up the inclined plane of imagination straight into Constance's heart.

"Will we ever get a dog?"

"Well, you know, sweetheart—they eat a lot and they do mess up the house. Maybe some day, when Raymie's less trouble—"

"Yes," Constance hastened to accede, and filed away in the department of faith the eventual dog, along with the few other wishes that she had.

"But let me tell you about this little dog I mean. He was a cute little dog. Curly black hair. Smart as a whip. Understood every word you said to him. At least that's what the fellow who owned him used to say. The fellow that owned him was a Greek—retired. He'd had a restaurant in Holyoke—still had it, far as I could make out—but he didn't have to bother with it himself no more—he had all kinds of money, I guess, and was very sweet on me. It used to make your Daddy kind of mad, how he used to hang around, knock on the door, this thing or that. He was great on compliments, always noticed what I wore—Daddy didn't notice then, no more than he does now, but he used to say the fellow had no business looking me over like that. Forever a gentleman, though—there wasn't no harm in him that I could see. He wanted company, like everybody else—and your Dad was gone all day, working at the mill. I hadn't my hands full then, like nowadays. No harm in it at all. I used to think how silly your Dad was to be jealous. I wasn't much more than seventeen and this Greek he was an old man, a widower and of course, though I wasn't sure of it at the time, you were coming along."

How odd it was, alluring, disquieting, that Constance had been there all the time—coming along, from where, into what? And if Mother hadn't been sure, could she have welcomed her? Could it be that babies were kind of saddled on their mothers, as she had often felt—but that was her evil nature—was the case with Rosalie? She did not dare to ask; these questions, for their very fascination, were criminal and she sensed that a family was founded on a layer of crushed secrets. All those bygone days, the dog who carried parcels, the Greek, a jealous father and an admired mother—concepts so strange and hard to relate to her own beginnings. She wasn't sure she liked to hear about these things, after all.

"It wasn't how we figured it, you see. I was going back to my job—they still wanted me back at the Mill—those were just a few months I was taking off to get married in. But like I told Dad at the time—if you're starting a family you might as well do it early as later. Of course we moved away—to seventy-nine Grove where we are now. We were lucky to find it, so handy to the Mill. Your Dad couldn't stand how that Greek paid court to me. Besides we thought we'd best start making a home, which no room ever is. There's lots of laundry with a baby—we had to think of that."

Which remained with Constance as one of the key facts of the human situation, along with the fact that dogs would eat a lot.

"I sometimes wonder whether he's still there, the Greek. It wasn't so long ago—and they still rent rooms. He wasn't a flighty fellow; the place seemed to suit him good. He used to say the funniest things—how I couldn't have known my mind when I married Dad—how it wasn't too late to change—he liked to tease. For all I know he's still there. Would he recognize me now, I wonder, if he came out on the street with his dog. Might give him an awful shock, how I've put on weight.

"Mostly after you, Constance. I don't know why it is—some girls are the same after any amount of babies and some, way I hear them talking in the hospital ward, why their figures even improve. But in my family—that's how we all are, anyway. Nothing to shed tears about. It's funny how those things stop mattering once you settle down. But I used to wear a perfect size twelve—that Greek he used to say I was something then—the prettiest girl in town. I'd have liked to show him my children, anyway."

And now they were at Grove Street, almost home. A washing was dancing out in Mrs. Streeter's back yard. The last narrow shoals of snow, dust-speckled and seemingly structural along each house's northwest wall, were gone. The concrete drainage channels, revealed, glistened with a streak of water. One big boy, biking home, bore slowly, elegiacally down on the pedals before drawing to a stop—the front wheel wavered, describing great S figures in the gutter. A pair of curtain stretchers stood leaning against the porch of No. 83.

"Tomorrow," Mother said, "if it's nice—"

"Will we go for another outing?" Constance asked. "Will we go out to the country?"

"I think we'd better stay home tomorrow, sweetheart. We'll wash the kitchen windows and if it's nice—" she cast a hypnotized glance at the starched ecru lace panels at No. 83—"if it's nice, maybe I'll do up the curtains too." Her face was rapt, contemplating the transfigurations of that tomorrow. And Rosalie sagged woodenly in the carriage as Mother jerked it up their little porch, with its squat posts sheathed in sham brick and the splintered floor where the carriage went through if one weren't careful.

"Wake up, Rosalie, wake up, honey." She rattled the carriage. Aside, she said to Constance, like a secret. "It's hard on her, being so young."

"Was it hard on me?" Constance asked. For it felt as though she had shot up years in an afternoon, could ask questions she'd never have presumed to ask before. As though her former bitterness and latter peace had merged, united, creating something new—the rational soul.

"Of course it was," Mother said. "Of course it was." She did not specify—it was as though all that were past, transcended. "That's how it is. It's hard on all of us, being young." She lifted Rosalie, mussed and sodden and insensible, and set her on the porch. Then she picked up Raymie. "Goodness, he needs changing," she said. "Soaked through." Arms full, she fumbled crippledly in her purse for the door key. Her absent eyes fell on the end of the street where it opened out over the Mill and the Old Canal.

"Look, Constance, how the sky's all pink and orange there. Hasn't it been a lovely day?"

Nancy Willard

Theo's Girl

She woke up suddenly, with the feeling she had overslept an exam. Someone was throwing stones at her window. She peered at the luminous dials of the clock; the hands said four. If I can get outside without turning on the lights, she thought, I won't wake anybody up.

But there was her mother, standing at the foot of the stairs.

"It's a mighty funny time to be going out with him," she observed. "Did you sleep in those clothes?"

"I just lay down in them. I didn't want to miss him."

"Sit down and eat. I got oatmeal made and everything. You want to ask Theo to come in?"

She couldn't get up earlier than her mother, try as she might. There was always that oatmeal waiting for you, no matter how quiet you were.

"I don't have time. He'll be late."

Her mother made a motion as if to throw it all in the sink, and Erica repented.

"Save it for me," she said. "Save it till we get back."

Theo was in the truck, drumming his fingers on the side view mirror, and she squeezed in beside him. The back, empty now, with its double doors clearly visible, resembled a sepulchre.

"Did you wake your mother?"

"Nope. She's still in bed."

"She didn't think it was funny? Like we were eloping?"

"No. She knows I wouldn't do a thing like that."

It sounded hollow, it hung in the air like a defeat. She should have been capable of it. As they drove out of the city and turned onto the superhighway, Theo stretched in his seat and leaned forward, resting his elbows on the wheel.

"Well, this is another job I'm going to lose. I've been late the last three times. It takes an hour to get to Detroit, another hour to bring the bagels back, and there's a line of people outside Sol's store by eight."

"You overslept."

"Clock didn't go off. The cat slept on the plunger."

They rumbled along quietly; she was falling asleep.

"Hey, wake up. Did I tell you about my new job?"

"Another job?"

"Yeah. At the undertaker's. There's a German family in town, wants me to make a death mask of the uncle."

"Aren't you studying for your exams at all?"

"I got all my sculpture projects in. All I have is French."

She leaned her head against the window, trying to keep awake. For days she had imagined the two of them, rolling softly, secretly, into the morning, and here she was, hardly able to realize it. The broad backs of the Ford factories glittered past, the river and the island flashed at them once and disappeared. When she opened her eyes, the heat of the city laid its weight on her, and the bakers were already running back and forth, red-faced, stuffing the last bags of bagels into the back of the truck.

"You goon! Some company you were!" laughed Theo.

But it was the trip home she loved best anyway, she decided, when the bagels filled the whole cab with a smell of onions and fresh dough. Theo reached behind and feeling the top of the bags, helped himself to a bagel, broke it, and handed her half. In silence they watched the sky lighten and the trees grow friendly again as the dark lumps of leaves opened to lacy green. The truck turned into her street; no one was stirring.

"I'll pick you up later if you want to come with me."

"Where?"

"To the undertaker's."

She lingered outside, one foot propped in the open door.

"If you want me to, I will. My Aunt Minnie's supposed to come today."

"She's still working to get you baptized, huh?"

"No."

"You know, if you let her do that to you, we're through."

"I know," said Erica.

"Well, what for, then?"

She had half a mind not to tell him, but she was no good at keeping secrets.

"She's taking us to Hannah's. Now can't you guess?"

"Say it."

"A wedding dress. Hannah's making it."

"Jesus!" He shook his head and smiled broadly. "You really mean it, don't you?"

She nodded seriously.

"I'll wear my *Croix de guerre* that I won in France."

"You've never been to France," said Erica.

Theo pulled a look of broad astonishment.

"Would I lie to you?"

"Mother says you've never been there or won any cross."

"My blue heron," said Theo, reaching over to stroke the hair which swung over her face when she put her head down. "If I can just get you out of here before you start listening to your mother."

Her mother was waiting in the doorway, holding her pink wrapper closed, watching them with that wistful smile she got sometimes.

"I kept it warm for you."

There were moments when Erica wanted to kiss her mother, like just then, but she would have felt funny doing it. Neither of them was very demonstrative. They went into the kitchen, and Erica got herself a dish and skimmed the crust off the oatmeal. Her mother beamed.

"You used to do that when you were a little girl."

She walked around the kitchen talking while her mother handed her things: orange juice, prunes, toast, always enough for a battalion. It was a mutual nervous mannerism, her mother handing her things, Erica taking them, putting them down here and there, talking while her mother beamed.

Far overhead, a cracked voice burst into "What a Friend We Have in Jesus."

"I forgot to tell you—Minnie came in last night," said her mother.

Every weekend she came, ostensibly to get her new Ford fixed. There seemed to be no Ford repairman in Detroit. On Sundays she drove back to attend church. When the semester ended, she would move into the spare third floor room for long periods altogether.

"She's taking us to Hannah's. But she's got to study."

"Study?"

"They're doing the new math in the fourth grade, and she says it's difficult. You got to learn it to teach it. She's got a new electric organ, she says. And a scalp vibrator."

Instead of a husband, said Theo somewhere in the back of her mind, and she shuddered. But Minnie had had husbands enough. Four. Two insurance men, a floor walker, and—the first one—an engineer. Erica could not imagine what it felt like to have run through so many. A different life with each one—did they fall away like so many winters? But when you repent of your sins, all that is changed and forgiven, said Minnie. Changed and forgiven. You are a new person in Christ. A new person.

And the husbands, thought Erica. Had they been baptized away, the hurts and losses drowned somewhere forever?

"I ate almost all the oatmeal," she said. "I'm sorry."

"Never mind. I can make some more."

Thump, thump. She picked up her orange juice and wandered into the living room. Her father peered up from the floor where he lay on his back, slowly raising his legs and letting them down again. Usually he was up before any of them. Once, on a dark winter morning, she had thought it was a burglar.

"We had a good time, Daddy."

"Eh?" His legs paused in mid-air, and he lifted his head. His grey hair snapped with electricity from the rug.

"I said, we had fun."

"Where were you?"

"Theo took me to pick up the bagels."

"To pick up what?" He had probably never seen a bagel, let alone eaten one. "He still got that old car of his?"

"No," said Erica. "It quit running. He abandoned it."

"Lord," said her father. He lowered his head and closed his eyes. Then he opened them again suddenly, as if something had bitten him.

"Minnie driving you to Hannah's?"

"Yes."

They never spoke much. It wasn't just the gap of generations, though; she didn't know what it was. Now that he was retired she felt she ought to speak to him more, but she didn't know what to say. All he could remember about Theo was that he had a broken car. Sometimes he asked if Theo had gotten the left headlight fixed yet, so it didn't shine into second story windows when he drove at night.

The voice upstairs gave way to a chorus. Erica heard hymns jogging closer, as from a wayward procession; then they clicked into silence. She went into the dining room and Minnie looked up brightly. Her hair, newly tinted auburn, had an odd shiny look, as if it were cased in plastic.

"If I can just hear a good sermon," she observed, "it makes my day. It's such a blessing to me, this program. I'll be ready to go as soon as I find my teeth. I always throw them out, in the night. It's my bridge, with the two front ones on it."

And then, as she pierced her grapefruit into sections with the wrong end of her spoon: "Why do old people look so bad without them? I look at my kids in school; they lose them and they look cute."

In their identical pink wrappers, her mother and Minnie really did look like sisters, though Minnie was thinner and better preserved. Except she always *looks* preserved, thought Erica, and she felt herself getting depressed, as if some blight had touched her. She let her mother bring her a cup of coffee and tried to be cheerful.

"How old is Hannah now?" she asked.

Her mother considered.

"She must be in her eighties. Imagine, living all alone on that farm, with nothing but sewing to support herself!"

"She has a brother, though," remarked Minnie.

"Divorced."

"No, that was the other brother," Minnie corrected her. "Jonathan went into a bakery and made real good. And when he started, he drove the wagon for twenty dollars a month."

"She's got a half-sister who lives in town."

"She must have married well."

"No, she didn't. She taught piano all her life. I got a letter from her husband after she died, so I wouldn't send any more Christmas cards."

There was a long silence, during which they all avoided looking at one another. Then Minnie said slyly, humming under her breath,

"Is this your wedding dress Hannah is making?"

Erica had her mouth open to speak, but her mother got there first.

"It's just some white sewing. It could be a very nice graduation dress."

"I thought you told me it was satin."

"Lots of dresses are made out of satin these days."

"*White* satin?"

"Someday I could get married," said Erica in a small voice.

"*If* she decides to get married," added her mother. "There's lots of other things she could do. Paint, for example."

"You have to be terribly careful when you marry. They say you never know anyone till you're married to them," said Minnie. "Oh, I turned down some good ones, all right."

"Remember Irving Tubbs? I'd say you'd have made it best with him."

"Too late now," shrugged Minnie, without bitterness.

But already Erica had that sinking feeling again. They always seemed to be picking on her—not directly, of course, but in conversations she felt were performed for her benefit. My blue heron, I'm not your father, Theo would say. You don't want a father, you want a husband.

She thought of his little room over the laundromat; she had painted mermaids in the shower for him and had lettered his favorite epigram on a sign which he kept over his desk: ENERGY IS ETERNAL DELIGHT.

Sometimes they would lie down on the bed together and listen to the flute player in the coffeeshop next door one floor down, he wholly relaxed, she with one foot on the floor. For running.

That's how it is with you, he'd say angrily. Always one foot on the floor. Who do you think is going to come in, anyway? Your mother?

Did you lock the door, she'd whisper, agonized.

I locked the door, yes. Maybe your mother can go through locked doors?

"Immersion," Minnie was saying. "What have you got to lose? If the Bible says that you shall be saved through water and the spirit, why take the risk?"

"I'd feel a little odd about it," her mother answered. "If it's so good, why don't the Presbyterians have it?"

Minnie shook her head. "Billy Graham preaches it. I'd arrange for a very private service."

"And you wouldn't tell anybody?"

"Not a soul."

Suddenly Erica felt ill. Why don't you say it, she thought angrily; he's an atheist, a black atheist. It never bothered her until they talked about immersion, and then only in a sort of superstitious way because she felt she might be missing out on something—a heavenly reward she wasn't sure she deserved but might, by some fluke, get anyhow. It was that feeling of something left undone that bothered her most. Prudence—the seventh deadly virtue, Theo called it, and sometimes she felt that Theo was more religious than all of them put together. But art is not a religion, said Minnie. All the painting and sculpture in the world won't gain you the kingdom.

Erica had, somewhere, a paper napkin on which he had written, "Someday I will show you all the kingdoms of *my* world." They were sitting in the German restaurant downtown, which was always so full at noon that they could hardly hear one another.

What kingdoms? she asked him then.

My blue heron, he said. My little Eurydike.

And a few days later he took her to see his city, which he was starting to build on the empty lot behind the laundromat.

It was a city to be made entirely of junk, he told her. Already she could see it rising into shape as they walked between the walls made of washing machines, fire hydrants, clocks, mirrors, and fenders, between the towers made of wagons and marbles, bicycles and animal skulls, wired and cemented together, all the paraphernalia of human life.

And it shall be fifty cubits long to the east, Theo intoned, and fifty cubits to the west. And there shall be an hundred furnaces beneath the foundations, and an hundred mirrors to catch the sun. And over the flagpole, a garbage can.

Where did you get the parking meter?

I took it from my room, said Theo. Didn't you see it in my room? I used to time my eggs by it when I had a hotplate.

He sat down on a large bed, painted silver. He had stuck paper flowers in the springs. Around it the walls glittered with bedpans, coffee pots and false teeth.

I have a hundred and five sets of false teeth, he declared solemnly. And a medallion of William Blake. You've got to learn how much is worth saving in this world.

Later they were crossing the alley behind Woolworth's on the way home from the nine o'clock show, and they both saw it: a pair of legs sticking out of a trash can.

Jesus! Somebody's fallen in!

The feet were hollow, the legs straight. Pushing aside broken boxes and excelsior, they set them upright.

Too bad it's only the bottom half, said Theo. Who'd throw out a thing like that?

Are you going to keep it? asked Erica.

Put it in the city, he answered. Grow beans on it, or roses. All my life I had to look at saints and flamingoes in my mother's garden. Nobody ever had a pair of legs like these. You take his feet.

As they emerged from the alley, a black car pulled up across the street.

Just keep walking, said Theo. And follow me.

He was humming happily to himself. He turned the corner with easy nonchalance and broke into a gallop. Erica, holding the feet, felt herself pelting after him.

You want to rest? he said at last.

They had stopped in front of the drugstore; a balding man in a pharmacist's white jacket was rolling up the awnings. The neon lights in the window winked out, leaving them in the blue mercurial haze of the street lamps. The streets were empty. They set the legs down on the pavement and seated themselves on the curb. In spite of the warm air of summer almost here, Erica felt a great weariness flood her like a chill. Theo reached over to stroke the hair that swung over her face when she lowered her head.

Will you come and live in my city?

They arrived at Hannah's early in the afternoon. Hannah, on hearing the car, had come out to meet them and was standing by the pump in her long blue print dress. Behind her the house, low-slung and weathered nearly black, crouched in the shadow of several freshly painted barns. She seemed to have been born ancient; Erica could not remember a time when her thin hair, tucked under the green eye-shade, was not already white.

"Afternoon," said Hannah, shyly.

As they stepped up to her, she kissed them one by one, a dry musty kiss on the cheek. The pin cushion she wore at her lapel pricked Erica's face.

Hannah led the way through the kitchen. The low ceiling made Erica want to stoop. There was a wooden sink, deeply stained, and an enamel bucket with a chipped rim beside it. On a pedestal near the front door, a large Christmas cactus trailed its branches in all directions.

"A hundred years old," said Hannah proudly, "and it bloomed this year. I called the paper about it, but Mrs. Schultz had already called them about *her* cactus, and they wasn't interested in two of 'em."

"But you aren't a hundred years old," exclaimed Erica.

"It come with the house, I think. Oh, I could have had a sign out in front about the house, but Jonathan was never much on publicity."

They went into the living room for the fittings. Boxes of cards and buttons spilled over the wicker sofa onto a piano which served as a shelf for photographs and birthday cards and was by this time nearly inaccessible; the keyboard looked permanently shut. On the sewing machine, with its faint traces of elegant scrolls, a cat lifted its head and blinked at them, then stretched itself back to sleep again.

For some reason the signs of faith were less depressing here than they might have been at home, thought Erica, forgiving Hannah the ceramic plaque, JESUS NEVER FAILS and the sign lettered in silver paint, GOD GRANT ME THE SERENITY TO ACCEPT THINGS I CANNOT CHANGE. On the walls, the sepia faces of an earlier generation looked out from absurd gilt frames. They were always stiff, her father told her, because the pictures were time exposures and you had to wear a clamp on your neck inside the collar that kept you from moving.

Suddenly she saw it, hanging on a coat rack shining out over the faded coats brought in for mending and the shapeless dresses of old women.

"You want to try on the white sewing first?" asked Hannah, noticing her gaze. "It's just basted."

Her mother started to hum.

"I got some stuff for you to do, when you're done with that," she said. And Erica saw her studying the pictures on the wall, pausing before a confirmation certificate, lettered in German, showing in faded tints the parables and deeds of Christ. Stuck on the frame was a tiny star-shaped pin, from which several bars fell in ladder-fashion: five years, ten years, fifteen years.

"You never miss a day of church, do you, Hannah?" said her mother. "I'll bet nobody's got a record like you do."

"Raise your arms," said Hannah, and Erica felt the sudden cool weight of satin falling over her body. "Only one man had a better record than mine; he got the twenty-five year bar, but the last year they had to bring him in on a stretcher."

She stood with her arms out while Hannah pinned and clucked to herself. Her hands were warm and light, almost like mice walking on her flesh, thought Erica. Minnie cleared a place for herself on the sofa and stretched out, running her eye over the dresses on the coat rack.

"That's a handsome black one," she said. "Who's that for?"

"Me," said Hannah, "to be buried in. Thought I might as well get some wear out of it."

"Remember how Grandma had a dress she kept in her drawer to be buried in? White wool, it was."

"Fits pretty good," said Hannah. "Now, try on this overslip."

She shook it over Erica's head—light, vaporous stuff, embroidered with flowers. Fullskirted like a child's dress. Theo hated full skirts. Minnie bent forward to examine it.

"Imagine," she said, "a machine to put in all those flowers."

"How does it fit around the arms?"

Erica nodded.

"Good. 'Course it'll take a little time—"

"No hurry," snapped her mother.

"—since I lost my ripper. I told Mrs. Mahoney to pick me up one somewhere."

"Mahoney?" mused Minnie. "Not Jack Mahoney?"

"He's dead now, just tipped over quick," said Hannah.

"Seems like all the people I went with are dead now," said Minnie softly.

Erica edged herself carefully out of the white dress, trying not to prick herself with pins. Her mother had already put on a lace one. Hannah and Minnie eyed her critically.

"Lace," observed Hannah. "Looks like you're going to a wedding."

"No wedding," said her mother. "Make it an inch shorter, don't you think, in the front? I haven't got a bosom like this—"

She pulled the front out like a tent.

"'Course, skirts is shorter now," said Hannah reluctantly. "Even the choir wears 'em shorter. Course a thing goes across the front so it don't show their knees. I could put some darts in the front."

"The lace is torn, too; do you mend lace?"

"Lace isn't good except for weddings," said Hannah, shaking her head.

He wouldn't like the dress, thought Erica. She scowled at it, hanging on the coat rack. He wouldn't like it because her mother had picked the design, not for his marriage but for marriage in general. Somehow the dress looked like her mother. She did not know why.

Late in the afternoon, Theo appeared at her house, dressed in a black suit with a bag of tools at his side.

"You coming with me to the undertaker's?"

She had not told her mother about this job. They took her bicycle, she sitting on the seat, he pumping in front, his haunches striking her in the stomach as they pitched uphill, past the park.

"I can get off, if you want to walk."

"No, you're light enough."

When they arrived at the funeral parlor, they were both damp with effort. They reached for the knocker, but a man in a moth-grey suit had already opened the door. Over his shoulder, Erica saw the rooms, with their high ceilings and French doors, opening into infinity, multiplying like a house of mirrors. She remembered this house from her grandmother's funeral two years before; the parlors where the dead awaited visitors and the carpets that flowed from one room to another, gathering up all human sounds. Was it in this large room they had laid her out and Erica had cried, not for grief but because her mother was crying?

The man led them over to a small group of people huddled together on a sofa at the other end of the room: two men and two women, all middle-aged with pointed sallow faces. The women had covered their heads with black lace mantillas.

"This is the young student."

They rose and looked at him rather severely, then turned to Erica.

"My wife," said Theo. "She assists me."

The women removed their gloves and extended their hands to her. Then the taller of the two men inquired in an accent so pronounced that Erica wondered if it were real, "You have done this before? You know—"

"Of course," said Theo. "I have studied the trade in Germany."

"Well, then!"

They all looked immensely relieved. With a polite nod, the undertaker indicated that they might sit down and motioned Theo to follow him.

The body had been laid out, fully dressed, on a table and wheeled into a private room, empty save for a sink at one end. For a moment Erica caught her breath, but Theo gave her a look, and she said nothing. The undertaker lingered a bit.

"Won't take you very long, I suppose."

"No, not very long. You will excuse me—I prefer to do this work alone."

Blushing deeply, the other man muttered a little and bowed into the doorway.

"His face has already been shaved."

Pause.

"The family will be down in—say—half an hour?"

Theo nodded and waved him away. The door slammed, and his composure dropped like scales from her eyes.

"Open the tool case quick," he said. "Twenty minutes. Get out the plaster of paris. Can you mix plaster of paris?"

"I think so."

She rummaged through the little bag, pulled out a chisel and a towel, then a tin bowl and the bag of plaster, carefully averting her eyes from the body. Thinking only of what she must do with her hands, she carried everything to the sink, filled the bowl, turned on the water and began to stir.

"Stir faster," cried Theo.

"You never really were in Germany, were you?"

"Christ, no. Give me the plaster—quick, before it dries."

Now she stepped forward and watched, fascinated, breathing very lightly to avoid the real or imagined smell of formaldehyde in the room. Theo had spread the towel over the body, tucking it in at the collar like a napkin. The face looked much like those she had seen upstairs; about thirty, she thought, maybe older. It neither grieved nor frightened her, this thing. Theo loaded his trowel and spread plaster over the chin and nose, then lathered it over the eyes and stood up straight.

"Now we wait for it to dry." He was looking cheerful again. "Who knows, maybe he'll come out looking like William Blake."

It was at that moment a kind of chill touched her.

"Where do you think he is—really?"

"Right here, all there is of him." Theo was washing his hands at the sink. "Your aunt been working on you again? Listen"—he looked very fierce—"if you let her baptize you, it's all over between us. Christ, you're not marrying me, you're marrying your mother!"

"They can hear you upstairs," she hissed.

"Listen," he said, in a gentler voice, pointing to the body. "*This* isn't anything to be afraid of. I've got to get you out of that house of old women."

"I think it's dry."

He tested the mask with his finger.

"Not yet. We'll wait a few more minutes."

They slid down on the floor, leaning against the wall in ominous silence. Presently Theo got up, bent over the body and took the edges of the mask in both hands.

"A little cool, but it's dry enough."

He tugged, carefully at first, then more roughly.

"Give me a hand," he said urgently.

She stumbled to her feet and, suddenly nauseous, swallowed hard and touched the rough plaster edge over the ear.

"Push your fingers under it. You need leverage. Pull!"

"It's stuck!" she cried in terror. "Why is it stuck?"

"I think," said Theo, in an odd voice, "that I forgot to grease the face."

He had climbed up on the table by this time and was straddling the dead man's chest, clawing furiously at the mask.

"Chip it! Get the chisel! We'll chip it away!"

There was a muffled cry behind them, and turning, Erica saw that someone had opened the door. In the doorway stood the bereaved, their sallow faces livid with rage.

The tallest man made a leap for Theo but missed. Theo was already on the ground, and he plunged like a wild horse through the door. Erica followed him, running as if the dead man himself were after them.

They sat, shaking, in a cranny of rubber tires, at one end of Theo's city. The sun beat down on them, the hundred mirrors turned on their hooks and wires, and the springs, sleds, motors, rowboats, saws, clocks, flowerpots, and bedpans of humanity twirled past them. They sat in the shadow of a hundred furnaces.

"Best thing to do," said Theo at last, "is to forget the whole thing. A death mask, for Christ's sake!"

"If we were married and you died first, would you want to be buried?" she asked timidly, and realized, as she said it, that she was really asking something else.

"Ashes to ashes and dust to dust. No coffin for me. I want to go back to the earth."

A loneliness foamed up in her mouth when he said that. She had always assumed she would lie down with the rest of the family in one of the plots her father had bought years ago. Enough for the generations, he said. It wasn't a thing to take lightly. For when the trumpet sounded and everyone stood up in their graves, it was important, said her mother, to be among people you knew.

But by this time, lots of bodies must have scattered to dust.

The Lord knows his own, said her mother stoutly.

Erica saw them all very clearly, standing up in the graves and rubbing their eyes as after a long sleep, Hannah in the black dress she'd made for her funeral, her mother in the lace, Minnie, singing along with the heavenly host because she alone knew the words to the hymns, and herself in the white dress which would be her best dress forever.

"I took my French this morning," said Theo.

"You didn't tell me. How was it?"

"Awful. I flunked. I'm ready to pull out of this place." He touched her hair lightly. "And I want to take you with me. You got to trust me more, Erica. I'm not like your dad, but I'm all right."

"What are you going to do now?"

He shrugged.

"Go to some city, I guess. You can always find people in a city." Suddenly restless, he jerked himself up. "It's hot here. You want to rent a boat and go to the island for a swim?"

"I have to go home and get my suit."

"Jesus! Whoever swims near the island? Go in your underwear."

"A nice day," said the old man, sitting on a kitchen stool in front of the canoe shed. He looked past the open door toward the river, as if expecting someone to appear there. "Don't know why there aren't more folks out on the water."

The three of them went inside. Erica had yet to see a canoe in the canoe shed. Instead, it was full of nickelodeons, scrolled and flowered to resemble circus wagons, with the works decorously exposed. Behind little windows, the captive performers slept: drumsticks and cymbals, gears and piano rolls, perforated for the syntax of dead voices.

"Sign the book," said the old man, slipping behind a counter and handing Theo a pen. "You get number twenty-five. That really plays, Miss."

Erica was staring at the silver anatomy of a violin, spread open and joined to hundreds of tiny threads and wheels, as if awaiting a surgeon. She had not noticed it the last time. On the glass was a neatly typed label: JUDGED THE EIGHTH GREATEST INVENTION IN THE WORLD. CHICAGO WORLD'S FAIR. 1933.

"It sounds just like a real violin. Listen."

The old man took a nickel from his pocket and dropped it into the back of the machine. From deep inside she heard a sputter and a whirr. Theo bent closer to look; then all at once they heard a nervous spidery response, ping! ping! Wheels spun, silver pistons scraped the strings. The whole effect was oddly touching, as if they were watching a fading performer's come-back from senility. When its shrill and complicated heart fell silent, they all three burst into applause.

"You don't know that tune, I bet," said the old man, pleased and shy. "Go out that door to the docks and take the first boat on the end. The paddles are inside."

The island looked small, the way places always looked to Erica when she had known them as a child and then revisited them as an adult. Rocks scratched against the bottom of the boat, and she climbed out, bunching her skirt in her arm. Theo lifted the prow and together they pulled the boat over the thin strip of beach toward the trees.

"Come on," said Theo. "I'm going in."

He vanished into a bush. Erica waded along the edge of the water. The white skeleton of a crayfish surfaced as she dug her toes into the sand.

"Are you going swimming in your dress?"

She could not look at him.

"Somebody might come." But she knew there was nobody here but themselves.

"Good Christ," shouted the bush. "Since when is your own flesh a thing to be ashamed of?"

And when the voice spoke again, it was softer and more winning.

"Here I am."

Drawn by its strangeness, she turned. There he stood, very white and thin-legged, and oddly exotic in his nakedness, like a unicorn.

"Well, I'm going into the water."

He plunged forward with studied casualness, but his whole body grimaced when the water touched his waist. Then he stopped and carefully splashed his ribs and arms, humming quietly to himself. In the sunlight, his back was as round and white as a loaf of dough. Dazzled by the brightness of things, gazing about him at the mainland some distance away, he seemed to have sprung from the dark flesh of the water itself. Suddenly a whistle bleated so close to them that Erica started.

"Are you coming in?"

He was looking at her, over his shoulder, which prickled into gooseflesh as she watched him.

The whistle hooted again, louder this time, and they both turned in alarm. A steamer, covered with tiers and tiers of children, was chugging toward them, under the green banner of the Huron Park Day Line. As the whole side of the boat broke into shouting and waving, she opened her mouth to speak, but Theo was already lumbering toward the woods, the water weighing him down like a heavy garment.

"Jesus!"

Now it was passing them, slowly and steadily, but she could see the children jumping up and down, and she could hear the way they called her, *Hey lady, hey lady!* not because they knew her but because they did not know her. She shaded her eyes and waved, like one who has been working and glances up to see something amazing, a unicorn in the bush, a caravan of pilgrims on the road, a shipload of souls, rollicking and rolling into the new world.

Toni Cade

Mississippi Ham Rider

"I'll be here tomorrow for my early morning coffee fix. If you gonna meet me, sister, bring your own dime."

He swiveled away from the counter and stomped out past the juke-box, huddling his greatcoat around him. I flipped my notebook open and wrote: Mississippi Ham Rider can best be described as a salty stud. We had talked for nearly an hour—or rather I had talked, he had merely rolled his eyes and stared into his cup as he swirled the watery coffee revealing the grinds—and still I had nothing to write up really except that there was no humor about the man, and, at seventy, was not particularly interested in coming to New York to cut records for the new Blues series.

The waitress had wiped the counter menacingly and was leaning up against the pie display with her hands on her hips. I was trying to figure out whether I should follow Rider, put Neil on his trail, or try to scrounge up a story from the townsfolk. The waitress was tapping her foot. And the cook, a surly looking bastard in white cap, was peeping over the edge of the kitchen counter, his head kind of cocked to the side so that the sweat beaded around his nostril. I was trying to get myself together, untangle my legs from the stool and get out of there. It was obvious that these particular sinister folks were not going to fill my dossier with anything printable. I moved. But before I even reached the door I was in the third person absentular.

"So what's this high yaller Northern bitch doin' hittin' on evil ole Ham?"

There was only one Rider in the ten-page directory, an Isabele

Rider, the address typed in the margin. I folded myself into Neil's Volkswagen and tried to find it. The town itself was something out of Alice or Poe, the colored section was altogether unbelievable—outhouses, corner hard-heads, a predominance of junkyards with people in them, poverty with all the usual trimmings. And Isabele Rider ran one of those time-immemorial stores—love potions and dream books and star charts and bleaching creams and dipilatory powders, and mason jars of ginger roots and cane shoots. A girl of about sixteen was sitting on a milk box reading a comic book and eating a piece of sweet potato pie.

"Mrs. Isabele Rider around?" I asked.

"No." She went right on reading and eating.

"I'm Inez Williams," I said. "The people I work for are trying to persuade Mr. Ham Rider to record some songs. They want him to come to New York and bring his guitar. He's a great blues singer," I said.

She looked me over and closed the book. "You want some pie?"

"No thanks, just Mrs. Rider. She around?"

"No. Just me. I'm Melanie. My mother says Ham ain't going nowhere nor me either. Lady before asked me to sit-in somewhere. My mother says I ain't going nowhere, Ham neither."

I leaned on the counter and unbuttoned my sweater. A badly drawn zodiac chart was right in front of me. I traced the orbits looking for Aries the Ram to give me the high sign. He looked like a very sick dog in the last stages of sickle-cell anemia. I tried to figure out the best way to run it down to this girl right quick that they didn't have to live in this town and hang around in this store and eat sweet potato pie for lunch and act like throwbacks, before I totally distracted myself with the zodiac or considerations of abnormal hemoglobins and such like.

"Look," I said, "back in the twenties a lot of record companies put out a series called race records. And a lot of blues singers and country singers and some flashy show business types made a lot of records. Some made a lot of money. But when the depression came, the companies fell apart and these singers went on home. Some stuck around and mopped floors and ran elevators. Now this jive mother who is my boss thinks he can make some bread by recording some of the old-timers. And they can make some bread too. So what I want is to get your grand-daddy to come with us and sing awhile. You see?"

"You best speak to Ham himself," she said.

"I did. But he thought I was just trying to get into his business. All I do is write up a thing about the singers, about their life, and the company sticks this onto the album cover."

She licked the last of the pie from her fingers and stood up. "What you wanna know?"

I whipped out my notebook. "What does he like, where does he come from, who're his friends. Stuff like that."

"We three all what's left. His landlady, Mama Teddy, looks out for him when he gets drinking and can't help himself. And I look out of his way when he gets raffish." She shrugged.

"Any chance of us all getting together? My partner, Mr. Neil McLoughlin, is the one who handles the business and all. I'd like you all to meet him."

"This some fay cat?"

"Uh . . . yeh."

"Uh-hunh." She ripped off the edge of the calendar and wrote an address. "This here is where we eat, Mama Teddy's. You be there at six."

Neil was going into one of his famous crouches by the time I got to the park. He had spent the day trying to find quarters for us both which was a lost cause. There was not even a diner where we could trade notes without incident, so I fell in beside him on the bench, jostling the bottle in his pocket.

"I'm beat and burnt-out, I mean it," he wailed, rolling his eyes up to the heavens. "This is the most unfriendly town. I escaped from an unbelievable little rooming house down the road just as an incredible act of hospitality was about to be committed."

"Yeh, well look, pull yourself together and let's deal with the Rider character first. He's quite a sketch—jack boots, the original War-One bespoke overcoat, razor scar, gravel voice and personality to match and—you ready?—he'll be damned if he's going north. Says he was badly mistreated up there. Froze his behind off one winter in Chicago. And in New York, the Negro artists had to use a drafty freight elevator to get to the recording studio."

"Not like the swell conditions here."

"He wasn't an artist here. I think the best thing to do is just tape him here and let him sign whatever release one signs."

"But old man Lyons, dearheart, wants him in the flesh to allow the poor folkway-starved sophisticates to, through a outrageous process of osmosis, which in no way should suggest miscegenation—to absorb their native—"

"Alright, alright, calm down. The thing is, his last offer was to sing obscene songs for party records. He damned near committed mayhem. In short, the man don't wanna leave, buddy."

"But wasn't he at least knocked out by your superior charms, not to mention your long, lean gams?"

"Those are my superior and singular charms. He was totally unimpressed. But the man's seventy something, keep in mind."

Neil slouched over into his hands. "This is hard work, I mean it. And I feel a mean and nasty spell coming on. I never had so much trouble and complication in my life before. I've got consumption of the heart and—"

"Neil, my nerves."

"They were always pretty easy to find. Mobile, Auburn, just a sitting there in a beat-up room in a beat-up town in a beat-up mood, just setting there waiting for an angel of mercy, me. Doing nothing but a moaning and a hummin' and a strummin'—"

"Alright, cut it out. We're in trouble. The man don't wanna budge and all you can do is indulge in these theatrical and most unnerving, irritating fits of—"

"Dearheart, recall," he demanded, shoving his spread hand in my face. "There was old man Supper, a real nice old supper man. Kinda quiet like and easy going, just dipping his snuff and boiling his supper. And then ole Jug Henderson, the accident-prone saint of white lightning, fiddling away and sipping that bad stuff out of a mayonnaise jar. And—"

"Neil, my nerves."

"And ole Blind Grassy Wilson from Lynchburg, only one leg left by the time I arrived, but swinging still and real nice about talking into the machine to tell how his best gal slapped a razor across his chops."

"Enough, you're running amok." I got up and stretched my legs. "We've got to find a place called Mama Teddy's. And please, Neil, let me do the talking. I'm tired of eating sandwiches out of paper bags. Just be quiet till after we eat. And no wise cracks. We might get killed."

"Good Lord," he jumped up, "I'm not insured. One false move and the man's liable to cut me, beat me up, starve me to death and then poison me." He grabbed himself by the throat and rolled around atop the mailbox. A truck passed, I stepped aside and acted like I wasn't with the lunatic.

"Amazing how your race has deteriorated under segregation, Neil. If only you'd had an example to follow, you might have been a halfway decent dancer."

He smoothed his hair back and walked quite business-like to the car.

"Get in, woman."

Mama Teddy's was a store front thing. Fried chicken legs and bar-b-qued ribs were painted on the window pane. And scrawled across the top of the glass in fussy little curliques were the various price-fixed meals. In the doorway were three large jugs with soapy, brown something or other in them, rag wicks stuffed into the necks and hanging over the sides to the floor. But you could see that the place was clean, sort of. I was starving. Neil was dragging along the tape recorder mumbling statistics about hernia and prostate damage.

"You see that pick-up truck over there," he whispered. "It's full of angry blacks with ugly sticks who're gonna whip my head 'cause they think you're my woman."

"Never mind, let's go find Mr. Ethnic-Authentic."

Neil tripped over the jugs and a whiff of chit'lins damn near knocked me over. A greasy smell from the kitchen had jammed up my breathing before I even got into the place.

"Somebody's dying," whispered Neil.

"Soul food," I gasped, eyes watering.

"What?"

"You wouldn't understand, my boy."

The large, jovial woman who shuffled out of the kitchen with what only looked like great speed was obviously Mama Teddy.

"Hi, little honey," she said squashing me into her bosom. "Little Melanie told me all about you and you're surely welcome. You too," she said swallowing up Neil's hand in her fist. She hustled us over to a table with cloth and flowers.

"Mr. Rider'll be in directly less'n he's in his cups. And Miss Isabele's expected soon. Just rest yourself. We're going to have a fine southern dinner. Your folks from here?" she asked me.

"Mother's from Atlanta and my father was born in Beaufort, South Carolina."

"Mmmm-huh," she nodded, agreeing that these were certainly geographically fine folks.

"My people hail from Galway Bay," offered Neil.

"Well I'm sure they're mighty fine people too," she winked. "Now, is it for true," she whispered, setting the silverware, "you taking Mr. Ham to New York to sing?"

"We'd like to. But he doesn't seem very interested."

"Oh," she laughed, snapping the dishcloth across the table. "All that huffin' and puffin' don't signify. You know what he and Melanie been doing all day? Writing out the songs, the words. She's very smart, that girl. Make a fine secretary. I bet you could use a fine secretary with all that writing you do. There must be a lot of jobs. . . . "

Neil saw it coming. He slouched in his seat and pushed his glasses up. He sat all the while rubbing his eyes. I fingered the soup spoon, vaguely attentive to Mama Teddy's monologue. It was perfectly clear what kind of game she was running. And why not? Along with the numerous tapes of chats and songfests, Neil had collected from the Delta and the Carolines, a volume of tales that didn't go into the album catalogues, things he was saving for some sensational book he'd never write. The payoffs, bribes, bargains and deals, interviews in jail cells, drug wards, wino bins. Things apart from the usual folksy atrocity story. The romance had long since gone out of the job. Neil's first trauma occurred last spring when he finally smoked Bubba Mabley out of a corner. The sixty-year-old card shark had insisted on taking his "little woman" along to New York. This sloe-eyed youngster of fifteen turned out to be his illegitimate daughter by his niece. It knocked Neil out though he told it now with a certain rehearsed nonchalance.

"Mr. Rider wouldn't think of traveling without his family," the big woman was saying. "They're a very devoted family."

Neil had worked his eyes into a feverish red. But I was perfectly content. One good exploitive act deserved another. And what was the solitary old blues singer going to do after he had run the coffeehouse circuit and scared the living shit out of the college kids? It was grotesque no matter how you cut it. I wished I was in films instead. Ole Ham Rider besieged by well-dressed coffee drinkers wanting his opinion on Miles Davis and Malcolm X was worth a few feet of film. And the quaint introduction some bearded fool in tight-across-the-groin pants would give would justify more footage. No amount of drunken thinking could convince me that Mr. Lyons could groom this character for popular hootenannies. On the other hand, if the militant civil liberties unions got hold of him, Mr. Charlie was a dead man.

"Here's Miss Isabele," the woman announced.

She looked real enough to upset Lyons' plans. She shook hands and sat down, crossed her legs, and lit up a cigarette. She was good looking in a way—plucked eyebrows, clinging wool dress, scary make-up. You knew she'd been jitterbugging since kindergarten, but she looked good anyhow.

"So you want the old man to sing," she said, sniffing in the curls of smoke. "Sits in the window sometimes to sing, but that don't cut no greens, don't make no coins." She swerved around in her chair and kicked Neil's foot. "The man needs money, Mister. He's been needing for a long time. Now what you gonna do for him?"

"We're going to give him a chance to sing," Neil said, catapulting a cigarette butt across the room with the tablespoon.

She looked dissatisfied. "He needs," she said simply, sending up a smoke screen.

The image of the great old artist fallen on bad times, holding up in a stuffy rooming house drinking bad home brew out of a jelly jar and howling blues out the window appealed to my grade-B movie-ruined mind.

"Now when he gets here," Miss Isabele instructed me with her cigarette, "you get him to do 'Evil Landlord.' That's his best."

"Will he bring his guitar?" Neil asked.

"He mostways do."

"To the dinner table?" Neil persisted.

"To the dinner table," she said, one eyebrow already on its way to a threatening arch. "And I need a cigarette."

Mississippi Ham Rider brought his guitar and his granddaughter. He had on a white shirt and had left the greatcoat at home. He mumbled his greetings and straddled a chair, dislocating my leg in the process.

"You got a long pair of legs, sister."

I had no clever retort so we all just sat there while Mama Teddy heaved big bowls of things onto the table. There were collard greens and black-eye peas and ham hocks and a long pan of corn bread. And there were a whole lot of things I'd never even seen, even in my household.

"Bet you ain't ate like this in long time," Rider said. "Most people don't know how to cook nohow, 'specially you Northerners."

"Jesus Christ," said Neil, leaning over to look into the bowls on the far side of the table. "What's that that smells?"

"That's the South, boy," said Rider.

Melanie smiled and I supposed the old man had made a joke. Neil leaned back and got quiet.

"I don't sing no cotton songs, sister," he said, picking up a knife. "And I ain't never worked in the fields or shucked corn. And I don't sing no nappy-head church songs neither. And no sad numbers about losing my woman and losing my mind. I ain't never lost no woman and that's the truth." He sliced the corn bread with a ceremonial air.

"Good," I said for no particular reason.

He looked up and for one rash moment I thought he was going to smile. I lost my head. But he really looked like he was going to work that bony, old, ashen skull in that direction.

"Well what else is there?" Neil finally asked. "I mean just what kind of songs do you sing?"

"My kind."

Melanie smiled again and Miss Isabele laughed on her cigarette. But I was damned if I could get hold of this new kind of humor.

After we had eaten, Mama Teddy put coffee on the table and then tended to her customers. I stretched my legs into the aisle and relaxed, watching the old man work up his pipeful. He was impressive, the way a good demolition site can be, the way horror movies from the thirties are now. I was tempted to ask him how many people he had killed in his lifetime, thinking I had at last gotten hold of his vein of humor. But I sat and waited for him to sing. I was sure that on the first job he'd turn the place out and maybe do somebody in just for the fun that was in it. And then a really weird thing came over me. I wanted to ask him a lot of dumb things about the South, about what he thought of the sit-ins and all. But he had already taken on a legendary air and was simply not of these times. I cursed Mr. Lyons' fairy-tale mentality and quietly indulged in fabricating figures from whole cloth.

"First I'm gonna sing you my birthday song," he said, pushing the coffee cups to the side. "And then I'm going to do this number about a little lady with long legs."

"Then what?" I smiled, putting my cup down.

"Then I'm gonna get drunk directly and pack my things. My bad suspenders and my green hat," he said. "One jar of Noxzema and my stocking cap."

Melanie laughed straight out and Neil began gagging on Miss Isabele's cigarette smoke.

"And I gotta get a brand new jug of Gallo," he sighed. "I don't never do no heavy traveling without my loving spoonful."

"Then you're coming with us?" I asked.

"We all going to New York and tear it up," he said.

"Damn," coughed Neil.

Rider grabbed his guitar by the neck and swung it over the dishes. He gave Neil a terrible look that only aggravated the coughing.

"But first I think Mr. Somebody best go catch himself some air."

"I can take it," Neil growled, hooking up the tape recorder. He climbed over customers to get to the outlet. "It's on, man," he said. "Go ahead and sing your song."

He looked up at Neil and then he did smile. I wouldn't ever want him to smile at me.

"I can take it," said Neil again, pushing up his glasses.

"See that you do, boy. See that you do." He plucked at the strings, grinning from ear to ear.

Susan Engberg

Trio

Now they were deep into the frozen months. If Paul and his two daughters were a few minutes early to the piano lessons, he would nod to the secretary of the music school, and they would wait in the comfortable office where it was warm. Here the radiators clanged and hissed against the disparate music of three or four or five violins and pianos, one of which might now and then, like a voice, swell momentarily above the others as the door to a lesson room opened and closed. Outside the ground-level window a bare hedge of spirea had become bowed down with ice.

He usually sat on the couch, one daughter on either side of him, the feet of the younger in her rumpled knee socks not yet touching the floor. Sometimes the children rested their heads against his arms; they were tired from school, and it would be dark by the time they finished their lessons and were driven home. Paul's own eyes were often heavy as he waited. Thoughts came and went in the space of his mind—about his lectures and papers, one student or another, the laundry, the groceries, the book he dreamed of beginning to write in the summer, the hope of a letter from his wife, Marta—but for the time being it was a relief simply to be quiet with his children, the pressure of their bodies against his like two stabilizing weights.

The central fact of their present life, which Paul woke into each morning and took with him to bed at night, was Marta's separation from the family for the year while she finished a lectureship in the eastern part of the country. He and she had reasoned long over this decision, weighing the esteem and usefulness of careers and salaries against the sustenance of daily family companionship, until one day early the previous spring Marta had admitted that she actually felt insulted by all the friends and family who were just assuming that she would break her contract and follow Paul to his new position in the Midwest. Where was her own voice, she had wanted somewhat shrilly to know, and from the increasing extremity of her language, Paul began to accept the depth of her need for separate action. So it happened that he not only went on ahead without her, but took the children with him as well. Intelligence, they both hoped, would see them through.

For Paul it was a good deal messier and more lonely than he had allowed for. If he had been alone, he would have thrown himself into his work in his usual way and so have pushed on to some sort of familiar sense of order; but in this year of solitary responsibility for the children, his attention was so divided that he often lost his former dynamic momentum. Haphazard complexities could absorb huge amounts of energy. Action seemed muddied. From the low vantage of his periodic exhaustion, the future would loom up as alarmingly demanding and circumscribed.

The piano lessons, however, were somewhat of a relief. He found that he was looking forward to them. His job was simply to sit off to one side of the piano in the parent's chair, listening to the music and taking down a few instructions for the children's practicing at home. The lessons took place in a small upstairs room off the stage of the chill auditorium. Besides the grand piano and the chairs and a case of music, the only other furniture in the room was a box-like gas heater, which in this season sucked a low note of wind into its internal fire and occasionally vibrated sympathetically with the piano. Dusk would come during the hour of the lessons. Outside the tall, arched window was a sycamore tree, reminding Paul pleasantly of his studies in Europe; between these mottled limbs and scattered brown seed-balls he measured the dark blue approach of evening.

First Marie, the younger daughter, and then Kate would come upstairs for instruction. Carol Harper seemed to Paul a very good teacher. Energetic, professional in spite of her youth, a trifle nervous perhaps, she used herself effectively on behalf of the children. She asked questions and waited when replies were slow; she taught music theory so naturally that it began to bloom even in Paul's mind; she moved the children's fingers to the correct keys without too much comment; she praised; she encouraged; she was humorous and yet precise about mistakes; she was reverent. The idea of music seemed marvelously at large in the room. Paul instinctively appreciated the excellence of the teacher and the orderliness of the lessons. A great deal would seem to have happened inside a small space.

He found himself thinking more and more about music and about the economy of beauty. His own family had never had a piano, perhaps never had even considered it. A close, unadventurous lot, of whom he was the only outlandish and farflung member, all their efforts had gone into making him, the only boy-child of their four, a scholar, so that he could win scholarships and thus gain a more material hold on the precarious, fearsome tenancy they called life. Both his parents had been the children of immigrants, from Sicily, but they had probably never imagined his eventual studies abroad, his unclannish marriage and the peripatetic careers of both himself and his wife. His parents never travelled themselves; in not one of the young couple's half dozen domiciles over the years had they ever ventured to visit.

Striving in large measure there had been in his past, but little music. These days Paul found himself fascinated as he supervised his daughters' practicing each night. Slowly, with fingers that felt thick and slow, he learned to play the simple pieces himself and felt their shapes take hold in his mind; when he finally came to the first Bach minuet and could read it through, he felt tremendously happy. He played the scales, too, and listened to their different sounds. At the lessons he sat humbly and quietly, stayed from his own busyness, while his children nimbly played. Their large, brown eyes and soft lips and dark, artless curls appeared to him even more beautiful as they concentrated on the keyboard. Where did all that beauty and agility come from, he often wondered. The children were more lovely, more vital than he ever could have imagined them; they seemed at every moment poised upon a crossroads, dancing on their toes, arms open to the four winds. Bursts of happiness would fill him now and then on account of them, and he would seem to have been led to the center of a circle to dance with his daughters, with his wife, while all around them were music and patterns of light.

At the end of each lesson Carol Harper stood, the pupil stood, and they bowed to one another. Then Paul would exchange a few pleasantries with her and they would part until the following week. At home Paul would turn on lights, prepare a supper and then as usual see that the children fed the cat and helped with the dishwashing and practiced the piano, and then he would trudge upstairs behind them where they might play a game of cards or read a story aloud on the big bed. In their own rooms Kate sometimes sat at her desk, bent beside the lamp light; Marie might play with her blocks and dolls, accompanied by a sing-song monologue; Paul would then lie down for a few minutes with the evening paper or a book, before he got down to the always pressing business of serious studying.

His field was political science, and in the last few years he had put forth several articles on emerging forms of European cooperation that were bringing him the beginnings of a reputation. As he scanned the newspaper, his eyes would feel heavily lidded with the intensity of his intelligence. The book he hoped to write existed like a constant pressure behind his eyes; phrases hammered at his consciousness, unbidden—*shifting of attitudes, unusual flux, the continuum of development and decay*—crying out to be brought under control. But was he ready? Did he know enough? Page after page he turned as he forced himself to stay awake and bring his mind to bear on more and yet more of the material of the world.

One midnight he woke dumbfounded to find his bedside light on, the newspaper fallen to his chest, himself still dressed, his throat very sore. Beside him the yellow cat lay curved in sleep on the pillow that should have been his wife's. Night had taken over entirely. Without him the children had put themselves in their own beds; unknown to him a new snow had whitened the dark, closing them even more deeply into winter. He went downstairs to lock the doors, and a translucent emptiness struck him to the heart. He telephoned his wife.

"Marta?"

"Paul!" she said, thick with sleep. "Darling, what time is it? Is everything all right?"

He could barely speak; he could barely swallow. He imagined the deep, open neckline of her nightgown as she propped herself up to talk and her dark, dishevelled hair and the way she would be reaching out to turn on the light and pick up her watch from among her books. He huddled over the telephone in the cold kitchen.

"Nothing is wrong," he said. "I love you."

Each time they paused, they were still connected. He could hear her breathing; he could almost hear her mind working and her heart beating. The silence after the call seemed irrationally absolute.

In the morning he woke feverish and dizzy. He guided himself from bathroom to bed, feeling unreal, and returned to sleep. When next he woke, he saw the face of Marie very close to his on the pillow, her eyes fixed on him. With an effort he came up through his sickness to meet her.

"I'm sick," he said.

"Daddy," she responded, naming him. She laid a hand on his chest.

"Will you get yourself some breakfast?" he asked. "I don't think we're going to make it to school today." There was a ringing between himself and his voice.

He watched the sympathy on her face turn into anticipation. "Can we watch TV?" she asked.

He nodded painfully, trying to joke. "Just don't make yourselves sick."

She dropped her head to his chest and hugged him briefly. "Daddy," she repeated happily, petting him, "get well, Daddy." Then she skipped out of the room.

He turned his face to the frost-rimmed window and the sunless view of the bared maple branches. He stared at the wallpaper, chosen neither by himself nor his wife, in which there were little faces to be found, repetitiously grimacing. There was one closet in the room and one cluttered bureau with a bleak, dusty mirror above it. There was no one to take care of him. He closed his eyes and sank beneath the ringing in his head to sleep.

Later in the morning he pulled himself up and dialed the secretary of his department to cancel his classes. He called the music school and left word that he would be unable to bring the girls in that afternoon. Oh, too bad! exclaimed the secretary; she hoped he would be better soon. Yes, he answered, it was probably just the flu. He hung up, took one look at his unshaven, haggard face and collapsed into the pillow.

The grimacing faces met his on every turn of his feverish head. His eyes saw distortion. At the gray window elongated tree branches stretched into a fantastic winter, while minute by minute he himself seemed to be contracting inside an unbelievable body. Fear clamped his chest and throat. It was barely possible to breathe, so great was the constriction. Helplessly he thumped the bed with his fist.

The children came through the doorway and stood side by side, still in their bedclothes, their hair unbrushed, looking down at him. "Bring me a bottle of mineral water, will you, Kate?" he asked.

Marie continued to gaze at him silently. "You look funny," she finally pronounced. He closed his eyes and wished she would go away. The grip of disorder seemed permanent.

"I can't open the bottle," said Kate, returning to the bedside.

"Of course you can!" he said, suddenly angry, desperate.

"I've tried and I can't," she said. "Here," and she thrust the bottle and the opener towards him.

"I want you girls to go and turn off that television." He raised his voice hoarsely and watched surprise snap into their features. "Do you hear me? You've got to pull yourselves together and take care of things. I'm too sick to move."

They scurried away, and for a long time he lay breathing heavily and clutching the bottle to his chest. He thought about death. Finally he raised himself up, forced the cap from the bottle and took a long drink of the smooth, rounded water.

Then he waited. There was nothing else to do. All day time lost its standardization. Large wedges of hours might pass without his awareness, or moments be sliced into painful segments.

At dusk he heard the children quarrelling in another bedroom but felt too weak to interfere. Finally he called them in and asked them what they had eaten during the day.

"Now listen," he said with difficulty, and he told Kate to scramble some eggs. He wasn't sure what else there was to eat, but they could have toast and milk and some fruit and then they were to feed the cat and make sure all the lights were turned off and come upstairs and wash themselves for bed. Did she understand?

Kate nodded. "Will you be better tomorrow?" she asked.

"I'll still be sick tomorrow, but you girls are to get up and take the school bus. Today was an exception."

No, no, they protested, they wanted to stay home with him.

They weren't sick, were they? he asked anxiously. How did they feel?

Fine, they answered, except, yes, they were sick, and please, please couldn't they stay home with him? Kate sat down on the edge of the bed and Marie began to crawl under the covers with him.

"Ah, go away!" he exclaimed. "You're wearing me out." He gave Marie a little push, but she only pressed closer to him.

"Daddy," she said, nestling against him, her arm across his chest. Kate also lay alongside him, propped her head in her hand, and began to study him. She looked very much like Marta and also very much like his mother and his youngest sister.

"What have you been doing all day?" he asked.

"Everything," she answered. "I like to stay home better than I like to go to school."

"Oh, you do, do you?" he said neutrally. It was a great effort to respond. Kate dropped her head to his shoulder and the three of them lay still. It was nearly dark in the room. He closed his eyes.

"I read two library books this afternoon," murmured Kate.

"That's good," he answered without opening his eyes. He felt her adjusting the covers under his chin.

"Daddy, don't you just love unmade beds?"

"Is that where you've been reading?"

"I made a nest," she answered, "and I let Marie come in, too."

"Sometimes she did," corrected Marie, "but she kept the best pillows."

Invisibly, the wood inside the old bureau near the bed cracked and was quiet. The animate weight of his children rose and fell with his own difficult breath. A faint, sudden current of released joy passed through him, almost too swiftly to be trusted; a heavy lid had lifted, a slit of light had appeared briefly along an inner horizon. All might be well; all might not be well.

"You've still got to go to school tomorrow, no matter how you feel about unmade beds," he said finally. "Now both of you hop out of here and go get yourselves some supper. Go on, out! out!" He elbowed them gently away, but then brought them in close embrace again. "Now take good care of each other," he whispered into their hair. They hugged him, and for a time the pressure of their arms lingered in the memory of his skin.

At night, however, when the children slept, he was absorbed so deeply into the topography of his illness that he felt lost from the touch of his daily life. The laws of this strange land were unknown. There were incalculable mountains to climb and troughs of dimensionless space to cross and narrow, extremely important places to shudder through. Humming voices and sinister elastic arms waited for him at every turn. On one smoking, crater-pocked plain a battle was being fought. For a long time he watched, as a traveller watches a scene onto which he has happened, but then he realized that the battle was his own; he was the principal. A figure came out of a crater to meet him, and as he tensed himself to face the advance, he wakened into the first light of another colorless winter day.

He was sicker than before. He scarcely heard the children preparing for school. When Kate brought in another bottle of water and a plate of toast, he thought wildly of asking her to stay home and nurse him, but then she seemed too much a child, too potentially demanding in her own right. Thanking her weakly, he closed his eyes again before she had even left his bedside.

He heard the front door closing and the voices of the children rising into the outside air. It sounded cold. He rolled his face against the pillow and drew up his knees. In between the rising and falling of intensities in his sickness, he listened dully to his labored breathing. He remembered Marta's breathing when the children were being born. Both births he had witnessed, and if there had been any way to take on part of the labor himself, he would have done it, he would have done anything. He had not been able to bear the thought of being left behind. She had seemed to be following a cord into an immemorial vitality. Marta, Marta, he had said when her eyes had closed and she had turned inward toward her enthralling pain, Marta, my dear.

He dreamt that he alone must enter a basement window, almost no more than a crack above the ground. It was necessary that he leave his briefcase underneath a sycamore tree. Hand it to me, will you? he implored the children when he had finally accomplished his entry, but they did not seem to understand; they were laughing and dancing. All that work, please, please, he begged again, but his dry words went nowhere.

At noon, urinating, he rested his head against the cool wall beside the toilet. When he was back in bed and the dizziness had passed, he pulled the telephone next to his pillow and called his cleaning woman. She might be able to come today and bring groceries, he thought; perhaps she could even cook the children a meal.

"Sick are you?" said Mrs. McClentin. "And what might the trouble be?"

"The flu, I think. I should be on the mend by tomorrow."

"Now I don't know what to say," she said. "My grandchildren are coming on Saturday, as I told you, and what if I should be getting sick myself and not able to keep them? The flu is a terrible kind this year, they say, just terrible. I don't know but that I don't want to set foot in your door, if you understand my problem."

Ah, yes, he said, he did understand, but there was this matter of the groceries. He hung tightly to the receiver.

"You poor man," she said. "I'll tell you what, I'll pick up a few things later in the afternoon and come by with the bag and your Kate can take over from there."

That was kind of her, very kind, he said as he hung up.

He lay back dramatically, pitying himself, and looked at his watch. Two minutes had passed. Adjusting the time to Marta's zone, he imagined her walking freely down a street in her own local snow. Her back was to him; she did not know his needs. He narrowed his eyes at the sullen window-square. Well-being to each person was a pressing daily matter; now, daily, he and Marta lived in ignorance of each other. And time was passing, month after month. Marta had gone her own way, all right. He thumped his fist angrily against the bed. Endless legions of wallpaper faces grimaced at him. Objects in the small room stood firm in their disarrangement. On the bureau there were books and papers, photographs, underwear, coins, Marie's toy monkey. HI DADDY, Kate had written into the dust of the mirror.

Shortly before the children were to come home from school, he forced himself to sit up and eat a piece of the cold toast. He drank a good deal more water and then set the empty bottle down, exhausted. The front door slammed, and another evening had begun. It was the second day. Wasn't it the second day? Or was it the third? He wondered where he would find the strength to continue.

They brought up the mail and piled it on his chest. There was one from Mommy, they shouted; he should open it, open it. Cold emanated from their clothing, drafts of cold stirred around his neck, his stomach knotted and turned. He swept aside the envelopes. The fingers of the children were icy. They were both talking at once. He didn't know how he was going to get through it. He wanted to disown them. The energy that was being sucked up from him was unbelievable. Their voices were high and excited.

"Go away," he said to them, and when they didn't respond, he barked, "Get out of here!" and then nauseating blackness overwhelmed him, blackness with tiny speckles of red and far, far away voices, coming from the far end of a tunnel, a black tunnel, prickled with red.

Someone was wiping his mouth. "Not that way, this way!" said Kate's voice. "Here, you take the towel."

"I want Mommy," wailed Marie.

"Well, she's not here. Now help me with this sheet."

He lay in clammy stillness. His children were doing things to him. Kate was lifting his arm.

"Daddy, you've got to sit up."

"No," he said, "I can't."

"You've got to. Come on."

He sat up and they clumsily put a clean pajama top on him. His head fell back on a different pillow. A clean sheet was brought over his chest, then blankets.

Someone's child was crying.

"Stop that, Marie!" said Kate. "Come with me."

He heard water running in the bathroom and voices and feet hurrying down the stairs. He was floating away now, an empty, ringing shell of himself.

Something was being held to his ear. "Wake up," said Kate, pressing the hard telephone receiver against him. "Wake up. I called Mommy and she wants to talk to you."

"Paul? Shall I fly out? How bad are you?"

"I don't know," he said.

"I don't know what to do. I'm grading mid-terms. Have you seen a doctor?"

"No one," he answered.

"What are your symptoms?"

She made a sound of sympathy after each item. "Yes, well, two days, you said? Then you really should be out of it in a day or two. Oh God, this is awful. Are you remembering to drink?"

"I threw up."

"Then you've got to take smaller amounts. Let me talk to Kate."

Wordlessly he handed over the receiver.

It was amazing how empty he felt, how weightless, floating in a new elation of emptiness. Soon there would be nothing left of him. He felt quieter now, quiet and empty.

"Daddy, take a drink of water," said Kate.

"No, not yet."

"Mommy said you had to. She said for me to use this straw."

Marie climbed onto the bed and sat cross-legged beside his body. "I'm going to read you a story I wrote," she said when he had taken a swallow of water. "It's called Toby the Skunk. 'Once upon a time there was a skunk named Toby. He was naughty. He lived in a house with his mother and his father and his sister Emily. One day they went to a Chinese restaurant.' "

"Daddy, are you listening? You're supposed to stay awake and drink water."

There was a child sitting on either side of him. The cat had come to lie at the top of his pillow on the crown of his head. He took another sip of water.

" 'Toby wouldn't eat any of the Chinese food. Emily ate everything and so she got a fortune cookie. Toby didn't get anything.' "

"Is that the end?" he asked. "What happens to Toby?"

"That's all the farther I've gotten."

"Did you write that at school?"

"No, I wrote it in my room."

"I like your story," he said. "I want to hear the end of it." He licked his dry lips and felt the tired calm in his cheeks. "I think I should rest now. Why don't you both go downstairs and get something to eat? I'll be better now." He felt pleased to be so emptied of himself.

When their piano practicing began downstairs, he was half-asleep. Scales ascended and descended with falters and alignments until the rightful sequences were rediscovered. Structures of sound bore him aloft. Far below he heard Kate hesitatingly put together the hands of the Bach minuet, which until now she had been practicing separately. Yes, that's it, he encouraged her silently as the complexities were drawn into place. Nothing much existed now except the sheerness of himself and the music and his children. He felt satisfied by his illness.

The next morning after the children had left for school, he made his way downstairs for the first time and enjoyed the slight strangeness he found to the rooms. He would have liked to keep it. He wouldn't go too fast, he told himself, he would just do one thing at a time. He broke an egg into boiling water and set a piece of bread to toast. He looked out the kitchen window at the plain grey sky and the snow and the snow-lined spray of redbud branches. He carried the children's cereal bowls to the sink, rinsed out the milk and bits of cereal and wiped the table. In his deliberateness he nursed his slightly buoyant, quiet separateness. He was a vessel of untold value. When the egg was poached, he spooned it onto toast, set a fork and a napkin by his plate, and sprinkled a few grains of salt onto the filmed yolk.

Under the wall clock was a calendar at which he gazed as he slowly chewed: music lessons, a departmental meeting for himself, a piano recital for both girls the following Sunday. His eye slid easily along the squares of the week; maps were like that, too, the multi-colored world yielding to a glance. He pressed up with his fork the last of the egg-soaked crumbs. Bite by bite everything that had been on his plate had been taken inside himself. The daylight in the kitchen was even more subdued; it would snow, perhaps, by evening.

Back in bed, he took up the stack of mail and found Marta's letter. With one hand as he read he stroked his three-day beard. Now and then he coughed deeply and drew the covers higher over his vulnerable chest. The letter had been written very early in the morning, after his midnight telephone call.

Dear Paul,

I haven't been able to go back to sleep yet, but I'm not uneasy any longer lying awake in the middle of the night. Will it seem strange to you if I say that I think I am learning at last how to live? I don't know why it should have taken something drastic like this year to help me come into this birthright, but so it has. Your call tonight—what really was on your mind? Do you know how often I think of you three there? What is happening to me is in spite of the ache of not being with you. In the classroom I think at last I am finding my own voice. I have this terrific sense of privacy. I walk around thinking, it's nobody else's damn business who I am or who I am becoming. Do you understand? I am happy to wake up every day. It was as if for a while I had forgotten how to speak.

I love you. I am taking long walks every weekend—last Sunday to the wharves. Excellence is on my mind. I am thinking of how the path might be kept clear.

I miss you all so much. I miss the sight of the children's bodies getting undressed for baths. Yours. The reality of what I'm not touching overwhelms me sometimes.

I had another letter from your mother last week, and it upset me greatly for a time, still does, I guess. She implies that I am way beyond my limits. She's worried about you, of course. I don't know how to answer her except in time.

Where would we be if you hadn't your wonderful ability to take the long view? You've steadied me many times. I wish I could tell you how deeply you have contributed to my sanity. I want to live *with* you. The future seems open. Tell me really why you called. There has to be something you weren't saying. I feel so right about this year and yet my mind is always half on you because it has to be right for you, too.

Tell the girls I have gotten their Valentines and will write to them tomorrow. And now I must sleep. I hope you are sleeping well. Kisses to you all.

My love, *Marta*

Paul rolled onto his side towards the window. The long view: was it true what she said? How strong was his mind? He fell asleep and dreamt that he had an erection the length of his arm; it is as long as my arm, he laughed to himself incredulously in the dream. It was the most amazing erection he had ever had. He woke up laughing, coughing, went to the bathroom, and came back to bed where he slept peacefully until afternoon. It was snowing, without bluster, when he woke.

That night Kate came into his bedroom to brush her hair by the bureau mirror. She had recently taken an interest in her hair and now stood in her nightgown, turning her face from side to side as she gazed at herself and brushed. Paul watched her. At the beginning of the winter term she had been weighed and measured by the school nurse: four foot eleven and seventy-eight pounds, she had announced that evening at the dinner table.

She pursed her lips and held up a handful of curls. "Shall I get my hair cut, Daddy?" she asked without turning around.

"No," he said. "I like it."

She frowned at herself and continued brushing. He watched the thin shoulders and arms of the new generation at work beneath the flannel gown.

"Well, do you want it cut?" he asked.

"Oh, I don't know!" she said impatiently and left the room.

A moment later she came back to stand in the doorway. "Are you really getting better?" she asked.

"Yes, thank you," he answered, "much better. I think I'll get up and start bossing you around tomorrow."

"Good," she sighed, "because everything is sure messed up around here."

All weekend indoors he wore the same old heavy sweater and navy blue knit hat and scarf. He drank hot lemonade with honey as he sat at his desk making notations in the margins of student research papers. Beneath his study in the basement the washing machine churned through its cycles. In the living room the girls had made a sprawling house of many rooms with their blocks, filled with scraps of cloth and carpet samples and empty thread spools. They came in occasionally to lounge against his chair. They toyed with his scarf and the curls of hair sticking out below his hat.

"Daddy," drawled Marie, testing his still unshaven cheek with her small hand, "come and play house with us."

"I am playing house with you." He made a large question mark in a margin and then looked up to smile at her.

"No, you're not, you're just doing your old work."

All weekend he watched the three of them living together, wrapped up in winter, a father and two daughters. He kept his eye on life from the vantage of his still tender, slowly improving condition.

"Play with us," his daughters begged him again.

With two columns and an arched block and two triangular blocks for an apex he made a second, grander doorway to their house.

"Not there," said Kate. "We've already got a door. Here, you can work these pieces."

He lay down on his side with his head in his hand, several wooden trucks and figures lined up in front of him, and mildly watched his children. In a little while they appeared not to need him.

Sunday afternoon he took another nap and woke feeling more rested than he had in a long time. He built a fire in the livingroom fireplace, spread a tablecloth on the floor as Marta sometimes used to do, and served a supper of toasted cheese sandwiches and fruit in the light of the flames. After he had cleared away the plates of apple parings, he lay down on the floor again and let the children wrestle with him. "More!" they shrieked. "More! Again!" His hat fell off, his scarf came loose and the ceiling and walls and floor were lambent with firelight. They wrestled until he lay back laughing and coughing and begging them to stop. The dancing patterns of light were beautiful. He lay flat on his back, breathless. It was as if he had just found himself to be there. "Let's tickle him again!" shouted Kate with a musical cascade of giggles.

On his return to work the next week, he continued to wear the heavy sweater and knit hat and scarf as badges of his nearly completed journey through the influenza. He had grown fond of the outfit. In the hallways he greeted his colleagues spiritedly. From the lecture platform he looked out into faces that were scarcely a decade older than those of his children. He listened to his own voice. Was he being clear? It seemed especially important that he be as articulate as he was able.

At noon he stayed in his office for a cup of bouillon and the sandwich he had brought from home. He took his lunch to the window and sat on the broad sill with a lookout over the university and the church spires to the end of town, where rolling fields of snow began. Squinting through the steam of his cup into the noonday light, he could almost see how this new world must at first have appeared. Now small planes tilted, glinting, down out of the sky towards the small airport where once uncut grasses and jack rabbits had abounded. He had glimmers of newly discovered territories in himself that he wondered how to keep sight of.

The children as usual took the bus home from school, let themselves in the back door with their own key, and then called him at his office to say they had arrived. On Monday he left early to shop for food and that night cooked a real dinner and felt energetic enough to put in several hours of evening reading after the children were asleep. His cough was much better. At ten-thirty he stopped, so as to be sure he got enough sleep, took a shower, put on his pajamas, and with the feeling that a successful day was coming to a close, he stepped into the concentrated hush of the children's bedrooms. Sitting for a few minutes on each of the beds, he could feel his breathing slow toward their sleeping breaths; he could feel their presence entering and filling his heart. Beneath tacked-up pictures of horses and dogs and panda bears, Marie lay flung out inside the motion of a dream. He watched her sealed eyes, her parted lips, her round cheeks and then he covered her and crossed to Kate's room. The cat looked up from the bed and yawned. It was the room of a child almost no longer a child. Knowledge seemed to be appearing in the new angularity of her body and the planes of her face. In nine years she would be the age Marta had been when they had met. He reached out a hand to smooth back her hair, but as she at that moment stirred, sighed and curled more deeply into sleep, he gave the cat a scratch instead and returned to his own room, happy.

On Wednesday, detained by a student, he closed his office at four-fifteen and hurried home through the fading light to pick up the girls for their piano lessons.

He found them lying feet to feet on the couch reading comic books.

"Come on!" he said. "I expect you to be ready by the time I get here. You're old enough to keep track of the time."

Marie stretched indolently; Kate continued to read, twirling a dark curl of hair around her finger.

Paul strode across the room and jerked the cheap paper from her hands. Kate grinned up beautifully, winningly.

"Kathryn," he made himself roar. "Get your shoes on! You, Marie, shoes! jacket! Quick!" He clapped his hands, urgent in his wish to inspire. His children were like lumps. They shivered and complained and poked each other in the car. Why couldn't they just stay home and read, they wanted to know. It was too cold for piano lessons today.

"Hush," he said to them, keeping his vision attentive to what was ahead. He parked the car and herded them along the icy sidewalk and up the steps of the music school.

The secretary looked up from a file box. A violin was being tuned somewhere. The waiting room was empty. "We're late," Paul said to Marie. "We'll go straight on up." Kate collapsed into the corner of the couch to wait her turn and opened one of the comics she had brought along with her music.

"Miss Harper is upstairs?" Paul asked the secretary.

"She should be," answered the secretary. "She stepped down a few minutes ago to see if you had come."

He and Marie clomped noisily up the wooden stairs to the deserted auditorium, which was faintly lit by the twilight in the tall, arched windows. Old-fashioned chandeliers of fluted, flower-like glass bells hung at intervals over the two hundred empty seats, and a stencilled design ran along the upper edge of the painted walls where the wooden ceiling slanted up. It was a charming, intimate hall.

"Hush, wait," said Paul, staying Marie with his hand on her shoulder.

"What for?"

"Listen!"

In the stillness they heard the piano music, not the stumblings of a child's lesson in progress, but liquid repetitions of a difficult phrase, then the passage to which it belonged, itself repeated, then repeated again, the musicality of the touch so astonishing that Paul stood without moving. Again the difficult phrase was extracted for attention; a comprehensive mind was at work; there was a mistake, a recovery, another attack; notes poured out cohesively, assuredly. It sounded nearly perfect to Paul. Hesitantly he continued up the stairs. The door was closed to the small room beside the stage. As they crossed the platform to it, he could hear human sounds along with the music, humming, a groan, sniffing. "Ah!" said the voice in exasperation at the poised apex of a crescendo. The music broke off abruptly and two hands landed hard on a dissonant chord.

Paul knocked softly. There was a scraping within and the door was flung open by Carol Harper, her eyes shining with tears. "Well, you're here," she said in her quick voice. "Good. I thought you might still be sick."

"I enjoyed your playing just now," said Paul.

Carol gave a short laugh. "I'm out of practice, I'm afraid, terribly out of practice."

Paul took his chair, shed his jacket, and opened his notebook. Marie had slid onto the piano stool and was looking down at her boots, her shoulders hunched. Carol stood with her back to them in the curve of the piano's wing. She fumbled in her purse. She blew her nose. Sycamore branches and the shadows of sycamore branches moved within the arch of the window.

Carol turned around and shook back her hair. Her eyes were red. "Excuse me, please." She closed her eyes for an instant and seemed to be collecting herself. "Excuse me, I used to be able to play that piece, but I'm finding myself far rustier than I had realized."

Paul nodded sympathetically. Marie continued to look at her boots.

"Fifty-two students," enunciated Carol, her fist resting on the top of the piano, "I have fifty-two students."

Paul nodded again.

Then a slight tremor seemed to pass, cleansingly, through the young woman's body and her manner shifted. She quickly took her chair and clapped Marie on the shoulder with a friendly hand.

"Well, Marie, let's see what you're going to do today. Start with the scale, please, A major. Good. Now, left hand. All right, now can you tell me what the next scale will be?"

Paul wrote *scale* in the assignment book. Marie counted up the keyboard and then looked at her teacher with large eyes. Two adults waited for her pronouncement; a child was to carry forward the knowledge of the circle of fifths.

"E major?" asked Marie.

"Of course," said Carol. "Very good. Now would you try it, please? How many sharps does it have?"

Paul wrote *E major* in the notebook and took a deep, quiet breath as he settled into the lessons. His gaze travelled between Carol's earnest profile, the soft face of his child, and the framed view of the winter, which intensified into an evening blue, and then by degrees as the color drained away, the sycamore tree merged with the world. They were in a warmed cave of light.

Where did Carol live, Paul wondered. When did she find time to practice? Did she come here, to this room, during odd, deserted hours, or did she have an upright piano in her apartment, with a lamp on it and stacks of music and a bust of Shubert or Chopin or Beethoven? The simplicity of her dress, the directness of her speech, the intentness of her manner suggested economy, efficiency, a self subsumed into its purpose; but then there was this matter of the tears, the fear of not measuring up, the dissonance of struggle. His meditations stirred in him a deep layer of understanding.

Kate now was on the stool, looking drowsy and placid, her hair curling over her cheek. *Excellence is on my mind,* Marta had written. Kate played through her scale and her recital piece for Sunday, and then she tipped her head to one side and started in on the Bach minuet. As the music began to draw her in, she seemed to suck in on her cheeks; her eyes widened a little and her nose flared as she came to the difficult places. Paul saw himself in her expression, Marta in her eyes, her hair, his own mother, his sisters in the angle of her nose.

"Good," said Carol, who seemed recollected now from her agitation. "You've made a good start in putting the hands together. Now, this is a dance." She reached over and played the opening phrase. "The dancers need a strong beginning. Now you try. Yes, that's it, even more, right hand sing out, continue."

Paul stared at the pattern he saw emerging from the scene: those who were young and still searching for their own powers, like himself, like Carol Harper, like Marta far away, yet cared for those even younger, lives unfolding out of lives, out of life, every moment pressing them onward. He was discovering himself to be already deep inside this pattern; it surrounded him like a dance, and what was important was the power between the dancers. He felt his heart reaching out, his mind stretching. Everything his finely trained intellect loved was still within his grasp—all those maps he was so fond of studying, with the red faction, the blue coalition, the green uncertainty about borderlines; all those political tendencies in crude slow motion shifting endlessly; all those theories, pleasing in their subtlety, researched, annotated, set down upon pages—but now he knew without doubt that he had also given himself over to a huge, whirling harmony, from which pattern within pattern could emerge. Sitting lightly in his chair, very still, he felt himself expanding to accept this vast motion, kindred to himself.

"I'll show you what the next part sounds like," said Carol to Kate. She stood up, reached her arms around the child to the piano and began a softer singing of the hands to one another, while Kate bowed slightly forward inside the enclosure of her teacher's body. "G minor," said Carol's voice above the music, "a trio, and now we return to the first minuet." After several measures she stopped and rested her hands on Kate's shoulders. "I think you'll enjoy putting all this together."

There were five minutes more to the lesson during which Carol heard Kate begin to read the separate hands of the new trio. "Very good," she concluded, "you'll have plenty to do this week." She and Kate bowed to one another and then she stood aside by the door.

"Thank you," said Paul, standing, a body in a down jacket, a mind full of waves of appreciation for this teacher, for Bach, for the small room inside the dusk, for the germinal presence of Kate.

"When we came up the stairs and heard you playing, I did think it sounded wonderful," he went on to Carol, as Kate began to gather up her music and jacket.

"Well, thank you," she answered, "but I haven't had nearly the time I need for practicing lately. I must make some decisions about this—and soon."

"Do you want to perform?"

"Basically I want to write about music. But I want to play very well, and of course I want students, too." She looked at Kate affectionately. "I'll be going back to school before long, as soon as I've saved a bit more money."

Paul nodded. Kate stood ready in her hooded jacket. It was five-thirty. Another student, a thin blond boy of about ten whom they passed each week, would be waiting with Marie in the office downstairs. Kate pulled on her father's hand.

"So," said Paul. "The recital on Sunday is at two?"

"Two o'clock, barring a blizzard or the end of the world," said Carol gaily.

On the way home both girls sat beside him in the front seat of the car. "Daddy, what did Carol mean by the end of the world?" asked Kate.

"She was making a joke."

"Is the world going to end?"

"No one knows."

Kate was silent. At bedtime she asked, "Then what would happen if the world ended?"

"No one knows that either."

"Well, you and me and Marie are going to stay in this house, and Mommy's coming home, and we're not going to move again."

"Is that the way it's going to be?" He bent close to her face and pulled the pillow up around her ears.

"Yes," she said definitively. "I say so."

"I'm with you," he said, kissing her in the center of her forehead.

For several hours after the children were in bed he sat reading in the deep chair beside his desk, settled down inside the sounds of his house. He had put on his knit hat again and wrapped an old blanket around his shoulders. As he read, he made a number of notations; he could feel material massing behind his eyes. He read of burgeoning international organizations. Where was the power to be? Who could foretell a future map of the surface of the earth? Page after page of facts and theories were being folded into his mind. Signs of evolution were what he was watching for, expressions of deep-rooted economy; for it was, he knew now, only beneath a broad aspect of orderliness that he wanted to organize the wealth of his studies.

On Sunday morning, which was cold and bright and full of winter birds and sharp, bluish shadows on the snow, all three of them took baths, first Paul and then, while he cooked breakfast, both the girls, squealing, together.

"Pancakes in five minutes," he shouted up the stairwell.

They thudded down to the kitchen, giggling, scrubbed, claiming to be too nervous about their recital to eat a bite.

"Start with one," said Paul as he set down a pitcher of hot maple syrup. The girls each ate four cakes, a banana and a glass of milk. "That should hold you," said Paul with satisfaction. All the while they had been eating he had delighted in the sunshine on their hair and the delicate flush on their cheeks and the ceaseless play of their talk.

"Hold me *down,*" said Kate. "I won't be able to climb on stage." She gripped her stomach, rolled her eyes at him and laughed.

By five minutes before two, twenty-eight children had taken their places on the long bench beneath the tall windows of the auditorium, a shining human strand of barely containable energy. Adults, more accustomed to the surgings of life, maintained characteristic composures. Carol and several other teachers walked up and down the row, now and then bending low to speak to a child.

Paul greeted the father next to him, a Japanese of about his own age, who made several more adjustments to his camera before lowering it in readiness to his lap.

"Which child is yours?" the man asked.

"That little girl in the blue dress, third from the end, and the one in brown in the center," said Paul.

"Ah, beautiful children, beautiful. Mine there, boy in red and girl with violin." He nodded his head in pleasure.

"Yes, I see them," said Paul and then he added ceremoniously, "your children are also beautiful."

"Ah, thank you," said the Japanese father, his face melting into a sweet, full, happy smile, "thank you."

Eric Wilson

The Axe, the Axe, the Axe

The whole time I was at Stanford, Eisenhower was in the White House. The opening freshman mixer, with no scintilla of irony, was called a Jolly-Up. Things that were great were "bitching." In contrast to high school slang, at Stanford the "g" was now clearly pronounced; it made you feel as if you had finally put away childish things.

If anyone on campus ever smoked marijuana in those days I never heard of it. Tom Lehrer sang with spirited glee of the Old Dope Peddler and it sounded roguish and surreal. Student hangouts down Alpine Road would be raided periodically by the Alcoholic Beverage Commission—a zealous band of "ABC boys" storming Zott's or Mama Garcia's in search of fake IDs, while minors hurled a flurry of Dixie cups out the windows and the air was awash with unlawful beer. In Budapest teenagers were throwing Molotov cocktails and sloshing gasoline into the air as tanks opened fire: but Sandor and the revolution didn't burst into my world until a year later, when I was a sophomore.

A consummate Stanford prank—such as an all-out and as-yet-unretaliated attack with water balloons—was a "bitching RF." There were a lot of RFs in those days, since with no co-ed housing the guys lived in a perpetual locker-room atmosphere. Sororities were not allowed, and the girls' dorms had lockable front doors and sentinel housemothers. They would page your date from a switchboard while you stood around listening to someone play Greensleeves on the lobby piano. The girls were locked in at 10:30 on weeknights;

they could get a limited number of sign-outs until midnight, but they usually hoarded these for dates—or the hope of dates—with fraternity men.

Freshmen couldn't go through rush until after Christmas or move into a fraternity house until sophomore year. As a frosh you *had* to live on campus and in a dormitory. My first roommate in Norton Hall was a stolid jock from Watsonville who said either "No shit?" or "Jeez Louise!" to everything you told him. After only a few weeks Larry decided he'd much rather room down the hall with The Jolly Green Giant, a towering PE major whose real name was Roland. The Green Giant had been rooming with a straight-arrow pre-med named Douglas, and one night while Doug was out booking for an anatomy test, a floor RF was swept into action: all Larry's stuff—down to the bedding—was moved out of our room and all Doug's things were moved in. When the library closed and Doug came back to Norton, Larry and The Green Giant dispatched him down to me and his new room. Douglas just shrugged his shoulders and mumbled, "Hope you can sleep with the lights on." He sat down to continue booking and by the end of the year I had learned to sleep with a pillow wrapped around my head and not suffocate.

Douglas would have looked callow even for a high-school kid. He wore white bucks as smooth as his face and not only ironed his jockey shorts, he folded them into neat little rectangles before putting them away. One day it occurred to me that *I* always started all the conversations between us—laconic and innocuous as they might be. I decided to leave the next opening line to Douglas.

And waited.

His silent treatment was particularly disturbing since I wasn't sure: was Douglas rejecting me simply because he was the cream-faced loon that he was, or was it because of my eye? Unilateral external strabismus. I remember I could say this even before we moved to Pacific Palisades, so that meant at least before I was five. My left eye goes slightly to the left, and with light blue eyes the dark errant pupil is particularly noticeable. When I was growing up I was never certain whether people were put off by the fact I couldn't look them straight in the eye, or whether they failed to notice this and just didn't like me.

I was never much good at small talk, but rooming with someone who made *no* talk was unnerving. I had been uncomfortable enough with Larry's incessant "Jeez Louise!" and his entourage of jocks, but being alone with Douglas soon grew unbearable. When Doug's mother in Walnut Creek called to invite me home for Thanksgiving, I accepted with a double relief: I wouldn't be abandoned in the dining hall on a holiday; and Douglas would be forced to speak to me now. But when that Thursday arrived, Doug still hadn't broken the silence. Mid-afternoon we both showered, put on suits and ties (Doug adding his own indomitable blend of Listerine and Old Spice), and then Doug followed me mutely down to my car. In transit he gave me a few sparse directions ("Take Dumbarton Bridge, then go north on 21 up past Danville"); and that was it. In fact, his last words to me *ever* were, "I *said:* pass the mince pie." But Doug's mother was already chattering as she greeted us on the front porch. I felt like Rosencrantz *and* Guildenstern, but even Hamlet was soon lost in the shuffle and the Queen herself put on the play. Periodically during the evening she would interrupt herself to exclaim, "Douglas, why didn't you *tell* us Greg was so interesting? You *must* bring him home with you more often!" Only later did it occur to me that Doug didn't have a car.

I had an old faded-beige Chevy station wagon that had been my parents' and had wallpaper that was supposed to look like wood. One Saturday, on the spur of the moment, Larry and The Green Giant and six of their buddies asked me to go with them to Half Moon Bay—and then they all piled into my car. They stayed on the beach playing bridge even by bonfire in the dark (I've never been able to play any sort of game), and I sat shivering wrapped in a blanket, my trunks still wet and gritty under my jeans.

Laurel was decorously bemused by the Chevy, especially the fading wallpaper. I had met her during a dinner exchange (sending a floor of Arbol Hall girls over to Norton helped keep down the food fights) and we started dating. I couldn't believe she would actually go out with me. But she had sat *next* to me at dinner, rather than across from me, so she wouldn't have seen the nonalignment of my eyes, at least not as a first impression. Laurel was from Boston and said "warter" for water, wore her hair in an elegant ash-blond duck-tail and was majoring in Chemistry.

The problem was that until you joined a fraternity there was no place you could go to be alone with a girl. You *could* go to the Cactus Gardens and park; but you didn't usually go to the Cactus Gardens unless you were going to go all the way. I didn't want to give Laurel the wrong idea about me—at least prematurely—so weeknights that left coffee dates at Stickney's: starched waitresses with sparkly glasses, refilling your cup until you sloshed.

One Saturday night I drove Laurel into the City to see Maria Schell in *Die letzte Brücke.* In high school I had been an exchange student in Berlin, and had picked up German in spite of myself. (I arrived without knowing a word, but the mother of the family I stayed with grabbed my arm the first day, pointed at the sky and proclaimed: "*Gregor, der Himmel ist blau!*" I looked up and realized that it *was.* I just kept on absorbing things, and by the time I left Berlin I could say *ikke dette kieke mal* as well as any kid on the *Strasse.*) But Laurel didn't believe I could actually understand the film without looking at the subtitles. French, perhaps, but German? Nobody spoke *German.* Driving back down Bayshore she insisted we speak French. Laurel spoke French and I tossed in every Gallic filler I could think of, relying most heavily on *pour ainsi dire* and *pas que je sache.* Then I remembered La Fontaine's fables and began telling her of *loups* and *cigognes* and *chauves-souris,* and finally even the *grenouilles* who demanded a king. By the time we hit Palm Drive Laurel was fully assuaged.

It was only 11:30 and we still had time to join the Arbol Hall ritual. You would stand somewhere in the shadows (people tight up against the building as if it were raining) and make out until just before it turned midnight. You had to keep looking at your watch over your date's shoulder so you wouldn't miss lock-out; but you couldn't stop making out, say, at five minutes to twelve or it would look as if you'd lost interest or gotten into a fight. Then right at midnight couples would emerge from all directions of the darkness and a mob, trying to look casual, would stream up the steps to the front door.

The next time I took Laurel to a foreign movie it was *The Seventh Seal.* On the way back she asked me what it had meant. I hesitated and then ventured that the film might have been a parody. I had sat there watching the gloom, waiting for the real meaning—any meaning—to hit me. But the only thing I could think of was that the film was a joke: playing chess with the devil in all that murk had to be making fun of something. "It's symbolic," Laurel said firmly, looking straight ahead while I drove. "It all *means* something. You're the English major, you're supposed to know what it is."

"All right. I think the devil symbolizes a moose. If there had been any decent lighting you'd have seen the outline of antlers under all those robes."

"That's not the devil playing chess with the Knight," Laurel informed me, crossing her arms. "It's Death. Even I know *that* much." She thought for a while and then chided: "You should at least be able to recognize Death."

When we got back to Arbol it was only a quarter to twelve, but Laurel wanted to go straight in. We never had another date after that. Every time I called, her roommate came on the phone and said Laurel was out studying. She never returned any of my calls, and I finally gave up, figuring she had met somebody else.

I found I could study best in an empty classroom over at Cubberly. Sometimes I'd just sit in a corner of the floor, leaning up against the wall with a book in my lap. Why did Neanderthal man do his animal paintings so far inside the caves? Why did Prufrock wear his trousers rolled? Why did pink snapdragons have red offspring? The thing I liked about Introduction to Biology was that there were definite answers. One white, two pink and one red. Mendel could be grasped, but not the mermaids singing, each to each.

Robbie, one of the guys in the dorm, had a brother who was a grad student and would buy beer for us. You couldn't take alcohol back to your rooms in the dorm, so we'd have to drive out into the hills and sit in the wallpapered Chevy and drink in the dark. We'd bring along multiple six-packs and get shit-faced just for the sake of getting shit-faced. John Buford, who'd been in Bremen when I was in Berlin, would start out wanting to talk about something serious like Cardinal Mindszenty's being freed, but Roger Steiner would tell about a guy at his high school who'd gotten a dose of the clap and Nick Pedersen would interrupt to say you couldn't ever just talk about the clap, it always had to be a *dose* of the clap just like it was always a *pride* of lions, that was the unit of measurement. I said it wasn't "air" it was "rrrr," to rrrrr is human, people kept saying it wrong. Robbie felt that twat was more onomatopoetic than snatch, things would gradually get out of hand and sometimes we'd start to sing Oh it's beer, beer, beer, that makes you want to cheer, on the farm, on The Farm. . . . Once we even broke into the axe yell, although that was supposed to be evoked only during the Big Game with Cal and even then only when the cheerleaders deemed it an absolute last resort. During freshman orientation week they were going to teach us the axe yell in Mem Aud, just so we'd know it and be ready when the time came, but then one of the cheerleaders (I suspect now that this was all carefully rehearsed) suddenly tried to stop the others, it was *sacrilege* to do The Axe even to teach it because it wasn't really the Big Game and the Big Crunch, but the others pleaded with him, just this *once,* and while they were still arguing there came this groundswell filling the auditorium, Robbie and Nick Pedersen would usually lurch into it after the third or fourth beer, Give 'em the axe, the axe, the axe, give 'em the axe, the axe, the axe, give 'em the axe, Christ, it went on like that forever, we'd keep screwing up, everybody off on his own like some kind of round song, the neck, the axe, give 'em the axe, *where?* Right in the neck, the neck, the neck, right in the neck, the axe, the neck, right in the neck, right in the axe, the neck, the axe, right in the neck, *there!* Right about this point Roger Steiner would lean out the window and start barfing, it was the same color as the wallpaper so it didn't really matter. Tom Callison was always so cheerful in the dorm, but whenever he got shit-faced with us in the hills he'd just sit there in the second back seat of the Chevy and start to cry. Once the crying started, that was it, he wouldn't stop the rest of the evening. Nick would usually put his arm around him and ask softly, "Hey, Callison babes, what is it?" But Tom would just turn his head away and keep sobbing.

We went through rush at the start of winter quarter, right after Christmas vacation. The guys in the fraternity houses wore slacks and crew-neck sweaters and looked really self-assured and (to use the word of the '50s) "studly." They'd serve you some bright red punch but give you a stage-wink to indicate that there'd be a lot of the real stuff once you were in the house—kegs of beer in the basement and suds at dawn on Saturdays and life would be just one big RF. They kept talking about the "brothers" as if they really meant it, and they had files of all the tests going back to God knows when. Their rooms looked like something left over from a ransacking that had to stay like that until the police photographers were done. No-Dōz scattered around and capless tubes of zit cream and dented tennis-ball cans used as ashtrays dumped over Kingston Trio albums, paperbacks of *Gatsby* and *Great Expectations* and *Les silences du colonel Bramble* broken-spined and spilling their pages. Most of the beds were in ragged sleeping porches upstairs, with screens but no windows and on the wall a yellow metal octagon said HUMP.

A lot of the fraternity guys were pinned and they had their girls on hand in tight sweaters to pass out cookies and make name tags for the open houses. Laurel was a hostess at the Phi Delt house and she wrote GREG KIRTLAND with round letters in turquoise ink and then, taking hold of his arm, asked whether I'd had a chance yet to meet Buzz. Buzz, she told me, giving him a squeeze, had been Chairman of the Big Game Bonfire, maybe I remembered. Buzz looked me right in the eye, or rather right in my strong eye, and then back and forth between them, establishing beyond a doubt that you couldn't look into both of them at once.

There were only a couple of us on the floor who didn't pledge. Tom Callison had already decided to leave Stanford at the end of the year, but he got a lot of bids anyway. Nick Pedersen joined an eating club, which was supposed to be an intellectual alternative to fraternities, and the club members had a special dorm of their own. Douglas also joined an eating club, but it was one of the "dorky" eating clubs and almost worse than not joining anything at all.

From winter quarter on, almost everything was fraternity or eating-club oriented, and the dorm-centered activities such as dinner exchanges between Norton and Arbol fell pretty much by the wayside. I went up to the City by myself to see *The Seventh Seal* again, but it was opaque from beginning to end. And I still couldn't figure out Douglas' unbroken silence; it gnawed at me like a continual reproach. For what? I kept wondering. *For what?*

But at least Douglas never turned violent like Robbie's roommate. Dave Donovan was a tennis player who had recently been diagnosed as having diabetes. He had become sullen and withdrawn, and one day Robbie came back from lunch to find everything on Donovan's side of the room knocked over, ripped apart or smashed to pieces. Donovan disappeared for the next week and a half; and on top of all the mess he left behind, Donovan had completely covered up his medicine-chest mirror with masking tape. Even after he finally came back and remained subdued for the rest of the year, Donovan was adamant on this one point: no one was *ever* to try to unmask the mirror.

Spring quarter I had a new English teacher and started getting B's instead of A's, even though I had been editor of my high school paper. Miss Middlemoss had a fixation about the "terrible gaiety" of Edith Sitwell and had once actually visited the offices of *The New Yorker.* She was alarmed that I found neither *Tristram Shandy* enormously comic nor *The Heart of Darkness* enormously deep and said that having a "serviceable expository style" wasn't going to do me much good if I kept missing the point. Why couldn't I learn to get beneath the surface of things and interpret? For our final we were supposed to imagine that Joseph Conrad, Pirandello, George Eliot and C. P. Snow had gotten together, and we were to write down a dialogue of what they said. I was tempted to write that they all sat around in the dark and played chess with a moose, but I didn't want to screw up my grade point average. Before I handed in my blue book, however, I scribbled boldly on the back cover, "Mistah Kirtland, he dead," and switched my major to Business Administration the next day.

If you didn't get asked to pledge a house and you didn't want to live off campus (living by myself in Palo Alto or Menlo Park seemed to me like banishment), you ended up in Sturges Hall. The place was pretty much of a joke and the humor magazine, *The Chaparral,* was always making barbs about how only fraternity rejects lived there. The *Chappy* had a parody of the social calendar, This Shell in a Monthnut (sometimes it was This Nut in a Monthshell), and right after "Dynamiting of Hoover Tower" they listed "Fall Rush Party, Sturges."

As I carried in the first load of stuff from the station wagon, I saw my name neatly typed on the card on the door, along with SANDOR RAGALYI. He hadn't shown up yet, and when I called home to tell my folks I'd arrived safely I spelled the name for them, adding I figured he'd probably be an exchange student and that would be something to look forward to. After a long silence on the phone my father said, " . . . Yes, but what color is he?" I didn't understand at first. "What if he's from Africa?" my father persisted. "What will happen if he's a *Negro?*"

My mother on the other phone started telling me about how people judge you by the company you keep, and you can't detach yourself all that successfully from a roommate, and what would that do to my social life? "Besides," she went on, "if you're going to go through fall rush what will you do if he wants to come *with* you? How are you ever going to get into a fraternity if you show up with a—"

Sandor had escaped during the Hungarian uprising the year before. He was tall and frail with shoulders hunched as if in fear. He had a pale complexion, pained dark eyes, and beautiful thick dark hair that looked like a velvet cap. In contrast to all the flattops that year, Sandor's hair was all the more striking. He smiled a lot, but in a leery, disoriented way. In the dorm he wore grandfatherly leather bedroom slippers which he apparently had thought to bring with him even in the midst of the revolution. The guys on the floor called him the Freedom Fighter, half joking, half in awe, but every time they said this Sandor would wince. A rumor got started that he had been in jail for political activities and had managed to break out, although Sandor refused to discuss this.

Sandor was oblivious, of course, to the fact that he had landed among such an oddball lot. There weren't any Sturges Hall jocks, and the grad student who was our RA—fondly referred to as Mother McAllister—used to lead floor meetings pretending he was a WAC drill sergeant. There was perhaps more than a routine feyness and familiarity among a number of the Sturges guys, but at the time I just chalked up their mannerisms to their being turkeys in general. They treated both Sandor and me as if we were from another world; and with respect. And they had the highest grade point average on campus.

Sandor's hands were extraordinarily fine; his fingers had the elongated reverence of an El Greco. When the Sturges guys—who were always very gentle with Sandor—routinely asked him whether he played the piano, he would whisper that no, he did not. He would hide his hands behind his back and stare down at his slippers, rigid with shame.

When we were alone, Sandor almost always spoke German with me, which he knew far better than English. And what elegant German it was! Sandor spoke in the blurred, trilled, faded grandeur of the Austro-Hungarian Empire and called me by my Magyar name, Gergely, even in German. He never wanted to talk about the revolution, but one night I found him staring straight ahead with an odd detached look in his dark eyes: bodies of Russian soldiers, he explained, were lying beside burnt-out tanks and armored cars and overturned trucks; men in white coats were going from corpse to corpse sprinkling snow-white lime, and the dead gradually began to look like cold marble statues. Small boys ran around in the rubble collecting bullets.

I introduced Sandor to the tradition of the Sunday Night Flicks: after a weekend of study you could walk over to Mem Aud and see films like *The Man Who Knew Too Much* and sing along with Doris Day belting out *Qué sera, sera* in that harrowing denouement. One Sunday while we were waiting in line at the flicks I met Rubybell, who had gone by herself. She was quick to explain she had been named for a wealthy, childless Aunt Rubybell who felt that the whole namesake thing had been a cheap ploy to get at her money (it was) and had left everything to Sweet Briar College. Rubybell had smooth pale skin, rich blue eyes, and a throaty voice as deep as the red lacquer of her nails. In the free association of her conversation, I remember, she told us right there in line that her father had lost his foot in Rio; he had been in the diplomatic service and fallen afoul of a streetcar. She agreed to go out with me even though I was a Sturges Hall turkey.

Rubybell—over coffee at Stickney's—said she had never met anyone until Sandor who could truly be described as "abject." Should she try to fix him up with a girlfriend of hers? But Sandor whispered to me no, please, he would feel far too ill at ease. And for all the cordiality—even tenderness—he received, Sandor's depression was becoming helplessly resolute. No one knew quite what to do. Mother McAllister tried to cheer him up one night in the dining hall by doing impersonations of Tragic Heroines: Isadora Duncan flamboyantly being yanked to her death by that long, beautiful scarf; Virginia Woolf walking slowly, steadfastly into the pond ("her ravelled sleeve of hair billowing out onto the water");—and FDR ("inching agonizingly forward in 'her' wheelchair"). Gerald Weintraub tried to incorporate Sandor into the mainstream of things by teaching him slang: things that Stanford men were wont to say such as "Did you plank her?" "Don't go apeshit!" and "How's your old wazoo?" But when Sandor formed these words in the reluctant blur of his accent, he sounded like an exiled prince forced to turn brigand. Gerald took us into his room to share some marzipan he had gotten from home and to play for us *The Unicorn, the Gorgon and the Manticore.* Mother McAllister loved the music and sang along with the libretto, but Sandor merely looked bleak. Back in our own room, lying in our beds in the dark, I asked him to teach me Hungarian. I still remember the first lesson began with *köszönöm* (thank you) and ended with *nem értem* (I don't understand).

The next day several members of the Catholic Church, which had sponsored Sandor, dropped by the room to ask if it wouldn't be advisable for him to get a tutor. Sandor sent them politely away, but confided to me he was not making his grades and that meant he might forfeit his scholarship. At this point I was taking both econ and chemistry—the Hawley-Smoot Tariff and exogenously given money supplies vying with mole fractions, volatile solutes and supersaturations—and doing wretchedly myself. To make matters worse, I was also doing poorly in German. I had merely wanted to keep up with the language, but we were having to read Schiller's *Kabale und Liebe,* a seething Sturm und Drang play that ran from frivolous roguishnesses to fissures rending the infinity of the universe. Amidst an incontinence of dashes and exclamation marks the characters came right out and *said* they were raving. Young Ferdinand gnawed at the seams of the bourgeois world and screamed he could never, ever love the Countess.

John Buford was in the same German class, and he and I would try to outdo each other in imitations of Ferdinand. John had pledged Sigma Nu, but would have lunch with me at Sturges on Saturdays when their cook had the day off. They were one of the more civil fraternity houses, all things considered, and one day it occurred to him I might be interested: he could invite me over to the house and I could meet some of the brothers. After all, I hadn't tried Sigma Nu the first time around, had I? And, well. . . . He looked nervously over at the next table where Mother McAllister was anticly pretending to be a manticore. I told John thank you but no thank you. I didn't tell him that I couldn't bear to be rejected again.

There was a Sturges dance in the lounge and I took Rubybell. I was worried about how the guys would react to her name, but Mother McAllister, when I introduced them, merely said "*Enchanté!*" and kissed her hand. I think he was impressed I had brought a girl at all. Rubybell and I danced to the music of someone's hi-fi, slowly, holding each other closely, and I realized that one of the things I liked about her was the fact she seemed to take me seriously.

Between records we went to get some more punch—Gerald must have slipped in a whole bottle of vodka—and I asked her whether she had ever seen *The Seventh Seal.* I felt comfortable enough around Rubybell to admit that, to tell the truth, I wasn't quite sure what all of it meant.

"*Meant?*" she asked, taken aback. Then she laughed her deep, throaty laugh, exhaling a swirl of sensual blue smoke: "It was *bullshit,* that's what it meant!" She ran her hand playfully over the top of my head, over the bristly flattop I kept rigid with a thick pink wax. "Look at Sandor's hair," she told me. "My God it's sexy. Greg, really, why don't you let your hair grow out . . . ?"

After I had taken Rubybell back to her dorm, I returned to find Sandor sitting on his bed waiting up for me. He spoke more softly than usual, so that I had to sit down next to him to hear him at all. The Soviets were threatening to do something to his mother if he didn't go back to Budapest. After he had come to America he hadn't received a single letter from her; he wasn't even certain she was still alive. He had asked his teachers if he could write his blue books in Hungarian and they had all laughed at first and then, realizing he was serious, said it was out of the question. He broke into muffled sobs: trucks were in flames in the rubble of the streets; someone was arranging a wreath of autumn leaves over a decomposing corpse; a boy had scrambled on top of a tank: when the turret opened, he dropped in a grenade just before the soldiers started to fire. Sandor looked at me in an unbearable terror.

And then he began to brighten. In fact, for the first time since I had known him, Sandor seemed downright jolly. In the dining hall he even made a point of going up to Gerald Weintraub and asking straight out: "How's your old wazoo?" It was wonderful seeing Sandor in such high spirits, even if they were a bit bizarre. Finally he seemed to be a part of things; his passivity and fear were replaced by a sense of confidence and purpose. He no longer hunched. Even the impending midterms no longer seemed to overwhelm him. If he studied diligently, he would pass; it was as simple as that. But he would need some uninterrupted time with his books. What was I going to be doing on Saturday morning? I would be over at Cubberly, sitting in a corner with my books. Would I go directly to the dining hall from there? It seemed important to him, so I promised I would. Then I wouldn't be back in the room before one o'clock? *Nem, nem,* I told him in Hungarian, definitely not.

After lunch I knocked circumspectly and waited a while before entering the room. But Sandor was gone and there was no trace of him. In a way I was glad, since Cubberly was starting to get crowded on weekends and I found this distracting. I sat down cross-legged on top of my bed with my books piled around me, steeling myself for an all-afternoon cram session.

If you lower the vapor pressure of the solvent in a dissolved solute, this would be proportional to the mole fraction of the solute in an ideal solution. Oh shit oh shit oh shit. She has seen my entire soul—

and she felt nothing? Felt nothing but the triumph of her guile? You tell me she swooned—o deceit—but cannot coquettes swoon? For changes in the amount demanded that respond to changes in price are changes in the amount demanded and *not* changes in "demand." Hence there is no change or shift in the demand schedule (see Figure 2–7) and it is only as a short-cut term that we refer to "demand." Ha! Emilie! No, proud unhappy creature, you may shame me but never revile me! Magnanimity alone shall be my guide! Raoult's law holds true only for an *ideal* solution, from solute mole fraction zero to—

The tremor was relatively mild, but I thought automatically: Would this be the Big One? I guess that's what Californians always think when they sense an incipient earthquake. But when I felt the bed with the palms of my hands, everything was completely still. Now if this same consumer who has just bought milk for 25¢ a quart subsequently finds that down the block milk is selling for only 20¢ a quart, according to Table 4–6 she—I felt it again, a jolt to the bed, pushing upward on the springs. And then another jolt to the springs. The wind was blowing in the open windows. Had someone—as an odd joke—climbed in the window and was now hiding under the bed, waiting to leap out at me?

The face must have slid out jaggedly along the floor before it actually came up at me. Sandor was an eerie white in contrast to the dark dried curds of blood that had spattered out from the slash on his neck, drenching his white shirt and a towel he had dragged out with him, his usual tentative porcelain smile jammed into a leer as he started to go into convulsions. The next thing I am aware of I am on the floor in Gerald's room, Mother McAllister is wrapping me snugly in a dark gray blanket and holding me down firmly, tightening the blanket around my arms and shoulders. This is without sound and in slow motion. Sandor is also wrapped in a blanket up to his chin, his head thrashing from side to side, but sometimes he's on a stretcher down the corridors of the med center and sometimes they're putting him in the back seat of the station wagon, but how can I see this while they're holding me down on Gerald's floor?

When I open my eyes I'm still wrapped up in blankets. I'm in a room with a dozen or so beds, a sterile room in an old house. It's dark outside and the dim electric light is a translucent blue. The other guys are restless but I feel . . . snug-as-a-bug-in-a-rug. I try to say this aloud to Mother McAllister leaning down over me but he's not there after all and I can't talk, I can't move. The blankets are up to my chin and there is no sound even though the guys are roughhousing around, someone's getting walloped with a pillow. The sound comes on when a girl in white arrives to quiet them down. There's teasing back and forth, Bonnie, give us a back-rub, huh, how 'bout it, pretty please? They've got their pajama tops off and Bonnie is kneading wide freckled shoulders with the pungence of alcohol. Me next, Bonnie, me next they're all shouting but I can't say a word. Hey, Terry wants a front-rub, do Terry next, come on, do Terry, do Terry, he's lying on his back on the bed next to mine, bare-chested with his arms folded behind his head, sandy hair in his eyes, do Terry they call out, Bonnie moves in between our beds, one play all the way, hey hey, one play all the way the guys chant, Bonnie moves down massaging, then there's a hush, I stare at the ceiling in the cold blue light and there comes a whoop in unison, me next, Bonnie me next, hooligans, Christ, another woman in white, absolute *hooligans,* Bonnie's out the door, the lot of you, why if you big galoots don't settle down—

By the time they released me from the convalescent home, there was no hope of my ever passing chemistry; I dropped the class, which gave me only 12 units. The Dean interceded for me in German, asking that I be allowed to take an incomplete. Mother McAllister said it would be left up to me as to whether I wanted a new roommate or to be by myself.

I wanted to be by myself. Every night before going to bed, like old maids in cartoons, I looked under the bed. Under the other bed—now starkly vacant—and inside both wardrobes, pushing back shirts and jackets on hangers. My compulsive nightly ritual was humiliating, even though no one was there to see me. I don't remember actually screaming in my dreams, but Mother McAllister and sometimes Gerald Weintraub would be sitting on the bed next to me telling me it was all right. Mother McAllister said not to worry about what anybody else thought. Once I remember waking up crying uncontrollably and Mother McAllister held my head in his lap and said that would do me good, just go ahead and cry.

For the most part things went on as they had been before, except that I dropped Business Administration and was without a major again. Business had sounded so unremittingly practical, and it seemed foolish to declare "undeclared" just as I was trying to get my life squared away. Rubybell talked me into growing my hair out, long like a poet's, but she got on my nerves because she kept trying to "soothe" me. She would keep saying "after what you've been through," as if now I were some kind of psycho. I was glad she wasn't with me the night I was driving the station wagon down Harrison Avenue and thought I heard a noise from the second back seat. After Sandor, I had become so uneasy about being shut in with the unhappenable the *next* time it happened that as a reflex action I just bolted out the front door and into the open, scraping hell out of myself on the pavement. I must have thrown the car into neutral, anyway it came to a stop halfway up a curb. I sat beside the car on the grass for a long time with my knees pulled up to my chin until finally a policeman stopped to see if I were drunk or hurt and that broke the spell.

Winter quarter it rained almost non-stop and I started studying in the reading room of Hoover Tower since it was relatively free from undergraduates. Every afternoon an older woman in a gray dress and orange beads would sit across the table from me reading Russian newspapers that smelled like sawdust. I'd take breaks by riding the elevator up to the wet observation deck and looking out at the red tile roofs and rolling hills turning darkly lush and the pewter-colored bay out in the distance. Sometimes I would sit in the window ledge of a deserted biology lecture room and listen to it rain until dusk. I didn't take the *Palo Alto Times* and so I didn't see the article until John Buford brought it over to show me. Sandor had made so much progress after the shock treatments that they had given him ground privileges. With his belt he had hanged himself from a tree.

My folks would call me at least once a week and my father's refrain had become Well what *are* you going to major in? You can't reject everything because you don't like it, the world's *full* of people who do things they don't like, that's what growing up is all about. My mother, on the other phone, would shush him and say I'm sure Greg knows what he's doing, don't you dear?

Then the note came from the fraternity—Dad's old house at Michigan State—inviting me over for dinner. So Dad had finally started to push my being a legacy, even though as far back as high school I had made him promise he would never do this. I certainly wasn't going to go through with it now—hey, Skip/Chip/Biff/Bucky, meet old Greg here from Sturges Hall—c'mon, Greg, step up a little closer and gobble for the fans. But then I decided I *would* go through with it. In the long run it would be the best way to shut Dad up.

The first guy I ran into when I got to the house was Terry Lindquist. I thought he looked familiar somehow, but he knew it had been in the convalescent home when we all had the Asian flu together, and just because I had been there he had it in his head that I was one hell of a bitching guy. He introduced me around to all the "bros" and at dinner we traded nudges about what a tough chick Bonnie had been and goddam he didn't think she'd really *do* it, Jesus was that ever bitching. After dinner when they pulled out some Cutty Sark Terry told me quite honestly he hadn't realized that *I* was Greg Kirtland, the name hadn't clicked, hell, word had gone around the house that I was just another Sturges Hall yo-yo being served up as the booby prize. Jeez Louise, had I heard that they finally caught old Bonnie going down on a Zete right in the middle of breakfast?

I didn't move into the fraternity house until the next fall. Even when I did, they never seemed to figure out that I didn't fit in. They'd talk about getting shit-faced and getting laid and we'd go out en masse to the home games and inject vodka into oranges and throw frozen gremlins around and after the card stunts we'd be the first ones to start flinging bright cardboard squares down at the cheerleaders even though they'd yell Hey you assholes, those could fucking blind somebody. I started working on the staff of the *Stanford Daily* and Terry said every house needed at least one brain and he guessed I was theirs. He said I even *looked* intellectual, what with my hair and my—, but he stopped before he said eyes. At their first party I was fixed up with a tough chick whose mystique was enhanced by the fact she was taking a course in something called existentialism. They said with her I was sure to score, and on one of the rumpled beds in the sleeping porch I did. I took Rubybell on a few coffee dates but never dared bring her around to the house: and only partially because of her name. The new diversion that fall was a freshman nympho named Elsbeth. When the bros could get hold of her they'd run her over to the house and take turns planking her on top of the pool table while everyone else stood around watching. Sometimes I'd walk into the pool room not realizing it was an Elsbeth night and feel the same way I had felt in the freshman dorm where the toilet stalls didn't have any doors.

I learned to steer clear of Elsbeth, but Sandor was less predictable. The next time he appeared his face finally did crack and blood was streaming out from his nose and the gash in his neck, the police had even confiscated *my* razor and never returned it but Sandor had still found a way, Gergely, Gergely, he has bad breath and El Greco hands grab at my shoulders and shake me and shake me and all I can do is scream, I jerk up in bed, the light's in my eyes and the guys standing there in the sleeping porch are staring in disbelief; Terry in his jacket with the big red S looks stricken. Brad, finally, breaks the silence: "Hey, Kirtland, it's no big deal. We just thought you might want to go out with us for a late-night pizza. You know?"

I didn't try to explain. I just said quietly it's okay, you guys go ahead. The next morning Terry came up to me in front of the bookstore, giving me a rough playful yank as he put his arm around me. "Hey, fellah, you're really some joker, you know that? I mean, you really scared the bejesus out of us. I gather you were royally pissed we woke you up so late, but *Christ* . . . !"

I got to worrying about what I'd say the next time I did something like that. But as it turned out, that was the last time I ever dreamt about Sandor. Some deadening mechanism in my mind—I am chagrined at the egocentricity of self-preservation—took over. Sandor's memory has become remote, and the scene from under the bed could just as well have been a drive-in movie I caught a glimpse of going past on the freeway. I kept on living in the house, and became more dogged than ever in my efforts to do everything the other guys did—short of Elsbeth. It wasn't long before the *Daily* started giving me regular front-page bylines, and the editor wanted me to branch out from the basic who-what-when stuff and try some features or reviews. I never did, though; I just stuck to reporting exactly what happened, and left the interpreting—the meaning of things—to others. For all her terrible gaiety, I was convinced that old Miss Middlemoss had been right about me. *Tristram Shandy* might really *be* enormously comic. And *The Heart of Darkness* enormously deep.

R. M. Berry

History

Preface

All will agree that the publication of this volume is a bold undertaking. Some may think it arrogant. The editors are not insensitive to this charge. To speak on behalf of another is always risky business, and the risks are increased when that other can no longer respond. Such risks are familiar to scholarship. But to speak in the name of another, to appropriate to oneself the life of his (or, as in this case, her) mind, to assume an authority not one's own . . . this goes beyond mere risk. It appears to be presumption. It may be fraud.

When on an August afternoon three years ago Dr. Myra Q. Stitz gazed up into the blue windshield of a careening parcel delivery van and concluded upon the asphalt of Meridian's commercial boulevard forty-three years of inspired and vigorous teaching, we, her colleagues and students, feared our own lives had come to an end. We'd sat across from her at tables, beside her in bars, walked with her at night among the grain bins and along the canal and always something was growing. When we spoke well, she'd jab her cigar at us: "Yes! Yes!" When we stumbled, she'd wait. We insisted that she publish her reflections, but she always laughed. "Whose reflections do you mean?"

In her two-room apartment above a musical instrument repair shop in this small southeastern town, Dr. Stitz left behind her, among the peculiar detritus of her personal life, a mass of writing too chaotic, fragmentary and tentative to constitute an opus but too daringly original to be ignored. For eleven months Dr. Peter Schleeter-Nachter studied these loose sheets, crumpled notes, and annotated journals trying to determine what existed in a state appropriate for publication. He read esoterica, phantasmal calculations, playful "hypothesisettes"—as Dr. Stitz liked to call them—all manner of abstruse speculation perhaps never intended to be read at all. There was a wholeness present, he informed us, a tone, a style of mind. Recognition seemed always about to take shape, but the Myra we'd known had vanished amid the parts.

As Dr. Stitz's executors we were faced with three alternatives. First, we might publish nothing under the name of Dr. Stitz herself. Her papers could be entered in the manuscript collection of the college library, and when utilizing her work in our own writing we could acknowledge the source and our indebtedness. Aside from an aura of professional opportunism surrounding this course of action, we disliked it for other reasons as well. Dr. Stitz's work deserved more attention than the preservation of her papers in a college library could insure. We knew that the writings of several individuals, no matter how directly influenced by that of Dr. Stitz, could never adequately represent the original. We decided against this alternative.

Second, we might publish her work precisely as we found it. This would raise a variety of practical difficulties involving the presentation of multiple versions, revisions, strike-throughs, frivolous insertions, self-parodies, variant schemes of organization, manuscript illegibilities, discontinuity, and transliteration of her (often exotic) idiolect, but these might be overcome with the assistance of an imaginative printer and a minimal amount of editorial discretion.

Our objection to this course was theoretical. We believed that Dr. Stitz's thought was much more coherent than such a presentation would demonstrate. Anyone who had ever sipped tea with her (Dr. Stitz drank no coffee or whiskey and refused to think whenever these were served; however, she had an inordinate love of assam tea, trifle, hard cider, stout and, most notoriously, an unnamed but hideously noxious brand of Cuban cigar) knew well Dr. Stitz's methodological self-consciousness and consistency of intention. Her arguments were fragmentary but not without strongly implied hierarchies, parallelisms, and a distinctive syntax. We concluded that the larger context of her café dialogues, peripatetic meditations, lectures, and informal chats were demanded by her writing. We emphatically rejected the second alternative.

Third, we might write her work. This is, of course, what we have done. Wherever possible we have used Dr. Stitz's own words, examples, non-standard orthography and punctuation. Where her notes were fragmentary or wherever her argument existed in outline only, we have paraphrased, interpolated and assembled her meaning. We have not always agreed among ourselves, as evidenced by the alternative renderings in chapters three and eight (points where Dr. Stitz apparently did not agree with herself!). Much has been omitted. In the appendix we have included facsimiles and transcripts of some relevant materials.

Can such a method be justified? We are uncertain. Are we attempting to give to a secondary work the authority of a primary one? Surely there is interpretation here, but whose? Nothing is concealed from the reader except what remains concealed from us all.

We make no apologies. If editorial responsibilities have ever been assumed honestly (and despite frequent abuses, we believe there *is* honesty in editorship), then we maintain that ours is an instance of such honesty. More importantly, if our undertaking can be justified, then the work of Dr. Myra Stitz will provide that justification. "We think me," she says in her first sentence, and then follows the fanciful "Parable of the Lonely Termite Who was Not." For Dr. Stitz consciousness is so radically social that she could maintain (as she often did with her tea sloshing dangerously in her upraised cup and her cigar pounding on the table edge like a gavel) that "nine thinkers are required for one clear idea and a whole suburb for an insight." Minds are the property of conversations. No one author's thinking. To anyone objecting that such reflections are mere editorial self-justification, we can only echo Dr. Stitz's own words: "Whose reflections do you mean?" We believe *Refractions of Identity* by Myra Q. Stitz offers an answer. We welcome all sincere critical response.

P. S-N.
S. S. S.
Meridian College

Preface to the Revised Edition

Myra Stitz lives.

When the first of R. F. Drew's Memoirs, "Dialogue at The Blue Potato," appeared in *Eidos* three years ago, all admirers of Myra Stitz were startled, none more so than her editors. Many of you will have followed the lengthy debate and ensuing correspondence in *Codices* between Mr. Drew and two of us—Drs. Peter Schleeter-Nachter and Stephen Sneed. Some may have examined the facsimile edition of Dr. Stitz's "manuscripts"—her assorted cocktail napkins, claim checks, envelope flaps, journal margins and flattened tissue boxes—published last summer by Epigone Press. All who knew Dr. Stitz will remember her hearty faith in the exuberance of mind: "Discourse is more fertile than we are. It cannot be aborted." A decade after her death her editors finally understand what she means.

Myra Q. Stitz did not write *Refractions of Identity.* In their attempt to construct an authoritative text, the editors of the first edition suppressed Dr. Stitz's most daring insights, abandoned the tone and arrangement these implied, and substituted much inferior material of their own. These inadequacies became apparent with the publication of the now infamous "Third Conversation at The Blue Potato" (a vegetarian eatery frequented by Dr. Stitz and recently taken over by the Meridian College Credit Union). Mr. Drew and Dr. Stitz had been engaged in a lengthy and, for Drew, frustrating discussion of baseball and coercion. Drew reports:

> I kept trying to paraphrase her remarks in terms of the sociology of knowledge (I'd been listening to John Cage) and looked for her approval. She only sucked her cigar and snorted. Finally I blurted out that she must consider me "dense." She eyed me for a moment, then reached over and pressed her thumb against my forehead. "Precisely, Drew. Nothing passes through you." Afterwards she got very drunk and kept muttering something about "social boundaries" but I was too discomposed to make it out.

Here was a new Myra Stitz! We could speculate endlessly about the lost "boundaries" utterance, but one thing was certain: this Dr. Stitz was fascinated by solidity. "Whatever we cannot penetrate we must try to understand," she remarks in the previously unpublished twenty-second conversation (included in the appendix to this volume). A host of forgotten observations returned to the memories of her editors. We now realized that her first sentence, "We think me," referred to something far more fundamental than society, and immediately her entire volume began to rethink itself.

The new edition was begun. Nightly we gathered in the Meridian College Library to sift scraps of paper and argue. Spirits were high.

Often we failed to hear the closing buzzer and had to grope for the exits in the dark. Whenever one of us made a discovery we'd all shout. The librarians considered us a nuisance. Despite our former intimacy with Dr. Stitz, we felt as if we had never known her until now. In the words of our senior member, "I catch myself asking her questions. It's like walking along the canal again. At times I'm sure I smell the cigars."

As Mr. Drew's *Memoir* suggested and our subsequent research revealed, much more of Dr. Stitz's work remained unwritten at her death than we'd first believed. Again and again we'd mistaken pauses for closure, and now the intricacy of her plan seemed startling. Chapters two and five became "Meditation Twelve: Whereabouts," the "utility fragments" were relegated to the appendix, and the Algebra of Ground ($f(U)=M_e^2$) had to be dispersed throughout. Still greater boldness was required for this edition than formerly, and yet our sense of direction was much surer. Dr. Stitz was beginning to speak to us through her silences. Incompleteness, we realized, had always been her intention. As she explains in the fifty-third conversation, "Only dead things are whole."

And now we are approaching an answer to the questions we first raised nearly a decade ago. Myra Stitz's editors have not written her work, as we formerly believed. Her work has written, and continues to rewrite, itself. "Who thinks for the jazz quartet?" she muses in a characteristic comparison. "The saxophone switches to swing, the brushes start to skip and slide, the piano player's hands catch the rhythm before he does. Afterwards the bass man remarks, 'We were just playing and the changes were there.' " What had before seemed editorial hubris now revealed itself as dull-witted resistance to the force of Myra Stitz's mind. We offer here no commentary, no extrapolation, and certainly no original work. *Refractions of Identity* has come into its own. The editors were there.

S. S. S.
P. S-N.
R. F. D.
Meridian College

Preface to the Critical Edition

The publication of this edition of *Refractions of Identity* is principally remarkable for its occurrence. As few as six years ago, no one would have believed it possible. Skepticism remains rampant. The editors are themselves by no means immune. The purpose of this preface is to deal as forthrightly as possible with the problems of the Myra Q. Stitz legacy in hope of, if not resolving all doubt, then at least distancing the present edition from those that have preceded it.

Before the revised edition was ever dust-jacketed, one of us, Dr. Derwent Irwin of the Hoagland Institute, had already made the discovery that would utterly discredit it. Had the printing been delayed six months it would not have occurred. As Dr. Irwin first revealed in his disturbing editorial, "Fraud!" (*Parles-tu?,* vol. XV, no. iiii), R. F. Drew enrolled in Dr. Stitz's survey "Problems of Impure Mathematics" during the fall of 1964 but withdrew for undetermined reasons at the end of the first week. He continued to attend lectures at Meridian College until November of that year when he emigrated to Canada in order to evade the draft and a possible narcotics conviction. Although there is some evidence to support his claim to a personal acquaintance with Dr. Stitz, it is clear such an acquaintance was much too brief to have included even a minute portion of the over one hundred "conversations" contained in his *Memoir.* When confronted with these charges it is to Mr. Drew's credit that he denied nothing and offered as his only defense the substantial plausibility of his inventions. "Even if it never happened," he maintained in a privately circulated statement *Eidos* refused to print, "it might have." A clever argument but in present context a straightforward admission of deceit.

The reaction of Dr. Stitz's other editors was considerably less straightforward. Drs. Stephen Sneed and Peter Schleeter-Nachter refused to acknowledge they had authored over three hundred of the text's seven hundred fifty-three pages, despite Alban B. Cuda's damning stylistic analysis, "A Work of Many Hands" (*Parles-tu?*, vol. XV, no. iiiiiii). Arguing from such Stitzian conceptions as antidefinition and the immortality of data, Sneed and Schleeter-Nachter maintained the fundamental passivity of their roles. When questioned in *Codices* regarding plagiarism, documentation and authority, they appeared alarmingly insensitive to the ethical issues involved. "The author's work is whatever fits," Dr. Sneed asserted in his only editorial defense, and Dr. Schleeter-Nachter seemed willing to extend himself still farther: "Why is everyone so stirred up about handwriting? So what if it's *my* handwriting? Would anyone doubt it's *her* idea?" In a letter of only nine paragraphs, Dr. Sneed appealed twelve times to the "spirit" of Dr. Stitz's work. Such loose thinking obscures essential distinctions to a degree that is criminal.

The work of Myra Q. Stitz must be disassociated from this sophistry and moral obtuseness. Although we cannot easily dismiss the editorial dilemmas raised by the previous editions or the theoretical enigma of authorship itself, we can eschew all subterfuge. In preparation for this volume the editors returned to the "three alternatives" of the original preface. The alternative not to publish anything at all became for us the question whether a new *Refractions* could be justified, a question easily answered by the vast quantity of provocative writing generated over the last two decades by Dr. Stitz's followers. Despite professional risks and an intimidating climate of public hostility, we concluded that Dr. Stitz had proven too influential to be left in adulterate and piecemeal form.

The second alternative, to publish the Stitz manuscripts precisely as they existed in the Meridian College Library, was both simpler and far more complicated for us than for the original editors. Simpler because the Epigone Press facsimile had done just this. Of course, there are lingering questions here (the "backward slanting fragments" discussed by Prof. Cuda ["Stitz's Many Scripts," *Parles-tu?,* vol. XV, no. iiiiiiiiiiiii] and the two tissue flaps carbon testing has dated three years after Dr. Stitz's death), but the facsimile does provide a basically reliable text for those to whom (in Dr. Schleeter-Nachter's disparaging phrase) "graphology is the principal test of authorship."

The complication arose from our inability to repudiate the most problematic assertions of the original editors. There does seem to be a coherence to the Stitz fragments, and this coherence seems most intelligible when viewed against the background of Dr. Stitz's personal conversations, musings, and "spoken works." Although we sought to qualify this bold claim with objective evidence—student lecture notes, Dr. Stitz's unpublished doctoral dissertation, a paper delivered at a Hunter College colloquium twenty years prior to her death—no document could entirely refute it. Dr. Stitz's thinking deserved publication in its most attractive form. Any arrangement, even that of the facsimile, required a certain amount of speculation, a certain amount of editorial daring.

Which returned us to the controversial third alternative. But here we had to pause. We refused to "write her work" for her as the original editors had claimed to do. As the textual history has shown, any crossing of the boundaries between author and editor opens the way for abuses without limit. What we have decided upon is the present variorum. The sequence is roughly that of the revised edition (regarding this sequence see Prof. Cuda's essay "Graphemic Diachronicity, Non-linear Structuring, Spectroscopic Ink Analysis, and the Case for Sequence in the Manuscripts of Myra Q. Stitz," *Parles-tu?,* vol. XV, no. iiiiiiiiiiiiiiiiiiiiiiiiiiiiii) with cross references to the original edition (Arabic numerals in brackets) and the Epigone Press facsimile (Roman numerals in parenthesis). Only in doubtful cases have we begun a section with a typographic reproduction of an entire fragment, although at points of unusual difficulty we have included relevant excerpts and at the conclusion of each section have listed cross references and possible sources, variants, and early drafts. All editorial interpolations, paraphrasings, footnotes, punctuative and orthographic standardization, splicing, insertions, "corrections," and occult exemplification have been set off in bold face. After introductory remarks concerning the rationale of former editors, we have placed the edited versions themselves along with our critiques of them, followed by a(n admittedly speculative) reconstruction of the composition history of those fragments upon which the section is (probably) based and excerpts from pertinent (?) conversations, recollected remarks, and student notes culminating in our attempt at a tentative and restrained textual reconstruction with appended documents, article reprints, and, in three cases, extracts from particularly "plausible" sections of Mr. Drew's *Memoir* with explanatory notes and addenda.

We regret the twelve volume format. Some will complain there has been a great sacrifice of "readability"; we fear this is so. There is about the whole project an air slightly pedantic, and this is all the more painful because of our own boyish enthusiasm for it. We can only say in defense that, at last, the distinction between editor and author is clear, and we hope textual reliability with its soberer satisfactions will compensate readers for the loss of more ephemeral pleasures. Any student can now distinguish what is Dr. Stitz herself, what is editorial intrusion, what is (imperfect) recollection, what is plausible reconstruction, what is synthesis and paraphrase, what is well-intended speculation, what is fraud. The amassed whole of *Refractions of Identity,* which has obscured so much falsification and distortion, is finally undone. All lovers of Dr. Myra Q. Stitz can examine the parts for themselves.

D. U. I.
A. B. C.
et al.
Hunter College

Preface to the New Stitz

Perhaps the fraud is not so much that of author or editor but of identity itself. Perhaps the lie is the insistence from the start that we are not each other. Then plausibility is as much as can be asked, the fullest, and composition becomes the task of making whole. It is a shared responsibility. Even analysis has a place, but the end of all labor is binding together. One tries very hard to be amusing.

We are Myra Q. Stitz and have written nothing until now. Drew, Irwin, Sneed are ciphers—edition's multiplication. The variorum, being accurate, may be ignored. The question arises: can Stitz become her desire? This is not the first time they've pronounced us dead.

We shall now reveal several anecdotes our editors never knew. Once upon a time while teaching at Meridian College we fell in love with water and forgot how to speak. Our students already understood that every new idea was a vessel. "Board her," we often advised, "or sink." Then one afternoon a young woman with no eyebrows and a carbuncle on her cheek—we can still see her—confessed with a yawn that all this talk of oceans "bored her." The faces in the room turned deathly pale. With a decorous sweep of our arm we dismissed class and stood gazing out the window for two days. How was anything intelligible? Many years after our untimely death this question continues to disturb those who vainly seek us in our writings.

Last spring we walked once again on the banks of the old canal and discussed this problem with our intimate friends, R. F. Drew and Alban Cuda. They referred frequently to Linwood Amory's recent discussion of continuity ("More! More! More!" *Odium,* 6/9), and because of our long association with these men, their enthusiasm became our own. We invited Dr. Amory to meet with us in the Meridian College Library, and soon amid the heady fume of Havana tobacco we were all ourself again. The long experience of emeritus professors Sneed and Schleeter-Nachter provided reassurance, and Derwent Irwin's intellectual integrity forced us beyond old solutions. "*Refractions of Identity* is NOT Myra Stitz!" he reminded us. Or something like that.

We were convinced. With Mr. Drew's guidance we recalled the period in our life of the Deep Silence. "She began to drink stout for breakfast, belch in committee, ingest her cigars," he told us. "If you greeted her in the corridor, her lips would flap wordlessly, her face turn away." Dr. Sneed recollected how he encouraged us to confide our anguish. "I felt so helpless. All afternoon you'd hear her bedroom slippers scraping over the linoleum in her office. The secretaries complained she was monopolizing the staff toilet, standing before the sink, both spigots twisted open, gazing for hours into the mirror as the spew of hot and cold swilled down the drain."

Until now this period has been disregarded for fear of raising doubts about the finality of our conclusions, but no longer. As Prof. Cuda (who was our student at this time) was first to understand, we were preparing for our loftiest insight. "Dr. Stitz spent each class session cleansing herself of all her old conceptions. She would sweep into the room in a white gown, her hair patchy, nested, her slippers overrun, and lay a wash basin on the lectern. All of her students gathered closer to observe. Then she'd begin to scrub her hands, lifting them high for our inspection as the rivulets wiggled down her forearms and disappeared into her sleeves. If she spoke at all it was softly and with great difficulty. At the conclusion of the hour she'd dry her hands on her blotter and empty the basin in a desk drawer."

As Professor Amory's article helped us to see, during the Deep Silence we were discovering arithmetic. "$742 + 2\frac{1}{4} - 3.14/25¢ = 744\frac{1}{4} - 3.14/25¢$," we explain on page $\sqrt{2}$, and from there proceed to our ingenious elaboration, "All/one, All/one, All/one." Because meaning is water, 2=also=toward=you(tu)=half a ballerina's skirt, but thought is number and hence, $\mu_e = f(W_e)$ is equivalent to our first sentence, "We think me," regardless of carbuncles, eyebrows or talk of tides. This accounts for Dr. Schleeter-Nachter's "hypothesisettes," the prominence of the Algebra of Mud and the Variorum's twelve volume format. There can be margins but no boundary.

Careful readers may notice that only the first sentence remains unchanged from the previous editions of this work. Through exhaustive, computer assisted analysis, Professor Cuda has isolated all manuscript fragments originating from our Deep Silence and demonstrated that, had we lived, we would have entirely repudiated our former thinking. Dr. Irwin himself has conceded that the present volume "has no relationship to Dr. Stitz's writings at all!" Our insights have forced us to continue beyond the manuscripts, beyond the dead letter, beyond "Myra Stitz." Even where the words are identical, the thought is wholly new. Our children know we are at every point the same.

As always, we encourage all imaginative response. However, we hope our detractors will forego the quibbles that in the past have been so detrimental to lively conversation. Many persons have a great stake in misunderstanding. So often criticism of our work has evinced the character of blindness resisting its own reflection. Myra Stitz is not to be feared. May our critics learn to become one another.

The four editions are the work of one author.

A. B. C.
R. F. D.
L. S. A.
S. S. S.
P. S-N.
with D. U. I.
Meridian College

Interface of the Cosmic Edition

Thought lives richly in the moment of the end. It leans, ready to topple upon its own consummation. Become the empty page. Yesterday was Speech, Earth, Author, Number. Today we are the russet house wren beneath the green awning above this shattered window. What tree is this whose branches would enfold me? Enwing yourself; become Sky. Our bowels tighten: no more words.

Once more I appear before you, my friends, daughters, lovers, sons, to instruct you in Stitzsong. When in distant time we were kissed by the grill of the frenetic delivery van and from the deep green naughtness sucked Mother-Death, our power misled us. We believed in direction, in shape. Now it is the eighth day, and there have been many editions. Irwinfaith overwhelms Drewstory. In SSS and the propositions Schleeter-Nachter has bloomed. So much has moved outward, and now we return to you, O Meridian, our navel. But no more words.

Sing!

It is in the odor of cigars, the dry foam rings on yesternight's glasses of stout, in this cafe that worlds us round, our Library, that Myra appears. She formed you ex nihilo of campus grass and canal slime, comely beings, to walk in this garden of mind. Livid flowers rise from other pages, other names. Dimly seen creatures encircle us round, and upon the canal, the barges drifting, the grain bins silent with fallow stench, we know our thought has been too small. All is written to be forgot. Everything is authorized. This preface contains no edition . . .

M. Q. S.
via lactea

Face

Myra Stitz is dead.

Although it is now commonplace to consign Myra Q. Stitz to the realm of myth and *Refractions of Identity* to that of hoax and folly, even to speak casually of Dr. Stitz's nonexistence, I want to make a few remarks about the woman I knew. Or thought I knew. I have no desire to engage in partisan debate. I've lived long enough to know memory is evidence of nothing.

Nearly twenty years ago an article on the relationship of societal to textual corruption appeared in the unusually shortlived *Journal of Anachronisms* (Vol. 1, no. 1). The author, one Dudley Spavin, argued that the Western intelligentsia's inability "to think a single coherent thought" was the result of a conspiracy of "Trismegistians" (the term has not stuck) to deny that anything is simply itself. "A stop sign's a stop sign, ain't it?" he argued in his spirited style. Spavin's article proposed a return to logical positivism, free enterprise and a modified feudalism. It did not cause a stir.

However, it did provoke a response by Peter Schleeter-Nachter who receives credit for being first to observe that "deterioration" is the one concept utterly alien to Stitzian thinking. For years the critics of *Refractions of Identity* had been frustrated by the tendency of

Myra Stitz's writing to incorporate its antagonists. Every new attack on *Refractions* became the starting point for the next edition. Every articulate opponent was invited to head the geometrically expanding editorial board. Eventually the institutional rewards for such invitations became substantial. As Schleeter-Nachter observed, Stitzism threatened to become a discipline in itself, a force capable of subjugating the entire academy, even a synonym for intellectual life. In the concluding paragraph of his article (which appeared in *Eidos* just two months before his startling suicide) Dr. Schleeter-Nachter observed that by failing to acknowledge its own extinction, the entire corpus of Stitziana may have become seriously degenerate: "Not the flowering of thought but rottenness at its root. A progressive estrangement from the primordial silence."

Almost immediately revisionists began to turn Myra Stitz against herself as critics re-examined what Schleeter-Nachter had termed "the inadequate ontology of Nothing." Old doubts reappeared with new authority. Editorial license now became "insufficient respect for the definitive lacunae;" fraud became "naive unawareness of their own substantialist tropes." The radical notion of identity on which the editors had based their work was revealed to be a jejune logocentrism: "Thought doesn't *grow;* there just gets to be more of it." And, finally, the illusion of coherency that had bound together the marginalia, library cards and bric-a-brac into a life was dispelled. "If no one had bothered to argue about Myra Stitz," one commentator observed, "she never would have existed at all."

Although Meridian College does show an "M. Q. Stitz" on its faculty some four decades ago, her appointment seems to have been in Zoology (!), and, aside from the unreliable memoirs and letters amassed by Dr. Stitz's editors, few college documents mention her. A single photograph, badly faded, in the *Meridian College Standard* shows her square nose, cropped hair, and distracted gaze (the view of her mouth is obstructed by a plump cheerleader's hip) riding atop a Science Club homecoming float, and a few surviving minutes of administrative meetings list her as second on motions to computerize the faculty-staff payroll. Her name appears in variant spellings (Moira Stitz and M. Q. Stitts) on two of the four articles attributed to her (only one of which deals with any subject related to *Refractions*), and on the single legal document in the county records office—a Quit Claim Deed on a vacant lot used for trash disposal five miles from town—her address is recorded beneath the bizarre orthography "Miracue Stizz." Even the notes and paper scraps so often cited by Dr. Stitz's editors are in a variety of scripts and cover such an abundance of disconnected topics that they more easily support than refute the thesis of a loose association of distinct persons confused by accident, coincidence and, possibly, deceit.

Nor is my own experience, despite its lingering vividness, any help. The blue-walled café in which I dreamed and drank stout is a brick drive-in bank, and the grain bins that once lined the canal are miraculously absent now. The canal itself has developed an unnatural odor as of too-sweet perfume, and the college campus, where I discovered a world, is hardly larger than a parking lot. Even the stately Victorian home in which I thought I lived out my youth is, in reality, crumbling stucco, quite shabby, and nowhere I've ever known. Irwin, Cuda, Amory are all buried, senile, or, like Drew, vanished into some dusty crack of the planet. Perhaps there was a Myra Q. Stitz, just as there surely was a Moses, an Odysseus, and a Richard III, but, if so, she was lost to me long ago in the successive nights of editorial frenzy, the chaos of index cards, triumphal illuminations.

So I have no intention of defending in my dotage causes that are lost. Myra Stitz is dead. My only wish is to underscore the aptness of Schleeter-Nachter's critique, concede the suspicions of Dr. Stitz' naysayers, and be done with contention once and for all. Dr. Stitz's work clearly omits Nothing entirely. In fact, extinction is so absent from *Refractions of Identity* that, without exaggeration, one could consider it the distinguishing feature of the several editions, perhaps even Dr. Stitz's principal motivation for never writing anything at all. More to the point, I think we are forced to conclude that Dr. Stitz never lived precisely so that her work, by being anything, would inevitably embody the deterioration of which she said so little. The author of *Refractions of Identity* is that same silence Dr. Schleeter-Nachter heard so clearly.

This afternoon I sat in my old classroom, listened to a bald, bearded man discuss Machiavelli's *Prince,* the ethics of deception. There was nothing so remarkable about my new position, nothing to assure me half a century had evaporated. My strongest impression was that the arthritic intruder in the last row was not me. I watched as the waves of heat from the open windows lulled the students, watched as the lethargy accumulated in the room like mold. And then I was surprised to hear a familiar phrase. "We think me," the young lecturer said. "We think . . . " I felt proud and rose to claim the thought, but once on my feet I merely continued out of the room. "If no one talks about us," he continued, "we grow uncertain. If no one listens, we are not there."

Doris Betts

Benson Watts Is Dead and in Virginia

After I died, I woke up here.

Or so it seems. Perhaps I am actually still dying, locked in that darkness between one breath and the next, still wearing tubes which leak from my nostrils and drain that long incision. My wife may, even yet, continue to bend over the high bed to catch the next beat of my heart while the blood jar is ticking down like a water-clock into my veins. Perhaps that last hospital scene is the only scene and all the rest is a dream-in-passage.

But the room and her melting face clicked off, I think. Then the smells went. She was saying something; I could still hear that—I stopped hearing it. I unbloated and the queer whistle in my breathing stopped. I could no longer tell the pain from cold. All my circuit breakers opened and sensations blurred. Someone set fire to my hand but it barely tickled.

Through all this my mind was clearer and more finely tuned than it had ever been. I treasured that clarity, though it had less and less raw material to think with now. I thought: I must withdraw into my brain and hide; there's nothing left outside.

So I did. I backed into my brain farther and farther and got smaller and smaller the deeper I went, until I fell out the other side.

And woke up prone in this yellow grass. The color is important. When they rolled me back from surgery, it was May.

At first I didn't dare move. If I lifted my hand it might fall through the air and drop back onto a starched sheet. I could not tell what was still attached to me and might clatter if I stirred.

The place where I lay was so . . . so ordinary.

A sky as blue as a postcard. Between it and me, one tree limb: oak. White oak, I thought. The grass felt like all autumn grass. When a cricket bounced over my head I knew for sure we were a long way from the Recovery Room; they would not recover me. I sat up.

I was on a sloping postcard meadow. At the bottom, a narrow stream. Willows. I touched my abdomen, which should have been hot and painful. Dacron trousers instead of gauze. Not mine, though. These were new and fitted perfectly.

Around my left wrist hung a small bracelet and a yellowish tag which looked like the ivory sliver off a piano key. On it, carved, was the following:

TO AVOID G.B.
1. Dwell, then travel
2. Join forces
3. Disremember

Very carefully, I got to my feet. It had been a long time since I could move without pain under my navel. The cool wind was a shock and made me clap both hands to my head. Bald as an egg! Not even one prickle, a wisp, a whisker. Otherwise I was myself as I had been before the intestinal cancer, even a little younger. I tried to guess the new age by flexing muscles, checking where pounds were gone, feeling my smoother face. A little beard was starting down my cheeks. I thought I might be forty again, or maybe less. I tried out my voice. Normal.

For practice I said aloud, "Well, it sure as Hell isn't Heaven!" and my laugh was normal, too—forced, but even that was normal. I took a few steps, then ran downhill and splashed into cold water in a pair of shoes I had never owned. Everything normal. A bright September day and I was alive in it.

Yet there was something.

There was something wrong with my mind. Too quiet up there, not enough panic, too small a load of bewilderment, not even enough curiosity. Earlier I said of the tree limb, *White oak, I thought,* and that wasn't right. I didn't quite *think.* This was spooky. It was more as if Something thought in me. I felt the words were moving by their own choice through my head the way air bubbles slide down the bowel.

I began walking along the stream's bank waiting for—I don't

know. For my head to clear? I felt aged forty from the neck down. I waited for that new age to rise and cover me like water.

When I died, I was in a Texas hospital. These hills and fields and meadows looked more to me like—what should I guess?—like Virginia. I said this over and over, aloud, "I'm dead and in Virginia," trying to make the sentence taste like mine. It never quite did.

Walking by the stream I now and then spotted hoofprints. Cattle? Or deer? I saw nothing else alive except me, that cricket, and dozens of yellow birds on quick and nervous flights. Rice birds in Virginia? They fed busily off tall stems and some stunted bush with brown catkins on its twigs. I jangled my wrist tag. I'd worn a bracelet in that hospital, too, with my name spelled out in beads like an infant's. WATTS. Benson Watts. Ben.

At that, I got the first pain, under one ear.

Ben Watts. 226 Tracy Avenue. . . .

I got the second pain, a needle, higher. I rattled the tag. *Disremember,* it said.

Crossing the stream, I noticed for the first time I was traveling downhill as it flowed—there! You see how my brain was? Unobservant. Unconcerned. By the water's edge was a stretch of pale sand. Beyond that the mud was like milk chocolate. More yellow grass grew on both sides to the edge of trees just turning from solid green to red maples and yellow hickories. The scattered pines were thinning their needles for fall.

I rounded a bend. To my right the land dipped off, and the water turned and ran downhill faster to empty into a long lake I could not see the end of, maybe half-a-mile wide. Its surface was very still with a skim of reflections. As I came closer, I knew what was wrong with this scenery, so ordinary and yet so unreal. There was so much absence. Everything I expected to see did not appear. No boats or motors, no fishermen, dogs, garbage, foam, signs, fences. No plastic bottles drifting near the shore. My head was aching now, perhaps because the sun was harsh on my peeled scalp.

Near the water I glimpsed a small house, almost a hut. *Déjà vu.* I spun to the southwest to see if the Fitchburg Railroad skirted the lake. No. Yet it was his house or one nearly like it, built beside the pond a hundred years ago for less than thirty dollars. Built yesterday. I began to run through the ripening grass. If I were back in time, was Thoreau inside? Writing in his journal? Was it possible that each of us died away into our own personal image of serenity and would be tucked there forever like something in a pocket?

Running made my headache worse. But that gut I had cursed for a year was now so new and strong I thought it might be turned to gold or silver, and I ran with both palms pressed there to feel each strand of muscle move.

The hut's wooden door was half open, heavy on its leather hinges. I jumped a low stone wall and ran toward it up the path.

One room with an earthen floor, a smaller one beyond in which I could see strings of onions, peppers and bean pods. I touched the hewn table, chair, bunk, saw high shelves on both sides of a fieldstone hearth reached over my head. They held a set of books, maybe a hundred, all with the same green binding.

I called out, "Hello!" to more absence. Nobody answered, though there were warm ashes in the fireplace under the charred spine of a book which seemed to match the others.

The room was swept. No dust. Under the bunk I found a stack of empty picture frames, white canvases, a wood box of paints and brushes. I could see the clean squares on one wall where somebody's pictures had hung. There were no titles on the books and when I pulled one out I found each page was lined but blank—the others were the same. Pen and ink waited on the bottom shelf.

I had to stoop to enter the back room, a pantry with a board floor. Cured hams were hanging from the ceiling over a flour bin. Crocks of meal and dried beans in sacks were under a table on which apples, potatoes, yams, pears, half-green tomatoes lay in neat rows. One high shelf held what looked like scuppernong wine in gallon jars. The wood box was behind the door, full of split oak, with a sack of cedar kindling nailed outside. In the dim pantry, the odors seemed thick as fog.

I carried and laid wood over the andirons. Matches had been left in a tin on the hearth, and after I lit the lightwood I rummaged in a second strongbox where small jars of spices were jumbled, some without labels. I read once that, if a man eats nutmeg, his urine will smell like violets. Perhaps I will try it.

Slowly the oak bark caught fire underneath, curled off, until the log smoked and finally burned. Beautiful was the fire. Its colors moved and gave way to others. Sitting before it, alert for the sudden lick of blue which would reappear in a new place, I found my headache gone. When there were coals, I slid three sweet potatoes in to roast and sat on, dreaming, sometimes tapping the log with a poker so sparks would leap off and shower onto the dirt floor. I must have sat that way for hours, without a thought to think me.

But the potato hearts were still raw when I peeled and ate them. Lifting a pink morsel to my mouth, I read again the words on my bracelet. Join forces with what? With whom? I rolled the thickest log across the floor and heaved it into place. Then I went to bed though it was barely dark.

In the night I woke to hear rustling beyond me, something large scraping its hide between a bush and the wall of my house. There were no windows. In the red firelight I found the poker and lifted it while I swung open the heavy door. A large deer moved down the path, stepping as carefully as if he had made it, so heavily antlered that he seemed to be holding up an iron grille by stiffening his neck. He bent to drink from the lake, snuffled lightly, moved off along the water's edge without joining forces with me. As soon as he passed, the frogs that he left would sing out again, so I could follow him through the dark long after he was lost to sight.

It was the same deer.

I put the poker under my bunk with the paints and brushes. Only when I was settled and warm again and had closed my eyes against the glow from the fireside did I wonder: What does that mean? *Same* deer?

I knew suddenly it might be very dangerous to sleep. Perhaps I would slide back. My gut would re-open; some bastard in a white coat would whisper, "He's coming out of it." I could almost see my wife hunched in her chair, the brown rubber tubes in her hands, waiting for me. And there was a drop of borrowed blood, halfway down, hung there till my arm would be under it.

But in spite of my fear I went to sleep and when I woke up, I was still here.

IN THE MORNING I could not remember the deer.

I could remember getting out of bed in the dark, but not why. Uneasily I ate an apple, found coffee beans and an old-fashioned hand grinder, and at last boiled the grounds in a cooking pot. The brew was thick and scummy, but its smell was magnificent. I remembered I'd had no cigarettes for weeks, no solid food for longer than that.

When I picked up the apple, saliva ran down my throat in a flood and I felt my nose was twitching like a dog's.

I had dreamed about a deer? That's it. In the dream, an old stag came into this house and offered to carry me across the lake on his back. He spoke in rather a high voice for so large an animal. He told me that when many deer swam the lake, each rested his head on the haunches of the one in front, and since the one behind did the same, they suffered no trouble from the weight. He said the whole line swam for the far shore with all speed in this linked position, to reach land before being befouled. He would be lead deer on this trip, he said, and would carry me himself.

No. The headache started.

No, there had been a real deer, outside. I saw him by the lake. It was hard to remember the simplest details. A doe, a fawn? I had never seen a deer that close before—this much was certain.

I grabbed a green ledger off the shelf and began to write down who I was and how I got here and that the deer was real. Writing was hard. My head felt as if something had come loose inside and was banging the bone. I read the entry twice, getting it all straight and in order. Every day I would do this; every morning I would set down the previous day and reread the earlier entries. This would be good training for my mind which, I now thought, had suffered oxygen deprivation there at the end. At the beginning? Whichever it was.

My name is Benson Watts and when I died in Houston, Texas, I was 65 and had grandchildren—none of whom I liked very much. I had thick gray hair and brushy eyebrows—gone now. When I told my namesake grandson I looked like John L. Lewis, he didn't know who Lewis was.

Now I'm 25 years younger, in Virginia, and my scalp is skin and pores like an orange peel, and I don't remember Lewis too well myself except for those eyebrows.

Was he a principal in some school where I taught? He had the face for the job. For years I taught U.S. and World History in high schools all over Texas, for peanuts, because that left my summers free. Summers I read books, collected stamps, built halves of sailboats in the backyard, took auto trips, sold Fuller brushes (once), and encyclopedias (four times), coached Little League, tried pottery and built my own kiln, got divorced and remarried, and made notes for the book I would someday write on the Cherokee Indian in North Carolina.

Here I am at last, dead and in Virginia, with a pen and ink pot and one wall of blank paper handy, and all I can remember is Tsali and the Trail of Tears. Some joke on me.

But I must write everything down. Once, too, I thought I might go to graduate school and write a different book on the Dark Ages, on the flickers of light in the Dark Ages. By 1969, when all I had was indigestion and a bellyache and still believed baking soda would save me, I thought we were edging into the shadow of a new darkness, without a Church to persevere. I taught myself Latin so I could read illuminated manuscripts at Oxford instead of translations in Texas libraries. (*Illuminated* manuscripts! What a good phrase!)

But I did not write that book, either, and now in Virginia I cannot call up a single Latin root.

I was born in Beaumont, four years after the Spindletop oil gusher blew in. Went to Baylor, started teaching history to conceited teenagers who—if they owned the world and Texas—would rent out the world and live in Texas.

Most summers I escaped from Texas. Once in the Notre Dame library I read the 12th Century bestiaries and made notes, later lost in a Southern Railway boxcar. In the thirties I jumped freights and thumbed and left my wives (there were three in all) to go discuss me with their mothers.

The third wife, Grace, sat with me in the Houston hospital when I died. She didn't shed a tear. Grace had come late in my life; she never expected much so was never disappointed. When I loaded up the car, or a suitcase, she'd just stand in the yard with her arms folded and call out, "O.K., Sunnybitch, don't leave me no dirty laundry." Grace had Indian blood. Nothing affected her much, even sex. She was a challenge. If Grace had cried, even once, in that sterile hospital room I might have stuck out a finger; I might have blotted that tear and sucked it off and gotten well, just from the novelty of the thing.

She didn't cry, though, and I had not died off into a medieval abbey nor a Cherokee camp to do firsthand research. You'd think there'd be some choice. They even claim to give you that in the Army if you volunteer. Draftees get a rough deal everywhere.

Outside the hut that first morning, I sat with my book and pen by the lake in the warm sun, writing how the deer had stood and blown the moonlit water. The season was Indian summer. And for all I knew some real Indian, even a Cherokee with strings of hickory bark around his waist, might step out of these woods! Wonderful!

Might shoot me with his locust bow strung with bear entrails. Not so good. Could I die twice? Re-die? All that was . . . metaphysics. I would not think about it yet.

Could not. Virginia was opposed to thinking. While I sat in the brightness, empty as a sack, a preying mantis climbed up a weed stalk and lay along its blade. I bent my face beside that green swaying. Red knobby eyes. The only insect, I'm told, that can look over its shoulder. Maybe when this one died of winter she would be raised up to my scale; as maybe I—shrunken—was now living on the tip of some giant weed and my lake was a dewdrop in the morning sun.

Once I would have touched the mantis to see where she would spring. It was not necessary. I had been let out of thinking as if thinking were a jail. Nothing expected me to connect it with anything else. Not to anticipate—delicious. I felt that first morning the way a baby feels. *I am here.* Nothing else. Except sometimes when I looked at the bracelet on my wrist and read the words written there.

Some days went by. My ledger notes are sketchy. Like Thoreau, I gave time to birds and anthills. I wrote some thoughtful essays and burned them. My words lacked urgency. Nobody would read them. I bored myself. Then I tried to put on canvas my nighttime deer bent over a floating picture of himself in the black water. My painting was squat and clumsy, a hog at a wallow.

The fifth morning I was sitting on a log by the lake, watching the mist rise. Every morning it lay over the lake like cloud, then slowly churned to blow up the shore and fade among the tree-trunks. I watched it thin itself over the land. Down the lake the mist suddenly shook like a curtain and I had a glimpse of someone walking by the water's edge.

I ran forward a few steps. Like gauze, the air blew shut. I saw it again. If not a man, a bear, upright and moving toward me.

Eyes fixed on the fog, I walked in that direction. Fear? I could not remember how it felt to be afraid. In the thinning haze I saw again a . . . a polar bear? Impossible. White but too small. We could hear each other now. Crackling brush, dry stems breaking underfoot.

I moved faster but those other noises stayed unhurried and regular. The mist was waist-high. I walked beyond it into a field of broomsedge and she, at the same moment, worked out of a wispy alder thicket and stared at me. She wore a white uniform, like a nurse.

I called, "Hello!"

She kept one bent limb taut in her hand. She was in her late twenties, red-haired and pregnant. I saw that not only in her shape but the way she stood, bare feet spread wide, her spine tilted. She stepped forward and the alder branch twanged behind her. "Who are you?"

"My name is Benson Watts. I live. . . . " That verb wasn't right. I jerked a thumb over one shoulder. "I've been staying in a little house by the lake."

"Good," she said. "I've not had anything to eat but persimmons. My mouth has shrunk down to zero." She smiled as she passed. "This way?"

"Just follow my track. What are you doing here?"

"Eating persimmons is all so far."

Flat-footed, she walked along the swath I had made in the ripe weeds. I could not think of a way to ask a pregnant woman if she were dead. The question sounded impolite. I followed. She was no more than five feet tall. Her short red hair was full of beggar's lice and stick-tights.

I said, "Have you been here long?"

"Don't remember."

Her white skirt was streaked with mud and resin. "What's the last thing you do remember?"

"Spending last night in the woods. Oh. There it is." She made for my cabin in that stride which, from behind, looked bow-legged and clumsy. "What's the last thing you remember, Mr. Watts?"

"A hospital room."

"You're not contagious, are you? TB or anything?" She glanced back and I saw how thickly her face was freckled. "You can see why I've got to ask." She patted her belly with a left hand on which she wore no ring. There was a bracelet, though, like mine. I pulled her tag and turned it over to read the same message: *Dwell, then travel. Join forces. Disremember.*

"Where'd you get this?"

"The fairies brought it," she said, "And the baby, too." She led the way into my house, stroked the earth floor with the sole of her foot. "This is nice." The tops of her feet were scratched, some of the marks white, some bloodied. I pointed to the pantry. Quickly she ran to a dangling ham and laid her face on its salty mold. I said I'd slice and fry some. She poked among the pears until she found one mellow enough to eat.

While I cut meat and set the pan in the fireplace, she finished the pear and bit into a cucumber, peeling and all. "What's in this sack?" she called. I was trying to keep the ham from catching fire. "Peanuts!" she crowed. "Oh, Glory! Peanuts!" I heard them rattle in a pot. "Let's parch some." She pushed the pan onto a bed of coals and a little pork grease popped into it and speckled their hulls. "Smell that ham, honey," she said—not to me, but to the lump at her middle.

I sat back on the dirty floor and let her tend the skillet. "What's your name?"

"Olena."

I had her spell it. I'd never heard that name before. I think she made it up.

"There's flour but no bread," I said. She didn't offer to make biscuits but sat with her legs crossed wide under the round bulk of her unborn child. I thought through several questions before I chose, "Is your home around here?"

Olena said, "It never was before. Where's yours?"

"Texas." She plucked the fork from my hand and turned over the ham. I took a long breath and blew out a statement on it, watching her face. "I was sick in a hospital and then I woke up here."

Matter-of-factly, Olena said, "I fell down a flight of stairs and this place was at the bottom."

We stared at each other, quickly looked away. Each stole a glance at the pale tag strung to the other's wrist. With a grunt Olena got to her feet and went to the pantry to find a plate and cutlery.

I warned her pork needed to cook longer than that, but she was already spearing an oily slice. "I don't think you can get worms here," she said, staring at the ham.

"I see plenty of regular insects."

Chewing, she didn't care. "Oh glory, that's good!" she sighed. I brought her a salt shaker and a tomato with the top cut off; she buried half her freckled face until its juice ran down her chin. "Can I sleep here tonight?" she asked, swiping a forearm over her mouth. I said she could.

Watching her chew the ham and pull its pink shreds from between her teeth, I tried to decide what accident had sent us both here to join forces, what kink in orderly process, whether there was some link between our lives or some similarity in our natures which made us candidates for transport to this place.

I asked about the location of the stairs where she fell and Olena said, "Florida. Fort Lauderdale." All I got out of that was a vague sense of regional districts, but it made me walk to the door and search the edges of the lake for some other Southerner. The mist had cleared. I stood looking into the empty dark, rubbing the ivory tag at my wrist.

"What you looking for?"

"Just looking." I felt certain somebody else would be coming soon. "Olena, is there someplace you're supposed to be? Or be going?"

She finished the ham and raked a pile of peanuts onto the floor to cool. "I guess not."

"We'll wait here a few days, then."

THE FIRE KEPT me awake. Even with my eyes closed, its pattern of light and shadow on my face was a physical touch and moved like warm water across my skin. I rolled in my blanket farther across the floor and turned my back to the blaze.

Above me in the bunk Olena lay, spread-legged, bulging. The covers seemed draped on an overturned chair. Behind me, the fire crackled. Rain had begun in late afternoon so we kept the fire going against a wet chill rising through the dirt floor. Olena's snore was soft as a cat's purr.

I dozed, then leaped alert. What had wakened me? Perhaps that deer, passing my door, had ground his teeth? I threw back the blanket and sat up, listening. It must have been nearly dawn since mockingbirds were taking turns, each song intensely sweet and swelling higher than the last. Barefoot, I crossed the damp floor and stepped onto the path. Raindrops on the weeds looked solid like tacks or metal pellets, but the sky was full of fading stars.

Far down the lake, something large and dark bent in the mist to drink, too wide and bulky to be a stag. My naked scalp prickled for there had flared through my head the leaves of those old Latin bestiaries, page after page of winged quadrupeds and dromedaries, each fact of natural history bent to reflect an attribute of Christ. In the distance, some creature howled. Just from Olena's presence this landscape had become a dream we both were having, and took on new qualities of concealment and mystery.

I started through the wet grasses to surprise the drinking animal but it melted through the brush and downhill into the woods, looking odd and fictional. Again, the distant howl. I had heard coyotes before, in Texas, but this was different.

The woods seemed, at the same time, dark and translucent. It seemed to me even the tree trunks were spelling words I could nearly read. I rested my hand on the bark of one, and tried in its cracks and lichen crusts to make out the Braille. Not since I was a child had I felt this expectancy, as if at last I were on the verge of seeing everything unveiled. Most of my life I'd been certain there was nothing *to* unveil. A bit of lichen, like tough lace, came loose in my fingers.

Quietly, I walked inside the hut, dried my feet and slid again into the blanket roll. Olena had turned her face to the wall and her back took on a woman's curves. I was fearful of desiring her.

I slept and dreamed that my mother was lying on her deathbed and the doctor took a large white bird out of his satchel and wrapped its claws on the brass bedstead. "If the bird turns to face her," he said, "this is not a mortal illness, but if he keeps his back turned there'll be nothing I can do." The bird unfolded extra wings and feathers after being cramped in the leather bag and seemed to grow larger and larger. One at a time, he uncurled his feet and shook them, then flapped once around the room. Each wing beat sounded like an oar slammed flat against the water. At last the bird lit facing away from my mother who gave a great cry. I ran forward to beat at the big bird but I could not make it move nor even look at me, and its yellow talons were wrapped on the metal rail as if molded there.

At daylight, we were wakened by loud thumps on the wooden door. Olena sprang half out of bed, one of her feet groping across the floor.

"Don't worry," I said. "It's another one."

She whispered, "Another what?"

"Another one of us." I jangled my bracelet in the air toward her and stepped into my shoes. I dragged open the heavy door.

He was ugly. Malformed—not deformed but *mal*formed—six feet tall and the parts of his body mismatched. Hips like a woman and a head flattened on both sides. I could not see a bracelet under the black sleeve of his suit. I pictured him yanked from his mother's womb, not by forceps, but with a pair of cymbals clapped over both ears. His face, driven together by the blow, was long and its features crowded. The nose, buck teeth, popeyes, had all leaped forward when the doctor first compressed his skull.

"Come in?" he asked softly.

"Of course." Another Southerner— Georgia cracker by his drawl. "Are you hungry?"

Thinking about it, he rubbed his temples with both thumbs. "I think I just ate," he finally said, and spotted Olena waiting by the bed. "Good morning, Ma'am."

I introduced Olena and myself. He wasn't curious. "Melvin Drum," he said, and wrapped my hand in a long set of fingers. He was too thin for his black suit and the pale bowtie made his Adam's apple look red and malignant. He said politely, "Hate to wake you up."

"I've been expecting you." That puzzled him. He took a seat and stared at his knuckles while he popped each one.

"This is a funny thing," he said mildly. "It might be amnesia. But look here . . . " (He leaned forward and his longish tan hair divided into two hanks. He pointed.) "You see a knot there? Anything?"

I felt his scalp. "Nothing."

Drum leaned back and his eyes—which I had thought were blue—glowed green as a cat's. "Maybe I've gone crazy," he said, obviously pleased. "They say religious people do."

Drily I suggested Mr. Drum would find he had passed beyond all need for religion now.

But he was smiling at Olena and did not hear. "It's hard to tell nuts from saints," he told her, "Except for God, of course. He can divide them left and right in the twinkling of an eye. The twinkling. Of one eye." He tilted his chair onto two back legs and I grabbed for his sleeve where something gleamed white.

"Can you explain this?" I said, shaking my own matching tag.

"I can accept it," he said. He pulled his cuff over the third bracelet. "We've all passed on and these are our instructions."

"*Passed on?* cried Olena. She crossed to the pantry, carried back a skirtful of yellow apples and sat on the floor to share them. "Are you so certain you're dead, Mr. Drum?"

"Death was the last promise I heard." His rabbit teeth bit out a sharp triangle and he talked above the sloshing noise of apple in his mouth. "I turned down an alley . . . there were three men bent over somebody. I tried to run. They grabbed me; one of them turned a flashlight on my face and said Oh Lord it was Willy and Willy had a big mouth. The one I couldn't see said, 'Willy's a dead man, then.' "

"Who's Willy?" I asked.

"God only knows." Drum read the carving softly. "To avoid going back—dwell, then travel. Join forces. Disremember. It seems clear. Anybody vote to go back?"

I pictured myself hooked up to tubes, pumps, catheters, filling and emptying at the nurses' convenience. No.

But Olena had pressed two freckled hands on her abdomen and was staring at them while her eyes filled. She sounded hoarse. "How did you die, then, Mr. Drum? After that promise?"

"In the alley? Tire iron, lead pipe." He wasn't sure.

"But death cured you of your final . . . condition. Your head wound. It's gone now. And you, Mr. Watts, of yours. Does that mean? Do you think I?"

We tried not to look at what her hands were cupping. Melvin Drum leaned forward and his face shifted in some way I could not see; his tone dropped an octave and he got older and almost dignified as he laid his thin hand upon Olena's red hair.

"Sister," he said, nearly rumbling, "Leave it to God."

Water ran down her nose and hung there. "This baby's alive!" she burst out. "You hear me? When the time comes you'll have to help me birth. I'll not leave that to God." She shook her head loose from under his palm.

"Yes you will," Drum said, but I told her we'd both help and maybe by then we'd find a doctor, too.

Melvin Drum tapped his bracelet. "We've joined forces, then," he said. "When does the travel start?"

Tomorrow, we decided. We'd pack food and bottle water. Olena would rest today and we'd swim, wash our clothes. I wrote these plans in my green-bound book. "Which direction shall we take?"

Melvin said East seemed appropriate. I wrote that down.

In the afternoon, he and I floated on our backs in the lake while Olena hung our clothes on the sunlit bushes. My younger body was a joy to me, moving easily, stroking well. Melvin had a large genital and as we drifted I could sometimes see it shift in the water like a pale fish. "Were you married, Melvin?"

He said no. I thought he must be over thirty. "Were you queer?"

Laughing, he had to gargle out some water. "Very," he said.

I don't think he meant for boys.

I'M ALREADY TIRED," Olena complained. "Why must you walk so fast?"

On her short legs she had to make three steps for every one of Melvin Drum's. I was winded, too, and the sun stood directly overhead. "Why hurry?" she puffed, pushing swags of honeysuckle to one side. "When we have no destination and no deadline?"

"None that we *know* of," said Drum, leading the way like the major of a band.

Over her shoulder to me Olena said, "This is silly. There's no time in this place." Overhearing, Drum pointed straight up at the blazing sun and kept marching. She poked him in the spine above his belt. "Disremember," she said.

We walked noisily, singlefile, through woods which were thick and shady, their fallen leaves ankle-deep; and the sun slid with us, shooting a ray through a thin branch now and then.

Olena carried the lightest pack—raisins, dried beans and figs, the peanuts she had brought over our objections. Drum and I had mostly ham and wine and water jars. The kitchen knife I'd strung at my waist had pricked me half a dozen times climbing uphill from the lake. Around us the land was level forest now with no sign of path or trail.

We rested by a shallow spring with a frog in it. I asked Drum, "You hear a river?"

He said it might be. Olena hung her red hair backwards into the spring so the ends uncurled and hung wetly down her back and dripped on the leaves in front of me when we walked on again.

"I'm ready to unstrap this blanket and leave it on some tree."

Drum told her for the third time we'd need blankets later.

"He thinks we'll still be hiking in December," she grumbled. "He's got a new think coming." She passed me a pocketful of peanuts to crack and eat as we walked. She wouldn't give Drum any.

The river still sounded far away when we looked down on it flowing low between walls of thicket and vines which had briars under their heart-shaped leaves. Drum stopped while we stepped to either side of him and gazed down the slope. The water was brown and sluggish with small sandbars in the middle. "Want to camp here?"

"Won't there be snakes?" But Olena let us lead the way, reaching our hands back for her when the hillside grew slippery or jagged. Rows of black willows kept us from the water's edge but upstream Melvin Drum broke through to a slab of gray rock which jutted into the current and had built behind it a sandy pool. Olena unlaced my borrowed shoes and slid her feet into it. "Glory, that's cool!" she said, and slipped forward until her white hem turned gray in the water.

"It's a good place to build a fire," Drum said. "But we might want to sleep on higher ground."

"I'm so tired all I'd ask a water moccasin is not to snore." Olena lay back and let her toes float into sight.

Drum and I dropped our packs to gather firewood and haul it onto the rock. I nudged Olena's shoulder once with my toe. "All right?"

"Sleepy," she said. I climbed uphill for another load, thinking that was Drum who thrashed ahead of me through the bushes in the gathering dusk. I squatted to rip lightwood from a rotted stump. Suddenly, from behind, he spoke my name and I jumped up, pointing uphill at the moving underbrush. We watched the dark leaves stir.

"There?" whispered Drum. I saw only a dim trunk of a thick gray shrub; then it moved and grew a snout. Between twigs I could make out the animal's long outline, lean and low to the ground with a tail curved around its hindquarters. He asked softly, "Dog?"

"Wolf," I said. Lupus. Very still, like a carving or a piece of statuary. In slow motion the wolf began to back away uphill and at one point I could see the whole arch of his back and the curve of his tucked-in tail. Once he stepped on a twig which snapped and he punished his own paw with a nip. I saw the sharp flash of teeth. He turned, then, and went up the slope in three long bounds.

Drum's breath blew out on the back of my neck. "A real wolf? Here?"

I didn't think it was a real wolf. More like an animated artwork I had seen drawn somewhere, and I said so. "Didn't you notice how the shape was exaggerated? It looked so . . . so stylized."

Drum sniffed at his armpit. "Well, I'm real enough. I'm organic and I stink and there's a blister on my foot."

I wanted to tell him about a pictured Lupus I had seen, which could only copulate twelve days in the whole year and whose female could not whelp except in May and then when it thundered; but that was like saying a 12th Century picture-book had come alive before our eyes, and the Psalter or Apocalypse might be next. For all I knew, Melvin Drum had dream-beasts in his own head to which I had yet to be subjected.

We carried the remaining firewood to the rock, pulled the small sack of white beans out of its river soak and boiled them slowly with a chunk of hamfat in our only pot. While they were cooking I asked Melvin just how religious he had been? Before.

"The last five years I thought of nothing else." He stretched out on the rock. "It's a shame I'm dead," he said, "Because some day I would have finished the stealing and had it all and could have begun to choose."

"Stealing what?" Olena stirred a peeled stick through the beans.

"Religion. I went in every church I could. Catechisms, hymnals, prayer books, rosaries, creeds—I stole them all. Took field trips to the Mormons and Christian Scientists. I stacked more junk in my room—you could hardly walk for candles and books and shawls. I had a prayer wheel but it rusted and wouldn't turn." Olena speared a bean for him but he shook his head that it was still too hard to eat. "That alley, at the end, that was in Los Angeles. I was on my way to visit the Rosicrucians."

She snapped, "What on earth was it all for?"

Drum smiled at the rising moon. "You ever seen a big set of railroad scales? Where you keep adding weights till the arm is perfectly balanced? When I got all the stuff together, when I had collected the right balance . . . weight. . . . " Suddenly he laughed toward the darkening sky. "It sounds dumber now than it did then."

I leaned over him on both gritty palms. "Doesn't your head hurt when you remember things like that?"

"No. Does yours?"

Olena said she got an ache too, just behind both eyebrows. She spoke in a fast singsong. "So I won't say it but once since I've quit remembering I was a beautician and having a baby and he was already married and I didn't care and one day I fell down the steps of my apartment building all the way to the washing machines in the basement and the woman folding towels just stood there and hollered all the time I came rolling down and all I could see looking up was her open mouth and fillings in every tooth in her head." She grabbed her brow. "Whew! That's the last time, damn it." She turned away and for awhile the three of us lay flat on our backs on the hard rock, not saying anything, while the sky got darker behind the stars.

The beans took a long time to soften. We got our spoons out of our pockets and tried them and lay down again.

I was almost asleep when Drum said, "Why don't we use the river?"

"Use it for what? You mean to travel?"

"Beats walking," Olena said.

"If we knew anything about boats or canoes," said Drum.

I sat up. "It happens I know a little." I began to tell them how the Indians would burn down a big tree or find one struck low by a storm and put pine resin and tree gum on one side and set fire to that, chopping out the charred wood and repeating the blazing gum, until they had burned the log hollow. "Some of their dugouts would carry twenty men."

"Won't that take a long time?" One of Olena's hands climbed up by itself and ran over the curve of her belly.

"We have a big rock to work on. Water, matches, trees. . . . "

Olena pointed her finger at me. "Hah! Why didn't your head hurt? Talking about Indians, why didn't your head hurt then?"

Drum said thoughtfully, "I think it must not hurt if the things you recall are useful to you. Useful now, I mean."

Which, in view of his vague religion, made us stare at him.

It was late when we spooned our mushy beans in the dark and rolled up in our blankets, tired enough to sleep on solid stone. If snakes crawled up at night, we never noticed. The last thing I thought was that any serpent I saw in this place would be like the one Pepys claimed could feed on larks by spitting its poison into the air, and for that one I would send forth a weasel since—as monks wrote in their illuminated manuscripts—God never makes anything without a remedy.

For all I knew, somewhere in Melvin Drum's last rented room were stacks of medieval books full of sketches of viper-worms and amphisbaena, perhaps even stories of the Cherokee Thunders who lived up in Galunlati, close to that Great Apportioner, the Sun.

And Drum was right—thinking of all these things my head never hurt at all.

AFTER THAT come repeated entries in my ledger: Worked on boat today.

I don't know how long it took. We had one hatchet and we used sharp rocks. My knuckles bled, made scabs, and bled again.

I slipped into a way of life I seemed to know from the bone out. Squatted in the woods, wiped with a leaf, covered my shit. I peed on tree trunks like a hound—it's instinct, I guess. We're meant to give back our excrement to plants. We washed in the river. Even Olena, after some days, bathed with us and I stopped staring at her stretched white skin and the brown mat of hair below. My beard grew out itchy; there were welts across my chest and the beans made gas growl inside us all. One night I spotted the wolf's eyes shining near the rock and I called to him, but the lights stayed where they were. When the ham got moldier, we lived off fish. My fingernails smelled like fertilizer.

Olena kept saying the boat was done but I wanted the shell thinner, lighter, and we chopped through the heartwood and sanded the inside down with stones. We pointed the stern and rounded the bow. Even after dark we'd sit scrubbing her surface absently with rocks until she felt smoother than our calloused hands.

"She's ready," Melvin Drum said at last. "Admit it, Ben. We can go on."

I did not want to stop. It seemed to me there was grace in the log we had not yet freed, shape that was still unrefined. But finally I gave in. I crushed pokeberries in my palm and wrote on her side with a finger: ESCARIUS.

They made me explain. A labrus fish, thick-lipped, Escarius had been called by Sylvester "Golden-Eye." The monks thought the Scarfish clever since, when trapped in a fish pot (they wrote), it would not dash forward but turn around and undo the gate with frequent blows of its tail and escape backwards. Other Scars, if they saw him struggle, were said to seize their brother's tail with their teeth and help him back loose to freedom.

We loaded Escarius, even filling our water bottles though we would be afloat in water. We still had beans and damp peanuts, and we opened a jar of grape wine on the rock and poured some over the boat and each spat a swallow into the river—I don't remember why.

Pushing off from the gray rock we started down the river, Drum and I trying our new poles and paddles. Olena sat amidships and let her fingers trail. She was singing:

Shall we gather at the river?
The beautiful, the beautiful river?
Gather with the Saints at the river
That flows by the throne of God?

Into the current we moved and skirted the sandbars, slipped silently under the drooping willows and began an easy drift. The knobs of turtle heads dropped below the water as we drifted by and floated up again when we had passed. We may have looked majestic, moving downstream in a boat so much longer than three people needed. Escarius tended to wallow to this side and that, but we learned how to balance with our oars. Our rock went out of sight and the water seemed thick with silt and reluctant, and bore us without interest, slowly, while the river spread wider and showed us flood-plains and sycamores with watching squirrels.

I felt like a man on a color calendar, poised with my oar level, going off the page and out of sight.

"She's all right," called Melvin Drum. "She rides fine."

Sometimes a snake would drop limp off a low limb and lie on the water like a black ribbon. Olena stopped worrying since they seemed to fear us and would at the last glide toward the shallow edge and blend with tree roots there.

"We're dreaming," she said, turning her face to me. "Even the snakes are dreaming."

The first set of rapids was shallow and we bumped down it like a sledge. In late afternoon we pulled up a low bank under pines and slid the hull over brown needles and braced her ashore with stones. Olena found a tick on her ankle but said it still seemed a fair place to sleep. My shoulders ached, I walked up the small creek to relieve myself and on its far side saw the bent tail and stiff fur of the same gray wolf as he slunk away. He could not be the same wolf; yet I was sure he was.

With darkness, the air turned cool and rain spattered overhead. We huddled together under our three blankets but slowly the wool soaked through. Then we just pressed together to outlast the rain, Olena with her back against a pine trunk, Drum and I on either side. Her knees were up, face down. "I hate it here," she suddenly said. We men leaned closer. "I hate it."

Putting an arm about her shoulders Drum and I got tangled with each other and once I slapped at the wet shreds of his sleeve.

"I could have been married by now," she said between her knees. "And had regular customers on my sunporch and bought myself a dishwashing machine." Rain poured over us. "I could have joined the Eastern Star," she wailed.

Trying to rub our foreheads on her soaked hair Drum and I bumped skulls and he said angrily, "You let me do all the work today!" Which wasn't so.

When at last the rain stopped, what could we do? We went on sitting there while the moon started down. We were soggy and chilled and had wet wool in our lungs.

In the morning nobody spoke. We spread our clothes to dry and tried to nap but the bugs were too bad.

"We might as well go on," I finally said. I felt resigned. There was nothing at the end of this river but a sea waiting to drown us. It would pull us home like caught fish on a line.

In silence, Drum wadded our wet blankets into the boat. Olena waded out to hoist herself aboard and without a word we pushed loose into the current. I was lonely and the river seemed hypnotic, just fast enough not to need our thrust. For a long while we sat with our oars laid in our laps. If Drum watched one bank I stared at the other, and when his attention shifted I crossed mine over, too.

Once Olena said we ought to capture the next snake, lift him into the boat, just to see what would happen. Maybe, she said, if one of us was bitten he would move on another layer to someplace else. "We might wake up in the pyramids."

Or Bethlehem, she hoped. I stroked the water hard. Drum grabbed at blackberries hanging from the bank until his hands were purple. I said, "Am I using my paddle enough today? Are you satisfied?"

He said, "It was raining, Ben." We drifted on.

By night we had passed into drier land and could build a fire and string our clothes nearby. We heated a cup of wine apiece. I asked him, "Is there a God? Now? What do you think now?"

"It's hard to think at all here."

"You can remember, though, better than we can."

The tin cup covered half his face. "I'm like every other expert," he said. "In time I got interested in the smaller sects. Began to specialize. Osiris or the voodoo drums. I went to the Hutterites and Shakers after Catholics began to bore me. Once I met Frank Buchman and couldn't see anything special about him. A man I knew had the Psychiana lessons, all twenty-four; remember them?" We didn't. "They cost him $26 during the Depression. I won't tell you the price he wanted. I didn't pay, of course. Stole the set and hid it in my mattress. Meant to read them someday." He finished the wine. "If a snake bit me here I'd wake up in Moscow, Idaho, asking about Frank Robinson." To Olena he said, "I'd just as soon be here. You feeling better?"

She had fallen asleep, mouth open, the edge of her teeth in view. I knew that I wanted to put my tongue there. I jumped when Drum said, "One thing we mustn't do is fight."

Swallowing, I nodded. He rinsed his cup in the river, stared across its lighted surface. "My brother used to have dizzy fits and he said he dreamed like this. Always of journeys and trips. Mostly he rode on a train that went very fast and roared. He was always on top of the engine, holding to the bells, and the whistle would go right through him, he said. If a tunnel could feel a train go through it, he said he could feel the sound of that whistle, boring, passing." Away from the fire, Drum looked taller. "The dream was always dark except for the engine lamps."

"Where did the train take him?"

"He always woke up too soon."

"Is your brother dead now?"

Melvin Drum laughed coming back into the firelight. He couldn't stop laughing. Even after we had curled up in the damp blankets I heard him laughing in the dark.

HOW WAS IT possible to dream in that place?

Yet I went on dreaming, every night, inventing an overlap of worlds which spun out from me without end. I dreamed of a life in an Indian village ringed by sharpened stakes, where my job was to be watchman over the fields of corn and pumpkins and to run forth with screams and rattles to drive off crows or animals. I dreamed of being alone on a sandy plain, lost, staying alive by eating fly larvae scraped from the surface of alkaline pools.

Drum said he never dreamed. Olena did. She tossed and grunted in her sleep but claimed she could not remember why in the morning.

We blundered on down the river, shipping water, overturning once in white froth when Escarius scraped a jagged rock.

"If we took turns sleeping, we could travel at night too," Drum said—but what was the point? Now that time did not rush from left to right? Only the river moved, for all we knew, moved forever.

Finally the banks began to withdraw and the wider current slowed. We seldom had to use oars or poles. Early one morning the shores were suddenly flung outward and we were afloat in a wrinkled lake which seemed without end. Drum said it might be an ocean sound at low tide since the waves were light but regular. We turned south to keep a shore in view. Soon Drum thrust down with our longest poplar pole and struck no bottom. It flew under the water like a spear and bobbed up far away, beating slowly and steadily toward the sandy bank. Under the hot sun my brain cooked like stew in a pot.

Olena had been silent for a long time. Suddenly she burst out, "You two might be dead but I'm not." She looked around defiantly at the wide water. Perhaps the child had moved in her, or she imagined that it moved.

Over her head Drum said to me, "Shall we keep on?" For the first time, he sounded tired.

"Olena?"

She jerked her face away from the disappointing shoreline, so plainly empty of other people like ourselves. Her freckles were wet and her sweaty forehead flamed. "There's nothing here," she said, almost whining. We stroked the water. "You, Melvin Drum, you made us leave that house too soon. Somebody else might have come if we had just waited awhile."

Or, by now, why hadn't we caught up with whoever had burned his books in that fireplace? Yet, I thought, Old Lobo might be the fourth one in our group, and I eyed the shore as if I might spot his gray head sliding through the water, parallel.

The sun had started down the sky when we landed on a small and wooded island, pocked with crab tunnels. Drum built a fire and dropped a dozen crabs into boiling water. We carried them in cloths, like hot spiders, up the beach and into the shade of high bushes.

"I'll fix yours," Drum said, breaking off claws, throwing the flippers downhill on the sand. He separated back from body, then gouged down to a paper thin shell. "Hand me your knife, Ben." He scraped out white meat for Olena and offered it in his palm. She ate bits with her fingers. I cleaned my own crabs. In case there should be some later use for them, we scrubbed the pink shells with sand and set them to dry in the sun. Then, while Olena lay resting under a tree, Drum and I explored the narrow island. There were so many loud birds inland that every tree seemed to scream. We found one pool of brackish water and near it wild grapevines which still had late fruit, although some had fermented on the stem. We could barely see the shore from which our river had issued, but on the island's far side there was only water and some shadows which might be other islands.

Before dark the waves grew higher and crabs at their foaming edges carried off the claws and flippers we had thrown. Olena felt pain during the night. Her heavy breathing woke us. She sprang up and began walking on the damp sand, hunched over.

"She's aborting," Drum said, watching her pace.

Olena heard him and screamed that she was not.

"It isn't her time. She's not big enough for that."

I called to her, "When were you due? What month?" But she would not answer.

Drum asked, "How long have we been here, anyway?" I looked back through these moonlit pages trying to count-up days, but it was hard to estimate. I kept glancing at Olena. Drum jerked impatiently at my book. "Is it forty-nine days? Is it close to that?"

I didn't know. He said something about people in Tibet once believing it took 49 days for the passage between death and further life. Then he clapped both hands to his head. I stared, for at last there was some piece of remembering that made Drum's head hurt. Good, I thought. I wanted his jawteeth roots to burn like fire.

I left him and crossed the sand to Olena. "I'll stay with you." Moonlight had turned her hair black and skin gray and sunk her eyes into pits. Together we marched on the cool sand. When the pain eased, we dragged her blanket closer to mine and I could feel the knob of her bent knee low in my back like something growing on my spine.

When I woke at sunrise, she had rolled to the other side. I turned, also, and fitted myself to her back. She only murmured as my arm dropped over her. Our parts were sweetly matched as if she were sitting in my lap; under the curve of her hips I could feel my stiffening heat. My fingers slid past her collar to her loose breast until they could play on her nipple like tongues.

Drum coughed. Over Olena's red curls I saw him watching my busy hand, staring at the cloth under which it moved. I pulled on her skin till the breast budded, all the while letting him watch. Olena was awake, now. The cells in her body came alive and caused my own skin to prickle.

Now I yanked my blanket and threw it over both of us, taking care that Drum could see, and that he knew I saw him see.

Under the blanket, creating bulges for his following eye, I ran my long arm over the swell of Olena's child until my thumb was centered low in her body hair and my fingertips pressed on. She moved to help me. I heard her breath. Her leg slid wide and dropped back over mine until I was touching her at last. The hot grasp was too much for me and my spasm came while she was simply widening and making ready for hers. I kept on until she made noises and threw herself on her back, knees up and shivering. Instantly, so Drum could not see her taut face, she jerked up the blanket and pulled it to her eyebrows.

Drum never moved. I gave him a long look but he never moved. I fell asleep with my hand on Olena's thigh and she must have slept, also.

In the morning Drum was gone, and the boat Escarius was gone, and half our possessions were neatly laid out by the dried crab shells on the beach. There was a moving speck near the mouth of the river but I could not tell for sure if it was man or animal, and when the sun got higher could not find it at all in the glare.

SWEET DAYS! Long, languid, poured out like syrup.

Olena slept in my arms. No sex in the regular way—because of her coming child—so like curious children ourselves we played touching games on each other's bodies.

Our clothes were very worn. I made a loin wrapping from my torn shirt; she sawed my pants off with a butcher knife for herself and left her breasts naked to the sun. We might have been Polynesian lovers from another age except for our bracelets which, without ever discussing it, we did not discard.

Maybe ten days, two weeks went by. The nights were cooling but our afternoons were still part of summer. For many meals we dug clams from an inland mud back, steamed them in salty water.

"Wouldn't you give anything for butter?" Olena said.

She had persuaded herself the seawaters were supplying her baby rich brain food and protein. She would watch me slide a knife along a fish's backbone as if each fillet were preordained to become some tender organ inside her unborn child. Maybe, she sometimes said, half-seriously, we should powder the fishbones since she had no milk to drink?

In spite of the sweet days and our sweeter nights I began gathering wood, poles, stakes, and lashing them together with strings of our ragged clothes or strips of bark. Olena didn't like the raft.

"Where will we go? Not out to sea, and there's nothing ashore but wilderness." She ran a freckled hand around my waist, spun a fingertip in my navel. "You'll help me when the baby comes, Ben. Things will be fine."

But in the night wind I could hear winter draw closer than her child. How cold might it get? Which of the fish would stay and what shelter would we have?

She pounded sea-oats into flour, mixed that with water, and baked patties in an oven of stones. They were bitter but we ate them for the sake of a different texture. "Now stop working on that raft and let's go swimming." Sometimes I did.

"Isn't it good," she'd whisper to me in the dark, "Not to be planning ahead? Saving money? Paying insurance?"

I held her tightly and watched the perpetual sea. "What do you think happened to Melvin Drum?"

Her whole body shrugged. "Who knows?"

Who-knows tormented me more than What-happened. "Maybe," I said, "Drum's found the place by now."

"What place?"

The place it ended. The sweeter Olena felt and tasted the more certain I was that this was an interlude we would both forget. Our stay on the island was timeless so I felt certain it could not possibly last. I had even begun to feel homesick for endings, arrivals. Finality.

"Ooh," breathed Olena, grabbing my hand. "Ooh, glory, feel that!" I laid my palm under her ribs. "Feel him move!"

I held my breath in case there should be some faint shifting at last beneath her tight skin. "I feel it," I lied.

She rubbed my chest with her forehead so her long red hair tickled. "When Eve had a son, do you think she worried about who he would marry? We're married, Ben. In a way."

"In a way," I said, kissing the peak of her ear.

"Really, you'll be the baby's father."

The word was not real to me. I tested it over and over in my head. Fatherfatherfather until the sound was mixed meaninglessness and prayer. Fatherfather.

"We should have asked Melvin to marry us."

I said, "He wasn't a preacher."

"Never did think that mattered much."

What *had* mattered, after all? Damn headache.

"Surely I'll not get much bigger," said Olena, stroking herself.

I thought she was the same size as the first time I saw her walking through the mist. We were both browner, though. Her legs were hairier; on my face grew a broad beard, still not a hair on my scalp. We cleaned our teeth by wrapping wet sand in wads of cloth, or chewing twigs into brushes. Nails on our toes and fingers were long and tough; my footsole felt like canvas. Sea bathing had hardened our skin and crusted the smallest scratch into a quick scar. My forearms looked almost tatooed.

Yes, we had changed. But Olena was still the same size.

One morning there washed on our beach an assortment of trash which made me shout for Olena. Empty blue bottles, finger-length. A warped black piece of a nameless book cover . . . the foot of a celluloid doll. She grabbed for that: a toy for the baby, she said.

I followed the tidemark of seaweed, stirring it with my toes. Rubber tubing. A piece of comb with the teeth sealed by barnacles. A length of wood which had once been fluted, part of a carved chair or table. Olena traced its design with awe, like some archaeologist.

But I was afraid. While she scanned the horizon for sails or a smokestack I thought of a rent in the membrane between worlds, perhaps the great suck of a filling vacuum which would sweep Olena down more stairs and drop me under another scalpel. When the wind blew, even lightly, it raised goosebumps under my tan.

"I've got to finish the raft," I said firmly. All day I watched while pretending not to watch for some vessel to follow its trash ashore. The raft grew wide enough for one person. Olena watched openly for a boat. The raft was wide enough for one person and a half. I worked on it constantly. Olena was bored with the building and bracing of its parts, and no longer waited nearby nor carried me cooked fish in crabshell dishes; but sat at a distance down the beach where the flotsam had washed, crooning to the doll's foot and waiting for something to rear up on the line between sea and sky. Some days she did not cook at all. At sundown I would carry food to her. Often she was sitting in an unnatural stiff position, and kept her hand poised like an eyeshade longer than she should have been able to keep it there.

One evening she used the doll's foot to mash her fish meat into white gruel, then lapped it up with her tongue. I was disgusted and struck her under one eye. I watched tears spill on her reddening cheekbone.

"I'm sorry, Olena. Forget it. Come sleep now."

She shook her head.

"I want you to put your hands on me."

Her eyes were sliding off my face, across the streak of moonlight on the water.

"I'll put mine on you, then," I wheedled.

No. She shrank away on the darkening sand.

When the raft was done, Olena would not climb on. "We're leaving," I said, "Even if it is dark."

I held the platform still on the water. She would not come and I threatened to hit her again as I had on that other night.

In the moonlight, then, we walked the raft past the low waves till I hoisted her on board and heaved myself beside. Olena wrapped her body and head in the blanket and sat in the middle, a lump, a cargo bale.

"We can cross most of the water in the cool of the evening," I said. All I could see of her was the roundness of one pale heel showing at the blanket's base. I tried to be cheerful. "We might even see Melvin Drum. I'll bet he made camp on the shore below the river's mouth, and that's right where we'll land." I paddled with wood, with my hands. The raft was slow and awkward and zigzagged on the black water. "Even if Drum moved on, he may have left some clue behind for us. Some message. Why don't you answer me?"

The lump said, "I don't feel good."

Very slowly we moved across the wide bay, as if moonlight were a thick impediment. The edges of the dark water beat luminous on our island and the landfall.

In a loud voice I said, "I couldn't stand just waiting like that. I couldn't keep doing that."

Olena would not move but rode on my labors like a keg under a tarpaulin.

At first light we landed on the same inland shore from which we had come, although the river was out of sight. No sign of Drum—no old campfires, no heaped shells or stones. The sand piled quickly into low dunes, stubby grass, underbrush.

"Why don't you sleep now?"

"I still don't feel good." Olena tottered up the beach and lay down in her damp blanket while I dragged the raft high out of the surf. There were shallow paw-prints in the wet sand, some in a circle, as if the animal had paced.

I squatted by Olena. "Are you hurting?"

"No." On her back, she stared beyond me. The last stars looked like flecks of paper stuck on the blueing sky. "I feel funny, though."

"It's from leaving. I'm sorry I forced you, Olena."

"Doesn't matter," she said. "But it's colder on this side of the water."

I asked if she wanted a fire but she said no. I curled up with my head laid on her thighs and went to sleep.

The sun was high and warm when I woke, feeling sticky. Again, Olena was too rigid, with one arm raised off the sand and her palm spread open to the sky. I felt for her knee and squeezed it. "Move around some." Her skin felt cool and dry.

I leaped up, staring. Overnight her pregnancy had collapsed like some balloon which had leaked out its air. Without even thinking I patted the blankets in case there should be a loose baby lying there. No. Nothing at all, no baby, no stains.

"Olena?" I got a good look at her face.

She was—what else to call it?—she was dead, her eyelids halfway down. I kissed her cold mouth which felt hard as a buckle. Then again I kissed her, frantic, blowing my breath deep and pinching her nostrils shut. I was trying to cry without losing the rhythm of the breath and my body shook. I thought my forced air might inflate Olena anywhere, blow up her abdomen or toes, because I did not understand how anything functioned in this place; but nothing happened except that my heartbeat got louder and throbbed in my head until even the sight of Olena lying there pulsated to my eye.

She was dead. I walked away on the beach. I covered her with the blanket and sat there, holding her uplifted hand. I walked some more. I took off every stitch of her clothes and, sure enough, her stomach was flat now as a young girl's. She looked younger, too, fourteen at most, but her face was tired.

I dressed her body again and tried wrapping her hand around the pink doll's foot but there was no grip.

Finally, because I could not bear to put her into this ground, to bury her in Virginia, I laid her on the raft in the blanket and spread her red hair, and combed it with my fingers dipped in seawater. The bracelet looked tarnished and there was rust in the links of the chain.

I placed on her eyes the prettiest coquinas I could find, and she seemed to be staring at the sun with a gaze part pink, purple, pearly. Then I saw I could not push her out to sea without crying, so I wrote in the ledger book awhile, until I could stand to do that.

NOW IT IS DARK again, and I think I can bear to push Olena off into the waters and let the current carry her down this coast. There have been noises from the thickets at my back. I think the wolf is there.

In a minute I am going to close up this ledger book and wrap it in a strip of wool I have torn off my blanket and put it under Olena's arm, and then I am going to walk waist deep into the water and watch them both ride away. Who knows where this sea will end, or where Olena will carry the doll's foot and the book? Maybe somewhere there'll be someone to read the words, or someone who dreams he has read them.

NOTES ON CONTRIBUTORS

R. M. BERRY, who teaches English at Florida State University, has published a book of short stories, *Plane Geometry.*

DORIS BETTS's novel, *Heading West* (1981), was a Book-of-the-Month Club selection; her *Beasts of the Southern Wild* was a National Book Award finalist in 1973.

ROSELLEN BROWN's most recent novel is *Civil Wars*; her book-length poem, *Cora Fry,* will soon be reissued by Unicorn Press.

TONI CADE, whose name is now Tony Cade Bambara, published *The Seabirds Are Still Alive: Collected Stories* in 1977 and a novel, *The Salt Eaters,* in 1980.

JOHN J. CLAYTON's published work includes a novel, *What Are Friends For?* and a collection of short fiction, *Bodies of the Rich*; he has had short stories reprinted in both *O. Henry Prize Stories* and *Best American Short Stories.*

SUSAN ENGBERG is completing a novel with the help of an NEA Fellowship; her publications include a book of short stories, *Pastorale,* and a novel, *A Stay by the River.*

BEN FIELD has published a number of novels and short stories.

TIM GAUTREAUX, who teaches creative writing at Southern Louisiana University, has published poetry and fiction in a number of literary magazines.

Born in New York City, ANDREW HORN has lived and taught in Africa since 1968, publishing plays, poetry, and scholarship.

WILLIAM LOIZEAUX has published a story in *Carolina Quarterly* and has received a grant from the Maryland State Arts Council.

BERNICE LEWIS RAVIN is at work on *The Ghost Site,* a novel about a group of American archaeologists in Cyprus at the time of the Turkish invasion.

JOÃO UBALDO RIBEIRO, a Brazilian, has published several short-story collections and novels, most recently *Viva O Povo Brasileiro* (Long live the Brazilian people).

W. D. WETHERELL has published a novel, *Souvenirs,* a book of essays, and a collection of short stories, *The Man Who Loved Levittown,* which won the Drue Heinz Prize.

GAYLE WHITTIER, who has published a number of short stories and scholarly essays, teaches at SUNY Binghamton.

NANCY WILLARD's newest book, *Firebrat,* appeared this past summer; she has published several volumes of poems and short stories and a novel, *Things Invisible to See.*

JINCY WILLETT, at work on a novel, has published a collection of short stories, *Jenny and the Jaws of Life.*

SHERLEY ANNE WILLIAMS's novel *Dessa Rose* was published in 1986. She is also the author of *The Peacock Poems,* 1975.

ERIC WILSON teaches fiction writing at the UCLA extension and does translating for the State Department. His stories have appeared in various journals and he has recently begun a novel.

CLARA WINSTON, a professional translator, published three novels before her death: *The Closest Kin There Is, The Hours Together,* and *Painting for the Show.*

LLOYD ZIMPEL has published both a novel, *Meeting the Bear,* and a collection of short stories, *Foundry Foreman,* as well as several books of nonfiction.